DB2 10.1 Fundamentals

Certification Study Guide

Roger E. Sanders

MC Press Online, LLC

Boise, ID 83703 USA

DB2 10.1 Fundamentals: Certification Study Guide

Roger E. Sanders

First Edition
First Printing—July 2014

MC Press Online, LLC, 3695 W. Quail Heights Court, Boise, ID 83703-3861 USA
service@mcpressonline.com, (208) 629-7275 ext. 500

ISBN: 978-1-58347-349-8

To my godsons, Alexander and Chandler Stephenson

About the Author

Roger E. Sanders is the president of Roger Sanders Enterprises, Inc., and the author of 22 books on relational database technology (21 on DB2 for Linux, UNIX, and Windows; one on ODBC). He has worked with DB2 for Linux, UNIX, and Windows—IBM's relational database management product for open systems—since it was first introduced on the IBM PC as part of OS/2 1.3 Extended Edition (1991), and he has been designing and developing databases and database applications for more than 20 years.

Roger authored a regular column ("Distributed DBA") in *IBM Data Magazine* (formerly *DB2 Magazine*) for 10 years, and he has written numerous tutorials and articles for IBM's developerWorks® website as well as for publications such as *Certification Magazine* and *IDUG Solutions Journal* (the official magazine of the International DB2 User's Group). He has delivered a variety of educational seminars and presentations at DB2-related conferences and has participated in the development of 21 DB2 certification exams.

From 2008 to 2014, Roger has been recognized as an **IBM Champion** for his contributions to the IBM Data Management community; in 2010 he received recognition as an **IBM developerWorks Contributing Author,** in 2011 as an **IBM developerWorks Professional Author,** and in 2012 as an **IBM developerWorks Master Author, Level 2** for his contributions to the IBM developerWorks community. (Only four individuals worldwide have received this last distinction.) Roger lives in Fuquay Varina, North Carolina.

Acknowledgments

A project of this magnitude requires both a great deal of time and the support of many individuals. I would like to express my gratitude to the following people for their contributions:

Susan Weaver—WW Certification Program Manager
Information Management
Susan invited me to participate in the *DB2 10.1 Fundamentals* certification exam development process, and she provided me with screen shots of the IBM Certification Exam Testing software. Susan also reviewed the first chapter of the book and offered valuable feedback.

Susan Visser—Publishing Program Manager
Information Management, IBM Software Group
As always, Susan's help was invaluable—without her help, this book might not have been written. Susan convinced me to tackle this project (and put off taking a long overdue break from writing), and she encouraged me to keep going when the going got tough. (And it often did, which is why this book took me so long to complete.)

Robert "Bob" J. Picciano—General Manager
Senior Vice President, Information & Analytics, IBM Software Group
Bob provided me with the Foreword for this book.

I would also like to thank my wife, Beth, for her help and encouragement, and for once again overlooking all of the things that did not get done while I worked on yet another (my 24th) book.

Contents

Foreword

Roger Sanders has long been a contributor to the DB2 Community through his presentations, his articles, and especially his many books and certification guides. It is with great pleasure that I write the Foreword for his twenty-fourth book, *DB2 10.1 Fundamentals: Certification Study Guide*. This book is designed to help you prepare for the DB2 10.1 Fundamentals certification examination, but it also lays out many of the capabilities of DB2 in Roger's very straightforward manner.

DB2 10 represents a major step forward for clients with major advancements in technology, function, and simplicity to provide the next-generation database capabilities to handle today's most demanding applications, as well as the applications of tomorrow. DB2 10 builds on its heritage of multi-workload and mixed-workload capabilities, enabling clients to use one database for their OLTP, OLAP, and operational reporting workloads without compromise.

Our new BLU Acceleration technology, available in DB2 10.5, provides dramatically faster reporting, analytics, and simplicity that enables our clients to "create, load and go." Imagine the power of a supercomputer with the simplicity of a spreadsheet. With its innovative columnar dynamic in-memory capabilities, BLU Acceleration dramatically speeds up even the most complex queries and raises the bar even further.

BLU Acceleration enables large volumes of information to be analyzed quickly, allowing companies to embrace Big Data and derive new value from new sources of data. With the democratization of data and the digitalization of everything, access to this new natural resource needs to be made simple. Simplicity means we need to harness the power of all the resources around us; to accelerate our insights about our world through simplified modeling; within the scope of the available skills.

At IBM, we have enhanced our big data platform for increased consumability and performance for the tasks of analyzing information in motion or at rest, and DB2 10.1—and particularly DB2 10.5—delivers on those goals with both unparalleled speed and simplicity.

With his latest book, Roger will help you and your organization embrace the wealth of capabilities in DB2 10.1, and help you lead your organization to modernize your DB2 environment and your business. I encourage you to use Roger's unique insights and his "no nonsense" approach to their full advantage.

Robert J. Picciano
Senior Vice President, Information & Analytics
IBM Software Group

Introduction

One of the biggest challenges computer professionals face today is keeping their skill sets current with the latest changes in technology. When the computing industry was in its infancy, it was possible to become an expert in several different areas, because the scope of the field was relatively small. Today, our industry is both widespread and fast paced, and the skills needed to master a single software package can be quite complex. Because of this, many application and hardware vendors have initiated certification programs that are designed to evaluate and validate an individual's knowledge of their technology. Businesses benefit from these programs because professional certification gives them confidence that an individual has the expertise needed to perform a specific job. Computer professionals benefit because professional certification enables them to deliver high levels of service and technical expertise and, more important, can lead to advancement or new job opportunities within the computer industry.

If you have bought this book (or you are thinking about buying this book), chances are you have already decided you want to acquire one or more of the IBM® DB2® Professional Certifications available. As an individual who has helped IBM develop 21 DB2 certification exams, I can assure you that the tests you must pass to become a certified DB2 professional are not easy. IBM prides itself on designing comprehensive certification exams that are relevant to the work environment an individual holding a particular certification will have had some exposure to. As a result, all of IBM's certification exams are designed with the following questions in mind:

- What are the critical tasks an individual must perform to hold a particular certification?
- What skills must an individual possess to perform each critical task identified?

- What are the consequences if an individual is unable to successfully perform each critical task identified?

You will find that to pass a DB2 certification exam, you must possess a solid understanding of DB2—and for some of the more advanced certifications, you must understand many of its nuances as well.

Now for the good news. You are holding in your hands what I consider to be the best tool you can use to prepare for the *DB2 10.1 Fundamentals* exam (Exam 610). Because IBM considers me a DB2 Subject Matter Expert (SME), I was invited to participate in the Exam 610 development process. In addition to helping define key exam objectives, I authored roughly 16 exam questions, and I provided feedback on many more before the final exams went into publication. Consequently, I have seen every exam question you are likely to encounter, and I know every concept you will be tested on when you take the *DB2 10.1 Fundamentals* exam.

Armed with this knowledge and copious notes I composed during the exam development process, I created this study guide, which covers not only every concept you will need to know to pass the *DB2 10.1 Fundamentals* exam (Exam 610) but also the exam process itself and the requirements for each DB2 certification role currently available. In addition, you will find, at the end of the book, sample questions that are worded just like the questions on the actual exam. In short, if you see it in this book, count on seeing it on the exam; if you do not see it in this book, chances are, it will not be on the exam. Consequently, if you become familiar with the material presented in this book, you should do well on the *DB2 10.1 Fundamentals* exam.

About This Book

This book is divided into two parts:

- **Part 1: IBM DB2 Certification (Chapter 1)**

    This section consists of one chapter (Chapter 1), which introduces you to the IBM DB2 Professional Certification Program. In this chapter, you will learn about the different certification roles available, along with the basic prerequisites and requirements for each role. This chapter also shows you how to prepare for a DB2 certification exam, and it concludes with a discussion on how to navigate the testing software that IBM uses to administer most of their exams.

- **Part 2: DB2 10.1 Fundamentals (Chapters 2–7)**

This section consists of six chapters (Chapters 2 through 7), which provide you with the concepts you will need to master before you can pass the *DB2 10.1 Fundamentals* exam (Exam 610).

Chapter 2 presents the various DB2 editions and add-on products that are currently available and shows you which editions and products you should use to create a particular type of database environment. In this chapter, you will learn about the products that make up the *DB2 Family*, the characteristics of data warehouse and OLTP databases, and which DB2 products to use to create each type of database environment. You will also learn how to store, manage, and manipulate large object (LOB) and Extensible Markup Language (XML) data.

Chapter 3 introduces you to the authorizations and privileges that are available with DB2, and to the tools that are used to give (grant) and take away (revoke) authorizations and privileges to/from individuals, groups, and roles. In this chapter, you will learn about the two mechanisms that DB2 uses to control access to instances, databases, database objects, and data: *authorities* and *privileges*. You will also discover how to grant authorities and privileges to specific users, groups, and roles, as well as how to revoke authorities and privileges when it is appropriate to do so. And you will learn how to utilize tools like Row and Column Access Control (RCAC) and Label-Based Access Control (LBAC) to secure sensitive data in a way that meets the strictest of security requirements or that adheres to rigid government security standards.

Chapter 4 introduces you to the various objects that are available with a DB2 environment and shows you how to create and connect to DB2 servers and databases, as well as design and create temporal tables. In this chapter, you will learn about servers, instances, and databases, along with many other different, but often related, objects that make up a DB2 database environment. You will also discover how to create new DB2 databases and how to identify and connect to DB2 servers and databases using Type 1 and Type 2 connections. Finally, you will learn about temporal data management, as well as the different types of temporal (time travel) tables that can be created in a DB2 10 (DB2 for z/OS®) and DB2 10.1 (DB2 for Linux®, UNIX®, and Windows®) database.

Chapter 5 introduces you to the SQL statements and XQuery expressions that can be used to store, modify, delete, and retrieve both relational (traditional) and XML data. In this chapter, you will learn how to use INSERT, UPDATE, and DELETE statements to store, change, and remove data, as well as how to use the SELECT statement and its associated clauses to retrieve data and format the results. You will also discover how to query temporal (time travel) tables and how to create and invoke SQL stored procedures and user-defined functions. Finally, you will learn what transactions are and how transaction boundaries are defined.

Chapter 6 introduces you to the various data types and constraints that are available with DB2 and shows you how to obtain information about existing tables, indexes, and views. In this chapter, you will learn about the various data types that can be used to store data, as well as how to constrain data with NOT NULL, default, UNIQUE, CHECK, and referential integrity constraints. You will also discover how to create base and temporary tables, as well as how to identify the characteristics of tables, views, and indexes. Finally, you will learn how to use schemas and you will be shown how to create and use triggers to supplement one or more of the data constraints available.

Chapter 7 introduces you to the concept of data consistency and to the two important mechanisms DB2 uses to maintain data consistency in both single and multiuser database environments: *isolation levels* and *locks*. In this chapter, you will learn what isolation levels are, which isolation levels are available, and how to use isolation levels to keep transactions from interfering with each other in a multiuser environment. You will also discover how DB2 provides concurrency control through the use of locking, which types of locks are available, how to acquire locks, and which factors can influence locking performance.

Audience

The book is written primarily for IT professionals who have some experience working with DB2 10 for z/OS or DB2 10.1 for Linux, UNIX, and Windows and want to take (and pass) the *DB2 10.1 Fundamentals* certification exam (Exam 610). However, any individual who would like to learn the fundamentals of DB2 10/10.1 will benefit from the information in this book.

Conventions Used

You will find many examples of DB2 commands and SQL statements throughout this book. The following conventions are used whenever a DB2 command or SQL statement is presented:

[ ]   Parameters or items shown inside brackets are required and must be provided.

< >   Parameters or items shown inside angle brackets are optional and do not have to be provided.

| Vertical bars indicate that one (and only one) item in the list of items presented can be specified.

, ...   A comma followed by three periods (ellipsis) indicate that multiple instances of the preceding parameter or item can be included in the DB2 command or SQL statement.

The following examples illustrate each of these conventions:

Example 1

```
REFRESH TABLE [TableName, ...]
<INCREMENTAL | NON INCREMENTAL>
```

In this example, you must supply at least one *TableName* value, as the brackets ([ ]) indicate, and you can provide more than one *TableName* value, as the comma and ellipsis (, ...) characters that follow the *TableName* parameter suggest. INCREMENTAL and NON INCREMENTAL are optional, as the angle brackets (< >) signify, and you can specify either one or the other, but not both, as the vertical bar (|) indicates.

Example 2

```
CREATE SEQUENCE [SequenceName]
<AS [SMALLINT | INTEGER | BIGINT | DECIMAL]>
<START WITH [StartingNumber]>
<INCREMENT BY [1 | Increment]>
<NO MINVALUE | MINVALUE [MinValue]>
<NO MAXVALUE | MAXVALUE [MaxValue]>
<NO CYCLE | CYCLE>
```

```
<NO CACHE | CACHE 20 | CACHE [CacheValue]>
<NO ORDER | ORDER>
```

In this example, you must supply a *SequenceName* value, as the brackets ([ ]) indicate. However, everything else is optional, as the angle brackets (< >) signify; in many cases, a list of available option values is provided (for example, NO CYCLE and CYCLE), but you can specify only one, as the vertical bar (|) denotes. In addition, when some options are provided (for example, START WITH, INCREMENT BY, MINVALUE, MAXVALUE, and CACHE), you must supply a corresponding value for each option used, as the brackets ([ ]) that follow the option indicate.

SQL is not a case-sensitive language, but for clarity, the examples shown throughout this book use mixed case—command syntax is presented in upper case, and user-supplied elements such as table names and column names are presented in lower case. (This same format is used with all of the DB2 certification exams.)

Note: Although basic syntax is presented for most of the SQL statements covered in this book, the actual syntax supported can be much more complex. To view the complete syntax for a specific DB2 command or SQL statement or to obtain more information about a particular command or statement, refer to the IBM DB2 Version 10.1 Information Center (*publib.boulder.ibm.com/infocenter/db2help*) or the IBM Information Management Software for z/OS Solutions Information Center (*publib.boulder.ibm.com/infocenter/dzichelp/v2r2/index.jsp*).

1

IBM DB2 Certification

Certification has long been a popular trend in the Information Technology (IT) industry. Consequently, many hardware and software vendors—including IBM—have certification programs in place that are designed to evaluate and validate an individual's proficiency with their product offerings.

Recognized throughout the world, the *IBM Professional Certification Program* offers a wide variety of certification options for IT professionals who want to demonstrate their knowledge and expertise with a particular IBM product. And if you regularly use IBM hardware, software, or both, chances are you have heard of this program and have thought about becoming IBM certified. But, are you aware that IBM has more than 275 different certification roles to choose from? More important, do you know which certification role is right for you? (And, do you know how to prepare for and take the certification exams that are required for the certification role you wish to pursue?)

This chapter is designed to provide you with answers to these and other questions. It begins by introducing you to the certification roles that have been defined for individuals who use IBM's DB2 Information Management software. Then, it shows you how to prepare for the DB2 certification exams, and it concludes with a discussion on how to navigate the testing software that IBM uses to administer most of its exams.

DB2 10 and 10.1 Certification Roles

The *IBM Professional Certification Program* consists of several distinct certification roles that are designed to guide you in your professional development. To obtain a particular certification, you simply select the role you wish to pursue (based on your knowledge and experience working with a particular IBM product), familiarize yourself with the requirements that have been defined for that role, and then take the required certification exam(s) for the role you have chosen. This book focuses on the **IBM Certified Database Associate—DB2 10.1 Fundamentals** role (as well as the exam you must take and pass to obtain this certification); however, two DB2 Version 10 and three DB2 Version 10.1 certification roles are currently available:

- IBM Certified Database Associate—DB2 10.1 Fundamentals
- IBM Certified Database Administrator—DB2 10.1 for Linux, UNIX, and Windows
- IBM Certified Database Administrator—DB2 10 for z/OS
- IBM Certified System Administrator—DB2 10 for z/OS
- IBM Certified Advanced Database Administrator—DB2 10.1 for Linux, UNIX, and Windows

IBM Certified Database Associate—DB2 10.1 Fundamentals

The **IBM Certified Database Associate—DB2 10.1 Fundamentals** certification is intended for entry-level DB2 users who are knowledgeable about the basic concepts of DB2 10.1 for Linux, UNIX, and Windows and DB2 10 for z/OS. In addition to having some hands-on experience or training (either formal or informal) on DB2 10 or DB2 10.1, individuals seeking this certification should:

- ✓ Know which DB2 10 and 10.1. products are available, as well as the function of each product (at a high level)
- ✓ Know which DB2 10 and 10.1 product to use for a given type of database workload (online transaction processing [OLTP], decision support system [DSS], or data warehouse)
- ✓ Know how to store and manipulate nonrelational data, such as large objects (LOBs) and Extensible Markup Language (XML) documents
- ✓ Possess an in-depth knowledge about the authorities and privileges that can be used to protect databases and data against unauthorized access and modification
- ✓ Know how to grant and revoke authorities and privileges
- ✓ Possess a basic understanding of Row and Column Access Control (RCAC)

✓ Possess a basic understanding of roles and trusted contexts

✓ Know how to create and connect to DB2 servers and databases

✓ Know how to create, access, and manipulate basic DB2 objects, such as tables, indexes, and views

✓ Know how and when to create system-period, application-period, and bitemporal temporal (time travel) tables

✓ Possess an in-depth knowledge of Structured Query Language (SQL), as well as an understanding of the Data Definition Language (DDL), Data Manipulation Language (DML), and Data Control Language (DCL) statements that are available with DB2

✓ Know how to sort and group data

✓ Possess a strong understanding of transactions and know what constitutes a transaction boundary

✓ Know how to create and invoke SQL procedures and SQL user-defined functions (UDFs), as well as how to pass parameters to and retrieve results from SQL procedures and SQL UDFs

✓ Possess a basic knowledge of XQuery

✓ Know how to query temporal (time travel) tables

✓ Know how to use the various data types—including the Oracle® compatibility data types—that are available with DB2

✓ Know how and when to create temporary tables

✓ Know how and when to use the different types of constraints (NOT NULL, default, CHECK, UNIQUE, referential integrity, and informational) that are available with DB2

✓ Know how and when to create triggers

✓ Know how to use schemas

✓ Possess a basic understanding of the mechanisms (transactions, isolation levels, and locks) that are used to isolate the effects of transactions from one another in a multiuser environment

✓ Know which factors influence locking

✓ Know how and when to use the LOCK TABLE statement

✓ Be able to identify the characteristics of common DB2 locks that are used on both the Linux, UNIX, and Windows platform and the z/OS platform

✓ Be able to identify the appropriate isolation level to use for a given situation

✓ Know how and when to use Currently Committed semantics with the Cursor Stability isolation level

To obtain **IBM Certified Database Associate—DB2 10.1 Fundamentals**
certification, candidates must take and pass the *DB2 10.1 Fundamentals* exam (Exam
610). Figure 1.1 illustrates the road map for acquiring this certification.

Figure 1.1: IBM Certified Database Associate—DB2 10.1 Fundamentals certification road map

IBM Certified Database Administrator—DB2 10.1 for Linux, UNIX, and Windows

The **IBM Certified Database Administrator—DB2 10.1 for Linux, UNIX, and
Windows** certification is designed for experienced DB2 users who possess the knowledge
and intermediate-to-advanced skills needed to perform the day-to-day administration of
DB2 10.1 for Linux, UNIX, and Windows instances and databases. Along with being
knowledgeable about DB2 fundamentals and having significant hands-on experience as a
DB2 10.1 Database Administrator (DBA), individuals seeking this certification should:

- ✓ Know how to configure and manage DB2 servers, instances, and databases
- ✓ Know how to use the autonomic features that are available with DB2 10.1 for Linux, UNIX, and Windows
- ✓ Know how to perform administrative tasks using Data Studio
- ✓ Know how to create a new DB2 10.1 for Linux, UNIX, and Windows database
- ✓ Know how to create, access, modify, and manage DB2 database (data) objects

✓ Be able to convert an existing DB2 for Linux, UNIX, and Windows database to an automatic storage database

✓ Know how to use the ADMIN_MOVE_TABLE() procedure

✓ Possess a basic knowledge of DB2's partitioning capabilities

✓ Know how to store and manage XML data

✓ Be able to describe how classic and adaptive row compression works, as well as know how to enable a table or index for either type of compression

✓ Possess a basic knowledge of the new table features that were introduced in DB2 10.1

✓ Know how and when to use the multi-temperature data feature

✓ Know how and when to create NOT NULL, default, CHECK, UNIQUE, referential integrity, and informational constraints

✓ Know how and when to use the WITH CHECK OPTION clause of the CREATE VIEW statement

✓ Know how and when to create and use triggers

✓ Know how and when to use the SET INTEGRITY command

✓ Know how to use administrative views and SQL functions to monitor a DB2 10.1 database environment

✓ Possess a basic knowledge of the monitoring features available with Workload Manager

✓ Be able to use the auto-monitoring tools that are available with DB2 10.1

✓ Know how to use the DB2 Problem Determination Tool (db2pd)

✓ Know how to capture and analyze Explain information

✓ Know how to use the DB2 data movement utilities (EXPORT, IMPORT, LOAD, and db2move)

✓ Know how and when to use the Ingest utility

✓ Know how and when to use the REORGCHK, REORG, REBIND, RUNSTATS, and FLUSH PACKAGE CACHE commands

✓ Know how and when to use the DB2 Design Advisor

✓ Possess an in-depth knowledge of crash recovery, version recovery, and roll forward recovery

✓ Know how to perform database-level and table space-level backup and recovery operations

✓ Be able to configure and manage a High Availability Disaster Recovery (HADR) environment, as well as enable a standby server for read-only operations

✓ Possess a basic knowledge of the high availability (HA) features DB2 pureScale® provides

✓ Possess an in-depth knowledge of the authorities and privileges that can be used to protect databases and data against unauthorized access and modification

✓ Know which operations someone with Security Administrator (SECADM) authority can perform

✓ Possess a basic understanding of the Audit facility

✓ Possess a basic understanding of trusted contexts

✓ Possess an in-depth knowledge of RCAC

✓ Possess an in-depth knowledge of Label-Based Access Control (LBAC)

✓ Be able to configure database connectivity

✓ Know how to perform a DB2 Discovery request, as well as how to prevent DB2 Discovery requests from seeing servers, instances, and/or databases

✓ Know how to configure a DB2 server for Lightweight Directory Access Protocol (LDAP) connectivity

Candidates who have taken and passed either the *DB2 9 Family Fundamentals* exam (Exam 730) or the *DB2 10.1 Fundamentals* exam (Exam 610) can obtain **IBM Certified Database Administrator—DB2 10.1 for Linux, UNIX, and Windows** certification by taking (and passing) the *DB2 10.1 DBA for Linux, UNIX, and Windows* exam (Exam 611). All other candidates must take and pass both the *DB2 10.1 Fundamentals* exam (Exam 610) *and* the *DB2 10.1 DBA for Linux, UNIX, and Windows* exam (Exam 611). Figure 1.2 displays the road map for acquiring **IBM Certified Database Administrator—DB2 10.1 for Linux, UNIX, and Windows** certification.

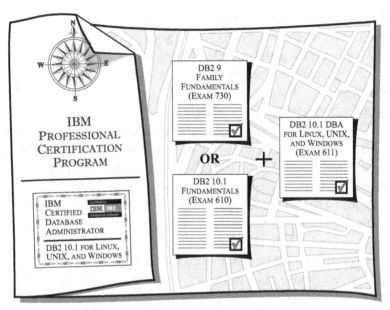

Figure 1.2: IBM Certified Database Administrator—DB2 10.1 for Linux, UNIX, and Windows certification road map

IBM Certified Database Administrator—DB2 10 for z/OS

The **IBM Certified Database Administrator—DB2 10 for z/OS** certification is intended for experienced DB2 10 users who possess the knowledge and skills necessary to perform the intermediate-to-advanced tasks related to the design and implementation, installation and migration, backup and recovery, and daily operation and administration of DB2 10 databases residing on z/OS platforms. In addition to having significant experience as a DB2 for z/OS DBA and extensive knowledge of DB2 (including an understanding of new features and functionality available in Version 10), individuals seeking this certification should:

- ✓ Know how to normalize data, as well as how to translate a logical data model (entity-relationship model, process model, or both) into a physical database design
- ✓ Be able to design tables, indexes, and views
- ✓ Understand the different performance implications of identity columns, row IDs, sequence objects, reorder row formats, and hash access
- ✓ Know how to design table spaces (choose the proper page size, specify clustering, and so forth), as well as how to obtain a table space's attributes
- ✓ Possess a basic knowledge of DB2's partitioning capabilities

✓ Know how to implement user-defined rules of integrity

✓ Know how to create and modify DB2 data objects

✓ Know how to store and manage LOB and XML data

✓ Have an in-depth understanding of the impact that different encoding schemes can have on performance

✓ Understand data distribution and replication

✓ Know which operation and recovery commands to use in normal conditions

✓ Know which commands and utility control statements to use in abnormal conditions

✓ Be able to identify, as well as perform, the actions necessary to protect databases from planned and unplanned outages

✓ Be able to load data into and unload data from one or more tables

✓ Know how and when to reorganize DB2 objects

✓ Know how to monitor DB2 objects by collecting statistics

✓ Know how to monitor and manage threads and utilities

✓ Be able to identify and respond to advisory and restrictive statuses on objects

✓ Understand the significance of checkpoints

✓ Know how to identify and resolve database problems

✓ Know how to perform health checks

✓ Be able to develop backup and recovery procedures

✓ Be able to describe the special considerations for database recovery in a data sharing environment

✓ Understand the concept of disaster recovery

✓ Possess a basic understanding of virtual storage constraints and limitations

✓ Possess an in-depth knowledge of the authorities and privileges that can be used to protect databases and data against unauthorized access and modification

✓ Be able to audit DB2 activity and resources, as well as identify the primary audit techniques that are available

✓ Be able to identify and respond appropriately to trace output or error messages that indicate security problems

✓ Possess a basic understanding of roles and trusted contexts

✓ Possess an in-depth knowledge of RCAC

✓ Be able to plan for performance monitoring by setting up and running monitoring procedures

✓ Know how to analyze performance

✓ Know how to analyze and respond to RUNSTATS statistics analysis

✓ Know how and when to perform a REBIND operation

✓ Be able to calculate cache requirements for new applications

✓ Know how to implement data distribution and replication
✓ Possess a basic knowledge of how DB2 interacts with Workload Manager
✓ Be able to interpret traces, as well as explain the performance impact of using DB2 traces
✓ Be able to identify and respond correctly to critical performance metrics
✓ Know how to analyze and tune SQL statements
✓ Know the difference between static and dynamic SQL, as well as how each type of SQL performs
✓ Know how to design a database for performance
✓ Understand the critical DSNZPARMs
✓ Be able to identify the migration and upgrade modes available
✓ Be able to identify and describe the data sharing components available

Candidates can obtain **IBM Certified Database Administrator—DB2 10 for z/OS** certification by taking (and passing) either the *DB2 9 Family Fundamentals* exam (Exam 730) or the *DB2 10.1 Fundamentals* exam (Exam 610) ***and*** the *DB2 10 DBA for z/OS* exam (Exam 612). Figure 1.3 shows the road map for acquiring **IBM Certified Database Administrator—DB2 10 for z/OS** certification.

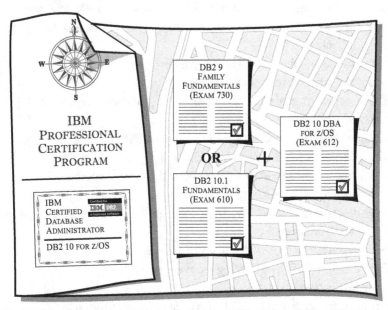

Figure 1.3: IBM Certified Database Administrator—DB2 10 for z/OS certification road map

IBM Certified System Administrator—DB2 10 for z/OS

The **IBM Certified System Administrator—DB2 10 for z/OS** certification is designed for individuals who possess the knowledge and skills to describe the architecture and administer the processes needed to plan, install, manage, tune, and secure DB2 for z/OS environments. In addition to having significant hands-on experience with DB2 for z/OS, along with possessing extensive knowledge about the product (including an understanding of the new features and functionality available in Version 10), individuals seeking this certification should:

- ✓ Be able to develop an installation or migration plan for a given scenario
- ✓ Be able to identify additional environments (Workload Manager, UNIX System Services, XML schema support, Resource Access Control Facility [RACF®] or equivalent, and so forth) that a particular installation or migration might require
- ✓ Be able to describe how to execute an installation or migration plan for a given scenario
- ✓ Know how to evaluate DSNZPARM settings
- ✓ Possess an in-depth knowledge of ways to protect DB2 subsystems and resources against unauthorized access and modification (including knowledge of new system authorities, distributed identity support, and connection-level security enforcement)
- ✓ Be able to describe the auditing techniques (policies) that are available with DB2 10
- ✓ Know how and when to use role-based security, as well as be able to explain the advantage of deploying it
- ✓ Know how to use and manage DB2 components and processes
- ✓ Know how and when to reorganize the catalog
- ✓ Know how and when to use the new options that are available with the REORG command
- ✓ Possess an in-depth knowledge of frequently used DB2 commands
- ✓ Know how to monitor and control DB2 threads
- ✓ Know how to perform system-level backup and recovery operations (Hierarchical Storage Management, FlashCopy®, and so on)
- ✓ Be able to describe how to recover from a system failure by performing a restart or conditional restart operation
- ✓ Be able to describe the process for disaster recovery
- ✓ Be able to describe DB2 data sharing recovery scenarios
- ✓ Know how to analyze performance
- ✓ Know how buffer pools and DSNZPARMs can affect performance
- ✓ Possess a strong knowledge of how to use statistics, monitoring tools, and trace definitions to monitor performance

✓ Know how to achieve efficient use of memory for a given situation
✓ Be able to identify Workload Manager settings that will improve DB2 performance
✓ Know how and when to use autonomic RUNSTATS as opposed to manual RUNSTATS
✓ Know which documentation to use to solve a particular problem
✓ Possess an in-depth knowledge of the operator commands and trace definitions that can be used for troubleshooting
✓ Know how to identify contention problems
✓ Possess an in-depth knowledge of the diagnostic utilities available
✓ Know how to identify and resolve DB2 data sharing problems

Candidates can obtain **IBM Certified System Administrator—DB2 10 for z/OS** certification by taking (and passing) either the *DB2 9 Family Fundamentals* exam (Exam 730) or the *DB2 10.1 Fundamentals* exam (Exam 610) **and** the *DB2 10 System Administrator for z/OS* exam (Exam 617). Figure 1.4 displays the road map for acquiring **IBM Certified System Administrator—DB2 10 for z/OS** certification.

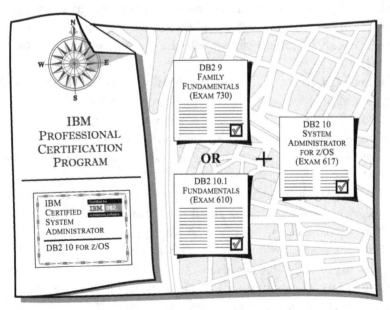

Figure 1.4: IBM Certified System Administrator—DB2 10 for z/OS certification road map

IBM Certified Advanced Database Administrator—DB2 10.1 for Linux, UNIX, and Windows

The **IBM Certified Advanced Database Administrator—DB2 10.1 for Linux, UNIX, and Windows** certification is designed for individuals who possess extensive knowledge about DB2 10.1 and have significant hands-on experience administering DB2 10.1 databases on Linux, UNIX, or Windows platforms. In addition to being knowledgeable about the more complex concepts of DB2 10.1 and being capable of performing advanced database administration tasks such as monitoring and tuning for optimum performance, planning for high availability, and managing network connectivity, individuals seeking this certification should:

- ✓ Be able to design, create, and manage database storage paths (for automatic storage databases)
- ✓ Be able to design, create, and manage table spaces for automatic storage databases
- ✓ Be able to design, create, and manage buffer pools
- ✓ Be able to design and configure a database for multi-temperature data
- ✓ Be able to use Data Studio to manage database environments
- ✓ Be able to design, create, and manage database partitioning using the Data Partitioning feature (DPF)
- ✓ Be able to design, create, and manage multidimensional clustered (MDC) tables
- ✓ Be able to design, create, and manage range-partitioned tables
- ✓ Be able to design, create, and manage insert time clustering (ITC) tables
- ✓ Be able to design, create, and manage range clustering tables
- ✓ Know how to develop a logging strategy, as well as be able to use transaction logs for recovery
- ✓ Know how to perform backup and recovery operations, as well as know how to use the advanced backup and recovery features that are available with DB2 10.1
- ✓ Know how to configure and use Workload Manager
- ✓ Be able to set up and maintain a HADR environment
- ✓ Know how to use DB2's diagnostic tools
- ✓ Be able to identify the appropriate DB2 diagnostic tool to use for a given situation
- ✓ Possess a strong knowledge of query optimizer concepts
- ✓ Know how to manage and tune database, instance, and application memory in conjunction with I/O
- ✓ Know how and when to use the different compression methods available
- ✓ Be able to correctly analyze, isolate, and resolve database performance problems
- ✓ Know how and when to create indexes to improve database performance

✓ Be able to take advantage of intrapartition and interpartition parallelism
✓ Know how and when to create a federated database environment
✓ Know how and when to use replication
✓ Be able to describe the major components needed in a DB2 pureScale environment, as well as know when DB2 pureScale should be used
✓ Know how and when to use the DB2 Audit facility

Candidates who obtained **IBM Certified Database Administrator—DB2 10.1 for Linux, UNIX, and Windows** certification by taking (and passing) either the *DB2 9 Family Fundamentals* exam (Exam 730) or the *DB2 10.1 Fundamentals* exam (Exam 610) ***and*** the *DB2 10.1 DBA for Linux, UNIX, and Windows* exam (Exam 611) can acquire **IBM Certified Advanced Database Administrator—DB2 10.1 for Linux, UNIX, and Windows** certification by taking (and passing) the *DB2 10.1 Advanced Database Administrator for Linux UNIX and Windows* exam (Exam 614). Figure 1.5 displays the road map for acquiring **IBM Certified Advanced Database Administrator—DB2 10.1 for Linux, UNIX, and Windows** certification.

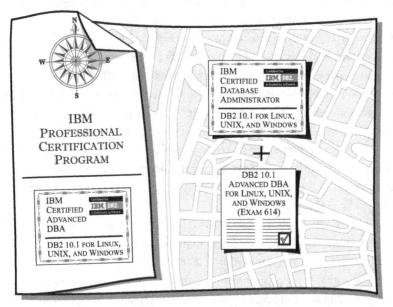

Figure 1.5: IBM Certified Advanced Database Administrator—DB2 10.1 for Linux, UNIX, and Windows certification road map for individuals holding IBM Certified Database Administrator—DB2 10.1 for Linux, UNIX, and Windows certification

Additional DB2 9.7 Certification Roles

In addition to the DB2 Version 10 and Version 10.1 certification roles that are currently available, two additional certification roles exist that are based on DB2 Version 9.7:

- IBM Certified Application Developer—DB2 9.7 for Linux, UNIX, and Windows
- IBM Certified Solution Developer—DB2 9.7 SQL Procedure

IBM Certified Application Developer—DB2 9.7 for Linux, UNIX, and Windows

The **IBM Certified Application Developer—DB2 9.7 for Linux, UNIX, and Windows** certification is intended for intermediate-to-advanced-level application developers who possess the knowledge and skills necessary to design, build, test, and deploy applications that interact with DB2 9.7 databases residing on Linux, UNIX, and Windows platforms. In addition to being knowledgeable about DB2 9.7 and having significant hands-on experience designing and developing applications, individuals seeking this certification should:

- ✓ Be familiar with the naming conventions that are used to identify DB2 objects, such as tables, aliases, and views
- ✓ Know when to use SQL routines, functions, and modules
- ✓ Know how and when to use DB2's built-in functions and stored procedures
- ✓ Possess an in-depth knowledge of the data types that DB2 recognizes
- ✓ Know which authorities and privileges are needed to access data from an application
- ✓ Possess an in-depth knowledge of the SQL statements that DB2 recognizes
- ✓ Be able to describe the differences between static and dynamic SQL
- ✓ Be able to construct queries that retrieve data from multiple tables and views
- ✓ Know how to use DML statements to insert, update, and delete data
- ✓ Be able to identify the types of cursors that can be used in an application (read-only, updatable, and ambiguous)
- ✓ Know how and when to use cursors, as well as know what a cursor's scope is
- ✓ Know how and when to use locators to manipulate LOB data
- ✓ Be able to manage transactions using COMMIT, ROLLBACK, and SAVEPOINT statements
- ✓ Be able to identify the appropriate isolation level to use for a given situation
- ✓ Possess a basic understanding of XML schema validation and XML schema evolution
- ✓ Know how to use the built-in XML functions that are provided with DB2
- ✓ Know how to handle white space in XML documents
- ✓ Be able to create an XML document from existing relational data

✓ Be able to execute and evaluate the results of an XQuery expression

✓ Know how to construct queries that retrieve both relational and XML data

✓ Know how to bind and rebind a package

✓ Know how and when to use parameter markers

✓ Know how to connect to a database from an Embedded SQL, Call Level Interface/ Open Database Connectivity (CLI/ODBC), Java® Database Connectivity (JDBC), SQL for Java (SQLJ), ADO.NET, or PHP application

✓ Know how to submit an SQL statement to DB2 for processing from an Embedded SQL, CLI/ODBC, JDBC, SQLJ, ADO.NET, or PHP application

✓ Know how to obtain query results, as well as manipulate data, from an Embedded SQL, CLI/ODBC, JDBC, SQLJ, ADO.NET, or PHP application

✓ Be able to analyze the contents of an SQL Communications Area (SQLCA) data structure

✓ Be able to obtain and analyze ODBC/CLI diagnostic information

✓ Be able to obtain and analyze JDBC trace, SQL exception, and JDBC error log information

✓ Be able to obtain and analyze ADO.NET diagnostic information

✓ Be able to obtain and analyze PHP diagnostic information

✓ Know how to create and register external stored procedures

✓ Know how to create external UDFs, including OLE DB and external table UDFs

✓ Be able to describe what will happen if an application attempts to modify data stored in a table that is part of a referential integrity constraint

✓ Possess a basic understanding of distributed units of work (two-phase commits)

✓ Possess a basic understanding of trusted contexts

✓ Know how to create, access, modify, and manage advanced DB2 database objects, such as sequences, global declared temporary tables, and multidimensional query tables (MQTs)

Candidates who have taken and passed either the *DB2 V8.1 Family Fundamentals* exam (Exam 700) or the *DB2 9 Family Fundamentals* exam (Exam 730) can obtain **IBM Certified Application Developer—DB2 9.7 for Linux, UNIX, and Windows** certification by taking (and passing) the *DB2 9.7 Application Development* exam (Exam 543). All other candidates must take and pass both the *DB2 9 Family Fundamentals* exam (Exam 730) *and* the *DB2 9.7 Application Development* exam (Exam 543). Figure 1.6 shows the road map for acquiring **IBM Certified Application Developer—DB2 9.7 for Linux, UNIX, and Windows** certification.

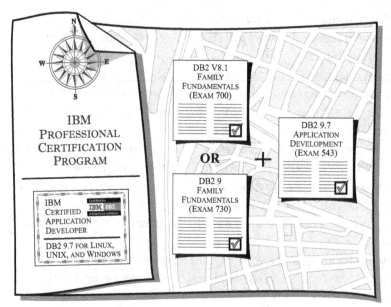

Figure 1.6: IBM Certified Application Developer—DB2 9.7 for Linux, UNIX, and Windows certification road map

IBM Certified Solution Developer—DB2 9.7 SQL Procedure

The **IBM Certified Solution Developer—DB2 9.7 SQL Procedure** certification is intended for intermediate-to-advanced-level developers who possess the knowledge and skills necessary to design, build, test, and deploy stored procedures, UDFs, and triggers that have been written using SQL, SQL Procedural Language (SQL PL), or both. In addition to being knowledgeable about DB2 9.7 and having significant experience programming in SQL and SQL PL (using IBM's development tools), individuals seeking this certification should:

✓ Know how to define variables and cursors
✓ Be able to code assignment statements
✓ Know how to use SQL control statements
✓ Be familiar with both SQL and SQL PL error handling
✓ Know when it is appropriate to use SQL procedures
✓ Know how to use the CREATE PROCEDURE statement
✓ Know the proper structure of an SQL procedure body
✓ Know how to return values and result data sets from SQL procedures
✓ Know how to code and use nested SQL procedures

- ✓ Be able to test and deploy an SQL procedure
- ✓ Know when it is appropriate to use SQL functions
- ✓ Know how to use the CREATE FUNCTION statement
- ✓ Know the proper structure of an SQL function body
- ✓ Know how to return both values and a table from an SQL function
- ✓ Know how to invoke an SQL function
- ✓ Be able to test and deploy an SQL function
- ✓ Know when it is appropriate to use a trigger (as opposed to an SQL procedure or function)
- ✓ Know how to use the CREATE TRIGGER statement
- ✓ Be able to identify the actions of a trigger
- ✓ Possess an in-depth knowledge of advanced uses of triggers
- ✓ Be able to test and deploy a trigger
- ✓ Know how and when to create and use declared global temporary tables
- ✓ Know how to use the ADMIN_CMD() procedure to execute administrative commands
- ✓ Know how to take advantage of system features
- ✓ Know how and when to use arrays and associated arrays
- ✓ Know how and when to use global variables
- ✓ Know how and when to use modules
- ✓ Know how to enable a database to support Oracle PL/SQL procedures
- ✓ Be familiar with DB2 application development tools such as IBM Data Studio
- ✓ Be able to debug stored procedures and UDFs using the DB2 development tools available
- ✓ Know how to capture and analyze Explain information

Candidates who have taken and passed either the *DB2 V8.1 Family Fundamentals* exam (Exam 700) or the *DB2 9 Family Fundamentals* exam (Exam 730) can obtain **IBM Certified Solution Developer—DB2 9.7 SQL Procedure** certification by taking (and passing) the *DB2 9.7 SQL Procedure Developer* exam (Exam 545). All other candidates must take and pass both the *DB2 9 Family Fundamentals* exam (Exam 730) ***and*** the *DB2 9.7 SQL Procedure Developer* exam (Exam 545). Figure 1.7 illustrates the road map for acquiring **IBM Certified Solution Developer—DB2 9.7 SQL Procedure** certification.

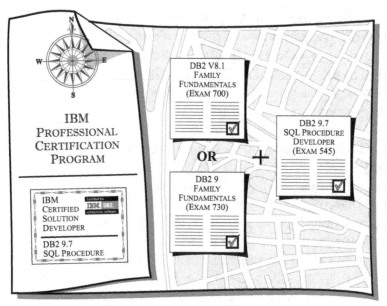

Figure 1.7: IBM Certified Solution Developer—
DB2 9.7 SQL Procedure Developer certification road map

The Certification Process

A quick examination of the road maps just presented reveals that, to obtain a particular certification from IBM, you must take and pass one or more exams that have been designed specifically for that certification role. (Each exam is a software-based test that is neither platform nor product specific.) Therefore, once you have chosen a certification role to pursue and have become familiar with the requirements (objectives) that have been defined for that role, the next step is to prepare for and take the necessary certification exam(s).

Preparing for the Certification Exams

If you have experience using DB2 10.1, DB2 10, or DB2 9.7 in the context of the certification role that you have chosen, you might already possess the skills and knowledge needed to pass the exams that have been created for that role. However, if your experience with DB2 is limited (or even if it is not), you can prepare for any of the certification exams available by taking advantage of the following resources:

Formal Education

IBM Learning Services offers a wide variety of courses that can help you prepare for certification. The IBM Professional Certification Program website (*www.ibm.com/certify*) provides a list of recommended courses for each certification exam. Simply locate and select the certification exam of interest and right-click the **Test preparation** tab when information about that exam appears. For more information on courses, schedules, training locations, and pricing, contact IBM Learning Services or visit its website.

Online Tutorials

IBM offers a series of interactive online tutorials to help you prepare for the DB2 10.1 Fundamentals exam (Exam 610) on its developerWorks website. The first tutorial in the series can be found at *www.ibm.com/developerworks/data/tutorials/db2-cert6101/index.html.*

IBM also offers a series of online tutorials for the DB2 10.1 for Linux, UNIX, and Windows Database Administration certification exam (Exam 611). The first tutorial in this series can be found at *www.ibm.com/developerworks/data/tutorials/db2-cert6111/index.html.*

Publications

You can find all the information you need to pass any of the DB2 certification exams available in the documentation that is provided with DB2; the product includes a complete set of manuals that you can access online via the DB2 Information Center or download from IBM's website in the form of PDF files. (The DB2 Product Family Library, at *www.ibm.com/software/data/db2/library*, contains links to this documentation as well as to version-specific DB2 Information Centers.)

Self-study books (like this one) that focus on one or more DB2 certification roles or specific DB2 certification exams are also available at your local bookstore, or you can order them from many online book retailers. (A list of possible reference materials for a particular certification exam can often be found on the **Test preparation** tab for that exam. And in some cases, ordering information is included with the listing.)

In addition to DB2 product documentation, IBM often produces manuals, known as Redbooks, that cover, among other things, advanced DB2 topics. These manuals are available as downloadable PDF files on IBM's Redbooks® website (*www.redbooks.ibm.com*). Or, if you prefer to have a bound hard copy, you can obtain one for a modest fee by following the appropriate link on the web page for the Redbook that interests you. (The downloadable Adobe® PDF files are available at no charge.)

Exam Objectives

The IBM Professional Certification Program website (*www.ibm.com/certify*) provides a list of topics that each certification exam covers. Simply locate and select the certification exam of interest and right-click the **Objectives** tab when information about that exam is presented. To find exam objectives for the *DB2 10.1 Fundamentals* exam (Exam 610), refer to Appendix A of this book.

Sample Questions and Practice Exams

Sample questions and practice exams offer a glimpse of the topics and the types of questions (as well as the wording) you are likely to encounter on a particular certification exam. More important, they can often help you determine whether you are ready to take a specific exam. (For this reason, sample questions, along with descriptive answers, are provided at the back of this book.)

Practice exams for most of IBM's certification exams are available via the IBM Professional Certification Program website (*www.ibm.com/certify*). Simply locate and select the certification exam of interest and right-click the **Test preparation** tab when information about that exam appears. Then, right-click the **Sample/Assessment test** link located at the top of the page, just below the tab. Usually, a fee of $30.00 US is charged for each assessment test taken.

It is important to note that IBM's certification exams are designed to be rigorous and extensive. Because of this, and because the range of material covered on a certification exam is usually broader than the knowledge base of many DB2 professionals, try to take advantage of as many exam preparation resources as possible. This will help ensure your success in obtaining the certification(s) you desire.

Arranging to Take a Certification Exam

When you are confident that you are ready to take a particular DB2 certification exam, your next step is to contact an IBM-authorized testing vendor and make the necessary arrangements. As of January 2, 2014, Pearson VUE is responsible for administering IBM's DB2 certification exams; however, in some cases IBM might administer them as well. For example, IBM frequently offers certification testing, for a nominal fee, at some of the larger IT conferences, such as the International DB2 User's Group (IDUG) conference and the IBM Insight (formerly IBM Information On Demand [IOD]) conference.

Pearson VUE's website (*www.pearsonvue.com/ibm*) offers a list of its testing centers—there are many to choose from throughout the world—and after finding a testing center that is convenient to you, you will need to create an account (or sign in if you already have an account) and make arrangements to take the certification exam desired. (You can also contact the vendor and make the necessary arrangements by phone; contact information for Pearson VUE can be found on their website.)

You must arrange to take a certification exam at least 24 hours in advance, and when you contact Pearson VUE, you should be ready to provide the following information:

- ✓ Your name (as you want it to appear on your certification certificate)
- ✓ Your unique testing identification number, if you have one (if you have taken an IBM certification exam before, this is the number that was assigned to you at that time; if not, Pearson VUE will supply one)
- ✓ A telephone number where you can be reached
- ✓ A fax number
- ✓ The mailing address where you want all hardcopy correspondence to be sent
- ✓ Your billing address, if it is different from your mailing address
- ✓ Your email address
- ✓ The number of the certification exam you wish to take (for example, Exam 610)
- ✓ The method of payment (credit card or debit card) you will use, along with any relevant payment information (such as credit/debit card number, expiration date, and card security code)
- ✓ Your company's name (if applicable)
- ✓ The testing center where you would like to take the exam
- ✓ The date that you would like to take the exam

Before you make arrangements to take a certification exam, you should have paper and pencil or pen handy so you can write down the test applicant identification number the testing center will assign you. You will need this information when you arrive to take the exam. (You should receive a confirmation email containing the number of the certification exam you are scheduled to take, along with corresponding date, time, and location information, at the email address you provided.)

•••

Note: If you have already taken one or more IBM certification exams, you should make the testing administrator (Pearson VUE or IBM) aware of this and ask them to assign you the same applicant identification number that was used before. This will allow the certification team at IBM to quickly recognize when you have met all the exam requirements for a particular certification role. (If you were assigned a unique applicant identification number each time you took an exam, you should go to the IBM Professional Certification Member website, *www.ibm.com/certify/members*, and select **Member Services** to combine all of your exam results under one ID.)

•••

Each certification exam costs $200.00 US, and you can arrange to take the exam immediately after you provide the appropriate payment information. If, for some reason, you need to reschedule or cancel your testing appointment, you must do so at least 24 hours before your scheduled test time. Otherwise, you will be charged the full price of the exam.

Taking an IBM Certification Exam

On the day you are scheduled to take a certification exam, you should arrive at the testing center at least 15 minutes before the scheduled time, to sign in. As part of the sign-in process, you will be asked to provide the applicant identification number you were assigned when you made arrangements to take the exam, as well as two forms of identification. One form of identification must be a current (not expired) government issued photo ID with your name and signature; the other must feature your name and signature. Examples of valid forms of identification include a driver's license or passport (government issued photo ID with signature) and a credit card (name and signature). The name on both forms of identification presented must match exactly the name that is in the Pearson VUE system.

Once you are signed in, the exam proctor will instruct you to enter the testing area and select an available workstation. The proctor will then enter your name and identification number into the workstation you have chosen, provide you with a pencil and some paper, and instruct you to begin the exam when you are ready. At that point, the Title screen of the IBM Certification Exam testing software should be displayed on the computer monitor in front of you. Figure 1.8 illustrates what this screen looks like.

Figure 1.8: Title screen of the IBM Certification Exam testing software

As you can see in Figure 1.8, the Title screen of the IBM Certification Exam testing software consists of the title "Professional Certification Program from IBM," the IBM Logo, and the name of the exam that is about to be administered (for example, the Title screen in Figure 1.8 indicates that the *DB2 10.1 Fundamentals* exam is about to be administered), along with some basic information on how to get started. Before proceeding, you should verify that the exam you are about to take is indeed the exam you expected to take. If the name of the exam that appears on the Title screen is different from the name of the exam you had planned on taking, bring this to the attention of the exam proctor immediately. When you are ready, begin by selecting the **Next** button located in the lower-right corner of the screen (refer to Figure 1.8). To do this, place the mouse pointer over the **Next** button and click the left mouse button.

After you have clicked **Next** on the Title screen, you will be presented with a Proprietary and Confidential Information screen, where you will be asked to agree that you will not disclose the contents of the exam in any manner, to anyone. Figure 1.9 illustrates what this screen looks like.

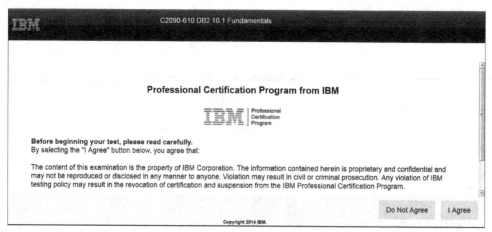

*Figure 1.9: Proprietary and Confidential Information screen of the
IBM Certification Exam testing software*

If you agree to the terms and conditions outlined on the Proprietary and Confidential
Information screen, select the **I Agree** button located in the lower-right corner of the
screen (refer to Figure 1.9). Once you have clicked **I Agree**, you will be presented
with the Begin Test screen of the IBM Certification Exam testing software. Figure 1.10
illustrates what this screen looks like.

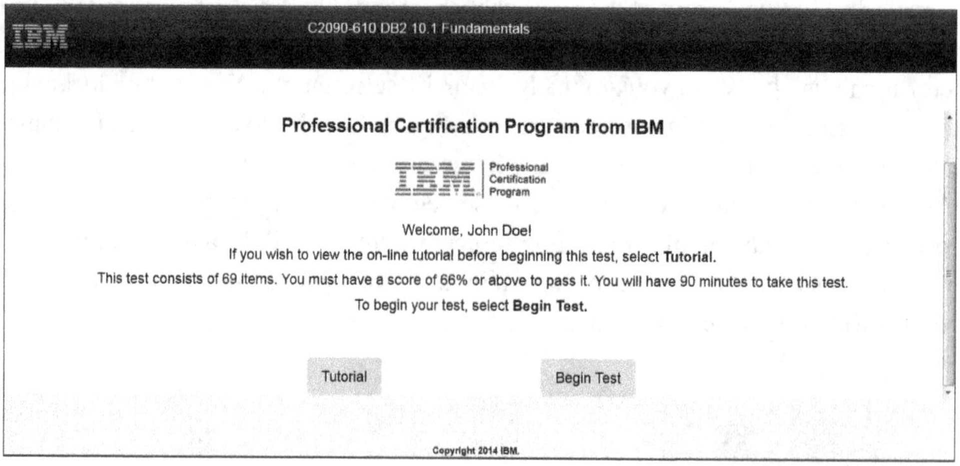

Figure 1.10: Begin Test screen of the IBM Certification Exam testing software

As you can see in Figure 1.10, the Begin Test screen consists of the title "Professional
Certification Program from IBM," the IBM Logo, and a welcome message containing

your name and some basic information about the exam you are about to take. Before proceeding, you should verify that your name is spelled correctly. The way your name appears in the welcome message displayed reflects how it has been stored in the IBM Certification database. Consequently, this is how all correspondence to you will be addressed, and, more important, this is how your name will appear on the certification credentials you will receive once you have met all the requirements for a particular certification role.

In addition to telling you which exam is about to be administered, the Begin Test screen lets you know how many questions you can expect to see on the exam, the score you must receive to pass, and the time frame in which the exam must be completed. Most DB2 certification exams contain between 60 and 70 questions, and you are allotted up to 90 minutes to complete them. However, even though each certification exam must be completed within a predefined time limit, you should never rush through an exam just because the "clock is running"; the time limits imposed are more than adequate for you to work through the questions at a relaxed and steady pace.

When you are ready to start the exam, select the **Begin Test** button located in the lower-right corner of the screen (refer to Figure 1.10). If, instead, you desire a quick refresher course on how to use the IBM Certification Exam testing software, click the **Tutorial** button located in the lower-left corner of the screen.

Important: If you plan to take a quick refresher course on how to use the IBM Certification Exam testing software, make sure you do so *before* you click Begin Test to begin the exam. Although help is available at any time, the clock does not start running until you select the Begin Test button. Therefore, by viewing help information before the clock has started, you avoid spending what could prove to be valuable testing time reading documentation instead of answering questions.

After you have clicked **Begin Test** on the Begin Test screen, the clock will start running, and the first exam question will be presented in a screen that looks similar to the one shown in Figure 1.11.

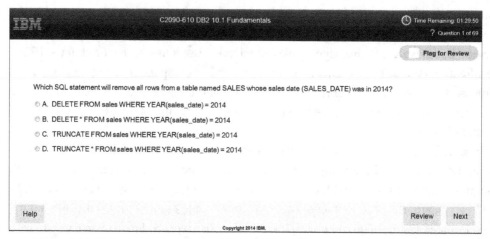

Figure 1.11: Typical question screen of the IBM Certification Exam testing software

Aside from the question itself, one of the first things you might notice if you look closely at the question screen is that the question number appears in the top-right corner of the screen. If you answer each question in the order they are presented, this portion of the screen can act as a progress indicator since it displays both the current question number *and* the total number of questions contained in the exam.

Immediately below the question number, you will find a special check box that is labeled **Flag for Review**. If you want to skip the current question for now and come back to it later, or if you are uncertain about the answer(s) you have chosen and would like to look at this question again after you have completed the rest of the exam, you should mark this check box (by placing the mouse pointer over it and pressing the left mouse button). After you have viewed every question once, you will be given the opportunity to review just the marked (flagged) questions again. At that time, you can answer any unanswered questions remaining and reevaluate any answers you have some reservations about.

Another important feature on the question screen is the **Time Remaining** information, which appears in the top-right corner of the screen, immediately above the question number. This area of the question screen provides continuous feedback on the amount of time you have available in which to complete (and review) the exam.

The most important part of the question screen, however, is the question itself and the corresponding list of possible answers provided. Take time to read each question carefully, and when you have located the correct answer in the list provided, mark it by selecting the answer radio button positioned just to the left of the answer text (by placing the mouse pointer over the desired answer radio button and pressing the left mouse button). After you have selected an answer for the current question (or marked it using the **Flag for Review** check box), you can move to the next question by clicking the **Next** button, located in the lower-right corner of the screen (refer to Figure 1.11).

If at any time you want to return to the previous question, you can do so by clicking the **Previous** button, located just to the left of the **Next** button, at the bottom of the screen (refer to Figure 1.12). And to obtain help on how to use the IBM Certification Exam testing software, click **Help**, located in the lower-left corner of the screen.

It is important to note that although you can use the **Next** and **Previous** buttons to navigate through the questions, the navigation process itself is not cyclic in nature—that is, when you are on the first question, you cannot go to the last question by clicking **Previous** (in fact, the **Previous** button will not be displayed if you are on the first question, which is why it is not shown in Figure 1.11). Likewise, when you are on the last question, you cannot go to the first question simply by clicking **Next**. However, you can quickly navigate back to the first question from the Item Review screen, which you can get to by clicking **Review**. (We will look at the Item Review screen shortly).

Although in most cases, only one answer in the list provided is the correct answer for the question shown, there are times when multiple answers are valid. On those occasions, the answer radio buttons will be replaced with answer check boxes, and the question will be worded in such a way to make it obvious how many answers are expected. Figure 1.12 shows an example of such a question.

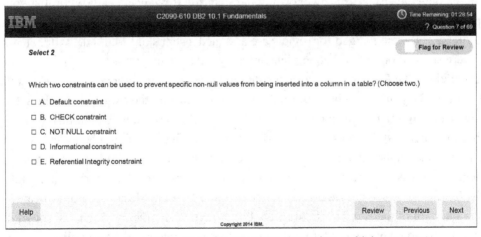

Figure 1.12: Question screen for questions expecting multiple answers

To answer these types of questions, select the answer check box positioned just to the left of the text of every correct answer you find. (Again, to do this, place the mouse pointer over each desired answer check box and press the left mouse button.)

When you have viewed every exam question available (by clicking **Next** on every question screen that appears), an Item Review screen similar to the one in Figure 1.13 may be displayed.

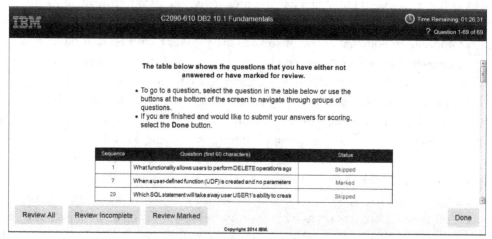

Figure 1.13: Item Review screen of the IBM Certification Exam testing software

The Item Review screen contains a listing of questions from the exam you have just taken that you either marked (by choosing the **Flag for Review** check box) or that you skipped or did not provide the correct number of answers for. (As you can see in Figure 1.13, items that were flagged for review are assigned a status of "Marked," while items that were skipped or that are incomplete are assigned a status of "Skipped.")

By clicking the **Review All** button located in the lower-left corner of the screen (refer to Figure 1.13), you can go back through all the questions on the exam. By clicking the **Review Incomplete** button (located just to the right of the **Review All** button), you can go back through just the questions that have been identified as being incomplete. When you review incomplete items in this manner, each time you click **Next** on a question screen, you proceed to the next incomplete question in the list until you eventually return to the Item Review screen. Likewise, by clicking the **Review Marked** button (located just to the right of the **Review Incomplete** button), you can quickly go back through just the questions you have marked. (Navigation works the same as when you click **Review Incomplete**.)

One of the first things you should do if the Item Review screen appears is resolve any incomplete items found. (When the exam is graded, each incomplete item is marked incorrect, and points are deducted from your final score.) Then, if time permits, you should go back and review the questions that you marked. It is important to note that when you finish reviewing a marked question, you should unmark it (by placing the mouse pointer over the **Flag for Review** check box and pressing the left mouse button) before proceeding to the next marked question or returning to the Item Review screen. This will make it easier for you to keep track of which questions you have reviewed and which you have not.

After you have resolved every incomplete item found, the **Review Incomplete** button will automatically disappear from the Item Review screen; similarly, when no more marked questions exist, the **Review Marked** button will disappear. Consequently, when you have resolved every incomplete and marked item found (or if there were no incomplete or marked items originally), you will be presented with a screen that looks like the one in Figure 1.14.

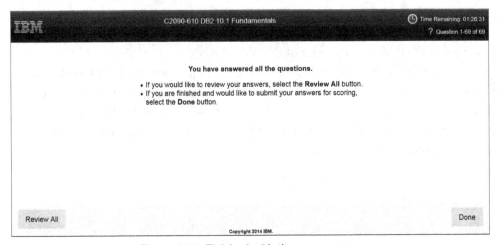

Figure 1.14: Finished with the exam screen

At this point, you can go through all the questions again by selecting the **Review All** button located in the lower-left corner of the screen (refer to Figure 1.14). Or, if you feel comfortable with the answers you have provided, you can end the exam and submit it for grading by clicking **Done**, which is located in the lower-right corner of the screen. After you select this button, a screen similar to the one in Figure 1.15 will appear.

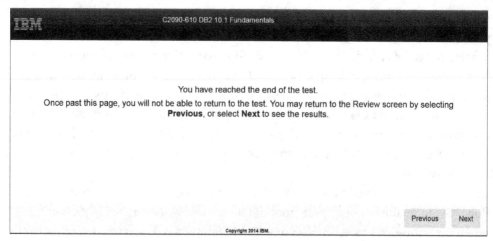

Figure 1.15: End exam session confirmation screen

This screen gives you the opportunity to confirm your decision to end the exam and submit it for grading, or to reconsider and continue resolving or reviewing exam items (questions). If you wish to do the former, click **Next** when this screen is displayed; if you wish to do the latter, click **Previous** to return to the Item Review screen. (Both buttons are located in the lower-right corner of the screen.)

Once you confirm that you do indeed wish to end the exam, the IBM Certification Exam testing software will evaluate your answers and produce a score report that indicates whether you passed the exam. This report will then be displayed on a Test Results screen similar to the one shown in Figure 1.16. At the same time, a corresponding hard-copy printout will be generated.

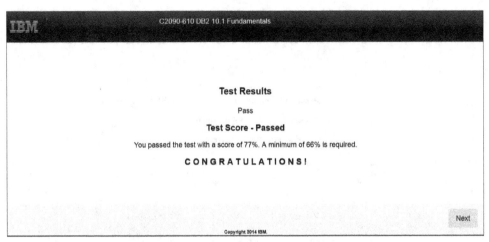

Figure 1.16: Test Results screen of the IBM Certification Exam testing software

As you can see in Figure 1.16, the Exam Results panel shows your test results (Pass or Fail) along with a message that contains the required score and the percentage score you received. If you received a passing score, this message will begin with the word "Congratulations!" However, if you received a score that is below the score needed to pass, the message you see will begin with the words "You did not pass the test."

Each certification exam is broken into sections, and regardless of whether you receive a passing or failing score, you should take a few moments to review the scores you received for each section. This information can help you assess your strengths and weaknesses. And if you failed to pass the test, this information can help you identify the areas that you should spend more time reviewing before you attempt to retake the exam. To view the section scores for the exam you just completed, simply click **Next**, which is located in the lower-right corner of the screen. You should then see a screen that is similar to the one in Figure 1.17.

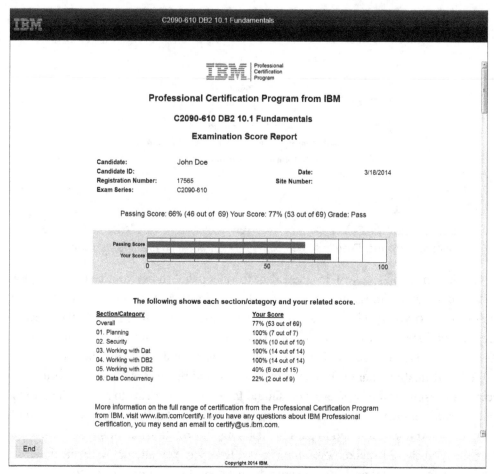

Figure 1.17: Examination Score Report screen

When you have finished reviewing your section scores, you can exit the IBM Certification Exam testing software by clicking **End**, which is located at the lower-left corner of the screen.

Shortly after you take a certification exam (usually within five working days), Pearson VUE will send your results, along with your demographic data (for example, name, address, phone number) to the IBM Certification Group for processing. If you passed the exam, you will receive credit toward the certification role the test was designed for. And if you have met all of the requirements that have been defined for that certification role, you will receive an email (at the email address you provided during registration) directing you to the IBM Certification Members website, where you can download a certificate suitable for framing (in the form of a PDF file), camera-ready artwork of the IBM certification logo, and guidelines for using the "IBM Certified" mark. If desired, you can also receive a printed certificate and/or a wallet-sized certificate via regular mail by going to the appropriate website (referenced in the email) and requesting these materials—you will be asked to provide your Fulfillment ID and Validation Number (also provided in the email) as proof that you have met all the requirements for certification.

Upon receipt of the welcome package, you are officially certified and can begin using the IBM Professional Certification title and trademark. You should receive the IBM Certification Agreement and welcome email within four to six weeks after IBM processes the exam results. If you failed to pass the test and you still wish to become certified, you must arrange to retake the exam (and you must pay the testing fee again). No restrictions apply on the number of times you can take a particular certification exam; however, you cannot take the same exam more than two times within a 30-day period.

2

CHAPTER

Planning

Ten percent (10%) of the *DB2 10.1 Fundamentals* certification exam (Exam 610)
is designed to test your knowledge of the various DB2 editions and add-on products
that are available from IBM. This portion of the exam is also designed to test your
ability to identify which edition and products to use to create a specific type of database
environment, as well as your knowledge of how to store and manipulate nonrelational
data. The questions that make up this portion of the exam are intended to evaluate the
following:

- Your knowledge of the DB2 10 and DB2 10.1 products currently available
- Your ability to identify the characteristics of both data warehouse and online
  transaction processing (OLTP) workloads
- Your ability to identify which DB2 products should be used to create a particular
  database environment (data warehouse or OLTP)
- Your knowledge of how to store and manipulate nonrelational data such as large
  objects (LOBs) and Extensible Markup Language (XML) documents

This chapter introduces you to the various DB2 editions and add-on products that are
currently available and shows you which editions and products to use to create a data
warehouse or OLTP environment. In this chapter, you will learn about the products that
make up the *DB2 Family*, the characteristics of data warehouse and OLTP databases, and

which DB2 products to use to create each of these types of database environments. You will also discover how to store, manage, and manipulate LOB and XML data.

The DB2 Family

In 1969, while working at IBM's San Jose Research Laboratory in San Jose, California, Edgar Frank "Ted" Codd introduced a relational model for database management in a paper titled "A Relational Model of Data for Large Shared Data Banks." And over the next four years, a variety of research prototypes such as University of California, Berkley's *Ingres* and IBM's *System R* (short for *System Relational*) were developed based on this model. In 1980, as part of an effort to port the System R prototype to their mainframe computer, IBM began work on a new product called *DATABASE 2* (otherwise known as *DB2*), and on June 7, 1983, the company made DB2 available to a limited number of IBM mainframe customers. In 1985, IBM made DB2 generally available to all customers who were using the MVS™ operating system.

In 1987, DB2 arrived on the personal computer (PC) in the form of a product called *Database Manager*, which was one of two special add-on products that were included as part of the Extended Edition version of OS/2 1.3; a year later, a version emerged in the form of *SQL/400* for IBM's new AS/400® server. (IBM developers working on System R created a nonrelational programming language named *SEQUEL*, which was later renamed *SQL*—an acronym for *Structured Query Language*—and the name *SQL/400* was derived by combining this acronym with part of the AS/400 server name.)

By 1992, DB2 had become a stand-alone product on OS/2 (and was now called *DB2/2*), and in 1993, IBM made DB2 generally available to customers running AIX® on IBM RS/6000® series servers. (Initially, this port was known as *DB2/6000*, but eventually both DB2/2 and DB2/6000 were replaced with a product named *DB2 for Common Servers*.) DB2 for Common Servers arrived on HP-UX and Solaris servers in 1994, on Windows servers in 1995, and on Linux servers in 1999. Along the way the name changed yet again, and DB2 for Common Servers became *DB2 Universal Database™*.

Today, essentially two flavors of DB2 are available: DB2 for Linux, UNIX, and Windows, sometimes referred to as *DB2 for LUW* or *DB2 for distributed platforms* and DB2 for z/OS. (With the release of DB2 Version 9, the *Universal Database* moniker was replaced with the names of the three most prominent operating systems the non-z/OS flavor of DB2 runs on.) Several editions of DB2 are available, and each edition has been designed to meet a specific business need. These editions, along with a suite of add-on products that provide additional functionality, are known collectively as the *DB2 Family*. The editions that make up the heart of this family are:

- DB2 Express-C
- DB2 Express Edition
- DB2 Workgroup Server Edition
- DB2 Enterprise Server Edition
- DB2 Advanced Enterprise Server Edition
- DB2 for z/OS

Figure 2.1 shows all of the aforementioned DB2 Family editions, along with the type of computing environment each edition is primarily designed for.

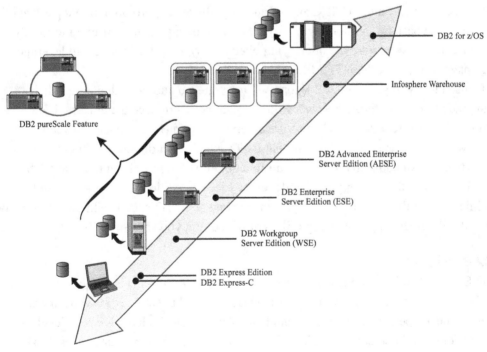

Figure 2.1: The DB2 editions available

•••

Note: Do not confuse DB2 for Linux on System z (also known as zLinux) with DB2 for z/OS. In this case, the DB2 product that runs on zLinux is DB2 for Linux, UNIX, and Windows—and any DB2 client or driver can connect to it, without the need of DB2 Connect™ software (an add-on product that provides connectivity between DB2 for Linux, UNIX, and Windows and DB2 for z/OS databases).

•••

It is important to note that you can easily move from one DB2 edition to another—provided you are not trying to move from an edition of DB2 that has been developed for Linux, UNIX, or Windows to an edition that has been developed for z/OS (or vice versa). That is because on Linux, UNIX, and Windows platforms, approximately 90 percent of the DB2 code base is common, with only 10 percent being slightly different to tightly integrate the software with the underlying operating system (for instance, to leverage huge pages on AIX or the NTFS file system on Windows).

Consequently, if you use DB2 Express-C to create a database and later decide to upgrade to DB2 Enterprise Server Edition, you merely replace the existing DB2 Express-C software with a DB2 Enterprise Server Edition (ESE) image. The end result will be a database environment that looks exactly as it did before, but that can take advantage of additional features and functionality that have been made available to it. This means that any application developed for one edition will work, without modification, with other editions. It also means that any DB2-specific skills that you have learned will remain applicable, regardless of the edition you are using.

DB2 Express-C

DB2 Express-C (also known as *DB2 Express-Community edition*) is a no-charge, entry-level database management system that is ideal for small businesses, IBM business partners, developers, instructors, and students who want to evaluate DB2 or develop applications that interact with DB2 for Linux, UNIX, and Windows databases. DB2 Express-C is quick to set up, easy to use, and contains many of the core features and functionality that are available with other DB2 editions, including:

- **IBM Data Studio:** An Eclipse-based integrated development environment that can be used to perform database and instance administration; create, deploy, and debug data-centric applications; and perform query-tuning operations

- **pureXML®:** Offers a simple, efficient way to store well-formed XML documents while providing the same level of security, integrity, and resiliency that is available for relational data; this allows XML data to be stored in its native, hierarchical format and be manipulated using XQuery, SQL, or a combination of the two
- **Backup compression:** Used to reduce the size of backup images by compressing all of the data in an image, including catalog tables, user tables, index objects, large objects, auxiliary database files, and database metadata, thereby reducing storage space requirements
- **Time Travel Query:** Lets you discover how data looked (or will look) at a specific point in time—special tables called *temporal tables* associate time-based, state information with relational data values; data in temporal tables can be valid for a time period that is defined by the database system, user applications, or both
- **Federation with DB2 for LUW and Informix® data sources:** Makes it possible to access objects like tables and views that reside in other DB2 for Linux, UNIX, Windows, and/or Informix databases as if they were local objects
- **SQL compatibility:** Lets you run applications written for Oracle, Sybase, and MySQL databases seamlessly against DB2 for Linux, UNIX, and Windows databases
- **DB2 Text Search:** Provides extensive capabilities for locating data that has been stored in textual columns in a DB2 database; by incorporating DB2 Text Search functions in SQL and XQuery statements, you can develop powerful and versatile text-retrieval programs
- **DB2 Spatial Extender:** Provides a way to generate and analyze spatial information about geographic features, as well as store and manage the data this information is based upon (a geographic feature is anything in the real world that has an identifiable location *or* anything that can be imagined as existing at an identifiable location)

DB2 Express-C is available in more than 16 different languages and can be installed on any server that is running the Linux or Windows operating system (32-bit or 64-bit versions). The server used can contain any number of processors/cores and any amount of memory. However, total resource utilization is limited to two processors/cores and 4 GB of RAM.

Owners of DB2 Express-C can purchase a low-cost, yearly subscription option (known as a *Fixed Term License* or *FTL*) that provides the following additional benefits and features that are unavailable with the no-cost version:

- 24/7 customer support, fix packs, and upgrade protection
- Increased resource utilization: four processors/cores and 8 GB memory
- Failover capabilities with High Availability Disaster Recovery (HADR)
- Enhanced security with both Row and Column Access Control (RCAC) and Label-Based Access Control (LBAC)
- SQL replication

DB2 Express Edition

DB2 Express Edition is a comprehensive, budget-friendly database management system that is designed to meet the needs of small and midsize businesses, academic institutions, and IBM business partners. With support for up to four processors/cores and 8 GB of RAM, DB2 Express Edition is ideal for building database environments that are robust, resilient, secure, and cost efficient. In addition to the features and functionality provided with DB2 Express-C, DB2 Express Edition includes the following:

- **Advanced Copy Services (ACS):** Enables the use of fast, disk-based replication technology that is available with some storage vendors for backup and recovery operations—use of this technology can drastically reduce the amount of time required to back up and restore large databases
- **Row and Column Access Control (RCAC):** Complements the authorities and privileges security model available with DB2 by controlling access to a table at the row level, the column level, or both the row and column level; can also be used to mask sensitive information so unauthorized users cannot see it
- **Label-Based Access Control (LBAC):** Provides multilevel data security by controlling who has read access, who has write access, and who has both read and write access to individual rows, individual columns, or individual rows and columns in a table; this feature is implemented by assigning unique labels to users and data and allowing access only when assigned labels match
- **Online reorganization:** Reorganizes tables and rebuilds indexes to eliminate fragmentation, compress data, or both; as the name implies, this work can take place while a database remains online and accessible

- **High Availability Disaster Recovery (HADR):** Provides ultrafast hardware and software failover capabilities by replicating data changes made to a source database (called the *primary database*) to one or more target databases (called *standby databases*) and failing over to one of the standbys, if for some reason, the primary becomes inaccessible
- **SQL Replication with DB2 for LUW and Informix data sources:** Captures changes made to source tables and views and writes them to staging tables— changes are then read from the staging tables and replicated to corresponding target tables in other DB2 for Linux, UNIX, and Windows or Informix databases

Like DB2 Express-C, DB2 Express Edition is available in multiple languages; however, unlike DB2 Express-C, DB2 Express Edition can be installed on servers that are running 32- or 64-bit versions of the following operating systems:

- Red Hat Enterprise Linux (RHEL) 5 or 6
- SUSE Linux Enterprise Server (SLES) 10 or 11
- Sun Solaris 10 (x86, 64-bit)
- Microsoft® Windows (Windows 7 Enterprise, Windows 7 Professional, Windows 7 Ultimate, Windows Server 2003, Windows Server 2008 Standard Edition, Windows Vista Business, Windows Vista Enterprise, Windows Vista Ultimate, or Windows XP Professional)

DB2 Workgroup Server Edition (WSE)

DB2 Workgroup Server Edition (WSE) is a scalable, full-function database management system that is ideal for small and midsize businesses, workgroups, and departments that consist of a small number of internal users. In addition to having the power and reliability to handle department-level workloads with ease, DB2 Workgroup Server Edition is packed with all the features that DB2 Express Edition offers as well as features that reduce the total cost of ownership (TCO), including:

- **The DB2 pureScale Feature:** Uses a shared-disk, cluster architecture that allows a database to be efficiently scaled across several servers (nodes)
- **Autonomic features:** Helps lower the cost of data management by automating basic administration tasks, increasing storage efficiency, improving run-time

performance, and simplifying the deployment of virtual appliances; the autonomic features available consist of:

>> **Automatic storage:** Simplifies storage management by allowing DB2 to determine the storage characteristics for table spaces (including the location of containers) and by automatically monitoring and managing table space container growth

>> **Self-Tuning Memory Manager (STMM):** Responds to significant changes in a database's workload by dynamically distributing available memory resources among several different database memory consumers

>> **Automatic maintenance:** Simplifies storage management by performing database backup operations automatically, keeping database statistics current, and reorganizing tables and indexes as necessary

>> **Self-configuration:** Automatically configures memory allocation, storage management, and business policy maintenance operations for DB2 databases

>> **Health monitoring:** Proactively monitors situations or changes in a database environment that can result in performance degradation or potential outages

- **Audit Facility:** Monitors data access and provides information needed for subsequent analysis; auditing can help discover unwanted, unknown, and unacceptable access to data as well as keep historical records of activities performed on a database system

- **IBM Workload Deployer:** Provides access to IBM middleware virtual images, making it easy to quickly and repeatedly create application environments that can be securely deployed and managed in a private cloud

DB2 Workgroup Server Edition is also available in 16 different languages and can be installed on servers that are running 32- and 64-bit versions of the same operating systems that DB2 Express Edition can be installed on. Unlike DB2 Express Edition, DB2 Workgroup Server Edition can also be installed on servers that are running IBM AIX 6 or 7.

One of the main advantages that DB2 Workgroup Server Edition offers over DB2 Express Edition (and DB2 Express-C) is that it can leverage more RAM and CPU processing power—DB2 Workgroup Server Edition is restricted to 16 processors/cores and 64 GB of memory. Another advantage is that the DB2 pureScale feature is included as part of DB2 Workgroup Server Edition. (If the DB2 pureScale feature is in use, RAM and CPU limits apply to the entire cluster.) It is important to note, however, that system requirements for DB2 pureScale are significantly different from those for DB2 Workgroup Server Edition. For instance, DB2 pureScale can only be installed on IBM p Series or x Series servers that are running either the AIX (p Series) or the Linux (x Series) operating system. DB2 pureScale also dictates that the General Parallel File System (GPFS™) file system is to be used.

DB2 Enterprise Server Edition (ESE)

Ideal for high-performance, robust enterprise environments, DB2 Enterprise Server Edition (ESE) is designed to meet the data server needs of midsize and large businesses that have hundreds of internal and/or external users. DB2 Enterprise Server Edition can be deployed on Linux, UNIX, and Windows servers (physical or virtual) of any size and, unlike with other DB2 editions, no restrictions apply to the number of processors/cores and amount of memory that can be used.

DB2 Enterprise Server Edition includes all the features and functionality that comes with DB2 Workgroup Server Edition, as well as some additional features:

- **Connection Concentrator:** Improves the performance of applications that require frequent, but relatively transient, simultaneous user connections by allocating host database resources only for the duration of an SQL transaction
- **Materialized Query Tables (MQTs):** Tables whose definitions are based on the results of a query; MQTs provide a powerful way to improve response time for complex queries, and they are similar to views in that their data comes from one or more base tables—MQT data is generated by executing the query the MQT is based upon, either at regular intervals or at a specific point in time that is dictated by the user; unlike with views, MQT data physically resides in the MQT itself
- **Multidimensional Clustering (MDC) Tables:** Offer an elegant way to cluster data along two or more dimensions; MDC tables can significantly improve query performance and drastically reduce the overhead of data maintenance operations—MDC tables are used primarily in data warehouse and large database environments, but they can be used in OLTP environments as well
- **Multi-temperature data management:** Utilizes *storage groups* (a named set of storage paths where data is to be stored) to represent different classes of storage (solid state disks, fibre channel drives, or serial ATA drives) that might be available to a database system—by using multi-temperature data management, it is possible to place frequently or constantly accessed data on faster storage devices and keep infrequently accessed data on slower (and cheaper) disks
- **Table partitioning:** A data organization scheme in which table data is divided across multiple storage objects (called *data partitions*) according to values stored in

one or more columns; each data partition can reside in a different table space, in the same table space, or in a combination of the two

- **Query parallelism:** Provides the ability to break a query into multiple parts and process those parts in parallel across multiple partitions of a partitioned database (that span one or more servers/workstations), thereby improving performance
- **Resource Description Framework (RDF):** A family of World Wide Web Consortium (W3C) specifications that employs Uniform Resource Identifiers (URIs) to create a relationship between data as a triple (for example, in the form of *subject-predicate-object* expressions) or as a quad—RDF is similar to NoSQL

As with other DB2 Editions, DB2 Enterprise Server Edition is available in multiple languages. And DB2 Enterprise Server Edition can be installed on servers that are running AIX, Linux (Red Hat or SUSE), Solaris, and Microsoft Windows—that is, on the same operating systems that DB2 Workgroup Server Edition can be installed on.

DB2 Advanced Enterprise Server Edition (AESE)

The most comprehensive DB2 edition available, DB2 Advanced Enterprise Server Edition (AESE) is a powerful database management solution that offers all the features and functionality available with DB2 Enterprise Server Edition, as well as the following additional features and benefits:

- **DB2 Storage Optimization Feature:** Helps decrease disk space utilization and storage infrastructure requirements by transparently compressing data using classic row compression (where data is compressed using table-level dictionaries), adaptive row compression (where data is compressed dynamically using page-level dictionaries), or a combination of the two; temporary tables are compressed when DB2 deems it necessary and indexes for compressed tables are compressed by default—DB2 Enterprise Server Edition users can take advantage of this functionality by purchasing the DB2 Storage Optimization feature
- **Continuous Data Ingest (CDI):** A high-speed, client-side DB2 utility that streams preprocessed data directly from named pipes or output files produced by ETL tools (or some other means) into DB2 tables
- **DB2 Workload Manager (WLM):** A comprehensive workload management feature that can help identify, manage, and control database workloads (applications, users, and so forth) to maximize database server throughput and resource utilization; with DB2 Workload Manager, it is possible to customize

execution environments so that no single workload can control and consume all of the system resources available

- **IBM InfoSphere® Optim™:** A family of data life-cycle management tools and solutions that can be used to design, develop, deploy, and manage database applications throughout the data life cycle (from requirements to retirement); the IBM InfoSphere Optim product family consists of:

  » **IBM InfoSphere Data Architect:** Offers a complete solution for designing, modeling, discovering, relating, and standardizing data assets; this tool is used for data modeling, transformation, and Data Definition Language (DDL) generation, as well as to build, debug, and manage database objects such as SQL stored procedures and user-defined functions (UDFs)

  » **IBM InfoSphere Optim Configuration Manager:** Provides advice on how to change database configurations; also stores states and changes in a repository, making it possible to compare current and historical data, which can be helpful when trying to understand and resolve problems related to configuration changes

  » **IBM InfoSphere Optim Performance Manager Extended Edition:** Can identify, diagnose, solve, and prevent performance problems in DB2 products and associated applications

  » **IBM InfoSphere Optim pureQuery® Runtime:** Can deploy advanced pureQuery applications that use static SQL; bridges the gap between data and Java technology by harnessing the power of SQL within an easy-to-use Java data access platform—it also increases security of Java applications, helping to prevent threats like SQL injection

  » **IBM InfoSphere Optim Query Tuner:** Often known as the *Query Tuner,* can analyze and make recommendations on ways to tune existing queries, as well as provide expert advice on writing new, efficient, high quality queries

- **Federation with DB2 for Linux, UNIX, and Windows and Oracle data sources:** Makes it possible to access objects like tables and views that reside in Oracle databases as if they were local objects

DB2 Advanced Enterprise Server Edition can be installed on servers that are running AIX, Linux (Red Hat or SUSE), Solaris, and Microsoft Windows—that is, on the same operating systems that DB2 Enterprise Server Edition can be installed on.

DB2 for z/OS

DB2 for z/OS is a multiuser, full-function database management system that has been designed specifically for z/OS, IBM's flagship mainframe operating system. Tightly

integrated with the IBM mainframe, DB2 for z/OS leverages the strengths of System z®
64-bit architecture to provide:

- **Reduced total cost of ownership:** Integration with the latest IBM System
  z9® processors, Modified Indirect Data Address Words (MIDAW) channel
  programming capability, Internet Protocol version 6 (IPv6) and Secure Socket
  Layer (SSL) support, along with improved hardware compression enable DB2 for
  z/OS to offer better functionality and performance
- **Continuous availability and business resiliency:** Unique improvements such
  as online schema evolution, the ability to dynamically add partitions and change
  data definitions, support for online unload and replace, and improved backup and
  recovery utilities enable DB2 for z/OS to offer the highest level of continuous
  availability possible
- **Extraordinary scalability:** New partitioning, clustering, and indexing options,
  along with important optimization improvements such as improved insert, update,
  and delete processing and buffer scalability enhancements, make DB2 for z/OS an
  excellent choice for large and growing databases
- **Ability to support complex data warehouses:** Improved optimization, the ability
  to rotate partitions, and new design options for indexes, clustering, materialized
  query tables result in faster response and reduced processing times for a host of
  query types
- **Portability and ease of migration:** Rich SQL enhancements such as new data
  types for decimal floating point, XML, and spatial data, along with new built-in
  functions, provide better compatibility within the DB2 Family and throughout the
  industry
- **Unmatched security and compliance assurance:** Legendary mainframe built-in
  security, trace features that provide end-to-end auditing capabilities, and enhanced
  data encryption mean that DB2 for z/OS can protect data in a way that adheres to
  growing compliance and audit requirements
- **Enhanced web support:** Improved Java Database Connectivity (JDBC) and
  SQL for Java (SQLJ) support, a new Java Universal Driver, enhanced Unicode
  support, WebSphere integration, and new pureXML functions make Java and web
  applications more robust and productive
- **Enhanced business analytics and data visualization solutions:** The ability
  to distribute reporting information quickly throughout the enterprise has been

exponentially increased via the WebSphere component of DB2 Query Management Facility™ (QMF™) Enterprise Edition; this Eclipse-based product extends QMF-supported platforms to Linux, Solaris, and HP-UX

Version 10 is a tremendous step forward for DB2 for z/OS because of its improvements in performance, scalability, availability, security, and application integration. As with previous versions, DB2 10 for z/OS takes advantage of the latest improvements in System z hardware and software to provide optimum performance—most customers can achieve out-of-the-box CPU savings of 5-to-10 percent for traditional workloads—and significantly cut IT infrastructure costs.

Database Workloads

Operations performed against relational databases are often classified according to the frequency in which they are performed and the volume of data they modify or retrieve. Together, these characteristics identify the type of workloads a particular database supports; most database workloads fall into two distinct categories: *online transaction processing* (OLTP) and *data warehousing*, which includes reporting, online analytical processing (OLAP), and data mining.

What differentiates a data warehousing system from an OLTP system? Data warehousing involves storing and managing large volumes of data (often historical in nature) that is used primarily for analysis. For instance, a data warehouse could be used to summarize a company's sales by region or to identify patterns in products that have been sold over the last five years. Consequently, workloads in a data warehouse environment can vary—they might consist of bulk load operations, short-running simple queries, long-running complex queries, random ad hoc queries, infrequent updates to data, or the execution of online maintenance utilities. To handle these types of workloads, most data warehouse environments have the following requirements:

- **Performance:** This is a system's ability to execute any action within a given time interval. In a data warehouse environment, the system should perform the initial population of tables and any required incremental updates in the shortest amount of time possible. Ad hoc queries should be satisfied, at any time, without degrading the performance of other mission-critical or time-sensitive operations. Similarly, complex and multidimensional queries should handle aggregations, full-table scans, and multiple table joins with little or no performance impact.

- **Scalability:** This is a system's ability to be readily enlarged or to handle increases in load without adversely affecting performance. Both the hardware and software components used in building a data warehouse should enable the environment to grow, as needed, without reducing performance.
- **Availability:** This relates to the proportion of time that a system is functional and working. A data warehouse should be available 24 hours a day, 7 days a week, 365 days a year. However, a data warehouse may be taken offline at regular intervals, and for a limited amount of time, to be updated or populated with a bulk-load operation.
- **Manageability:** This defines how easily administrators can manage a system, usually through tools that are available for monitoring, debugging, and tuning. A data warehouse environment should be flexible and extensible, while minimizing the administrative costs involved in keeping it online and accessible.

In contrast, OLTP systems are designed to support day-to-day, mission-critical business activities such as web-based order entry, stock trading, and inventory management. Consequently, OLTP workloads are often characterized by simple, single-record lookups and by SQL operations (typically inserts, updates, and deletes) that access or modify a small number of records and perform few, if any, input/output (I/O) operations. To better handle these types of workloads, most OLTP environments have the following requirements:

- **High performance:** In an OLTP environment, high throughput, measured in hundreds of transactions per second, is required. And subsecond end-user response time is desired. (Performance of OLTP workloads can often be enhanced by minimizing I/Os, optimizing CPU utilization, eliminating sorts, and improving transaction concurrency.)
- **High volume:** A typical OLTP environment might consist of hundreds to thousands of users issuing millions of transactions per day against databases that vary in size. Consequently, the volume of data affected may be very large, even though each transaction typically makes changes to only a small number of records. (Data tends to be current.)
- **High availability:** Unlike data warehouses, which can be taken offline at regular intervals, OLTP databases typically must be available 24 hours a day, 7 days a week, 365 days a year.

Optimized Solutions for Each Workload Type

Although you can use all the DB2 Editions available *except* DB2 Express-C and DB2 Express Edition to create both data warehouse and OLTP environments, IBM offers two solutions that are tailored specifically for one workload type or the other: *InfoSphere Warehouse* (for data warehousing workloads) and the *DB2 pureScale Feature* (for OLTP workloads).

IBM InfoSphere Warehouse

IBM InfoSphere Warehouse is a complete data warehousing solution that contains components that facilitate data warehouse construction and administration, as well as tools that enable embedded data mining and multidimensional OLAP. InfoSphere Warehouse is built on DB2 Enterprise Server Edition and the Data Partitioning Feature (DPF)—DB2 Enterprise Server Edition contains data warehouse–enhancing features such as MQTs, the starburst query optimizer, and support for multidimensional clustering tables. The Data Partitioning Feature provides the ability to divide very large databases into multiple parts (known as *partitions*) and store them across a cluster of inexpensive servers. (In the past, it was possible to add DPF to DB2 Enterprise Server Edition environments by activating a license key; however, starting with version 10.1, if you want DPF functionality, you must purchase InfoSphere Warehouse.)

Sometimes called a *database node* or simply a *node*, each database partition contains its own data, indexes, configuration files, and transaction log files. Because these components—as well as memory and storage—are not shared between partitions, an InfoSphere Warehouse utilizes what is referred to as a *shared-nothing* environment. Figure 2.2 shows what a simple InfoSphere Warehouse partitioned DB2 database environment looks like.

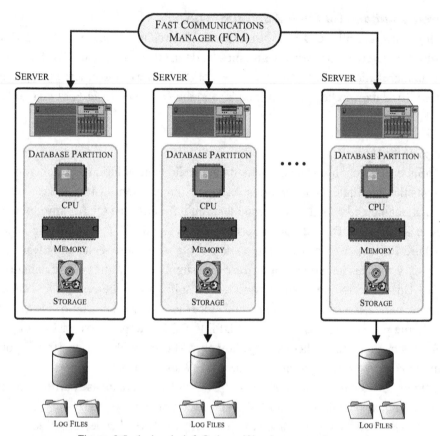

Figure 2.2: A simple InfoSphere Warehouse environment

With InfoSphere Warehouse, a database can be scaled as an organization's data needs grow simply by adding more database partitions. (The fact that the database is split across multiple partitions is transparent to applications and users.) InfoSphere Warehouse also enables DB2 to process complex queries more efficiently—data retrieval and update requests are decomposed automatically into subrequests and executed in parallel among all applicable partitions. In addition, InfoSphere Warehouse can improve data availability by reducing the impact of performing routine maintenance activities and by decreasing the time needed to do so; such activities can be performed one partition at a time.

The DB2 pureScale Feature

The DB2 pureScale Feature leverages IBM's System z Sysplex technology to bring active-active clustering services to DB2 for LUW database environments. This technology enables a DB2 for LUW database to continuously process incoming requests, even if multiple system components fail simultaneously (which makes it ideal for OLTP workloads where high availability is crucial).

Unlike InfoSphere Warehouse, the DB2 pureScale Feature is based on a "shared data" architecture. The DB2 engine runs on multiple servers or logical partitions (LPARs) as data "members," each member has its own set of buffer pools and log files (which are accessible to the other members), and each member has equal, shared access to the database's underlying storage. IBM's General Parallel File System (GPFS) makes shared storage access possible; Cluster Caching Facility (CF) software provides global locking and buffer pool management and serves as the center of communication and coordination between all members (synchronous CF duplexing ensures high availability); and integrated Cluster Services (CS) handles failure detection and provides recovery automation.

The DB2 pureScale Feature offers the following key benefits:

- **Practically unlimited capacity:** The DB2 pureScale Feature provides practically unlimited capacity by allowing for the addition and removal of data members, on demand. A DB2 pureScale database is scalable to 128 members and has a highly efficient centralized management facility that allows for very efficient scale-out capabilities. The DB2 pureScale Feature also leverages Remote Direct Memory Access (RDMA) technology to provide a highly efficient internode communication mechanism, which also enhances its scaling capabilities.

- **Application transparency:** Applications that run in a DB2 pureScale environment do not need to know anything about the members in a cluster or be concerned about which member they connect to. Clients see a single, common view of the database and can connect to any member; automatic load balancing and client reroute ensures that application workloads are distributed evenly across all available members. And because the DB2 pureScale Feature provides native support for the SQL syntax used by other database vendors, applications written for other relational database management systems can be run against a DB2 pureScale database with little or no changes.

- **Continuous availability:** The DB2 pureScale Feature provides a fully active-active cluster configuration; the HACMP™ Reliable Services Clustering Technology (RCST) quickly detects failures, while Tivoli® System Automation for Multi-platforms (SA MP) automates recovery. Consequently, if one member goes down, processing is automatically rerouted to and can continue on the remaining active members. During a member failure, only data being modified on the failing member is temporarily unavailable, and data recovery for that member can be completed in a matter of seconds. This is in contrast to other competing solutions in which an entire system freeze might occur as part of the database recovery process.

- **High performance:** The DB2 pureScale Feature uses a low-latency, high-speed interconnect to maximize performance. RDMA-capable interconnects like InfiniBand and 10Gb RoCE Ethernet allow one server to alter the memory contents of another without requiring the CPU in the target server to get involved. Consequently, no interrupt or other message processing is needed to keep changes made by data members synchronized.

Figure 2.3 shows what a DB2 pureScale environment consisting of three data members looks like.

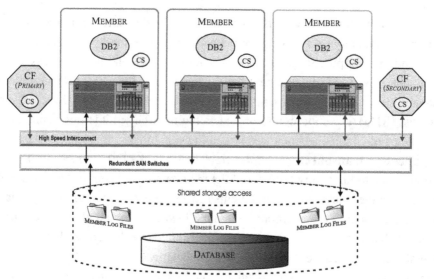

Figure 2.3: A simple DB2 pureScale environment

Managing Nonrelational Data

Now more than ever, organizations are using relational database management systems to store nonrelational types of data such as digital photos, scanned documents, audio clips, video clips, and both binary and ACSII-formatted files. Such data can be stored in DB2 databases using LOB and XML data types.

Large Objects (LOBs)

The term *large object* and the generic acronym LOB are often used to refer to large chunks of data that is considered either "nontraditional" or too large to be stored in one of DB2's more conventional built-in data types. With DB2, the following set of built-in data types are designed specifically for LOB data:

- **Binary large object (BLOB):** Used to store binary data values (such as documents, graphic images, pictures, audio, and video) that are up to 2 GB in size
- **Character large object (CLOB):** Used to store single-byte character set (SBCS) or multibyte character set (MBCS) character string values (such as documents written with a single character set) that are between 32,700 and 2,147,483,647 characters in length
- **Double-byte character large object (DBCLOB):** Used to store double-byte character set (DBCS) character string values that are between 16,350 and 1,073,741,823 characters in length
- **National character large object (NCLOB):** Used to store a sequence of bytes— between 16,350 and 1,073,741,823 bytes in length—in a Unicode database that uses UTF-16BE encoding; this data type is essentially the same as the DBCLOB data type and is provided for compatibility with Oracle applications

From an application perspective, the LOB data type used determines how LOB data is accessed. For instance, because BLOB data is usually indecipherable, applications have to know the format of a BLOB value and be customized to work with such values. However, CLOB data, DBCLOB data, and NCLOB data can typically be retrieved and manipulated with methods that are frequently used to work with character data.

LOB locators

Because LOB values can be quite large, transferring them from a database server to one or more application host variables can be time consuming and resource intensive (in terms of memory utilization). However, most applications process LOB values in pieces rather than as a whole, so often it is not necessary to transfer complete LOB values. Instead, applications can reference them using a device known as a *LOB locator*.

A LOB locator (also referred to as a *locator*) is a mechanism that refers to a LOB value from within a transaction. It is not a data type, nor is it a database object. Instead, it is a token value—in the form of a host variable—that does not persist beyond scope of the transaction it is created in. LOB locators do not store copies of LOB data—they store a description of a base LOB value, and the actual data that a LOB locator refers to is only materialized when it is assigned to a specific location, such as an application host variable or another table record.

After associating a LOB locator with a LOB value, an application can perform any number of SQL operations on the value (such as applying scalar functions like SUBSTR(), CONCAT(), VALUE(), or LENGTH() or querying the value with a LIKE clause) simply by specifying the LOB locator as input. The resulting output (that is, the actual data value returned) is typically a subset of the LOB value.

It is important to understand that a LOB locator represents a LOB value, not a location or row in a table. Consequently, once an application selects a LOB value into a locator, operations performed on the row containing the original LOB value will have no effect on the value that the locator references.

Inline LOBs

Some applications make extensive use of LOBs, and in some cases the LOB data they work with is relatively small—at most, just a few kilobytes. When this is the case, query performance can often be increased by storing LOB data in the same data pages as the rest of a table's rows, rather than in a separate LOB storage object (which is where LOB data is stored by default). Such LOBs are referred to as *inline LOBs*. Inline LOBs improve the performance of queries that access LOB data because no additional I/O is needed to store and access this type of data. Moreover, inline LOB data is eligible for compression.

Inline LOBs are created by appending the INLINE LENGTH clause to a LOB column's definition; LOB columns are defined using either the CREATE TABLE or ALTER TABLE statement. The INLINE LENGTH option applies to both LOB and XML columns—in the case of a LOB column, the inline length specified indicates the maximum size, in bytes (including four bytes for overhead), that LOB values stored in the row can be. This feature is implicitly enabled for all LOB columns that are added to new or existing tables; an implicit INLINE LENGTH value for each LOB column is defined and stored automatically as if it had been explicitly specified.

It is important to note that when a table has columns with inline LOBs, fewer rows fit on a page. Consequently, the performance of queries that return only non-LOB data can be adversely affected (because such queries have to retrieve more pages). Additionally, operations against inline LOBs are always logged; therefore, their use can increase logging overhead. Inline LOBs are most helpful for workloads in which queries frequently retrieve data from one or more LOB columns.

XML Documents

Extensible Markup Language (XML) is a simple, flexible text format that is derived from Standard Generalized Markup Language (SGML, ISO 8879). Originally designed to meet the challenges of large-scale electronic publishing, XML is playing an increasingly important role in the exchange of a wide variety of data on the web and elsewhere. Why? Because XML provides a neutral, flexible way to exchange data between different devices, systems, and applications; data is maintained in a self-describing format that accommodates a vast array of ever-evolving business needs.

One approach to storing XML documents in a relational database has been to "shred," or decompose, the documents and store their contents across multiple columns in one or more tables. The shredding of XML documents enables users to leverage their existing SQL programming skills, as well as take advantage of popular query and reporting tools, to work directly with selected portions of the "converted" data. This technique works well if the XML data being stored has a tabular format. However, the cost associated with decomposing XML data is often dependent upon the structure of the underlying document.

XML documents consist of a hierarchical set of attributes and entities, and many XML documents contain heavily nested parent-child relationships, irregular structures, or both. Consequently, the shredding of complex XML documents can require a large number of tables, some of which might need to have values generated for foreign keys in order to capture the relationships and ordering that is inherent in the original document. Moreover, querying such shredded documents can require complex SQL statements that consist of multiple join operations.

Another popular method is to store the entire contents of an XML file in a single column that has been defined as having a LOB data type. This approach eliminates the overhead of breaking an XML document into pieces and storing the parts across multiple tables. Furthermore, complex joins are not needed to reconstruct the original XML document because it was never decomposed in the first place.

However, the use of LOB data types—character or binary—to store XML documents has its drawbacks. For instance, finding and retrieving a subset of data from an XML document can be resource intensive. And when updates are required, you must replace the entire document, even if only a small portion needs to be modified. This can result in unacceptable server response times, particularly if the XML document you are modifying is large.

The DB2 pureXML feature offers a simple and efficient way to create a "hybrid" DB2 database that allows the storing of XML data in its native, hierarchical format. With pureXML, XML documents are stored in tables that contain one or more columns that have been defined with the XML data type. (Tables that contain XML data type columns can also have columns that have been assigned traditional data types.)

The "pure" support in pureXML consists of special storage techniques that provide efficient management of the hierarchical structures inherent in XML documents, indexing technology that accelerates the retrieval of subsets of XML data, capabilities for validating XML data and managing changing XML schemas, native support for XQuery and SQL/XML enhancements, integration with popular application programming interfaces (APIs), and extensions to popular database utilities. The result is a single relational database management system that offers the benefits of a traditional tabular database environment along with a native XML data store.

DB2's Comprehensive Tool Set

Each edition of DB2 comes with a set of tools designed to assist with the administration and management of DB2 instances, databases, and database objects, as well as to aid in the development of stored procedures, UDFs, and database applications. Many of these tools use a graphical user interface (GUI), and others are command-line oriented. But out of all the tools available, two stand out because of their ease of use and versatility: *IBM Data Studio* and the *DB2 Command Line Processor (CLP)*. Using these tools, individuals who have been given the proper authorization can do anything that they otherwise can do within a DB2 database environment.

The DB2 Command Line Processor

The DB2 CLP is a text-oriented application that can be used to issue DB2 commands, system commands, and SQL statements, as well as view the results of any statement and command executed. The CLP can be run in one of three different modes:

- **Command mode:** To run the CLP in command mode, simply enter a valid DB2 command or SQL statement, preceded by the characters db2 and separated by a space, from an operating system command prompt. For example, the command CONNECT TO sample would be entered as db2 CONNECT TO sample. If the command or statement contains characters that have a special meaning to the operating system in use, that command or statement must be enclosed with double quotation marks ("") to ensure that it will be properly executed (for example, db2 "SELECT COUNT(*) FROM employee"). If the command to be executed is too long to fit on a single line, a space followed by the line continuation character (\) can be placed at the end of a line that is to be continued, and the remainder of the command can follow on a new line.

- **Interactive Input mode:** When the CLP is ran in interactive input mode, the prefix db2 is automatically provided (as characterized by the db2 => prompt) for each command or statement entered. To run the CLP in interactive input mode on a UNIX system, simply enter the command db2 at the system prompt. However, on Windows, you must select **Command Line Processor** from the Windows Start menu, or run the command db2cmd, followed by the command db2. To exit interactive input mode, enter the command quit. Aside from that, the rules that apply to using the command mode of the CLP also apply to using the interactive input mode. It is important to note that if you need to execute an operating system command while running the CLP in interactive input mode, you must prefix the command with an exclamation mark (!). For example, to obtain a listing of the files found in the current directory on a UNIX system, you would enter the command !ls -al.

- **Batch mode:** When running the CLP in batch mode, it is assumed that all commands and SQL statements to be executed have been stored in an ASCII-format text file. (The characters db2 should *not* precede the commands or statements stored in this file.) To run the CLP in batch mode, enter the command db2 -f *xxxxxxxx* (where *xxxxxxxx* is the name of a file that contains the set of commands or statements that are to be executed) at the system prompt.

Figure 2.4 illustrates how the DB2 CLP looks on a Windows 7 server when it is first started in interactive input mode.

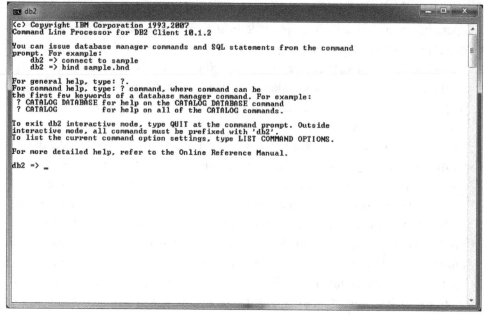

```
db2

(c) Copyright IBM Corporation 1993,2007
Command Line Processor for DB2 Client 10.1.2

You can issue database manager commands and SQL statements from the command
prompt. For example:
    db2 => connect to sample
    db2 => bind sample.bnd

For general help, type: ?.
For command help, type: ? command, where command can be
the first few keywords of a database manager command. For example:
  ? CATALOG DATABASE for help on the CATALOG DATABASE command
  ? CATALOG          for help on all of the CATALOG commands.

To exit db2 interactive mode, type QUIT at the command prompt. Outside
interactive mode, all commands must be prefixed with 'db2'.
To list the current command option settings, type LIST COMMAND OPTIONS.

For more detailed help, refer to the Online Reference Manual.

db2 => _
```

Figure 2.4: The DB2 Command Line Processor (in interactive input mode)

A variety of command-line options can be specified when the CLP is invoked. To obtain a list of all available options, execute the command LIST COMMAND OPTIONS, either from the system command prompt or from the CLP prompt (when running the CLP in interactive input mode).

Note: On Linux and UNIX servers, you must "source" the DB2 profile before you can use the CLP. Sourcing the DB2 profile is done automatically when you log on as the DB2 instance owner; however, if you log on as someone else, you must do the following before you will be allowed to use the CLP:

1. Locate the home directory for the DB2 instance owner.
2. In the instance owner home directory, look for a subdirectory named sqllib. Inside that subdirectory, you should see a file named db2profile.
3. Execute the commands in the db2profile file. For example, if the home directory for the DB2 instance owner is /home/db2inst1, you would execute a command that looks like this:

     . /home/db2inst1/sqllib/db2profile

Be sure to include the space between the period and the file name/ location—otherwise, the command will not work. Execution of the commands in the db2profile file does not produce any output; however, it starts CLP and leaves it running in command mode. By adding this command to a user's profile (usually stored in a hidden file called .profile or .bashrc within a user's home directory), you can ensure that the CLP is available whenever that user logs on.

• •

IBM Data Studio

One of the drawbacks to using any type of command-line interface tool is that the user must possess some level of knowledge about the commands the tool supports. And in the case of DB2, almost 300 commands and more than 75 SQL statements are available to choose from, which makes using the CLP effectively somewhat of a challenge if you do not have a lot of experience with DB2. That is why tools that have a well-designed graphical user interface (GUI) can be indispensable—they relieve users from the burden of having to know a long list of commands, and they make it easier for individuals just starting out with a software product to perform tasks they need to complete.

IBM Data Studio is an Eclipse-based, integrated development environment (IDE) that can be used to perform instance and database administration, routine development (SQL procedures, SQL functions, etc.), application development, and performance-tuning tasks. It replaces the DB2 Control Center, which has been around since Version 5 (DB2 for LUW), as the standard GUI tool for DB2 database administration and application development. Unlike the DB2 Control Center, Data Studio provides collaborative database development tools for DB2 for LUW, DB2 for z/OS, Informix, Sybase, MySQL, Oracle, SQL Server, and others; it also supports a variety of programming languages. As with the DB2 Control Center, IBM Data Studio is available at no extra charge. However, it does not come prepackaged with DB2—instead, you must download it separately.

IBM Data Studio is part of the IBM InfoSphere Optim family of data life-cycle management tools and solutions. Together, these tools provide an integrated environment for managing databases and developing database applications throughout the data and application life cycle. For example, InfoSphere Data Architect provides a robust data modeling solution that integrates seamlessly with Data Studio. InfoSphere Optim Query Workload Tuner expands on the basic query-tuning features found in IBM

Data Studio. And IBM Data Studio users can take advantage of InfoSphere Optim Performance Manager to ensure that applications are built from the ground up with database performance in mind. In addition, IBM Data Studio now incorporates advanced administration, development, and monitoring capabilities from InfoSphere Optim Database Administrator, InfoSphere Optim Development Studio, and Data Studio Health Monitor, all of which are no longer being further developed.

If you are familiar with Eclipse-based applications, you will likely feel comfortable with the IBM Data Studio interface. After spending some time with the tool, users coming from the DB2 Control Center should find IBM Data Studio intuitive and relatively easy to use as well. (For example, like the DB2 Control Center, IBM Data Studio allows users to connect to a DB2 database using a wizard—users are still required to provide login credentials to establish the connection.) Figure 2.5 shows what the basic interface for IBM Data Studio, Version 4.1 looks like.

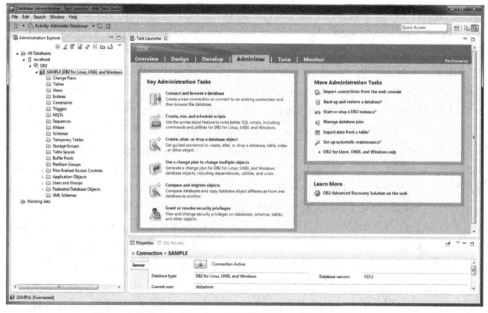

Figure 2.5: Basic interface for IBM Data Studio, Version 4.1

There are three different IBM Data Studio components to choose from:

- IBM Data Studio administration client
- IBM Data Studio full client
- IBM Data Studio web console

The administration client is a lightweight tool for administering databases and meets most of the basic development needs for DB2 for LUW and DB2 for z/OS database environments. The full client expands the functionality of the administration client to support the development of Java, SQL Procedural Language (SQL PL) and PL/SQL routines, XML, and other technologies. And the web console complements both clients by providing the ability to monitor database health and availability, as well as to manage scheduled jobs, via a web browser. All three components can be installed on servers running Red Hat Linux, SUSE Linux, Windows, and the AIX (Data Studio web console only) operating system.

3

Security

Fifteen percent (15%) of the *DB2 10.1 Fundamentals* certification exam (Exam 610) is designed to test your knowledge of the mechanisms DB2 uses to protect data and database objects against unauthorized access and modification. The questions that make up this portion of the exam are intended to evaluate the following:

- Your ability to identify ways in which access to instances, databases, and user data can be restricted
- Your ability to identify the authorization levels and privileges that are available with DB2
- Your ability to identify how specific authorizations and privileges are given (granted) to others
- Your ability to identify how specific authorizations and privileges are taken away (revoked) from others
- Your knowledge of how to define and use roles
- Your knowledge of how to use Row and Column Access Control (RCAC) to prevent unauthorized access to sensitive data
- Your knowledge of how and when to use trusted contexts

This chapter introduces you to the authorizations and privileges that are available with DB2. It also provides you with information about the tools that are used to give (grant) and take away (revoke) authorizations and privileges to/from individuals, groups, and roles.

In this chapter, you will become familiar with the two mechanisms that DB2 uses to control access to instances, databases, data objects, and data: *authorities* and *privileges*. You will also learn how to grant authorities and privileges to specific users, groups, and roles, as well as how to revoke authorities and privileges when it is appropriate to do so. And you will learn how to use tools like RCAC and Label-Based Access Control (LBAC) to secure sensitive data in ways that meet the strictest of security requirements or that adhere to rigid government security standards.

Controlling Database Access

Identity theft—a crime in which someone wrongfully obtains another person's personal data (such as a Social Security number, bank account number, or credit card number) and uses it in a fraudulent or deceptive manner for economic gain—is the fastest-growing crime in our nation today. Criminals obtain the information needed to steal an identity in a variety of ways: through overheard conversations made on cell phones; through telephone and email "phishing" scams; by stealing wallets, purses, and personal mail; by taking discarded documents from the trash; and by exploiting careless online shopping and banking habits. If that is not frightening enough, studies show that up to 70 percent of all identity theft cases are "inside jobs"—that is, they are perpetrated by a co-worker or by an employee of a business that individuals frequently patronize. In these cases, all that is needed to commit identity theft is access to a company database.

That is why it is essential that a relational database management system be able to protect data against unauthorized access and modification. With DB2, a combination of external security services and internal access controls are used to perform this vital task. Furthermore, three different layers of security are employed: the first controls access to the instance a database was created under, the second controls access to the database itself, and the third controls who has access to the data and data objects that reside within the database.

Authentication

The first security portal most users must pass through on their way to gaining access to a DB2 instance or database is a process known as *authentication*. The purpose of authentication is to verify that users really are who they say they are. And in most cases, an external security facility that is not part of DB2 is used to perform this task. This facility might be part of the operating system, which is the case when DB2 is deployed on Linux, AIX, Solaris, HP-UX, and recent versions of the Windows operating system. Or it can be a separate add-on product such as Distributed Computing Environment (DCE) Security Services. In either case, the external security facility used often must be presented with two specific pieces of information before a user can be authenticated: a unique *user ID* and a corresponding *password*. The user ID identifies the user to the security facility, and the password, which is information that is supposedly known only by the user and the security facility, verifies that the user is indeed who he or she claims to be.

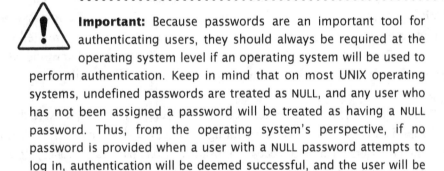

• •

Important: Because passwords are an important tool for authenticating users, they should always be required at the operating system level if an operating system will be used to perform authentication. Keep in mind that on most UNIX operating systems, undefined passwords are treated as NULL, and any user who has not been assigned a password will be treated as having a NULL password. Thus, from the operating system's perspective, if no password is provided when a user with a NULL password attempts to log in, authentication will be deemed successful, and the user will be given access to the operating system as well as to DB2.

• •

Where Authentication Takes Place

Because DB2 can reside in environments that consist of multiple clients, gateways, and servers (each of which can be running a different operating system), deciding where authentication is to take place can sometimes be challenging. For this reason, DB2 often relies on the security facility that either the client or the server's operating system provides to control how users are authenticated.

With DB2 for Linux, UNIX, and Windows, a parameter in each DB2 Database Manager configuration file (which is a file that is associated with every instance) controls where and how authentication takes place. The value assigned to this parameter, often referred to as the *authentication type*, is set initially when an instance is first created. (On the server side, the authentication type is specified during the instance creation process; on the client side, the authentication type is stipulated when a remote database is cataloged.) Only one authentication type exists for each instance, and it controls access to that instance, as well as to all databases that fall under that instance's control. The following authentication types are available with DB2 10.1 for Linux, UNIX, and Windows:

- **CLIENT**: Authentication occurs at the client workstation or database partition where a client application is invoked, using the security facility that the client's operating system provides (assuming one is available). The user ID and password supplied by users wishing to access an instance or database are compared with the user ID and password combinations stored at the client or node to determine whether access is permitted.

- **SERVER**: Authentication occurs at the server workstation using the security facility that the server's operating system provides. The user ID and password supplied by users wishing to access an instance or database are compared with the user ID and password combinations stored at the server to determine whether access is permitted. Unless otherwise specified, this is the default authentication type used.

- **SERVER_ENCRYPT**: Authentication occurs at the server workstation using the security facility that the server's operating system provides. However, the password supplied by users wishing to access an instance or database can be encrypted at the client workstation before it is sent to the server for validation.

- **DATA_ENCRYPT**: Authentication occurs at the server workstation using the SERVER_ENCRYPT authentication method. In addition, all user data is encrypted before it is passed from the client to the server and vice versa.

- **DATA_ENCRYPT_CMP**: Authentication occurs at the server workstation using the SERVER_ENCRYPT authentication method. And all user data is encrypted before it is passed from the client to the server and vice versa. In addition, compatibility for down-level products that do not support the DATA_ENCRYPT authentication type is provided. (Such products connect using the SERVER_ENCRYPT authentication type, and user data is not encrypted.)

- **KERBEROS**: Authentication occurs at the server workstation using a security facility that supports the Kerberos security protocol. This protocol performs authentication as a third-party service by using conventional cryptography to create a shared secret key—the key becomes the credentials used to verify the user's identity whenever local or network services are requested. (This eliminates the need to pass a user ID and password across the network as ASCII text.) If both the client and the server support the Kerberos security protocol, the user ID and password provided by users wishing to access an instance or database are encrypted at the client workstation and sent to the server for validation.

- **KRB_SERVER_ENCRYPT**: Authentication occurs at the server workstation using either the KERBEROS or the SERVER_ENCRYPT authentication method. If the client's authentication type is set to KERBEROS, authentication takes place at the server using the Kerberos security system; if the client's authentication type is set to anything other than KERBEROS or if the Kerberos authentication service is unavailable, the server acts as if the SERVER_ENCRYPT authentication type was specified, and the rules for that authentication method are applied.

- **GSSPLUGIN**: Authentication occurs at the server workstation using a Generic Security Service Application Program Interface (GSS-API) plug-in. If the client's authentication type is not specified, the server returns a list of server-supported plug-ins to the client. (This list is stored in the *srvcon_gssplugin_list* database manager configuration parameter.) The client selects and uses the first plug-in it finds that is identified in the supported list; if no supported plug-in is found, the client is authenticated using the KERBEROS authentication method.

- **GSS_SERVER_ENCRYPT**: Authentication occurs at the server workstation using either the GSSPLUGIN or the SERVER_ENCRYPT authentication method. That is, if client authentication occurs through a GSS-API plug-in, the client is authenticated using the first client-supported plug-in found in the list of server-supported plug-ins supplied. However, if the client does not support any plug-ins in this list, it is authenticated by using the KERBEROS authentication method—if the client does not support the Kerberos security protocol, it is authenticated using the SERVER_ENCRYPT authentication method instead.

It is important to note that if the authentication type a client workstation employs will encrypt user ID and password information before sending it to a server, the server must use an authentication type that can decipher this information. Otherwise, the encrypted data cannot be processed, and an error will result.

Authorities and Privileges

After a user has been authenticated and an attachment to an instance (or a connection to a database) has been established, DB2 evaluates the set of *authorities* and *privileges* that have been assigned to the user to determine which operations, if any, he or she is allowed to perform. Authorities convey the right to perform high-level administrative and maintenance/utility operations on an instance or a database. Privileges, on the other hand, convey the right to perform certain actions against specific database resources (such as tables, indexes, and views).

Together, authorities and privileges control access to an instance, to one or more databases under a specific instance's control, to a database, and to a database's data objects and data. Users can work only with instances, databases, and objects they have been given authorization for—that is, only if they possess the specific authority or privilege needed.

Administrative Authorities

An *administrative authority* is a set of related privileges that controls which administrative and maintenance operations a user can perform against a DB2 instance or database. Individuals who have been given (granted) administrative authority are responsible both for controlling an instance or database and for ensuring the safety and integrity of any data that might come under that instance/database's control. The following administrative authorities are available:

- **System Administrator (SYSADM) authority:** The highest level of administrative authority available; users who have been granted this authority can run most DB2 utilities, execute most DB2 commands, and perform any SQL or XQuery operation that does not attempt to access data that is protected by RCAC or LBAC. Users with this authority also have the ability to create databases and database objects such as tables, indexes, and views.

  Individuals who hold SYSADM authority are implicitly given all the rights that are granted to users who hold any of the other system-level administrative authorities available.

- **Installation System Administrator (Installation SYSADM) authority:** Assigned to a limited number of users when DB2 is first installed, this authority conveys the same set of abilities that SYSADM authority provides. However, unlike with SYSADM authority, information about who holds Installation SYSADM authority is not stored in the system catalog. Consequently, users with this authority can perform recovery operations when the system catalog for a database is inaccessible or unavailable.

- **System Control (SYSCTRL) authority:** The highest level of system and instance control authority available; users who have been granted this authority can create and drop DB2 databases, use almost all of the DB2 utilities, and execute the majority of the DB2 commands available. However, they cannot access user data directly unless they have been explicitly granted the privileges needed to do so. (SYSCTRL authority is intended to provide select users with nearly complete control of a DB2 system without letting them access sensitive data.) Because a database connection is required to run some of the DB2 utilities available, users who hold SYSCTRL authority for a particular instance automatically receive the privileges needed to connect to any database that falls under that instance's control.

- **System Operator (SYSOPER) authority:** Provides select individuals with the ability to execute all DB2 commands available *except* ARCHIVE LOG, START DATABASE, STOP DATABASE, and RECOVER BSDS. Users with SYSOPER authority can also run the DSN1SDMP utility, as well as terminate any running utility job.

- **Installation System Operator (Installation SYSOPER) authority:** Assigned to one or two user IDs when DB2 is installed, this authority conveys the same set of abilities that SYSOPER authority provides. However, as with Installation SYSADM authority, information about who holds Installation SYSOPER authority is not stored in the system catalog, thereby allowing users with this authority to perform select operations when the system catalog for a database is unavailable.

- **System Maintenance (SYSMAINT) authority:** Provides select individuals with the ability to perform maintenance operations on an instance and any databases that fall under that instance's control. As with SYSCTRL authority, SYSMAINT authority is intended to let special users maintain a database that contains sensitive data they most likely should not view or modify. Consequently, users who receive this authority cannot access user data unless they have been explicitly granted the privileges needed to do so. Because a database connection is required to run some of DB2's maintenance utilities, users who have SYSMAINT authority for a particular instance automatically receive the privileges needed to connect to any database that falls under that instance's control.

- **System Monitor (SYSMON) authority:** Provides select individuals with the ability to take database system monitor snapshots of an instance and its databases. Users who have been granted this authority can execute the various LIST commands that are available for obtaining information about databases and database objects. However, they are not permitted to access user data directly unless they have been explicitly granted the privileges needed to do so. Because a connection to a database must exist before the DB2 snapshot monitor can be used, users who have SYSMON authority for a particular instance automatically receive the privileges needed to connect to each database under that instance's control.

- **Database Administrator (DBADM) authority:** The highest level of database authority available; users who have been granted this authority can create database objects (such as tables, indexes, and views), issue database-specific DB2 commands, and execute built-in DB2 routines (with the exception of audit routines). Users with DBADM authority also have the ability to access data stored in tables and views, including system catalog tables and views—provided that data is not protected by RCAC or LBAC.

    Users who hold DBADM authority implicitly receive all the rights that are given to users who hold many of the other database-level administrative authorities available.
- **Database Control (DBCTRL) authority:** Provides select individuals with the ability to create database objects, issue database-specific DB2 commands, run DB2 utilities (*including those that change data*), and terminate any running utility *except* DIAGNOSE, REPORT, and STOSPACE.
- **Database Maintenance (DBMAINT) authority:** Provides select individuals with the ability to create database objects, issue database-specific DB2 commands, run DB2 utilities that do not change data, and terminate any running utility *except* DIAGNOSE, REPORT, and STOSPACE.
- **Package Administrator (PACKADM) authority:** Provides select individuals with BIND, COPY, and EXECUTE privileges on all packages in one or more specific collections. Users who have been granted this authority can also use the BIND subcommand to create new packages in certain collections.
- **System Database Administrator (System DBADM) authority:** Provides select individuals with the ability to create, alter, and drop database objects; issue database-specific DB2 commands; and run the following DB2 utilities: CHECK INDEX, CHECK LOB, COPY, COPYTOCOPY, DIAGNOSE, MODIFY RECOVERY, MODIFY STATISTICS, QUIESCE, REBUILD INDEX, RECOVER, REPORT, and RUNSTATS. Users with this authority can also access and modify data stored in system catalog tables and views. However, they cannot access user data, and they cannot grant and revoke authorities and privileges.
- **Security Administrator (SECADM) authority:** Provides select individuals with the ability to manage security-related database objects, such as those needed to implement RCAC and LBAC. Users who possess this authority can also grant and revoke database-level authorities and privileges, execute DB2's audit system routines, and access data stored in system catalog tables and views. However, individuals who possess SECADM authority cannot access user data.

- **Access Control (ACCESSCTRL) authority:** Provides select individuals with the ability to grant and revoke privileges on objects that reside in a specific database. Like users with SECADM authority, individuals with ACCESSCTRL authority can access and modify data stored in system catalog tables and views. However, they cannot access or modify user data.
- **Data Access (DATAACCESS) authority:** Provides select individuals with the ability to access and modify data stored in user tables, views, and materialized query tables. Users with this authority can also execute plans, packages, functions, and stored procedures.
- **SQL Administrator (SQLADM) authority:** Provides select individuals with the ability to monitor and tune SQL statements—that is, to execute EXPLAIN SQL statements and PROFILE commands, run the RUNSTATS and MODIFY STATISTICS utilities, and execute system-defined stored procedures, functions, and packages. DB2 for Linux, UNIX, and Windows users with this authority can also run the following commands: CREATE EVENT MONITOR, DROP EVENT MONITOR, FLUSH EVENT MONITOR, FLUSH OPTIMIZATION PROFILE CACHE, FLUSH PACKAGE CACHE, PREPARE, REORG, and SET EVENT MONITOR STATE.
- **Workload Management Administrator (WLMADM) authority:** Provides select individuals with the ability to manage workload management objects, such as service classes, work action sets, work class sets, and workloads.

It is important to note that although many of these authorities are available across all editions of DB2, some are operating system/platform dependent. Specifically, SYSMAINT, SYSMON, and WLMADM authorities are available only with DB2 for Linux, UNIX, and Windows; Installation SYSADM, SYSOPER, Installation SYSOPER, DBCTRL, DBMAINT, PACKADM, and System DBADM authorities are available only with DB2 for z/OS.

A word about the separation of management and security-related tasks

With earlier versions of DB2, individuals who held the administrative authorities needed to manage instances and databases also had the ability to access the databases they managed, which meant they potentially had access to confidential and/or sensitive information. They also had the ability to grant and revoke authorities and privileges to others. Today, it is possible to separate security administration from system administration, database administration, and data access. Separating management tasks from security administration can simplify system administration and strengthen the security of a database environment.

By default, when a DB2 for Linux, UNIX, and Windows user with SYSADM authority creates a database, that user is automatically granted SECADM authority for that database. Similarly, with DB2 for z/OS, SYSADM authority and SECADM authority are combined (under SYSADM authority). However, the process used to separate SYSADM authority from SECADM authority differs depending upon the operating system being used. With DB2 for Linux, UNIX, and Windows, a user with SECADM authority must explicitly grant SECADM authority to a user, group, or role; the user who receives SECADM authority must then revoke the authority from everybody else. (Only users with SECADM authority are allowed to grant and revoke SECADM authority to/from others.) With DB2 for z/OS, the process is simpler. To separate SECADM authority from SYSADM authority, you must set the SEPARATE_SECURITY system parameter on panel DSNTIPP1 to YES during installation or migration.

Privileges

As mentioned earlier, *privileges* convey the right to perform certain actions against specific database resources. Two distinct types of privileges exist: *database* and *object*. Database privileges apply to a database as a whole and control which actions a user is allowed to perform against a particular database. With DB2 for Linux, UNIX, and Windows, the following database privileges (also referred to as *database authorities*) are available:

- **BINDADD**: Allows a user to create packages in a certain database (by precompiling Embedded SQL application source code files against the database or by binding application bind files to the database)
- **CONNECT**: Allows a user to establish a connection to a certain database
- **CREATETAB**: Allows a user to create new tables in a certain database
- **CREATE_EXTERNAL_ROUTINE**: Allows a user to register user-defined functions (UDFs) and procedures that are external (for example, that reside in a shared library) with a certain database so other users and applications can execute them
- **CREATE_NOT_FENCED_ROUTINE**: Allows a user to create unfenced UDFs and procedures and store them in a specific database—unfenced UDFs and stored procedures are UDFs/procedures that are considered "safe" enough to be run in the DB2 Database Manager operating environment's process or address space; unless a UDF or procedure is registered as unfenced, the DB2 Database Manager insulates the UDF's or procedure's internal resources such that they cannot be run in DB2 memory space

- **EXPLAIN**: Allows a user to generate Explain query plans
- **IMPLICIT_SCHEMA**: Allows a user to implicitly create a new schema in a certain database—if a user with this authority attempts to create an object without specifying a schema qualifier, the object will be assigned a schema name that is different from any of the schema names that already exist in the database
- **LOAD**: Allows a user to bulk-load data into one or more existing tables in a certain database
- **QUIESCE_CONNECT**: Allows a user to establish a connection to a certain database while it is in a quiesced state (that is, while access to the database is restricted)

With DB2 for z/OS, the following database privileges are available instead:

- **CREATETAB**: Allows a user to create new tables in a certain database
- **CREATETS**: Allows a user to create new table spaces for a certain database
- **DISPLAYDB**: Allows a user to display the status of a certain database
- **DROP**: Allows a user to drop or alter a certain database
- **IMAGCOPY**: Allows a user to prepare for, make, and merge copies of table spaces in a certain database, as well as remove records of any table space copies made
- **LOAD**: Allows a user to bulk-load data into one or more existing tables in a certain database
- **RECOVERDB**: Allows a user to recover objects in a certain database and report an object's recovery status
- **REORG**: Allows a user to reorganize objects in a certain database (that is, to run the REORG utility)
- **REPAIR**: Allows a user to generate diagnostic information about and repair data stored in a certain database's objects
- **STARTDB**: Allows a user to start a certain database
- **STATS**: Allows a user to gather statistics, check indexes and referential constraints for associated objects, and delete unwanted statistics history records from the system catalog tables
- **STOPDB**: Allows a user to stop a certain database

Object privileges, on the other hand, apply to specific database objects (for example, tables, indexes, and views). Because the nature of each database object varies, the individual privileges that exist for each object differ. The remainder of this section describes the various object privileges that are available.

The authorization ID privilege (DB2 for Linux, UNIX, and Windows only)

The authorization ID privilege allows a user to set the session authorization ID to one of a set of specified authorization IDs available (by executing the SET SESSION AUTHORIZATION statement). Only one authorization ID privilege exists—the SETSESSIONUSER privilege.

Buffer pool privileges (DB2 for z/OS only)

Buffer pool privileges control what users can and cannot do with a particular buffer pool. (A buffer pool is a portion of memory that has been allocated to DB2 for the purpose of caching table and index data as it is read from disk.) The following buffer pool privileges are available:

- **USE OF BUFFERPOOL**: Allows a user to use a certain buffer pool
- **USE OF ALL BUFFERPOOLS**: Allows a user to use every buffer pool available

The table space privilege

The table space privilege controls what users can and cannot do with a particular table space. (Table spaces control where data in a database physically resides.) Only one table space privilege exists—the USE (or USE OF TABLESPACE) privilege, which, when granted, allows a user to use a certain table space.

• •

Note: In DB2 for Linux, UNIX, and Windows environments, the USE privilege cannot be used to give an individual the ability to create tables in the system catalog table space or in any temporary table spaces that might exist.

• •

The storage group privilege (DB2 for z/OS only)

The storage group privilege controls what users can and cannot do with a particular storage group. (With DB2 for z/OS, a storage group refers to a set of volumes on disks that holds the data sets in which tables and indexes are stored.) Only one storage group privilege exists—the USE (or USE OF STOGROUP) privilege, which, when granted, allows a user to use a certain storage group.

Schema privileges

Schema privileges control what users can and cannot do with a particular schema. (A schema is an object that is used to logically classify and group other objects in a database; most objects are identified by using a naming convention that consists of a schema name, followed by a period, followed by the object name.) The following schema privileges are available:

- **CREATEIN**: Allows a user to create objects within a certain schema
- **ALTERIN**: Allows a user to change the comment associated with any object in a certain schema or alter any object that resides in the schema
- **DROPIN**: Allows a user to remove (drop) any object within a certain schema

With DB2 for Linux, UNIX, and Windows, the objects that can be manipulated within a schema include tables, views, indexes, packages, data types, functions, triggers, procedures, and aliases. With DB2 for z/OS, those objects consist of distinct data types, UDFs, triggers, and procedures.

Table privileges

Table privileges control what users can and cannot do with a particular table in a database. (A table is a logical structure that presents data as a collection of unordered rows with a fixed number of columns.) The following table privileges are available:

- **CONTROL**: Provides a user with all table privileges available; with this privilege, a user can remove (drop) a certain table from the database, execute the RUNSTATS and REORG commands against the table, execute the SET INTEGRITY statement against the table, and grant and revoke individual table privileges (with the exception of the CONTROL privilege) to/from others—*this privilege is available with DB2 for Linux, UNIX, and Windows only*
- **ALTER**: Allows a user to change a certain table's definition and/or the comment associated with the table, as well as create or drop a table constraint
- **SELECT**: Allows a user to retrieve data from a certain table, as well as create a view that references the table
- **INSERT**: Allows a user to add data to a certain table
- **UPDATE**: Allows a user to modify data in a certain table; this privilege can apply to the entire table or be limited to specific columns within the table
- **DELETE**: Allows a user to remove data from a certain table

- **INDEX**: Allows a user to create an index for a certain table
- **REFERENCES**: Allow a user to create and drop foreign key constraints that reference a certain table in a referential integrity constraint; this privilege can apply to the entire table or be limited to specific columns within the table, in which case a user can only create and drop referential constraints that reference the columns identified
- **TRIGGER**: Allows a user to create triggers for a certain table—*this privilege is available with DB2 for z/OS only*

View privileges

View privileges control what users can and cannot do with a particular view. (A view is a virtual table that provides an alternative way of working with data that physically resides in one or more tables; views are frequently used to restrict access to specific columns in a table.) The following view privileges are available:

- **CONTROL**: Provides a user with all view privileges available; with this privilege, a user can remove (drop) a certain view from the database, as well as grant and revoke individual view privileges (with the exception of the CONTROL privilege) to/from others—*this privilege is available with DB2 for Linux, UNIX, and Windows only*
- **SELECT**: Allows a user to use a certain view to retrieve data from its underlying base table(s)
- **INSERT**: Allows a user to use a certain view to add data to its underlying base table(s)
- **UPDATE**: Allows a user to use a certain view to modify data in its underlying base table(s); this privilege can apply to the entire view or be limited to specific columns within the view
- **DELETE**: Allows a user to use a certain view to remove data from its underlying base table(s)

It is important to note that with DB2 for Linux, UNIX, and Windows, the owners of a view will receive CONTROL privilege for that view only if they hold CONTROL privilege for every base table the view references.

Note: To create a view, a user must hold, at a minimum, SELECT privilege on each base table the view references.

The index privilege (DB2 for Linux, UNIX, and Windows only)

The index privilege controls what users can and cannot do with a particular index. (An index is an ordered set of pointers that refer to one or more key columns in a base table; indexes are frequently used to improve query performance.) Only one index privilege exists—the CONTROL privilege, which, when granted, allows users to remove a certain index from a database.

Unlike the CONTROL privilege for other objects, the CONTROL privilege for an index does not automatically give users the ability to grant and revoke index privileges to/ from others. That is because the only index privilege available is the CONTROL privilege, and only users with ACCESSCTRL or SECADM authority are allowed to grant and revoke CONTROL privilege.

Sequence privileges

Sequence privileges control what users can and cannot do with a particular sequence. (A sequence is an object that can be used to generate values automatically. Sequences are ideal for producing unique key values because they eliminate the concurrency and performance problems that can occur when unique counters residing outside a database are used for data value generation.) The following sequence privileges are available:

- **USAGE**: Allows a user to use the PREVIOUS VALUE and NEXT VALUE expressions that are associated with a certain sequence (the PREVIOUS VALUE expression returns the most recently generated value for the specified sequence; the NEXT VALUE expression returns the next value for the specified sequence)
- **ALTER**: Allows a user to perform administrative tasks on a certain sequence, such as restarting the sequence or changing the increment value for the sequence; this privilege also lets a user add or change the comment associated with a certain sequence

The distinct type privilege (DB2 for z/OS only)

The distinct type privilege controls what users can and cannot do with a particular distinct data type. (A distinct type is a user-defined data type that is based on an existing built-in

DB2 data type.) Only one distinct type privilege exists—the USAGE OF TYPE (or USAGE OF DISTINCT TYPE) privilege, which, when granted, allows a user to use a certain distinct data type.

The function privilege (DB2 for z/OS only)
The function privilege controls what users can and cannot do with a particular UDF or CAST function that has been generated for a distinct data type. (A function is a routine that can be invoked from within an SQL statement that returns a value or a table.) Only one function privilege exists—the EXECUTE privilege, which, when granted, allows a user to invoke a certain function.

The procedure privilege (DB2 for z/OS only)
The procedure privilege controls what users can and cannot do with a particular procedure. (A procedure, also known as a *stored procedure*, is a routine that can be called to perform specific operations. Procedures often consist of multiple SQL statements and are typically used to enforce business rules.) Only one procedure privilege exists—the EXECUTE privilege, which, when granted, allows a user to invoke a certain stored procedure.

The routine privilege (DB2 for Linux, UNIX, and Windows only)
The routine privilege controls what users can and cannot do with a particular routine. (A routine can be a UDF, a stored procedure, or a method that different users can invoke.) Only one routine privilege exists—the EXECUTE privilege, which, when granted, allows a user to invoke a certain routine, create a function that is sourced from the routine (if the routine is a UDF), and reference the routine in an SQL statement.

Package privileges
Package privileges control what users can and cannot do with a particular package. (A package is an object that contains information that DB2 uses to efficiently process SQL statements embedded in an application.) The following package privileges are available:

- **CONTROL**: Provides a user with all package privileges available; with this privilege, a user can remove (drop) a certain package from the database, as well as grant and revoke individual package privileges (with the exception of the CONTROL privilege) to/from others—*this privilege is available with DB2 for Linux, UNIX, and Windows only*

- **BIND**: Allows a user to bind or rebind (recreate) a certain package, as well as add new versions of a package that has already been bound, to a database (with DB2 for z/OS, the BIND privilege also allows a user to execute the BIND, REBIND, and FREE PACKAGE subcommands, along with the DROP PACKAGE SQL statement)
- **COPY**: Allows a user to copy a certain package—*this privilege is available with DB2 for z/OS only*
- **EXECUTE**: Allows a user to execute or run a certain package; because all privileges needed to execute the SQL statements in a package are implicitly granted at run time, users who hold EXECUTE privilege for a particular package can execute that package even if they do not possess the privileges needed to execute the SQL statements stored in it

The collection privilege (DB2 for z/OS only)

The collection privilege controls what users can and cannot do with a particular collection. (A collection is an object that is used to logically classify and group packages.) Only one collection privilege exists—the CREATE IN privilege, which, when granted, allows a user to name a certain collection, as well as execute the BIND PACKAGE subcommand.

Plan privileges (DB2 for z/OS only)

Plan privileges control what users can and cannot do with a particular plan. (Whereas a package contains control structures that DB2 uses to run SQL statements efficiently, a plan relates an application process to a local instance of DB2 and specifies processing options; an application plan can contain a list of package names, the bound form of the SQL statements used, or both.) The following plan privileges are available:

- **BIND**: Allows a user to bind, rebind, or free a certain plan (by executing the BIND, REBIND, and FREE PLAN subcommands)
- **EXECUTE**: Allows a user to execute a certain plan when running the corresponding application

The JAR file privilege (DB2 for z/OS only)

The JAR privilege controls what users can and cannot do with a particular JAR file. (A JAR file is a file that contains a collection of classes for a Java routine.) Only one JAR privilege exists—the USAGE privilege, which, when granted, allows a user to use a certain JAR file.

System privileges (DB2 for z/OS only)

System privileges control what users can and cannot do with a DB2 system. The following system privileges are available:

- **ARCHIVE**: Allows a user to archive the current active log, provide information about input archive logs, modify the checkpoint frequency specified during installation, and control allocation and deallocation of tape units for archive processing
- **BINDADD**: Allows a user to create new plans and packages
- **BINDAGENT**: Allows a user to bind, rebind, or free a plan or package, as well as copy a package on behalf of the grantor—the BINDAGENT privilege is intended for separation of function, not for added security
- **BSDS**: Allows a user to recover the bootstrap data set (by executing the RECOVER BSDS command)
- **CREATEALIAS**: Allows a user to create an alias for a table or view
- **CREATEDBA**: Allows a user to create a new database and have DBADM authority over it
- **CREATEDBC**: Allows a user to create a new database and have DBCTRL authority over it
- **CREATESG**: Allows a user to create a storage group
- **CREATE_SECURE_OBJECT**: Allows a user to create secure objects, such as secure triggers or secure UDFs—if a trigger is defined for tables that are enforced with RCAC, it must be secure; similarly, if a UDF is referenced in the definition of a row permission or column mask, it must be secure; additionally, if a UDF is invoked in a query and its arguments reference columns with column masks, the UDF must be secure
- **CREATETMTAB**: Allows a user to define a created temporary table
- **DEBUGSESSION**: Allows a user to control debug session activity for SQL stored procedures, Java stored procedures, and non-inline SQL functions
- **DISPLAY**: Allows a user to display system information by using the DISPLAY ARCHIVE, DISPLAY BUFFERPOOL, DISPLAY DATABASE, DISPLAY LOCATION, DISPLAY LOG, DISPLAY THREAD, and DISPLAY TRACE commands
- **EXPLAIN**: Allows a user to generate Explain query plans
- **MONITOR1**: Allows a user to receive trace data that is not potentially sensitive
- **MONITOR2**: Allows a user to receive all trace data, regardless of its sensitivity

- **RECOVER**: Allows a user to recover threads (by executing the RECOVER INDOUBT command)
- **STOPALL**: Allows a user to stop DB2
- **STOSPACE**: Allows a user to obtain information about storage space usage
- **TRACE**: Allows a user to control tracing (using the START TRACE, STOP TRACE, and MODIFY TRACE commands)

The server privilege (DB2 for Linux, UNIX, and Windows only)

The server privilege controls whether a user can work with a particular federated server data source. (A DB2 federated system is a distributed computing system that consists of a DB2 server, known as a *federated server*, and one or more data sources the federated server sends queries to. Each data source consists of an instance of some supported relational database management system, such as Oracle, plus the database or databases the instance supports.) Only one server privilege exists—the PASSTHRU privilege, which, when granted, allows a user to issue Data Definition Language (DDL) and Data Manipulation Language (DML) SQL statements (as pass-through operations) directly to a data source via a federated database server.

Nickname privileges (DB2 for Linux, UNIX, and Windows only)

Nickname privileges control what users can and cannot do with a particular nickname. (When a client application submits a distributed request to a federated database server, the request is forwarded to the appropriate data source for processing. However, such a request does not identify the data source itself; instead, it references tables and views within the data source by using *nicknames* that map to specific table and view names in the data source. Nicknames are not alternative names for tables and views in the same way that aliases are, but are pointers that a federated server uses to reference external objects.) The following nickname privileges are available:

- **CONTROL**: Provides a user with all nickname privileges available; with this privilege, a user can remove (drop) a certain nickname from the database, as well as grant and revoke individual nickname privileges (with the exception of the CONTROL privilege) to/from others—*this privilege is available with DB2 for Linux, UNIX, and Windows only*
- **ALTER**: Allows a user to add, reset, or drop a column option for a certain nickname; also lets a user change a nickname's column name or data type, as well as modify the comment associated with the nickname

- **SELECT**: Allows a user to retrieve data from the table or view within a federated data source that a certain nickname refers to
- **INSERT**: Allows a user to retrieve data from the table or view within a federated data source that a certain nickname refers to
- **UPDATE**: Allows a user to modify data in the table or view within a federated data source that a certain nickname refers to; this privilege can apply to the entire table or be limited to specific columns within the table
- **DELETE**: Allows a user to remove rows of data from the table or view within a federated data source that a certain nickname refers to
- **INDEX**: Allows a user to create an index specification for a certain nickname
- **REFERENCES**: Allows a user to create and drop foreign key constraints that reference a certain nickname in a referential integrity constraint

Variable privileges (DB2 for Linux, UNIX, and Windows only)

Variable privileges control what users can and cannot do with a particular global variable. (A global variable is a named memory variable that can be retrieved or modified by using SQL statements; global variables enable applications to share relational data among SQL statements, without the need for additional application logic to support such data transfers.) The following variable privileges are available:

- **READ**: Allows a user to read the value of a certain global variable
- **WRITE**: Allows a user to assign a value to a certain global variable

The XML schema repository (XSR) object privilege (DB2 for Linux, UNIX, and Windows only)

The XML schema repository (XSR) object privilege controls what users can and cannot do with a particular XSR object. (XSR objects are used to validate and process XML instance documents that are stored in an XML column.) Only one XSR object privilege exists—the USAGE privilege, which, when granted, allows a user to use a certain XSR object.

The workload privilege (DB2 for Linux, UNIX, and Windows only)

The workload privilege controls what users can and cannot do with a particular workload. (Workloads are a key part of a DB2 workload management solution and are used to identify a source of work.) Only one workload privilege exists—the USAGE privilege, which, when granted, allows a user to use a certain defined workload.

●●●

Note: Users with ACCESSCTRL, DATAACCESS, DBADM, SECADM, or WLMADM authority are implicitly granted the USAGE privilege on all available workloads.

●●●

Granting Authorities and Privileges

Individuals can obtain authorities and privileges in a variety of ways:

- **Implicitly:** With DB2 for Linux, UNIX, and Windows, when a user creates a new database, he or she automatically (implicitly) receives DBADM authority for that database, as well as all database privileges that are currently available. Likewise, when a user creates a database object, he or she automatically receives all privileges that exist for that object, along with the ability to grant any combination of those privileges—with the exception of the CONTROL privilege—to others.

    With DB2 for z/OS, a user can acquire privileges implicitly through object ownership. Generally, when an object is created, the object's owner can be defined as a user's primary or secondary authorization ID. Or the object's owner can be the role the user is associated with in a trusted context.

    In some cases, a user can implicitly receive authorities and privileges when a higher-level privilege is explicitly granted. For example, if a DB2 for Linux, UNIX, and Windows user is explicitly given CONTROL privilege for a table, he or she will implicitly receive all available table privileges. Implicitly granted privileges are permanent and persist outside the scope in which they are granted.

- **Indirectly:** When a user executes a package that performs operations that require certain privileges (for example, a package that deletes a row of data from a table will require DELETE privilege on the table), he or she is indirectly given those privileges for the express purpose of executing the package. Indirectly granted privileges are temporary and do not exist outside the scope in which they are granted.

- **Explicitly:** Most authorities and privileges can be explicitly given (granted) to select individuals by someone who has the authority to do so. To explicitly grant authorities and privileges, a user must possess SECADM authority, ACCESSCTRL authority, or in the case of DB2 for Linux, UNIX, and Windows, CONTROL privilege on the object that privileges are to be granted for. Alternatively, a user can explicitly grant any privilege associated with an object that they have ownership of or any privilege that was granted to them with the WITH GRANT OPTION.

The GRANT Statement

One way to explicitly give authorities and privileges to others is by executing the GRANT statement. Syntax for the GRANT statement varies according to the type of authority or privilege being granted. However, the basic syntax looks something like this:

```
GRANT [Authority | Privilege <Options>, ...]
  ON [DATABASE <DatabaseName, ...> | SYSTEM]
  TO [Recipient, ...]
```

or

```
GRANT [Authority | Privilege, ...]
  [ON | OF | IN] [ObjectType] [ObjectName]
  TO [Recipient, ...]
  <WITH GRANT OPTION>
```

or

```
GRANT [ALL <PRIVILEGES> |
    Privilege <(ColumnName, ...)>, ...]
  [ON | OF] [ObjectType] [ObjectName]
  TO [Recipient, ...]
  <WITH GRANT OPTION>
```

or

```
GRANT <ROLE> [RoleName, ...]
  TO [Recipient, ...]
  <WITH ADMIN OPTION>
```

where:

Authority	Identifies one or more authorities to grant
Privilege	Identifies one or more privileges to grant

DatabaseName	Identifies, by name, one or more databases to grant authorities and privileges for—*this parameter must be specified for DB2 for z/OS only; it is not used by DB2 for Linux, UNIX, and Windows*
Options	Identifies one or more options that are associated with the authority or privilege to be granted; for example, the <WITH | WITHOUT DATAACCESS> and <WITH | WITHOUT ACCESSCTRL> options can be specified when the DBADM authority/privilege is granted
ColumnName	Identifies, by name, one or more specific columns that the authorities and privileges specified are to be associated with
ObjectType	Identifies the type of object the authorities and privileges specified are to be granted for
ObjectName	Identifies, by name, the object the authorities and/or privileges specified are to be granted for
RoleName	Identifies, by name, one or more roles to grant
Recipient	Identifies who is to receive the authorities and privileges that are being granted; the value specified for this parameter can be any combination of the following:

[*AuthorizationID*]	Identifies a particular user, by authorization ID, whom the authorities and privileges specified are to be granted to
<<USER> *Name* >	Identifies a particular user, by name, whom the authorities and privileges specified are to be granted to—*this clause is recognized by DB2 for Linux, UNIX, and Windows only; it cannot be used with DB2 for z/OS*
<<GROUP> *Name* >	Identifies a particular group, by name, that the authorities and privileges specified are to be granted to—*this clause is recognized by DB2 for Linux, UNIX, and Windows only; it cannot be used with DB2 for z/OS*
<<ROLE> *Name* >	Identifies a particular role, by name, that the authorities and privileges specified are to be granted to—*the keyword* ROLE *is optional if this clause is used with DB2 for Linux, UNIX, and Windows; it is required if this clause is used with DB2 for z/OS*

PUBLIC   Indicates that the authorities and privileges
                                    specified are to be granted to the group
                                    PUBLIC

As mentioned earlier, only users with ACCESSCTRL or SECADM authority are allowed
to grant and revoke the CONTROL privilege for an object. Consequently, if the ALL
PRIVILEGES clause is specified with the GRANT statement used, all authorities and
privileges for the designated object—*except* the CONTROL privilege—will be granted to
each recipient indicated. CONTROL privilege must be granted separately.

If the WITH GRANT OPTION clause is specified with the GRANT statement used, the
individual receiving the designated authorities and privileges will receive the ability to
grant those authorities and privileges to others. Similarly, if the WITH ADMIN OPTION
clause is specified with the GRANT statement used, the individual being granted a role will
receive the ability to grant that role to others.

More about roles

A *role* is a database entity that is used to group two or more authorities or privileges (or a
combination of authorities and privileges) together so they can be simultaneously granted
or revoked. When roles are used, the assignment of authorities and privileges is greatly
simplified. For example, instead of granting the same set of authorities and privileges
to every individual in a particular job function, you can assign a set of authorities and
privileges to a role that represents the job and then grant membership in that role to every
user who performs that particular job.

Roles also enable you to control database access in a manner that mirrors the structure
of your organization—you can create roles that map directly to specific job functions
within your company. And because you can grant users membership in roles that
reflect their responsibilities, as their responsibilities change, you can easily move their
membership from one role to another.

Many of the authorities and privileges available, with the exception of SECADM
authority, can be granted to a role. And if a role's authorities and privileges are changed,
all users who have membership in that role will automatically have their authorities and
privileges updated. The authorities and privileges held by each individual user do not
have to be altered to reflect the change.

GRANT Statement Examples

Now that you have seen the basic syntax for the GRANT statement, let us look at some examples.

Example 1: Give a user whose authorization ID is USER1 the ability to create a view on a table named SALES:

```
GRANT SELECT ON TABLE sales TO user1
```

Example 2: Give a user whose authorization ID is USER1 the privileges needed to remove records from a table named INVENTORY, as well as the ability to give those privileges to others:

```
GRANT DELETE ON TABLE inventory
   TO USER user1
   WITH GRANT OPTION
```

Example 3: Give a user whose authorization ID is USER1 the privileges required to run an Embedded SQL application named HR.CALC_BONUS that calls a package named HR.CALCULATIONS:

```
GRANT EXECUTE ON PACKAGE hr.calculations
   TO user1
```

Example 4: Give a user whose authorization ID is USER1 the ability to assign a comment to a sequence named PRODUCT_ID:

```
GRANT ALTER ON SEQUENCE product_id
   TO USER user1
```

Example 5: Give two users (whose authorization IDs are USER1 and USER2) the privileges needed to perform DML operations on a table named DEPARTMENT using a view named DEPTVIEW:

```
GRANT SELECT, INSERT, UPDATE, DELETE ON deptview
   TO user1, user2
```

Example 6: Grant all privileges (except CONTROL privilege) for a table named EMPLOYEES to a role named ADMIN; then, give a user whose authorization ID is USER1 membership in the ADMIN role:

```
GRANT ALL ON TABLE employees TO ROLE admin;
GRANT ROLE admin TO USER user1;
```

Revoking Authorities and Privileges

Just as the GRANT statement can be used to grant authorities and privileges, the REVOKE statement can be used to remove any authorities and privileges that have been granted. And as with the GRANT statement, syntax for the REVOKE statement varies according to the type of authority or privilege being revoked. The basic syntax for the REVOKE statement looks something like this:

```
REVOKE [Authority | Privilege]
   ON [DATABASE <DatabaseName, ...>]
   FROM [Forfeiter, ...]
```

or

```
REVOKE [ALL PRIVILEGES | Authority | Privilege, ...]
   [ON | OF | IN] [ObjectType] [ObjectName]
   FROM [Forfeiter, ...]
```

or

```
REVOKE <ADMIN OPTION FOR>
   <ROLE> [RoleName, ...]
   FROM [Forfeiter, ...]
```

where:

Authority	Identifies one or more authorities to revoke
Privilege	Identifies one or more privileges to revoke
DatabaseName	Identifies, by name, one or more databases for which authorities and privileges are to be revoked—*this parameter must be specified for DB2 for z/OS only; it is not used by DB2 for Linux, UNIX, and Windows*
ObjectType	Identifies the type of object the authorities and privileges specified are to be revoked for
ObjectName	Identifies, by name, the object the authorities and/or privileges specified are to be revoked for
RoleName	Identifies, by name, one or more roles to revoke
Forfeiter	Identifies who is to lose the authorities and privileges that are being revoked; the value specified for this parameter can be any combination of the following:

[*AuthorizationID*]	Identifies a particular user, by authorization ID, whom the authorities and privileges specified are to be revoked from
<<USER> *Name* >	Identifies a particular user, by name, whom the authorities and privileges specified are to be revoked from—*this clause is recognized by DB2 for Linux, UNIX, and Windows only; it cannot be used with DB2 for z/OS*
<<GROUP> *Name* >	Identifies a particular group, by name, that the authorities and privileges specified are to be revoked from—*this clause is recognized by DB2 for Linux, UNIX, and Windows only; it cannot be used with DB2 for z/OS*
<<ROLE> *Name* >	Identifies a particular role, by name, that the authorities and privileges specified are to be revoked from—*the keyword* ROLE *is optional if this clause is used with DB2 for Linux, UNIX, and Windows; it is required if this clause is used with DB2 for z/OS*
PUBLIC	Indicates that the authorities and privileges specified are to be revoked from the group PUBLIC

If the ALL PRIVILEGES clause is specified with the REVOKE statement used, all authorities and privileges for the object indicated—*except* the CONTROL privilege—will be revoked from each forfeiter specified. Therefore, if CONTROL privilege is to be revoked, it must be revoked separately (by someone with ACCESSCTRL or SECADM authority).

If the ADMIN OPTION FOR clause is specified with the REVOKE statement used, the ability to grant the specified role(s) to others will be taken away from the forfeiter(s) indicated.

REVOKE Statement Examples

Now that you have seen the basic syntax for the REVOKE statement, let us look at some examples.

Example 1: Remove the ability to create tables in a table space named HR from a user whose authorization ID is USER1:

```
REVOKE USE OF TABLESPACE hr
  FROM user1
```

Example 2: Remove the ability to use a UDF named MPH_TO_KPH from a user whose authorization ID is USER1:

```
REVOKE EXECUTE ON FUNCTION mph_to_kph
  FROM USER user1
```

Example 3: Remove the ability to modify information stored in the ADDRESS and HOME_PHONE columns of a table named EMPLOYEES from a user whose authorization ID is USER1:

```
REVOKE UPDATE (address, home_phone)
  ON TABLE emp_info
  FROM user1
```

Example 4: Remove the ability to add data to a table named SALES from a user whose authorization ID is USER1:

```
REVOKE INSERT ON TABLE sales
  FROM user1
```

Example 5: Prevent users in the special group PUBLIC from adding, changing, or deleting data stored in a table named EMPLOYEE:

```
REVOKE INSERT, UPDATE, DELETE
  ON TABLE employee
  FROM PUBLIC
```

Example 6: Remove a user whose authorization ID is USER1 from a role named ADMIN role:

```
REVOKE ROLE admin FROM USER user1
```

Row and Column Access Control (RCAC)

Traditionally, if a database administrator needed to restrict access to specific columns or rows in a table, he or she relied on views. For example, if a table containing employee information held sensitive information such as Social Security numbers and salaries, access to that data might be restricted by creating a view that contained only the columns that held nonsensitive data. Then, only authorized users would be given access to the table, while everyone else would be required to work with the view. (This was accomplished by granting appropriate table privileges to select users and the necessary view privileges to everyone else.)

Using views for access control works well when data access rules and restrictions are relatively simple. However, this approach becomes ineffective if several views are needed or if view definitions are complex. And it can be costly, particularly if a large number of views must be manually updated and maintained. Even when data access rules are relatively simple, the use of views for access control has one significant drawback—users with direct access to a database, and users who hold DATAACCESS authority, can often gain access to the sensitive data that one or more views have been designed to protect.

Implemented through SQL and managed by a DB2 security administrator, Row and Column Access Control—sometimes referred to as *fine-grained access control*, or *FGAC*—resolves these issues by stipulating rules and conditions under which a user, group, or role can access rows and columns of a table. With RCAC, all users access the same table (as opposed to accessing alternative views), but access is restricted based on individual user permissions and rules that a DB2 security administrator has specified in a security policy that has been associated with the table. Two sets of RCAC rules exist: one set operates on rows (known as *row permissions*), and the other operates on columns (referred to as *column masks*). These rules can be used together or separately to control how data is accessed.

Row Permissions

A *row permission* is a database entity that describes a specific row access control rule for a certain table. Written in the form of a query search condition, a row permission specifies the conditions under which a user, group, or role can access individual rows of data in a table. Row permissions can be created on all tables except materialized query tables; row permissions are created by executing the CREATE PERMISSION statement. The basic syntax for this statement is as follows:

```
CREATE PERMISSION [PermissionName] ON [TableName]
  FOR ROWS WHERE [SearchCondition]
  ENFORCED FOR ALL ACCESS
  [ENABLE | DISABLE]
```

where:

PermissionName	Identifies the name to assign to the row permission that is to be created
TableName	Identifies, by name, the base table the row permission is to be created for
SearchCondition	Identifies one or more logical conditions that evaluate to TRUE (1) or FALSE (0); the search condition specified must follow the same rules the search condition in a WHERE clause of a query adheres to, with some minor exceptions—notably, the search condition specified cannot contain references to other database objects, and user, group, or role can be referenced

If the ENABLE clause is specified with the CREATE PERMISSION statement used, the resulting row permission will be enabled for row access control as soon as it is created. However, because you can use the CREATE PERMISSION statement to create a row permission *before* row access control has been activated for a table, the row permission might not take effect immediately. If row access control is not currently activated for the table specified, the row permission will become effective only after row access control for the table has been activated. (To activate row access control for a table, execute the ALTER TABLE statement with the ACTIVATE ROW ACCESS CONTROL clause specified.) Activating row access control for the table will make the row permission effective immediately, and all packages and dynamically cached statements that reference the table will be marked as invalid.

Thus, to create a row permission named SREP_ROW_ACCESS that allows only members of the role SREP (which is a role that has been created for sales representatives) to see records stored in a table named SALES, you would execute a CREATE PERMISSION statement that looks something like this:

```
CREATE PERMISSION srep_row_access ON sales
   FOR ROWS WHERE
      VERIFY_ROLE_FOR_USER (SESSION_USER,'SREP') = 1
   ENFORCED FOR ALL ACCESS
   ENABLE
```

Of course, the resulting row permission (SREP_ROW_ACCESS) will not be enforced unless row access control has been activated for the table named SALES.

If multiple row permissions are defined for a single table, the search condition in each row permission is logically ORed together to form the row access control search condition that will be applied whenever users access the table. The final row access control search condition acts as a filter and is processed before any other operations (such as an ORDER BY operation) are performed. In addition, the final row access control search condition ensures that any row an authorized user inserts or updates in the table conforms to the definition of all row permissions that have been defined.

●●

Note: In most cases, only users with SECADM authority are allowed to create, alter, and drop row permissions. The one exception is if the SEPARATE_SECURITY system parameter for DB2 for z/OS is set to NO. In this case, users with either SYSADM *or* SECADM authority are allowed to create and manage row permissions.

●●

Column Masks

A *column mask* is a database entity that describes a specific column access control rule for a certain column in a table. Written in the form of an SQL CASE expression, a column mask indicates the conditions under which a user, group, or role can access values for a column. Depending upon the CASE expression used, a column mask can also control the value that unauthorized users, groups, or roles will receive whenever a protected column is queried.

As with row permissions, column masks can be created on all tables except materialized query tables. Column masks are created by executing the CREATE MASK statement. The basic syntax for this statement is as follows:

```
CREATE MASK [MaskName] ON [TableName]
  FOR COLUMN [ColumnName]
  RETURN [CASEExpression]
  [ENABLE | DISABLE]
```

where:

MaskName	Identifies the name to assign to the column mask that is to be created
TableName	Identifies, by name, the base table the column mask is to be created for
ColumnName	Identifies, by name, the column that the column mask is to be created for
CASEExpression	Identifies a CASE expression that is to be evaluated to determine the appropriate value to return for the column (the result of the

CASE expression is returned in place of the column value in a row; therefore, the result data type, NULL attribute, and length attribute of the CASE expression result must be identical to that of the column specified)

If the ENABLE clause is specified with the CREATE MASK statement used, the resulting column mask will be enabled for column access control as soon as it is created—provided column access control has been activated for the table. If column access control has not been activated for the table indicated, the column mask will become effective only after column access control for the table has been activated. (To activate column access control for a table, execute the ALTER TABLE statement with the ACTIVATE COLUMN ACCESS CONTROL clause specified.)

Thus, to create a column mask named SSN_MASK that allows only members of the role HR to see Social Security numbers stored in a column named SSN (in a table named EMPLOYEES) and that allows everyone else to see just the last four digits of Social Security numbers, you could execute a CREATE MASK statement that looks something like this:

```
CREATE MASK ssn_mask ON employees
  FOR COLUMN ssn
  RETURN
    CASE
      WHEN (VERIFY_GROUP_FOR_USER (SESSION_USER,'HR') = 1)
        THEN ssn
      ELSE 'XXX-XX-' || SUBSTR(ssn,8,4)
    END
  ENABLE
```

Although multiple columns in a table can have column masks defined, only one column mask can be created per column. When column access control is activated for a table, the CASE expression in the column mask definition is applied to determine the values that will be returned to an application. The application of column masks affects the final output only; it does not affect operations in SQL statements (such as predicates and ordering).

•••

Note: Usually, only users with SECADM authority are allowed to create, alter, and drop column masks. The one exception is if the SEPARATE_SECURITY system parameter for DB2 for z/OS is set to NO. In this case, users with either SYSADM *or* SECADM authority are allowed to create and manage column masks.

•••

Activating Row and Column Access Control

You can activate row and column access control for a table at any time. If row permissions or column masks already exist, activating row and column access control simply makes the permissions or masks become effective—provided they were created with the ENABLE clause specified. If row permissions or column masks do not yet exist, activating row access control for a table will cause DB2 to generate a default row permission that prevents any SQL access to the table from occurring. Activating column access control causes DB2 to wait for column masks to be created.

No database user is inherently exempted from row and column access control rules. Therefore, users with direct access to a database, as well as users who hold DATAACCESS authority, cannot get to sensitive data that row and column access control measures have been defined to protect.

Label-Based Access Control (LBAC)

Label-based access control (LBAC), also known as *multilevel security*, is a security feature that uses one or more security labels to control who has read access, who has write access, and who has both read and write access to individual rows and/or columns in a table. LBAC is implemented by assigning unique labels to users and data and allowing access only when assigned labels match; it is similar, in both form and function, to the security models that the United States and many other governments use to protect important information. Such models often assign hierarchical classification labels like CONFIDENTIAL, SECRET, and TOP SECRET to data based on its sensitivity. Access to data is then restricted to just those users who have been assigned the appropriate label (for example, SECRET) or to users who have been assigned a label that is at a higher level in the classification hierarchy.

To implement an LBAC solution, it is imperative that you have a thorough understanding of the security requirements that need to be enforced. Once the security requirements are known, someone with SECADM authority (DB2 for Linux, UNIX, and Windows) must define the appropriate *security label components*, *security policies*, and *security labels*. Then, that individual must grant the proper security labels to the appropriate users. Finally, someone with LBAC credentials must create an LBAC-protected table or alter an existing table to add LBAC protection. (With DB2 for z/OS, the process is significantly different.)

Security Label Components

Security label components represent criteria that can be used to determine whether a user should have access to specific data. Three types of security label components can exist:

- **SET**: A set is a collection of elements (character string values) where the order in which each element appears is not important.
- **ARRAY**: An array is an ordered set that can represent a simple hierarchy. With an array, the order in which the elements appear is important—the first element ranks higher than the second, the second ranks higher than the third, and so on.
- **TREE**: A tree represents a more complex hierarchy that can have multiple nodes and branches.

Security label components are created by executing the CREATE SECURITY LABEL COMPONENT statement. The basic syntax for this statement is as follows:

```
CREATE SECURITY LABEL COMPONENT [ComponentName]
   SET {StringConstant, ...}
```

or

```
CREATE SECURITY LABEL COMPONENT [ComponentName]
   SET [StringConstant, ...]
```

or

```
CREATE SECURITY LABEL COMPONENT [ComponentName]
   TREE (StringConstant ROOT
      <,StringConstant UNDER StringConstant, ...>)
```

where:

ComponentName   Identifies the name to assign to the security label component that
                   is to be created

StringConstant   Identifies one or more string constant values that make up the set,
                    array, or tree of values the security label component will use

Thus, to create a security label component named SEC_COMP1 that contains an array of
values listed from highest to lowest order, you could execute a CREATE SECURITY LABEL
COMPONENT statement that looks something like this:

```
CREATE SECURITY LABEL COMPONENT sec_comp1
   ARRAY ['MASTER_CRAFTSMAN', 'JOURNEYMAN', 'APPRENTICE']
```

On the other hand, to create a security label component named SEC_COMP2 that
consists of a tree of values that describe a company's organizational chart, you would
execute a CREATE SECURITY LABEL COMPONENT statement that looks more like this:

```
CREATE SECURITY LABEL COMPONENT sec_comp2
   TREE ('CEO' ROOT,
         'SALES_MGR' UNDER 'CEO',
         'HR_MGR' UNDER 'CEO',
         'ENG_MGR' UNDER 'CEO',
         'SALES_STAFF' UNDER 'SALES_MGR',
         'HR_STAFF' UNDER 'HR_MGR',
         'ENG_STAFF' UNDER 'ENG_MGR')
```

Security Policies

Security policies determine exactly how LBAC is to protect a table. Specifically, a
security policy identifies the following:

- The security label components to use in the security labels that will be part of the
  policy

- The rules to use when security label components are compared (at this time, only one set of rules is supported: DB2LBACRULES)
- Optional behaviors to use when data protected by the policy is accessed

Every LBAC-protected table must have one (and only one) security policy associated with it. Rows and columns in a table can only be protected with security labels that are part of the associated security policy, and all protected data access must adhere to the rules of that policy.

Security policies are created by executing the CREATE SECURITY POLICY statement. The basic syntax for this statement is as follows:

```
CREATE SECURITY POLICY [PolicyName]
   COMPONENTS [ComponentName , ...]
   WITH DB2LBACRULES
   <OVERRIDE NOT AUTHORIZED WRITE SECURITY LABEL |
    RESTRICT NOT AUTHORIZED WRITE SECURITY LABEL>
```

where:

PolicyName	Identifies the name to assign to the security policy that is to be created
ComponentName	Identifies, by name, one or more security label components that are to be part of the security policy

The OVERRIDE NOT AUTHORIZED WRITE SECURITY LABEL/RESTRICT NOT AUTHORIZED WRITE SECURITY LABEL clause specifies the action to take when a user who is not authorized to explicitly provide a security label value for write access attempts to write data to the protected table. By default, the value of a user's security label, rather than an explicitly specified value, is used for write access during insert and update operations (OVERRIDE NOT AUTHORIZED WRITE SECURITY LABEL). However, if the RESTRICT NOT AUTHORIZED WRITE SECURITY LABEL clause is specified with the CREATE SECURITY POLICY statement used, insert and update operations will fail if the user is not authorized to write an explicitly specified security label to the protected table.

So, to create a security policy named SEC_POLICY that is based on the SEC_COMP1 security label component that was created earlier, you would execute a CREATE SECURITY POLICY statement that looks like this:

```
CREATE SECURITY POLICY sec_policy
  COMPONENTS sec_comp1
  WITH DB2LBACRULES
```

Security Labels

Security labels describe a certain set of security criteria and are applied to data to protect it against unauthorized access or modification. When a user attempts to access or modify protected data, his or her assigned security label is compared against the security label that is protecting the data to determine whether access or modification is allowed.

Each security label is part of exactly one security policy, and a security label must exist for every security label component found in that security policy. Security labels are created by executing the CREATE SECURITY LABEL statement. The basic syntax for this statement is as follows:

```
CREATE SECURITY LABEL [LabelName]
  [COMPONENT [ComponentName] [StringConstant, ...]  , ...]
```

where:

LabelName	Identifies the name to assign to the security label that is to be created; the name specified must be qualified with a security policy name and must not match an existing security label for the designated security policy
ComponentName	Identifies, by name, a security label component that is part of the security policy that was specified as the qualifier for the *LabelName* parameter
StringConstant	Identifies one or more string constant values that are valid elements of the security label component that was specified in the *ComponentName* parameter

Thus, to create a set of security labels for the security policy named SEC_POLICY that was created earlier, you could execute a series of CREATE SECURITY LABEL statements that look like this:

```
CREATE SECURITY LABEL sec_policy.master
  COMPONENT sec_comp 'MASTER_CRAFTSMAN'

CREATE SECURITY LABEL sec_policy.journeyman
  COMPONENT sec_comp 'JOURNEYMAN'

CREATE SECURITY LABEL sec_policy.apprentice
  COMPONENT sec_comp 'APPRENTICE'
```

Granting Security Labels to Users

After the security labels needed have been created, you must grant the proper security label to the appropriate users. You must also indicate whether a particular user is to have read access only, write access only, or full access to data that is protected by the security label being granted. Someone with SECADM authority (DB2 for Linux, UNIX, and Windows) can grant security labels to users by executing a special form of the GRANT SQL statement. The syntax for this form of the GRANT statement is as follows:

```
GRANT SECURITY LABEL [LabelName]
  TO [Recipient]
  FOR [READ | WRITE | ALL] ACCESS
```

where:

LabelName	Identifies, by name, the security label that is to be granted; the label name specified must be qualified with the security policy name that was used when the security label was created
Recipient	Identifies who is to receive the security label being granted; the value specified for this parameter can be any combination of the following:

[*AuthorizationID*]	Identifies a particular user, by authorization ID, whom the security label specified is to be granted to
<<USER> *Name* >	Identifies a particular user, by name, whom the security label specified is to be granted to— *this clause is recognized by DB2 for Linux,*

	UNIX, and Windows only; it cannot be used with DB2 for z/OS
<<GROUP> *Name* >	Identifies a particular group, by name, that the security label specified is to be granted to—*this clause is recognized by DB2 for Linux, UNIX, and Windows only; it cannot be used with DB2 for z/OS*
<<ROLE> *Name* >	Identifies a particular role, by name, that the security label specified is to be granted to

Thus, to give a user named USER1 the ability to only read data that the security label SEC_POLICY.EXEC_STAFF protects, you would execute a GRANT statement that looks like this:

```
GRANT SECURITY LABEL sec_policy.exec_staff
   TO user1 FOR READ ACCESS
```

Implementing Row-Level LBAC Protection

To configure a new table for row-level LBAC protection, you must include a column with the DB2SECURITYLABEL data type in the table's definition and associate a security policy with the table by using the SECURITY POLICY clause of the CREATE TABLE statement. For example, to create a table named SALES and configure it for row-level LBAC protection using a security policy named SEC_POLICY, you would execute a CREATE TABLE statement that looks something like this:

```
CREATE TABLE sales
   (po_num     INTEGER NOT NULL,
    date       DATE,
    sales_rep  INTEGER,
    amount     DECIMAL(12,2),
    sec_label  DB2SECURITYLABEL)
   SECURITY POLICY sec_policy
```

Alternatively, you can add a DB2SECURITYLABEL column to an existing table and associate a security policy with it by using the ALTER TABLE statement. For instance, to configure an existing table named SALES for row-level LBAC protection using a security policy named SEC_POLICY, you would execute an ALTER TABLE statement that looks like this:

```
ALTER TABLE sales
  ADD COLUMN sec_label DB2SECURITYLABEL
  ADD SECURITY POLICY sec_policy
```

However, to execute either statement, you must have been granted a security label for write access that is part of the SEC_POLICY security policy. Otherwise, the attempt to create the DB2SECURITYLABEL column will fail.

Implementing Column-Level LBAC Protection

Just as you must associate a security policy with a table (using the SECURITY POLICY clause of the CREATE TABLE or ALTER TABLE statement) when configuring a table for row-level LBAC protection, you must associate a security policy with the table you want to secure with column-level LBAC protection. However, instead of including a column with the DB2SECURITYLABEL data type in the table's definition, you must configure each of the table's columns for protection using the SECURED WITH clause of the ALTER TABLE statement. For example, to configure a table named EMPLOYEES for column-level LBAC protection using a security policy named SEC_POLICY, you would execute an ALTER TABLE statement that looks something like this:

```
ALTER TABLE employees
  ALTER COLUMN emp_id SECURED WITH confidential
  ALTER COLUMN f_name SECURED WITH unclassified
  ALTER COLUMN l_name SECURED WITH unclassified
  ALTER COLUMN ssn    SECURED WITH confidential
  ALTER COLUMN salary SECURED WITH confidential
  ALTER COLUMN bonus  SECURED WITH confidential
  ADD SECURITY POLICY sec_policy
```

In this case, the security label "unclassified" will protect data in columns F_NAME and L_NAME, and the security label "confidential" will protect the data in the remaining columns. It is important to note that if you attempt to execute this ALTER TABLE statement as a user with SYSADM or SECADM authority, the operation will fail. That is because the only user who can secure a column with a security label is a user who has been granted write access to data that is protected by that security label. Consequently, in this example, someone who has been granted write access to data that is protected by the security label unclassified will need to alter the F_NAME and L_NAME columns. And someone who has been granted write access to data that is protected by the security label "confidential" will need to make the rest of the changes needed. In order for one person to make all the changes shown, he or she must be granted exemptions to the LBAC rules before they will be allowed to make the changes desired.

A Word About Trusted Contexts

Another security enhancement available with DB2 is a feature that is known as a *trusted context*. A trusted context is a database object that describes a trust relationship between a DB2 database and an external entity, like a web server or an application client. The following information is used to define a trusted context:

- A system authorization ID that represents the authorization ID that an incoming connection must use to be considered "trusted"
- The IP address, domain name, or security zone name an incoming connection must originate from to be considered "trusted"
- A data stream encryption value that represents the level of encryption that an incoming connection (if any) must use to be considered "trusted"

It is important to note that trusted context objects can only be defined by someone with SECADM authority.

Trusted contexts are designed specifically to address the security concerns involving the use of three-tier (client, gateway, server) configurations. Usually, with such configurations, all interactions with a database server occur through a database connection that the middle tier (gateway) establishes by using a combination of an authorization ID and a credential that identifies the middle tier to the server. In other words, the authorities and privileges associated with the middle tier's authorization ID control what clients can and cannot do when working with a database at the server. When trusted contexts are used, each user's authorization ID is used instead, thereby ensuring that each user is only allowed to interact with a database according to the authorities and privileges that he or she has been granted.

So how do trusted contexts work? When a database connection is established, DB2 compares that connection's attributes against the definitions of each trusted context object defined. If the connection attributes match a trusted context object, the connection is treated as a *trusted connection*, and the connection's initiator is allowed to acquire additional capabilities. These capabilities vary depending upon whether the trusted connection is *implicit* or *explicit*.

An implicit trusted connection results from a normal connection request and allows users to inherit a role that is unavailable to them outside the scope of the trusted connection. An explicit trusted connection is established by making a connection request within an application. After an explicit trusted connection is established, an application can switch the connection's user to a different authorization ID. (Switching can occur with or without authenticating the new authorization ID, depending upon the definition of the trusted context object associated with the connection. If a switch request is made using an authorization ID that is not allowed, the explicit trusted connection is placed in an "unconnected" state.)

DB2 for z/OS extends this concept to allow the assignment of a trusted context to a role. An authorization ID that uses such a trusted context can inherit the privileges assigned to the role, in addition to the authorities and privileges that have already been granted to that authorization ID.

4

Working with Databases and Database Objects

Twenty percent (20%) of the *DB2 10.1 Fundamentals* certification exam (Exam 610) is designed to test your knowledge of the different DB2 objects available and to assess your ability to create and connect to DB2 servers and databases. The questions that make up this portion of the exam are intended to evaluate the following:

- Your ability to identify DB2 objects
- Your knowledge of the basic characteristics and properties of DB2 objects
- Your ability to construct a new DB2 database
- Your ability to identify and connect to DB2 servers and databases
- Your ability to identify the results produced when select Data Definition Language (DDL) statements are executed
- Your knowledge of temporal data management and temporal (time travel) tables

This chapter introduces you to the various objects that are available with DB2 environments. It also shows you how to create and connect to DB2 servers and databases, as well as how to design and create temporal tables. In this chapter, you will learn about servers, instances, and databases, along with many other objects that make up a DB2 database environment. You will also discover how to create new DB2 databases and

how to identify and connect to DB2 servers and databases using Type 1 and Type 2
connections. Finally, you will learn about temporal data management and the different
temporal (time travel) tables that can be created in a DB2 10 (DB2 for z/OS) and DB2
10.1 (DB2 for Linux, UNIX, and Windows) database.

Servers, Instances, and Databases

DB2 sees the world as a hierarchy of objects. *Servers* running DB2 software occupy the
highest level of this hierarchy, *instances* comprise the second level, and *databases* make
up the third. Figure 4.1 shows what this hierarchical relationship looks like in a DB2 for
Linux, UNIX, and Windows environment.

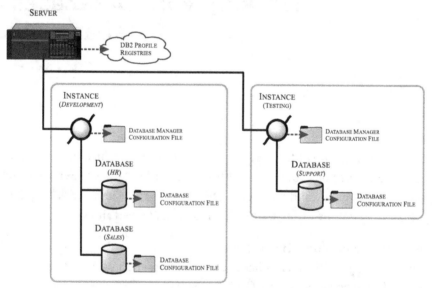

*Figure 4.1: Hierarchical relationship between systems, instances, and databases
in a DB2 for Linux, UNIX, and Windows environment*

When DB2 is first installed, program files for a background process known as the
DB2 Database Manager are physically copied to a server and, typically, an instance of
this process is created and initialized as part of the installation process. (This instance is
started immediately after creation and, by default, it will be restarted whenever the server
is rebooted.)

Instances are responsible for managing system resources and databases that fall
under their control. And although only one instance exists initially, with DB2 for Linux,
UNIX, and Windows, multiple instances can be created on a single server. When multiple

instances are used, each instance behaves as if it were a separate, stand-alone DB2 server, even though it might share the same DB2 binary program files with other instances. (If one instance is running a DB2 version that is different from the others, that instance will have its own set of program files that corresponds to the different DB2 version.) In addition, each instance has its own environment, which can be configured by modifying the contents of an associated DB2 Database Manager configuration file.

A database is an entity that contains many physical and logical components, all of which aid in the storage, modification, and retrieval of data. Multiple databases can exist and, like instances, each database has its own environment. To a certain extent, a database's environment is also governed by a set of configuration parameters, which reside in an accompanying database configuration file.

Other DB2 Objects

Although servers, instances, and databases are the primary components that make up a DB2 database environment, many other different, but often related, objects exist. Typically, these objects are classified as being either *system objects* or *data objects* (sometimes referred to as *database objects* or *data structures*).

Data Objects

Data objects control how user data is stored and, in some cases, how data is organized inside a database. Some of the more common data objects available include:

- Schemas
- Tables
- Views
- Indexes
- Aliases
- Sequences
- Triggers
- User-defined data types (UDTs)
- User-defined functions (UDFs)
- Stored procedures
- Packages

Schemas

Schemas provide a way to logically group objects in a database; you use them to organize data objects into sets. When objects that can be qualified by a schema are created, they are given a two-part name—the first (leftmost) part of the name is the *schema name* or *qualifier*, and the second (rightmost) part is the user-supplied object name. Syntactically, these two parts are concatenated and separated by a period (for example, HR.EMPLOYEES).

When select data objects (that is, table spaces, tables, indexes, distinct data types, functions, stored procedures, and triggers) are created, they are automatically assigned to (or defined into) a schema, based on the qualifier that was provided as part of the user-supplied name. Figure 4.2 illustrates how to assign a table named EMPLOYEES to a schema named HR during the table creation process.

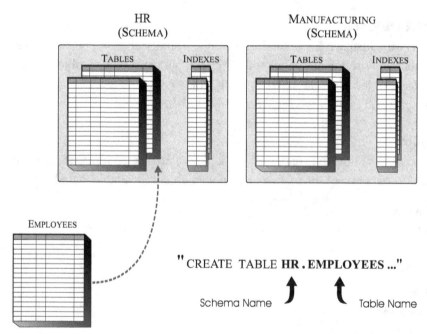

Figure 4.2: Assigning a table object to a specific schema

If a schema name or qualifier is not provided as part of an object's name, the object is automatically assigned to a default schema, which typically has the name of the authorization ID of the individual who created the object.

It is important to note that with DB2 for Linux, UNIX, and Windows, objects cannot be created in the schemas that are automatically produced when a database is created (that is, in a schema whose name begins with the letters "SYS"). With DB2 for z/OS, objects cannot be created in a *system schema*, which is any set of schemas that are reserved for use by the DB2 subsystem.

Tables

A *table* is an object that acts as the main repository for data. Tables present data as a collection of unordered *rows* with a fixed number of *columns*. Each column contains values of the same data type, and each row contains a set of values for one or more of the columns available. The storage representation of a row is called a *record*, the storage representation of a column is called a *field*, and each intersection of a row and column is called a *value* (or *cell*). Figure 4.3 shows the structure of a simple table.

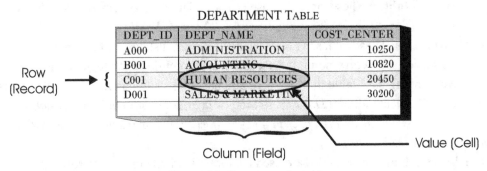

Figure 4.3: Structure of a table

With DB2, the following types of tables are available:

- **Base tables (or regular tables):** These tables hold persistent user data; they are the most common type of table used in a DB2 database.
- **Multidimensional clustering (MDC) tables:** MDC tables are physically clustered on more than one key or dimension simultaneously. (*This type of table is available with DB2 for Linux, UNIX, and Windows only.*)
- **Insert time clustering (ITC) tables:** ITC tables are conceptually and physically similar to MDC tables, but they cluster data according to the time in which rows are inserted. (*This type of table is available with DB2 for Linux, UNIX, and Windows only.*)
- **Range-clustered tables (RCTs):** RCTs use a special algorithm to associate record key values (which are similar to index key values) with the location of rows in the table; each record in a RCT table receives a predetermined record identifier (RID),

and this identifier is used to quickly locate individual records. (*This type of table is available with DB2 for Linux, UNIX, and Windows only.*)

- **Partitioned tables:** These tables use a data organization scheme in which data is divided across multiple storage objects, called *data partitions* or *ranges*, according to values found in one or more partitioning key columns.

- **Temporal tables:** These tables can be used to manage multiple versions of data as well as track effective dates for data that is subject to changing business conditions. Data stored in temporal tables can be valid for a time period that is defined by the database system (*system-period temporal tables*), customer applications (*application-period temporal tables*), or a combination of the two (*bitemporal tables*).

- **Auxiliary tables:** These tables are used to hold data for a specific column in a base table. (*This type of table is available with DB2 for z/OS only.*)

- **Clone tables:** These tables are created in a different instance of the same table space as the corresponding base table, are structurally identical to the corresponding base table in every way, and have the same indexes, BEFORE triggers, and LOB object values. (*This type of table is available with DB2 for z/OS only; clone tables can be created only in a range-partitioned or partition-by-growth table space that DB2 manages.*)

- **History tables:** These tables are used to store historical versions of rows for system-period temporal tables.

- **Result tables:** These are DB2-defined tables containing a set of rows that DB2 retrieves from one or more base tables or that DB2 generates, directly or indirectly, in response to a query.

- **Materialized query tables (MQTs):** MQTs derive their definitions from the results of a query (SELECT statement), and their data consists of precomputed values taken from one or more tables the MQT is based upon. MQTs are similar to views in that their data comes from one or more base tables. Where they differ is in how their data is generated and where that data is physically stored. An MQT's data is generated by executing the query the MQT is based upon, either at regular intervals or at a specific point in time that is user controlled. An MQT's data physically resides in the MQT itself, rather than in the MQT's underlying base table(s). MQTs can greatly improve performance and response time for complex queries, particularly queries that aggregate data over one or more dimensions or that join data across multiple base tables.

- **Temporary tables:** These tables are used to hold data temporarily. Two kinds of temporary tables are available:
  - » **Declared global temporary tables:** These tables are used to hold nonpersistent data temporarily, on behalf of a single application. Declared global temporary tables are explicitly created by an application when they are needed and implicitly destroyed when that application is terminated.
  - » **Created global temporary tables:** These tables are used to hold nonpersistent data temporarily, on behalf of one or more applications. Unlike declared global temporary tables, definitions for created global temporary tables are stored in the system catalog, and an empty instance of the table is created the first time it is referenced in an OPEN (cursor), SELECT, INSERT, UPDATE, or DELETE statement. Each connection that references a created global temporary table has its own unique instance of the table, and the instance is not persistent beyond the life of the connection.
- **Typed tables:** These tables' column definitions are based on the attributes of a user-defined structured data type. (*This type of table is available with DB2 for Linux, UNIX, and Windows only.*)

Because tables are the basic data objects used for storing information, many are often created for a single database.

Note: Often, you can reduce the storage space needed for a table by compressing the data stored in it. Data compression is based on the principle that large amounts of data tend to be highly redundant. When a table (DB2 for Linux, UNIX, and Windows) or a table space (DB2 for z/OS) is enabled for compression, DB2 looks for repeating patterns in the data and replaces those patterns with 12-bit symbols, which are then recorded along with the patterns they represent in a *compression dictionary*. Once a compression dictionary is created, it is stored in the table (or page, if adaptive compression is used) along with the compressed data, and whenever the table is accessed, the dictionary is loaded into memory and used to decompress the data.

With DB2 Version 10 (DB2 for z/OS) and Version 10.1 (DB2 for Linux, UNIX, and Windows), base tables, temporary tables, and indexes can be enabled for compression.

Views

Views provide an alternative way of describing and displaying data stored in one or more tables. As with base tables, views can be thought of as having columns and rows. Essentially, a view is a named specification of a result table that is populated each time the view is referenced in an SQL operation. Figure 4.4 shows a simple view that presents data values from two different base tables.

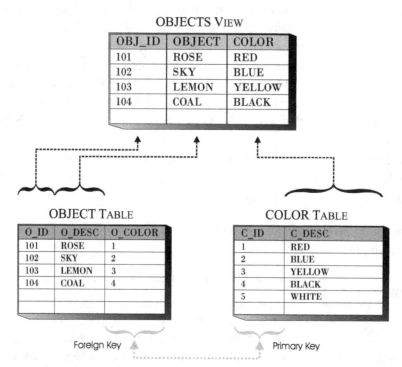

OBJECTS VIEW

OBJ_ID	OBJECT	COLOR
101	ROSE	RED
102	SKY	BLUE
103	LEMON	YELLOW
104	COAL	BLACK

OBJECT TABLE

O_ID	O_DESC	O_COLOR
101	ROSE	1
102	SKY	2
103	LEMON	3
104	COAL	4

COLOR TABLE

C_ID	C_DESC
1	RED
2	BLUE
3	YELLOW
4	BLACK
5	WHITE

Foreign Key   Primary Key

Figure 4.4: A view that presents data stored in two base tables

Although views look similar to base tables, they do not contain data. Instead, they obtain their data from the table(s) or view(s)—views can be derived from other views—they are based upon. Consequently, only a view's definition is stored in a database. Even so, in most cases, views can be referenced in the same way that tables can be referenced. That is, they can be the source of queries as well as the target of insert, update, and delete operations. (Whether a particular view can be used to insert, update, or delete data depends upon how the view was defined—views can be defined as being *insertable*, *updatable*, *deletable*, or *read-only*.)

When a view is the target of an SQL operation, the query that was used to define the view is executed, the results produced are returned in a table-like format, and the operation is then performed on the results. Therefore, when a transaction performs insert, update, and delete operations against a view, those operations are actually executed against the base table(s) the view is based upon. If the view is derived from another view, the operation cascades down through all applicable views and is applied to the appropriate underlying base table(s).

It is important to note that a single base table can serve as the source of multiple views; the SQL query you provide as part of a view's definition determines the data that is to be presented when a particular view is referenced. Because of this, views are often used to control access to sensitive data. For example, if a table contains information about every employee who works for a company (including sensitive information like bank account numbers), managers might access this table via a view that allows them to see only nonsensitive information about employees who report directly to them. Similarly, Human Resources personnel could be given access to the table by means of a view that lets them see only information needed to generate paychecks for every employee. Because each set of users are given access to data through different views, they each see different presentations of data that resides in the same table.

Indexes

An *index* is an object that contains pointers to rows in a table that are logically ordered according to the values of one or more columns (known as *key columns* or *keys*). Figure 4.5 shows the structure of a simple index, along with its relationship to the table it derives its data from.

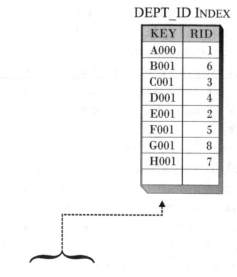

Figure 4.5: A simple index that has a one-column key

Indexes are important because:

- They provide a fast, efficient method for locating specific rows of data in large tables. (In some cases, the index itself can contain all the information needed to resolve a query, in which case, table data does not have to be retrieved.)
- They provide a logical ordering of the rows in a table. (When indexes are used, the values of one or more columns can be sorted in ascending or descending order; this is beneficial when queries that contain ORDER BY and GROUP BY clauses are executed.)

- They can enforce the uniqueness of records in a table. (If an index is defined as being UNIQUE, rows in the table associated with the index are not allowed to have more than one occurrence of the same value in the set of columns that make up the index key; any attempt to perform an insert or update operation that compromises the uniqueness of the key will result in an error.)
- They can force a table to use *clustering* storage, which causes the rows of a table to be physically arranged according to the ordering of their key column values. Usually, a clustering index will improve query performance by decreasing the I/O needed to access data. When a logical set of rows are physically stored close together, read operations typically require less I/O because adjacent rows are more likely to be found within the same extent (data pages are written in groups called *extents*) instead of being widely distributed across multiple extents.

Although some indexes are created automatically to support a table's definition (for example, to enforce unique and primary key constraints), indexes are typically created explicitly by using SQL, Data Studio, or the DB2 Design Advisor. A single table can contain a significant number of indexes (up to 32,767 with DB2 for Linux, UNIX, and Windows); however, every index comes at a price. Because indexes store key column and row pointer data, additional storage space is needed for every index used. Furthermore, write performance is negatively affected—each time a transaction performs an insert, update, or delete operation against a table with indexes, every index that is affected must be updated to reflect the changes that were made. Because of this, indexes should be created only when there is a clear performance advantage to having them available.

Indexes are typically used to improve query performance. Therefore, tables that are used for data mining, business intelligence, business warehousing, and by applications that execute many (and often complex) queries but that rarely modify data are prime candidates for indexes. Conversely, tables in Online Transaction Processing (OLTP) environments or environments where data throughput is high should use indexes sparingly or avoid them altogether.

Aliases

An *alias* is an alternate name for a table, view, or other alias. After it is created, an alias can be referenced in the same way that its corresponding table or view can. However, an alias cannot always be used in the same context as a table or view. For example, an alias cannot be used in the check condition of a check constraint or to reference a user-defined temporary table.

As with tables and views, you can create, drop, and associate comments with an alias. However, unlike with tables (but similar to views), aliases can refer to other aliases via a process known as *chaining*. Aliases are publicly referenced names, so no special authority or privilege is required to use them. Still, appropriate authorization *is* needed to access the table or view an alias refers to.

So why would you want to create and use an alias? Because by using aliases, you can construct SQL statements in such a way that they are independent of the base tables or views they reference. An SQL statement that references an alias behaves no differently than a similar SQL statement that references the associated table or view. Therefore, by using an alias, it is possible to create a single SQL statement that works with a variety of tables and views—the target of the alias can be changed dynamically, and as long as the underlying structure of the new target is similar to that of the old target, SQL statements that reference the alias do not have to be altered.

Sequences

As the name implies, a *sequence* is an object that is used to generate a sequence of numbers, in either ascending or descending order. Unlike identity columns, which produce data values for a specific column in a table, sequences are not tied to any specific column or to any specific table. Instead, sequences behave as unique counters that reside outside of the database. However, because DB2 generates the values that are needed for a given sequence, performance bottlenecks that often occur when an application relies on an external counter are eliminated.

In addition to delivering better performance, sequences offer the following advantages over external counters:

- They are guaranteed to generate unique values (assuming the sequence is never reset and does not allow values to cycle).
- They are guaranteed to produce unique values independently of any running transactions.
- They can be used to generate values of any exact numeric data type that has a scale of zero (that is, SMALLINT, BIGINT, INTEGER, or DECIMAL).
- They can produces consecutive values that differ by any increment value specified (the default value is 1).
- They ensure that the values produced are fully recoverable; if DB2 should fail, the sequence is reconstructed from transaction logs so that unique values will continue to be generated.

- They can cache values to improve performance.
- They provide versatility—one sequence can be used for several tables, or multiple, individual sequences can be created for every table that needs uniquely generated values.

Another benefit of using sequences is that you can use SQL (the ALTER SEQUENCE statement) to dynamically modify many of a sequence's attributes. For instance, you can restart a sequence, change the way in which values are incremented, establish new minimum and maximum values, increase or decrease the number of sequence numbers that are cached, change whether a sequence cycles, and alter whether sequence numbers are required to be generated in their original order *while the sequence remains online and accessible.* It is important to note, however, that if a different data type is needed or desired, a sequence must be dropped and recreated—the data type of an existing sequence cannot be dynamically changed.

Once they are created, sequences can generate values in one of three ways:

- By incrementing (or decrementing) by a specified amount, without bounds
- By incrementing (or decrementing) by a specified amount to a user-defined limit, and then stopping
- By incrementing (or decrementing) by a specified amount to a user-defined limit, and then cycling back to the beginning and starting again

To facilitate the use of sequences in SQL operations, two expressions are available: PREVIOUS VALUE and NEXT VALUE. The PREVIOUS VALUE expression returns the most recently generated value for the sequence specified, while the NEXT VALUE expression returns the next value that a certain sequence will produce.

Triggers

A *trigger* is an object that is used to define a set of actions that are to be executed whenever an insert, update, or delete operation is performed against a table or updatable view. Triggers are often used to enforce data integrity and business rules; however, they can also be used to automatically update other tables, generate or transform values for inserted and updated rows, and invoke functions to perform specific tasks such as issuing errors or alerts.

Before you can create a trigger, you must identify the following components:

- **Subject table/view:** The table or view that the trigger is to be associated with
- **Trigger event:** An SQL operation that, when performed against the subject table or view, will cause the trigger to be activated (*fired*); the trigger event can be an insert operation, an update operation, a delete operation, or a merge operation that inserts, updates, or deletes data
- **Trigger activation time:** Component that indicates whether the trigger should be fired *before*, *after*, or *instead of* the trigger event
- **Set of affected rows:** The rows of the subject table or view that are being added, updated, or removed
- **Triggered action:** An optional search condition and a set of SQL statements that are executed when the trigger is fired—if a search condition is specified, the SQL statements are executed only if the search condition evaluates to TRUE
- **Trigger granularity:** Component that specifies whether the triggered action is to be executed once, when the trigger event takes place, or once for each row the trigger event affects

As was mentioned earlier, a trigger can be fired in three different ways: before the trigger event takes place, after the trigger event completes, or in place of the trigger event. Because of this, triggers are often referred to as being BEFORE triggers, AFTER triggers, or INSTEAD OF triggers. As the name implies, BEFORE triggers are fired before the trigger event occurs and can see new data values that are about to be inserted into the subject table. For this reason, BEFORE triggers are typically used to validate input data, to automatically generate values for newly inserted rows, and to prevent certain types of trigger events from being performed.

AFTER triggers, however, are fired after the trigger event occurs and can see data values that have already been inserted into the subject table. AFTER triggers are frequently used to insert, update, or delete data in the same or in other tables, to check data against other data values (in the same or in other tables), and to invoke UDFs that perform nondatabase operations.

Unlike BEFORE and AFTER triggers, INSTEAD OF triggers are executed against a subject view, rather than a subject table. Because INSTEAD OF triggers are executed in place of the trigger event, they are typically used to ensure that applications can perform insert, update, delete, and query operations against an updatable view only; INSTEAD OF triggers prevent such operations from being performed against a table.

User-defined data types

As the name implies, *user-defined data types* are data types that database users create. Depending upon the edition used (DB2 for Linux, UNIX, and Windows or DB2 for z/OS), up to two types of UDTs are available: *distinct* and *structured*.

A *distinct data type* (or simply *distinct type*) is a UDT that is derived from one of the built-in data types that are provided with DB2. Distinct types are useful when it is desirable for DB2 to handle certain data differently from other data of the same type. For example, even though you can use a decimal data type to store currency values, a distinct type will prevent currencies such as Canadian dollars from being compared against United States dollars or United Kingdom pounds.

Although a distinct data type shares a common internal representation with a built-in data type, it is considered a wholly separate type that is different from all other data types available. Furthermore, because DB2 enforces strong data typing, the value of a distinct data type is compatible only with values of the same distinct type. Consequently, distinct types cannot be used as arguments for most built-in functions. (Likewise, built-in data types cannot be used in arguments or parameters that expect distinct data types.) Instead, UDFs that provide similar functionality must be developed if that capability is needed.

When a distinct data type is created, by default, six comparison functions (named =, <>, <, <=, >, and >=) are also created—provided the distinct type is not based on a LOB data type. (Because LOB values cannot be compared, comparison functions are not created for distinct types that are based on LOB data types.) These functions let you compare two values of the distinct data type in the same manner that you can compare two values of a built-in data type. In addition, two casting functions are generated that allow data to be converted between the distinct type and the built-in data type the distinct type is based upon.

A *structured data type* (or *structured type*) is a UDT that contains multiple attributes, each of which has a name and data type of its own. (*Structured types are available with DB2 for Linux, UNIX, and Windows only.*) A structured data type often serves as the data type of a typed table or view, in which case each column of the table or view derives its name and data type from an attribute of the structured type. A structured data type can also be created as a *subtype* of another structured type (referred to as its *supertype*); in this case, the subtype inherits the supertype's attributes and can optionally add additional attributes of its own.

Just as six comparison functions and two casting functions are normally created to support a distinct data type, six comparison functions (also named =, <>, <, <=, >, and >=)

and two casting functions can be created for a structured type. However, unlike with distinct data types, these functions are not created automatically.

User-defined data functions

User-defined functions are special objects that are used to extend and enhance the support provided by the built-in functions that are supplied with DB2. As with UDTs, UDFs (also called *methods*) are created by database users. Unlike built-in functions, UDFs can exploit system calls and DB2 administrative APIs.

Depending upon the edition used (DB2 for Linux, UNIX, and Windows or DB2 for z/OS), up to five different types of UDFs can be created:

- **SQL:** A function whose body is written entirely in SQL. An SQL function can be scalar in nature (scalar functions return a single value and can be specified in an SQL statement wherever a regular expression can be used), or it can return a row or table.

- **Sourced (or Template):** A function that is based on some other function that already exists. Sourced functions can be columnar, scalar, or tabular in nature; they can also be designed to overload a specific operator such as +, −, *, and /. When a sourced function is invoked, all arguments passed to it are converted to the data types that the underlying source function expects, and the source function itself is invoked. Upon completion, the source function performs any conversions necessary on the results produced and returns them to the calling application. Typically, sourced functions are used to provide built-in function capability for distinct UDTs.

- **External Scalar:** A function that is written using a high-level programming language such as C, C++, or Java that returns a single value. The function itself resides in an external library and is registered in the database, along with any related attributes.

- **External Table:** A function (written in a high-level programming language) that returns a result data set in the form of a table. As with external scalar functions, the function itself resides in an external library and is registered in the database, along with any related attributes. External table functions can make almost any data source appear as a base table. Consequently, the result data set produced can be used in join operations, grouping operations, set operations, or any other operation that can be applied to a read-only view.

- **OLE DB External Table:** A function (written in a high-level programming language) that can access data from an Object Linking and Embedding Database (OLE DB) provider and return a result data set in the form of a table. A generic built-in OLE DB consumer that is available with DB2 for Linux, UNIX, and Windows can be used to interface with any OLE DB provider; simply register an OLE DB table function with a database and refer to the appropriate OLE DB provider as the data source—no additional programming is required. (*This type of UDF is available with DB2 for Linux, UNIX, and Windows only.*)

Once a UDF is created (and registered with a database), it can be used anywhere a comparable built-in function can be used. That is, scalar UDFs can be used where built-in scalar functions can be used, and UDFs that return rows or tables can be used anywhere built-in table functions can be used.

Stored procedures

In a basic DB2 client/server environment, each time an SQL statement is executed against a remote database stored on a server workstation, the statement itself is sent through a network from the client to the server. The database at the server then processes the statement, and the results are returned, again through the network, to the client. This means that two messages must go through the network for every SQL statement that is executed.

Breaking an application into separate parts, storing those parts on the appropriate host (that is, the client or the server), and having them communicate with each other as the application executes can minimize network traffic. This can also enable applications to execute faster—code that interacts directly with a database can reside on the database server, where computing power and centralized control can provide quick, coordinated data access. And application logic can be stored at a client, where it can make effective use of all the resources the client has to offer.

If an application contains transactions that perform a relatively large amount of database activity with little or no user interaction, those transactions can be stored separately on a database server in what is known as a *stored procedure*. Stored procedures allow work that is done by one or more transactions to be encapsulated and stored in such a way that they can be executed directly at a server by *any* application or user who has been given the necessary authority. And, because only one SQL statement is required to invoke a stored procedure, fewer messages are transmitted across the network—only the data that is actually needed at the client is sent across.

Just as there are different types of UDFs available, there are different types of stored procedures. Depending upon the DB2 Edition used, up to three different types of stored procedures can be created:

- **SQL (or Native SQL):** A stored procedure whose body is written entirely in SQL or SQL Procedural Language (SQL PL).
- **External SQL:** A stored procedure whose body is written entirely in SQL, but that DB2 supports by generating an associated C program for. External SQL procedures are created by executing a CREATE PROCEDURE statement with the FENCED or EXTERNAL option specified. (*This type of procedure is available with DB2 for z/OS only.*)
- **External:** A stored procedure whose body is written in a high-level programming language such as Assembler, C, C++, COBOL, Java, REXX, or PL/I. Whereas SQL procedures offer rapid application development and considerable flexibility, external stored procedures can be much more powerful because they can exploit system calls and administrative APIs. However, this increase in functionality makes them more difficult to produce. In fact, the following steps are needed to create an external stored procedure:
  1. Create the body of the procedure, using a supported high-level programming language.
  2. Compile and link the procedure to create a shared (dynamic-link) library.
  3. Debug the procedure; repeat steps 1 and 2 until all problems have been resolved.
  4. Physically store the library containing the procedure on the database server.
  5. Modify the system permissions for the library so that all users with the proper authority can execute it.
  6. Register the procedure with the appropriate DB2 database.

It is important to note that when a stored procedure is used to implement a specific business rule, the logic needed to apply that rule can be incorporated into any application simply by invoking the procedure. Thus, the same business rule logic is guaranteed to be enforced across multiple applications. And if business rules change, only the logic in the procedure has to be modified—applications that call the procedure do not have to be altered.

Packages

A *package* is an object that contains the control structures DB2 uses to execute SQL statements that are coded in an application. (A *control structure* can be thought of as the operational form of an SQL statement.) High-level programming language compilers do not recognize, and therefore cannot interpret, SQL statements. So, when SQL statements are embedded in a high-level programming language source code file, they must be converted to source code a compiler can understand. A tool known as an *SQL Precompiler*, which is included in the DB2 Software Development Kit, is used to perform this conversion.

During the precompile process, a high-level programming language source code file containing SQL statements is converted to source code that a compiler can process. A package containing the control structures needed to execute the statements in the source code file is produced as well. The process of creating and storing a package in a DB2 database is known as *binding*, and by default, binding occurs automatically when the precompile process is complete. However, by specifying appropriate SQL precompiler options at precompile time, it is possible to store the control structures needed to create a package in a file that can be bound to the database later. Another tool, called the *SQL Binder* (or simply the *Binder*), can be used to create and store a package in a DB2 database, using the contents of such a file. (This is referred to as *deferred binding*.)

System Objects

DB2 has a comprehensive infrastructure that is used to provide, among other things, data integrity, exceptional performance, and high availability. And a large part of this infrastructure consists of *system objects*, which unlike data objects, are controlled and accessed primarily by DB2. Some of the system objects available include:

- Buffer pools
- Table spaces
- The system catalog
- Transaction log files
- The DB2 directory
- The bootstrap data set
- The data definition control support (DDCS) database
- Resource limit facility tables
- The work file database

Buffer pools

A *buffer pool* is an object that is used to cache table and index pages. The first time a row of data is accessed, a DB2 agent retrieves the page containing the row from storage and copies it to a buffer pool before passing it on to the user or application that requested it. (If an index was used to locate the row, the index page containing a pointer to the row is copied first; the pointer is then used to locate the data page containing the row, and that page is copied to the buffer pool as well.) And in most cases, when a page of data is retrieved, DB2 uses a set of heuristic algorithms to try to determine which pages will be needed next and those pages are copied from storage, too. (This behavior is known as *prefetching*). Once a page has been copied to a buffer pool, it remains there until the space it occupies is needed or until the database is taken offline. This is done to improve performance—data that resides in a buffer pool can be accessed much faster than data that resides on disk.

As subsequent requests for data are made, DB2 searches every buffer pool available to see whether the data requested already resides in memory. If the data is found, it is forwarded to the user or application that requested it; if not, the process of locating and copying data pages from storage is performed again. If a row is to be updated or deleted, the page containing the row is copied to a buffer pool (if it is not already there) before the update or delete operation is performed. The page is then marked as being "dirty" until it is written back to storage, which typically occurs when the transaction that made the modification is committed. Dirty pages that are written to storage are not automatically removed from the buffer pool they were stored in. Instead, they remain in memory in case they are needed again.

Before a page can be copied into a buffer pool, space for that page must be available. So, if a buffer pool is full, DB2 will selectively remove existing pages (referred to as "victim" pages) to make room for others. DB2 chooses victims by examining when a page was last referenced, by determining whether the page is for a table or an index, by evaluating the likelihood that the page will be referenced again, and by determining whether the page is dirty.

To guarantee data integrity, dirty pages are always written to disk before they are removed from memory. Therefore, if a buffer pool contains a significant number of dirty pages, performance can be adversely affected. That is because transactions may be forced to wait for dirty pages to be written to disk before they can continue. To prevent too many dirty pages from accumulating, DB2 uses special agents called *page cleaners* to periodically scan a buffer pool for dirty pages and asynchronously write them to disk.

Page cleaners ensure that some amount of buffer pool space is always available for future read operations.

Table spaces

Table spaces provide a layer of indirection between a data object (such as a table or an index) and the physical storage where that object's data resides. With DB2 for Linux, UNIX, and Windows, a table space consists of one or more *containers*, which can be an operating system directory, an individual file, or a raw logical volume/disk partition. A single table space can span many containers, but each container can belong to only one table space. With DB2 for z/OS, a table space is typically a set of volumes on disks that consist of a number of VSAM linear data sets.

Table spaces are divided into equal-sized units, called *pages*, which can be 4 KB, 8 KB, 16 KB, or 32 KB in size. (Unless otherwise specified, a page size of 4 KB is used by default.) And with DB2 for Linux, UNIX, and Windows, pages are grouped into contiguous ranges called *extents*. When a table space spans multiple containers, data is written in a round-robin fashion, one extent at a time, to each container used. This is done to evenly distribute data across all of the containers that belong to a given table space. Figure 4.6 shows the relationship between table space containers, pages, and extents (in a DB2 for Linux, UNIX, and Windows environment).

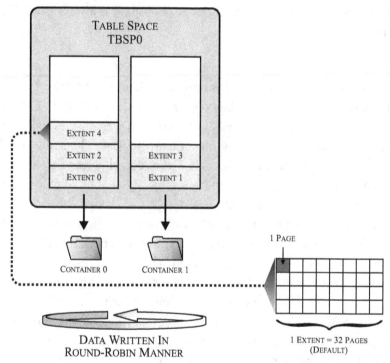

Figure 4.6: Table spaces, storage containers, pages, and extents

Depending upon the edition used, up to five different types of table spaces are available. With DB2 for Linux, UNIX, and Windows, the following types of table spaces can exist:

- **System Managed Space (SMS):** SMS table spaces are used to store temporary data. Only directory containers can be used for storage, and the operating system's file manager is responsible for controlling how space is used. The SMS storage model consists of many files (each representing a table, index, or large object data) that reside within the file system space—a DBA specifies the files' location, DB2 assigns the files their names, and the file system is responsible for managing growth.

- **Database Managed Space (DMS):** DMS table spaces are used to store regular, large object, and XML data. Only file, raw device/raw logical volume, or disk partition containers can be used for storage, and the DB2 Database Manager is responsible for controlling how space is used.

- **Automatic Storage (AS):** AS table spaces are used only if a database is configured to use automatic storage. Automatic storage table spaces consume space in the storage paths that have been defined for a database and grow automatically as the table space is filled. Although at first glance, automatic storage table spaces appear to be a third type of table space, they are actually an extension of SMS and DMS table spaces: regular and large table spaces are created as DMS table spaces with one or more file containers; system temporary and user temporary table spaces are created as SMS table spaces with one or more directory containers.

With DB2 for z/OS, the following types of table spaces can be created instead:

- **Partitioned table space:** This type of table space is used to divide the space available into separate units of storage called *partitions*; each partition contains one data set of a single table.
- **Segmented table space:** This type of table space is used to divide the space available into groups of pages called *segments*; each segment contains rows from only one table. (Every segment is the same size.)
- **Universal table space:** This type of table space provides better space management (particularly for varying-length rows) and improved bulk delete performance by combining characteristics of partitioned and segmented table spaces. A universal table space can hold one table.
- **Large object (LOB) table space:** This type of table space is used to store large object data such as graphics, video, or very large text strings. A LOB table space is always associated with the table space that contains logical LOB column values.
- **XML table space:** This type of table space is used to store XML data. An XML table space is always associated with the table space that contains logical XML column values.

It is important to note that each table space is associated with a buffer pool. One buffer pool is created automatically as part of the database creation process (with DB2 for Linux, UNIX, and Windows, this buffer pool is named IBMDEFAULTBP; with DB2 for z/OS, it is named BP0), and by default, all table spaces are associated with this buffer pool. You can assign a different buffer pool to a table space at any time; however, before such an assignment can be made, the buffer pool must already exist and both the buffer pool and the table space must have matching page sizes.

The system catalog

The *system catalog* (or *DB2 catalog*, or simply *catalog*) is a set of special tables that contain information about everything that has been defined for a database system that is under DB2's control. DB2 uses the system catalog to keep track of information like object definitions, object dependencies, column data types, constraints, and object relationships (specifically, how one object is related to another). With DB2 for Linux, UNIX, and Windows, a set of system catalog tables are created and stored in a database as part of the database creation process; with DB2 for z/OS, the system catalog resides in a system database named DSNDB06. (With DB2 for Linux, UNIX, and Windows, several system catalog views are created as well, and it is recommended that you use these views to query the system catalog. You can also use a limited number of these views to modify select system catalog data values.)

DB2 updates the information stored in the system catalog whenever any of the following events occur:

- Database objects (such as tables, indexes, and views) are created, altered, or dropped.
- Authorizations and privileges are granted or revoked.
- Statistical information is collected.
- Packages are bound to the database.

In most cases, when an object is first created, its characteristics (referred to as its *metadata*) are stored in one or more system catalog tables. However, in some cases, such as when triggers and constraints are defined, the actual SQL used to create the object is stored in the catalog instead.

Note: With DB2 for z/OS, the *communications database* (CDB) is also part of the system catalog. The CDB consists of a set of tables that contains information that is used to establish conversations with remote database management systems—the *distributed data facility* (DDF) uses the CDB to send and receive distributed data requests.

Transaction log files

Transaction log files (sometimes called *log files* or simply *logs*) are files that DB2 writes data changes and other significant database events to. Using a process called *write-ahead logging*, DB2 keeps track of changes that are made to a database *as they occur*. So how does write-ahead logging work? When a transaction adds a new row to a table via an insert operation, that row is first created in the appropriate buffer pool. If the transaction performs an update or delete operation instead, the page containing the record that is to be altered is copied to the appropriate buffer pool, where it is then modified accordingly.

Then, as soon as the desired insert, update, or delete operation is complete, a record reflecting the insertion or modification is written to the *log buffer*, which is simply a designated storage area in memory. (If a transaction performs an insert operation, a record for the new row is written to the log buffer; if it performs a delete operation, a record containing the row's original values is written to the log buffer; and if it performs an update operation, a record containing the row's original data, together with the corresponding new data, is stored in the log buffer.) When the transaction that performed the insert, update, or delete operation is terminated, a record indicating whether the transaction was committed or rolled back is written to the log buffer as well.

As transactions are executed, any time the log buffer becomes full, buffer pool page cleaners are activated, or transactions are terminated, records stored in the log buffer are immediately written to one or more log files on disk. This is done to minimize the number of log records that might be lost in the event a system failure occurs. Eventually, after all log records associated with a particular transaction have been externalized to log files, the effects of the transaction itself are written to the database. Figure 4.7 illustrates this process.

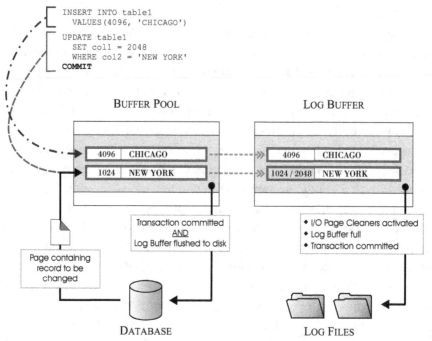

Figure 4.7: The transaction logging process

Because log files are updated frequently and because changes made by a particular transaction are externalized to the database only when the transaction successfully completes, DB2 can replay changes recorded in log files to return a database to a consistent state after a catastrophic failure occurs. When the database is restarted, log records are analyzed, and each record that corresponds to a transaction that was committed is reapplied to the database. Records for uncommitted transactions are either ignored or backed out (which is why "before" and "after" information is recorded for update operations).

The DB2 directory (DB2 for z/OS only)

The *DB2 directory* contains information that DB2 uses during normal operation. This directory consists of a set of tables that reside in table spaces that are stored in a system database named DSNDB01—the table spaces used are stored in a Virtual Storage Access Method (VSAM) linear data set. Table 4.1 shows the names of the table spaces used, along with the type of information each table space contains.

Table 4.1: Table spaces used by the DB2 directory	
Table space name	**Description**
SCT02	Contains the internal form of SQL statements that are coded in an application
SPT01 (Skeleton Package)	Contains the internal form of SQL statements that exist in a package
SYSSPUXA	Contains the contents of a package selection
SYSSPUXB	Contains the contents of a package explain block
SYSLGRNX (Log Range)	Tracks the opening and closing of table spaces, indexes, or partitions; by tracking this information and associating it with relative byte addresses (RBAs) as contained in the DB2 log, DB2 can reduce the amount of log data that must be scanned for a particular table space, index, or partition, thereby shortening recovery time
SYSUTILX (System Utilities)	Contains a row for every utility job that is running (the row persists until the utility is finished); if the utility terminates without completing, DB2 uses the information in the row to resume the utility where it left off when it is restarted
DBD01 (Database Descriptor)	Contains internal information (called *database descriptors* or *DBDs*) about the databases that exist within the DB2 subsystem; each database has exactly one corresponding DBD that describes the database, as well as its table spaces, tables, check constraints, indexes, and referential integrity constraints. DB2 constructs a DBD for a database when the database is first created; DB2 updates DBDs whenever their corresponding databases are updated
SYSDBDXA	Contains the contents of a DBD section

Only DB2 can access the DB2 directory. However, much of the information contained in this directory resides in the system catalog, which, as we saw earlier, can be queried using SQL.

Bootstrap data set (DB2 for z/OS only)

The *bootstrap data set* (or BSDS) is a VSAM key-sequenced data set that contains information that is critical to DB2. Specifically, the BSDS contains:

- An inventory of all active and archive log data sets that are known to DB2; DB2 uses this information to track active and archive log data sets and to locate log records to satisfy log read requests during normal DB2 system activity, as well as during restart and recovery processing—DB2 for z/OS writes log records to a disk data set called the *active log*; when the active log is full, the contents of the log are copied to a disk or magnetic tape data set called the *archive log*
- A wrap-around inventory of all recent DB2 checkpoint activity; DB2 uses this information during restart processing

- The distributed data facility (DDF) communication record, which contains information that is needed to use DB2 as a distributed server or requester
- Information about buffer pools

Because the BSDS is essential to recovery in the event a subsystem failure occurs, DB2 automatically creates two copies of the BSDS during installation, and if possible, places them on separate physical volumes.

The data definition control support (DDCS) database (DB2 for z/OS only)

The *data definition control support (DDCS) database* refers to a user-maintained collection of tables that DDCS uses—DDCS is a DB2 security measure that provides additional constraints to existing authorization checks. DDCS is used to manage access to data, as well as to restrict the submission of specific DDL statements to selected application plans and package collections.

During installation, the DDCS database is created automatically and assigned the name DSNRGFDB. Once the DDCS database is available, an individual with the proper authority must populate its tables before it can be used as intended.

Resource limit facility (DB2 for z/OS only)

The *resource limit facility* is used to control the amount of processor resources that SQL statements can consume. For example, this facility can be used to disable bind operations during critical times to avoid contention with the system catalog. Resource limits can be applied to insert, update, delete, truncate, and merge operations. They can also be applied to queries; however, query limits pertain only to dynamic SQL operations. (The resource limit facility does not control static SQL statements regardless of whether such statements are issued locally or remotely.)

You can establish resource limits that apply to all database users, or you can set different resource limits for individual users. It is also possible to establish some resource limits for all users *and* other resource limits for individual users only. After resource limits are established, a process known as *predictive governing* lets you apply the limits before a statement is executed, whereas a process referred to as *reactive governing* lets you apply them while a statement is running. (Predictive governing and reactive governing can be used alone or in combination.)

The work file database (DB2 for z/OS only)

The *work file database* is a special database that is used as storage when SQL statements that require working space (such as sort operations) are processed. This database is also used as storage for created and declared global temporary tables.

During installation, DB2 creates a work file database automatically—in a non-data-sharing environment, the work file database is named DSNDB07. In a data-sharing environment, each member in the data-sharing group has its own work file database, and the name assigned to this database can vary. DB2 also creates several table spaces in the work file database at the time of installation. However, additional work file table spaces can be created, if needed. In addition, the work file database (or one or more of the table spaces in it) can be dropped, recreated, and/or altered as desired.

Creating a DB2 Database

Of all the objects that make up a DB2 database environment, it is probably safe to say that the most important object is the database itself. Many of the system objects available exist to support one or more databases, and most data objects cannot be created unless a database exists. A DB2 database can be created in one of two ways: with Data Studio (which is used primarily with DB2 for Linux, UNIX, and Windows) and by executing the CREATE DATABASE command. In its simplest form, the syntax for the CREATE DATABASE command looks like this:

```
CREATE DATABASE [DatabaseName]
```

where:

DatabaseName   Identifies a unique name that is to be assigned to the database that is to be created

The only value you must provide when using this form of the CREATE DATABASE command is a database name. This name:

- Can consist of only the characters "a" through "z", "A" through "Z", "0" through "9", "@", "#", "$", and "_" (underscore)
- Cannot begin with a number
- Cannot begin with the letter sequences "SYS", "DBM", "IBM" (*DB2 for Linux, UNIX, and Windows*), or "DSNDB" (*DB2 for z/OS*)
- Cannot be the letters "DSN" followed by five digits (*DB2 for z/OS only*)

- Cannot be the same as the name of another database that exists within the same instance (DB2 for Linux, UNIX, and Windows) or at the current server (DB2 for z/OS)

When this form of the CREATE DATABASE command is executed, the characteristics of the database produced, such as page size (DB2 for Linux, UNIX, and Windows) and member (DB2 for z/OS), are defined according to a set of predefined default values. To change any of these default characteristics, you must use a more complex form of the CREATE DATABASE command. With DB2 for Linux, UNIX, and Windows, the basic syntax for this form of the CREATE DATABASE command is:

```
CREATE [DATABASE | DB] [DatabaseName]
  <AUTOMATIC STORAGE [YES | NO]>
  <ON [StoragePath, ...] <DBPATH [DBPath]>>
  <ALIAS [Alias]>
  <USING CODESET [CodeSet] TERRITORY [Territory]>
  <COLLATE USING [CollateType]>
  <PAGESIZE [4096 | Pagesize <K>]>
  <DFT_EXTENT_SZ [DefaultExtentSize]>
  <RESTRICTIVE>
  <CATALOG TABLESPACE [TS_Definition]>
  <USER TABLESPACE [TS_Definition]>
  <TEMPORARY TABLESPACE [TS_Definition]>
  <WITH "[Description]">
```

where:

DatabaseName	Identifies a unique name that is to be assigned to the database that is to be created
StoragePath	If AUTOMATIC STORAGE NO is specified, identifies one or more locations (drives and/or directories) where both data and metadata files associated with the database are to be physically stored; otherwise, this parameter identifies one or more storage paths that are to be used to hold automatic storage table space containers

DBPath	If AUTOMATIC STORAGE YES is specified (the default), identifies the location where metadata files associated with the database are to be physically stored
Alias	Identifies the alias that is to be assigned to the database that is to be created
CodeSet	Identifies the code set that is to be used for storing data in the database (with DB2, each single-byte character is represented internally as a unique number between 0 and 255—this number is referred to as the *code point* of the character; assignments of code points to every character in a particular character set is known as a *code page*, and the International Organization for Standardization term for a code page is *code set*)
Territory	Identifies the geographical location that is to be used for storing data in the database
CollateType	Identifies the collating sequence (that is, the sequence in which characters are ordered for the purpose of sorting, merging, and making comparisons) that the database is to use
PageSize	Identifies the page size that is to be used by the default buffer pool (IBMDEFAULTBP) and the default table spaces (SYSCATSPACE, TEMPSPACE1, USERSPACE1) that are to be constructed for the database; this parameter also identifies the default page size to use when new buffer pools/table spaces are created and a page size is not specified with the CREATE BUFFERPOOL and/or CREATE TABLESPACE statements used—if you do not provide a value for this parameter, a page size of 4 KB will be used by default
DefaultExtentSize	Identifies the default extent size that is to be used when a new table space is created and an extent size is not specified with the CREATE TABLESPACE statement used
TS_Definition	Specifies the table space definition that is to be used to create one or more of the default table spaces (SYSCATSPACE, TEMPSPACE1, USERSPACE1) that are automatically constructed for the database
Description	Identifies a comment that is to be used to describe the database; this comment is stored in the database directory and helps identify the database; the description provided cannot be more than 30 characters in length and must be enclosed in double-quotation marks

With DB2 for z/OS, the complete syntax for the CREATE DATABASE command looks more like this:

```
CREATE DATABASE [DatabaseName]
  <BUFFERPOOL [BP_Name]>
  <INDEXBP [IBP_Name]>
  <AS WORKFILE <FOR [MemberName]>>
  <STOGROUP [SYSDEFLT | SG_Name]>
  <CCSID [ASCII |EBCDIC | UNICODE]>
```

where:

DatabaseName	Identifies a unique name that is to be assigned to the database that is to be created
BP_Name	Identifies, by name, the default buffer pool that is to be used for table spaces that are created within the database; if the database is a work file database, 8 KB and 16 KB buffer pools cannot be specified
IBP_Name	Identifies, by name, the default buffer pool that is to be used for indexes that are created within the database
MemberName	Identifies, by name, the member for which the database is to be created
SG_Name	Identifies, by name, the storage group that is to be used as a default storage group for the database—this storage group is used to support DASD space requirements for table spaces and indexes within the database

Thus, to create a DB2 for Linux, UNIX, and Windows database named SAMPLE that:

- Uses automatic storage
- Uses the paths "/mnt/fsystem1" and "/mnt/fsystem2" (which refer to file systems that have been created on Fibre Channel drives) to store its data and metadata
- Recognizes the United States and Canada code set
- Uses a collating sequence that is based on the United States and Canada code set
- Has a page size of 8 KB

you would need to execute a CREATE DATABASE statement that looks something like this:

```
CREATE DATABASE sample
  ON /mnt/fsystem1, /mnt/fsystem2
  USING CODESET 1252 TERRITORY US
  COLLATE USING SYSTEM
  PAGESIZE 8192
```

On the other hand, to create a DB2 for z/OS database named DSN8D10P that:

- Uses a storage group named DSN8G100 as the default storage group for its table spaces and indexes
- Uses a buffer pool named BP8K1 (which has a page size of 8 KB) as the default buffer pool for its table spaces
- Uses a buffer pool named BP2 as the default buffer pool for its indexes

you would execute a CREATE DATABASE statement that looks more like this:

```
CREATE DATABASE DSN8D10P
  STOGROUP DSN8G100
  BUFFERPOOL BP8K1
  INDEXBP BP2;
```

Establishing a Database Connection

When a DB2 for Linux, UNIX, and Windows database is first created, it contains only the system catalog. (When a DB2 for z/OS database is created, it is empty.) Consequently, before you can use a database to store data, you must first define data objects such as tables, indexes, and views. And before you can define new data objects (or do anything else, for that matter), you must first establish a connection to the database. Usually, a connection to a database is established by executing some form of the CONNECT SQL statement. The basic syntax for this statement is:

```
CONNECT
<TO [ServerName] | [Location]>
<USER [UserID] USING [Password]>
```

or

```
CONNECT RESET
```

where:

ServerName	Identifies, by name, the application server a connection is to be made to—*this parameter is recognized by DB2 for Linux, UNIX, and Windows only; it cannot be used with DB2 for z/OS*
Location	Identifies, by location, a server that is known to the local DB2 subsystem—*this parameter is recognized by DB2 for z/OS only; it cannot be used with DB2 for Linux, UNIX, and Windows*
UserID	Identifies an authorization ID (or user ID) that DB2 is to use to verify that the individual attempting to establish the connection is actually authorized to connect to the server specified
Password	Identifies the password that is associated with the authorization ID provided; it is important to note that passwords are case-sensitive

Therefore, if a user whose authentication ID is db2user and password is ibmdb2 wants to establish a connection to a database named SAMPLE, he or she can do so by executing a CONNECT statement that looks like this:

```
CONNECT TO sample USER db2user USING ibmdb2
```

Once a database connection is established, it will remain in effect until it is explicitly terminated or until the application that established the connection ends. You can explicitly terminate a database connection at any time by executing a CONNECT statement with the RESET clause specified. Such a statement looks like this:

```
CONNECT RESET
```

Type 1 and Type 2 Connections

Applications that interact with DB2 databases have the option of using two types of connection semantics. Known simply as Type 1 and Type 2, each connection type supports a very different connection behavior. For instance, Type 1 connections allow a transaction to be connected to only one database at a time. Type 2 connections, however, allow a single transaction to connect to and work with multiple databases simultaneously. Table 4.2 shows other differences between Type 1 and Type 2 connections.

Table 4.2: Differences between Type 1 and Type 2 connections	
Type 1 Connections	**Type 2 Connections**
The current transaction (unit of work) must be committed or rolled back before a connection to another application server can be established.	The current transaction does not have to be committed or rolled back before a connection to another application server can be established.
Establishing a connection to another application server causes the current connection to be terminated. The new connection becomes the current connection.	Establishing a connection to another application server places the current connection into the dormant state. The new connection then becomes the current connection.
The CONNECT statement establishes the current connection. Subsequent SQL requests are forwarded to this connection until another CONNECT statement is executed.	The CONNECT statement establishes the current connection the first time it is executed against a server. If the CONNECT statement is executed against a connection that is in the dormant state, that connection becomes the current connection—provided the SQLRULES precompiler option was set to DB2 when the application was precompiled. Otherwise, an error is returned.
The SET CONNECTION statement is supported, but the only valid target is the current connection.	The SET CONNECTION statement changes the state of a connection from dormant to current.
Connecting with the USER...USING clauses will cause the current connection to be disconnected and a new connection to be established with the given authorization ID and password.	Connecting with the USER...USING clauses is allowed only when there is no dormant or current connection to the same named server.

With DB2 for Linux, UNIX, and Windows, when a database connection is established from the DB2 Command Line Processor (CLP), Type 1 connections are used by default. With DB2 for z/OS, the opposite is true—Type 2 connections are used by default, instead. However, the connection semantics that Embedded SQL applications use is controlled by the following set of SQL precompiler and Binder options:

- **CONNECT [1 | 2]**: Specifies whether to process CONNECT statements as Type 1 (1) or Type 2 (2)
- **SQLRULES [DB2 | STD]**: Specifies whether to process Type 2 connections according to DB2 rules (DB2), which allow the CONNECT statement to switch to a *dormant* connection, or according to the SQL92 Standard rules (STD), which do not allow this behavior
- **DISCONNECT [EXPLICIT | CONDITIONAL | AUTOMATIC]**: Specifies which database connections are to be disconnected when a COMMIT operation occurs—those that have been explicitly marked for release by the RELEASE statement (EXPLICIT),

those that have no open WITH HOLD cursors and that are marked for release (CONDITIONAL), or all connections (AUTOMATIC)

With Call Level Interface (CLI) and Open Database Connectivity (ODBC) applications, the connection semantics used is controlled by assigning the value SQL_ CONCURRENT_TRANS (Type 1) or SQL_COORDINATED_TRANS (Type 2) to the SQL_ATTR_ CONNECTTYPE connection attribute (using the SQLSetConnectAttr() function).

A Word About DB2 Connect

DB2 Connect™ gives applications running on LAN-based workstations, personal computers (PCs), and mobile devices the ability to work with data stored in DB2 databases that reside on IBM System z, System i®, and IBM Power Systems™ platforms. An add-on product that must be purchased separately, DB2 Connect is a combination of several industry-standard application programming interfaces (which are implemented as drivers) and a robust, highly scalable, communications infrastructure.

Five editions of DB2 Connect are available, and each has been designed to meet a specific business need:

- **IBM DB2 Connect Application Server Edition:** This edition makes DB2 data stored on IBM System z or System i platforms available to large, multitier client/ server or web-based applications. It includes IBM Data Studio, which can speed application development and aid in problem resolution.
- **IBM DB2 Connect Personal Edition:** This edition makes DB2 data stored on System z, System i, and IBM Power Systems servers directly available to desktop applications. It enables applications to work transparently with data stored on multiple systems—without using a gateway; this edition includes IBM Data Studio and the InfoSphere Optim pureQuery Runtime environment, which can significantly improve database development, testing, and deployment.
- **IBM DB2 Connect Enterprise Edition:** This edition connects LAN-based systems and desktop applications to System z, System i, and IBM Power Systems databases. Host access can be consolidated through a gateway, making it easier to deploy web and multitier client/server applications. It includes IBM Data Studio and the InfoSphere Optim pureQuery Runtime environment.
- **IBM DB2 Connect Unlimited Advanced Edition for System z:** This edition makes it easy to access, manage, and optimize the performance of enterprise information, wherever it resides. Because it is licensed for unlimited deployment

on authorized servers, this edition is a cost-effective solution for organizations that use DB2 Connect extensively, especially where multiple applications are involved. It includes IBM Data Studio and InfoSphere Optim pureQuery Runtime for Linux, UNIX, and Windows, as well as InfoSphere Optim Configuration Manager for DB2. Collectively, these tools provide a secure, rapid application environment, along with centralized configuration management for data servers and clients.

- **IBM DB2 Connect Unlimited Edition for System i:** This edition integrates IBM System i (formerly eServer™ iSeries®) data with client/server, web, mobile, and service-oriented architecture (SOA) applications. It delivers unified application development, integrated data, and pervasive data functionality to System i users; this edition includes IBM Data Studio and the InfoSphere Optim pureQuery Runtime environment.

It is important to note that DB2 Connect is not actually responsible for connecting workstations to remote databases. Instead, it provides a way for applications to establish connections to databases using a variety of standard interfaces for database access, such as JDBC, SQLJ, ODBC, OLE DB, ADO, ADO.NET, RDO, DB2 CLI, and Embedded SQL. Thus, if an application written in Java wants to connect to a DB2 for z/OS database using DB2 Connect, it can do so by registering the appropriate DB2 JDBC driver with the workstation it will be run on, and then calling the getConnection() method of the resulting DriverManager object. (The JDBC interface is widely used because it allows applications to run, unchanged, on most hardware platforms.)

Another benefit that DB2 Connect offers is the ability to perform distributed requests across members of the DB2 Family, as well as across other relational database management systems (RDBMSs). A *distributed request* is a distributed database function that lets applications and users perform SQL operations that reference two or more databases or RDBMSs in a single statement. For example, a distributed request will allow a UNION operation to be performed between a DB2 table and an Oracle view.

To implement distributed request functionality, all you need is a DB2 Connect instance, a database that will serve as a federated database, and one or more remote data sources. (A *federated database* is a DB2 database whose system catalog contains entries that identify remote data sources and their characteristics; a *data source* is an RDBMS and its data.) After a federated system is created, information stored in the data sources that have been identified can be accessed as though it resided in one large DB2 database.

Temporal Data Management and Time Travel Tables

Industry regulations and pressure from competition is forcing businesses to keep larger amounts of data available for longer periods of time. And now, more than ever, companies are looking for better, more efficient ways to analyze both historical and current information so they can predict future trends. To help organizations achieve these goals, IBM introduced temporal data management technology in DB2 Version 10 (z/OS) and 10.1 (Linux, UNIX, and Windows). This new technology makes it much easier to track and query past, present, and future conditions. Instead of hard-coding time awareness into applications, triggers, and stored procedures, companies can now let DB2 manage multiple versions of their data, as well as keep track of effective dates for data that is subject to changing business requirements.

DB2's temporal data management technology consists primarily of new table design options and new query syntax and semantics (which is derived from emerging ANSI/ ISO SQL standards). However, before you can consider which new table design option to use, it helps to understand the time-management concepts that each new table type is based upon.

Basic Temporal Data Concepts

Temporal tables are designed to record an appropriate time period for every row stored in them. A *time period* (or *period*) is simply an interval of time that is defined by two specific dates, times, or timestamps—one date/time/timestamp identifies the beginning of the period and the other indicates when the period ends. The beginning value for a period is inclusive and the ending value is exclusive, which means that a row with a period from January 1 to February 1 is actually valid from 12:00 a.m. on January 1 until 11:59 p.m. on January 31. February 1 is not included in the period range.

When it comes to managing temporal data, the term *system period* refers to the period in which a particular row is considered current. And the term *system time* is often associated with tracking when changes are made to the state of a row (record). For example, when a new bank account is opened or an insurance policy is modified to reflect that a higher premium must be paid.

The term *application period*, however, refers to the period in which a particular row is considered valid. And the term *business time* (sometimes referred to as *valid time* or *application time*) is usually associated with tracking the effective dates of certain business conditions. For example, when a warranty takes effect (and when it expires) or when a particular item goes on sale (and how long it stays at the sale price).

Some organizations need to track both system-period and application-period information for rows stored in a single table. When this is the case, the table is considered to be *bitemporal*.

The table design options that are part of DB2's temporal data management technology were developed with these concepts in mind. Consequently, you can now create the following types of temporal (also referred to as *time travel*) tables:

- System-period temporal tables
- Application-period temporal tables
- Bitemporal tables

System-period temporal tables

A system-period temporal table is a table that maintains historical versions of its rows. Such tables are used to automatically track and manage multiple versions of data values. For this reason, every system-period temporal table must be associated with a history table—any time a row in a system-period temporal table is modified, DB2 automatically inserts a copy of the original row into the corresponding history table. This storage of original data values is what enables you to retrieve data from previous points in time.

System-period temporal tables are created by executing the CREATE TABLE statement with the PERIOD SYSTEM_TIME clause specified. (We will take a closer look at the CREATE TABLE statement in Chapter 6, "Working with DB2 Tables, Views, and Indexes.") In addition, the table definition provided must include "system time begin" and "system time end" columns, which are used to track when a row is considered current. Both columns must be assigned a TIMESTAMP(12) data type; however, they can be implicitly hidden. DB2 will automatically populate the "system time begin" column with the current timestamp, and it will store the value 12/30/9999 in the "system time end" column as rows are inserted into the table. If a row is subsequently updated or deleted, DB2 will update these columns accordingly, and then write a historical record to the corresponding history file. One other special column must also exist so DB2 can capture the start times of transactions that perform update or delete operations on a particular row. (This column must also be assigned a TIMESTAMP(12) data type and can be implicitly hidden, if so desired.)

Thus, to create a system-period temporal table named TAX_INFO that has one column for storing taxpayer IDs and another column for storing tax amounts owed, you could execute a CREATE TABLE statement that looks something like this:

```
CREATE TABLE tax_info
 (taxpayer_id  CHAR(4) NOT NULL,
  tax_amount   INT NOT NULL,
  sys_start    TIMESTAMP(12) NOT NULL
                  GENERATED ALWAYS AS ROW BEGIN,
  sys_end      TIMESTAMP(12) NOT NULL
                  GENERATED ALWAYS AS ROW END,
  ts_id        TIMESTAMP(12) NOT NULL
                  GENERATED ALWAYS AS
                  TRANSACTION START ID
                  IMPLICITLY HIDDEN,
  PERIOD SYSTEM_TIME (sys_start, sys_end))
```

However, once the resulting table is created, it cannot be populated until a corresponding history table is created and a link between the two tables is established. One way to create a history table for a system-period temporal table is by executing a CREATE TABLE statement that is identical to the statement used to create the system-period temporal table. (Of course, the name assigned to history table will need to be changed.)

Alternatively, you can create a history table by executing a CREATE TABLE statement with the LIKE clause specified. For example, to create a history table named HIST_TAX_INFO that has the same definition as the TAX_INFO table created in the previous example, you could execute a CREATE TABLE statement that looks like this:

```
CREATE TABLE hist_tax_info LIKE tax_info
```

When both a system-period temporal table and a corresponding history table are available, a link can be established between the two by executing an ALTER TABLE statement with the ADD VERSIONING clause specified. (We will take a closer look at the ALTER TABLE statement in Chapter 6, "Working with DB2 Tables, Views, and Indexes.") For example, to establish a link between the system-period temporal table named TAX_INFO and the history table named HIST_TAX_INFO that were created in the previous examples, you would execute an ALTER TABLE statement that looks like this:

```
ALTER TABLE tax_info
  ADD VERSIONING
  USE HISTORY TABLE hist_tax_info
```

Assuming this statement executes successfully, whenever a row is updated or deleted from the TAX_INFO table, DB2 will automatically insert a copy of the original row into the HIST_TAX_INFO table.

In most cases, working with system-period temporal tables (that is, inserting, updating, deleting, and retrieving data) is no different from working with other tables. However, queries against system-period temporal tables can contain a time-period specification, which will cause results for a specified time period (or point in time) to be returned. (We will take a closer look at working with system-period temporal tables in Chapter 5, "Working with DB2 Data Using SQL.")

Application-period temporal tables

An application-period temporal table is a table that maintains "currently in effect" values of application data. Such tables let you manage time-sensitive information by defining the time periods in which specific data values are considered valid.

Application-period temporal tables are created by executing a CREATE TABLE statement with the PERIOD BUSINESS_TIME clause specified. In addition, the table definition provided must include "business time begin" and "business time end" columns, which are normally populated with user- or application-supplied values that indicate the time period in which a particular row is considered valid. Both columns must be assigned a DATE, TIME, or TIMESTAMP data type; however, they can be implicitly hidden, if so desired. The "business time begin" column is used to store the date/time/timestamp that indicates the beginning of a row's validity, and the "business time end" column is used to store the date/time/timestamp that designates when a row is no longer considered valid.

Therefore, to create an application-period temporal table named INVENTORY that contains two columns, one for storing item IDs and another for storing item prices, you could execute a CREATE TABLE statement that looks something like this:

```
CREATE TABLE inventory
 (item_id    CHAR(4) NOT NULL,
  price      DOUBLE NOT NULL,
  bus_start  DATE NOT NULL,
  bus_end    DATE NOT NULL,
  PERIOD BUSINESS_TIME (bus_start, bus_end),
  PRIMARY KEY(item_id, BUSINESS_TIME WITHOUT OVERLAPS))
```

The resulting table can then be used to keep track of the price of different items for a given period of time. It is important to note that this particular example includes a unique primary key consisting of the ITEM_ID, BUS_START, and BUS_END columns. This primary key ensures that no overlapping time periods can exist for ITEM_ID values.

In most cases, inserting data into an application-period temporal table is no different from inserting data into a regular table. However, update and delete operations against application-period temporal tables can be significantly different—data can be updated or deleted for specific points in time that occur in the past, the present, or the future.

Querying application-period temporal tables is relatively straightforward. If you are not concerned about obtaining temporal data, the syntax and semantics of the SELECT statement used is the same as when other tables are queried. However, if you want to retrieve past, current, and/or future data values, you will need to construct a SELECT statement that contains a business time-period specification. (We will take a closer look at the SELECT statement, and at working with application-period temporal tables in Chapter 5, "Working with DB2 Data Using SQL.")

Bitemporal tables

A bitemporal table combines the historical tracking of a system-period temporal table with the time-specific data storage capabilities of an application-period temporal table. Consequently, bitemporal tables are used when a single table needs to maintain historical versions of its rows *and* keep track of data values that are currently considered valid.

Bitemporal tables are created by executing a CREATE TABLE statement with both the PERIOD SYSTEM_TIME clause and the PERIOD BUSINESS_TIME clause specified, and by including "system time begin," "system time end," "transaction start-ID," "business time begin," and "business time end" columns in the table's definition. Thus, to create a bitemporal table named INVENTORY that has one column for storing item identification

numbers and another column for storing item prices, you would execute a CREATE TABLE
statement that looks something like this:

```
CREATE TABLE inventory
 (item_id   CHAR(4) NOT NULL,
  price     DOUBLE NOT NULL,
  sys_start TIMESTAMP(12) NOT NULL
                GENERATED ALWAYS AS ROW BEGIN,
  sys_end   TIMESTAMP(12) NOT NULL
                GENERATED ALWAYS AS ROW END,
  ts_id     TIMESTAMP(12) NOT NULL
                GENERATED ALWAYS AS
                TRANSACTION START ID,
  bus_start DATE NOT NULL,
  bus_end   DATE NOT NULL,
  PERIOD SYSTEM_TIME (sys_start, sys_end)
  PERIOD BUSINESS_TIME (bus_start, bus_end))
```

Of course, you will also need to create a corresponding history table and establish a
link between it and the INVENTORY table before the INVENTORY table can be used.

Working with bitemporal tables (that is, inserting, updating, deleting, and retrieving
data) is no different from working with system-period and application-period temporal
tables. However, when retrieving data from a bitemporal table, you have the option of
constructing a query that contains a system time-period specification, a business time-
period specification, or both. (We will take a closer look at working with bitemporal
tables in Chapter 5, "Working with DB2 Data Using SQL.")

Working with DB2 Data Using SQL

Twenty percent (20%) of the *DB2 10.1 Fundamentals* certification exam (Exam 610) is designed to test your knowledge of the various SQL statements and XQuery expressions that are commonly used to store, manipulate, and retrieve data. The questions that make up this portion of the exam are intended to evaluate the following:

- Your ability to perform insert, update, and delete operations against a database
- Your ability to retrieve and format data using various forms of the SELECT statement
- Your ability to sort and group data retrieved by a SELECT statement
- Your ability to query system-period, application-period, and bitemporal temporal (time travel) tables
- Your ability to access Extensible Markup Language (XML) data using XQuery expressions and the built-in SQL/XML functions that are available with DB2
- Your ability to create and invoke an SQL stored procedure or an SQL user-defined function (UDF)
- Your knowledge of what transactions are, as well as how transactions are initiated and terminated

This chapter introduces you to the SQL statements and XQuery expressions that are used to store, modify, delete, and retrieve both relational (traditional) and XML data. In this chapter, you will learn how to use INSERT, UPDATE, and DELETE statements to store, change, and remove data, as well as how to use the SELECT statement and its associated clauses to retrieve data and format the results. You will also discover how to query temporal (time travel) tables and how to create and invoke SQL stored procedures and UDFs. Finally, you will learn what transactions are and how transaction boundaries are defined.

Structured Query Language (SQL)

Structured Query Language (SQL) is a standardized language that is used to work with database objects and the data they contain. Using SQL, you can define, alter, and delete database objects, as well as add data to, change data in, and retrieve or remove data from the objects you create. One of the strengths of SQL is that it can be used in a variety of ways. For example, you can execute SQL statements interactively using tools such as IBM Data Studio and the DB2 Command Line Processor (CLP). Or you can embed them in high-level programming language source code files. (Because SQL is nonprocedural by design, it is not an actual programming language; therefore, most applications that use SQL are built by combining the decision and sequence control of a high-level programming language with the data storage, manipulation, and retrieval capabilities of SQL.) Like most other languages, SQL has a defined syntax and its own set of language elements.

SQL statements can be categorized according to the function they have been designed to perform. Consequently, SQL statements typically fall under one of the following categories:

- **Embedded SQL Application Construct statements:** Used for the sole purpose of constructing Embedded SQL applications
- **Data Control Language (DCL) statements:** Used to grant and revoke authorities and privileges
- **Data Definition Language (DDL) statements:** Used to create, alter, and delete database objects
- **Data Manipulation Language (DML) statements:** Used to store data in, manipulate data in, retrieve data from, and remove data from select database objects
- **Transaction Management statements:** Used to establish and terminate database connections and transactions

You may recall that the two primary DCL statements—GRANT and REVOKE—were covered in Chapter 3, "Security," and that many of the objects that can be created with DDL statements were discussed in Chapter 4, "Working with Databases and Database Objects." Some of the DDL statements that are used to create those objects are covered in Chapter 6, "Working with DB2 Tables, Views, and Indexes." So, instead of covering DCL and DML statements here, this chapter begins by examining the DML statements that are available with DB2, and then focuses on transactions and the SQL statements that support them. (Because you do not need to be familiar with the Embedded SQL Application Construct statements to pass the *DB2 10.1 Fundamentals* certification exam, these statements are not addressed.)

SQL Data Manipulation Language (DML) Statements

In Chapter 4, "Working with Databases and Database Objects," you saw that a table is a logical object that acts as the main repository in a database, and that often many tables are defined. After one or more tables are created, the next step toward building a fully functional database is to populate those tables with data. And after a table is populated, at some point, you might need to retrieve, modify, or in some cases, delete the data that is stored in it.

This is where the DML statements come in to play. DML statements are used exclusively to store, modify, and delete data, as well as to retrieve data from tables, views, or both. Four DML statements are available:

- INSERT
- UPDATE
- DELETE
- SELECT

The INSERT Statement

When a table is first created, it is nothing more than a definition of how a set of data values are to be stored; no data is associated with it. But once created, a table can be populated in a variety of ways. For example, you can bulk-load it using utilities like Import and Load, or you can add data to it, one row at a time, by using an INSERT statement. The basic syntax for this statement is:

```
INSERT INTO [TableName | ViewName]
  <([ColumnName], ...)>
  VALUES ([Value | NULL | DEFAULT], ...)
```

or

```
INSERT INTO [TableName | ViewName]
  <([ColumnName], ...)>
  [SELECTStatement]
```

where:

TableName	Identifies, by name, the table data is to be added to
ViewName	Identifies, by name, the updatable view data is to be added to
ColumnName	Identifies, by name, one or more columns that data values are to be assigned to; each column name provided must identify an existing column in the table or updatable view specified
Value	Identifies one or more data values that are to be added to the table or updatable view specified
SELECTStatement	Identifies a SELECT statement that, when executed, will produce the data values that are to be added to the table or updatable view specified (by retrieving them from other tables, views, or both)

Therefore, to add a record to a base table named DEPARTMENT that has the following characteristics:

Column Name	Data Type
DEPTNO	CHAR(3)
DEPTNAME	CHAR(20)
MGRID	INTEGER

you could execute an INSERT statement that looks something like this:

```
INSERT INTO department
  (deptno, deptname, mgrid)
  VALUES ('A01', 'ADMINISTRATION', 1000)
```

It is important to note that the number of values provided in the VALUES clause must equal the number of column names identified in the column name list. Furthermore, the values provided will be assigned to the specified columns in the order in which they appear—in other words, the first value listed is assigned to the first column identified, the second value is assigned to the second column identified, and so on. Finally, each value supplied must be compatible with the data type of the column it is being assigned to. (In other words, a character string value can only be assigned to a column that has character string data type.)

If values are provided (using the VALUES clause) for every column found in the table, the column name list can be omitted. In this case, the first value provided is assigned to the first column in the table, the second value is assigned to the second column, and so on. Thus, the row of data that was added to the DEPARTMENT table in the previous example could just as easily have been added by executing an INSERT statement that looks like this:

```
INSERT INTO department
    VALUES ('A01', 'ADMINISTRATION', 1000)
```

Along with literal values, two special tokens can be used to assign values to individual columns. The first token, DEFAULT, is used to assigns a system- or user-supplied value to an identity column or a column that was defined as having a default constraint. The second, the NULL token, is used to assign a NULL value to any nullable column—that is, to any column that was *not* defined as having a NOT NULL constraint. (Identity columns, default constraints, and the NOT NULL constraint are covered in detail in Chapter 6, "Working with DB2 Tables, Views, and Indexes.")

Therefore, you could add a record that contains a NULL value for the MGRID column to the DEPARTMENT table presented earlier by executing an INSERT statement that looks like this:

```
INSERT INTO department
    VALUES ('A01', 'ADMINISTRATION', NULL)
```

By using another form of the INSERT statement (the second syntax version presented), the results of a query can be used to supply values for one or more columns as well. With this form, you supply a SELECT statement (known as a *subselect*) in place of a VALUES clause, and then assign the results of the subselect to the appropriate columns. This form of the INSERT statement performs a type of cut-and-paste operation in which values are retrieved from one base table or view and copied to another.

As you might imagine, the number of values that the subselect returns must match the number of columns identified in the column name list (or the number of columns found in the table or view if a column name list is not provided). And the order of assignment is the same as that used when literal values are supplied.

Consequently, you could add a record to the DEPARTMENT table presented earlier, using the results of a subselect, by executing an INSERT statement that looks like this:

```
INSERT INTO department (deptno, deptname)
    SELECT deptno, deptname FROM organization
```

Notice that the INSERT statement in the previous example did not provide values for every column found in the DEPARTMENT table. Just as there are times when you might want to insert complete records into a table or view, there may be times when you want or are forced to insert partial records. On such occasions, you can construct and execute an INSERT statement in which only the columns you have data for are specified in the column names list provided. However, for such an INSERT statement to execute correctly, all columns in the table the record is being inserted into that *do not* appear in the column name list must either accept NULL values or have a defaults constraint associated with them. Otherwise, the INSERT statement will fail and an error will be generated.

The UPDATE Statement

Data in a database is rarely static. Over time, the need to change or remove one or more values stored in a table can, and will, arise. This is where the UPDATE statement comes in—once a table has been created and populated, you can modify any of the data values stored in it by executing an UPDATE statement. The basic syntax for this statement is:

```
UPDATE [TableName | ViewName]
    SET [ColumnName] = [Value | NULL | DEFAULT], ...]
    <WHERE [Condition] | WHERE CURRENT OF [Cursor]>
```

or

```
UPDATE [TableName | ViewName]
  SET ([ColumnName], ...) =
    ([Value | NULL | DEFAULT], ...)
  <WHERE [Condition] | WHERE CURRENT OF [Cursor]>
```

or

```
UPDATE [TableName | ViewName]
  SET ([ColumnName], ...) = ([SELECTStatement])
  <WHERE [Condition] | WHERE CURRENT OF [CursorName]>
```

where:

TableName	Identifies, by name, the table that contains the data that is to be modified
ViewName	Identifies, by name, the updatable view that contains the data that is to be modified
ColumnName	Identifies, by name, one or more columns that contain data that is to be modified; each column name provided must identify an existing column in the table or updatable view specified
Value	Identifies one or more data values that are to be used to replace existing values for the column name(s) specified
SELECTStatement	Identifies a SELECT statement that, when executed, will produce data values that are to be used to replace existing values in the table or updatable view specified (by retrieving them from other tables, views, or both)
Condition	Identifies the search criterion that is to be used to locate one or more specific rows whose data values are to be modified; this condition is coded like the WHERE clause in a SELECT statement— we will look at the SELECT statement, along with the WHERE clause and its predicates, a little later
CursorName	Identifies, by name, the cursor that is currently positioned on the row whose data values are to be modified

> **Important:** In most cases, you should provide an appropriate *Condition* (or use the WHERE CURRENT OF [*CursorName*] clause) when using the UPDATE statement. Otherwise, the update operation specified will be performed on every row found in the table or updatable view referenced.

Thus, if you have a base table named EMPLOYEE that has the following characteristics:

Column Name	Data Type
EMPNO	INTEGER
FNAME	CHAR(10)
LNAME	CHAR(10)
SEX	CHAR(1)
HIREDATE	DATE
TITLE	CHAR(25)
DEPT	CHAR(3)
SALARY	DECIMAL(8,2)

you can modify the records stored in this table such that the salary of every employee who has the title of DATABASE ADMINISTRATOR is increased by 10 percent by executing an UPDATE statement that looks like this:

```
UPDATE employee SET salary = salary * 1.10
  WHERE title = 'DATABASE ADMINISTRATOR'
```

In addition to providing a way to change existing data values, the UPDATE statement can also be used to remove data stored in one or more columns—provided the columns are nullable. (Such delete operations are performed by changing the existing data value to NULL.) For example, to delete the values assigned to the DEPT column of every record found in the EMPLOYEE table presented earlier, you could execute an UPDATE statement that looks like this:

```
UPDATE employee SET dept = NULL
```

Similar to an INSERT statement, a subselect can be used with an UPDATE statement to supply values for one or more columns that are to be updated. This form of the UPDATE statement (the third syntax format presented) performs a type of cut-and-paste operation in which values are retrieved from one base table or view and copied over existing values stored in another.

As with the INSERT statement, the number of values the subselect returns must match the number of columns provided in the column name list. However, the subselect used *must not return more than one row*! If the subselect returns multiple rows, the update operation will fail and an error will be generated.

Consequently, to change the value assigned to the DEPT column of each record found in the EMPLOYEE table presented earlier, using the results of a subselect, you might execute an UPDATE statement that looks like this:

```
UPDATE employee SET (dept) =
  (SELECT deptno
    FROM department
    WHERE deptname = 'ADMINISTRATION')
```

It is important to note that update operations can be conducted in one of two ways: by performing what is known as a *searched update* or by performing what is referred to as a *positioned update*. So far, the examples presented have illustrated searched update operations. To perform a positioned update operation, a cursor must be created, opened, and then positioned on the row that is to be updated. (We will look at cursors shortly.) Then, to modify data stored in the row the cursor is currently positioned on, an UPDATE statement that contains a WHERE CURRENT OF [*CursorName*] clause is executed.

Positioned update operations change data in a single row only, whereas searched update operations can modify several rows at a time. Because of their added complexity, positioned update operations are typically used in custom applications.

The DELETE Statement

While the UPDATE statement can be used to delete individual values from a base table or updatable view (by replacing those values with NULL), it cannot be used to remove entire records/rows. To remove one or more rows of data from a table or updatable view, the DELETE statement must be used instead. The basic syntax for the DELETE statement is:

```
DELETE FROM [TableName | ViewName]
  <WHERE [Condition] | WHERE CURRENT OF [CursorName]>
```

where:

TableName	Identifies, by name, the table that contains the data that is to be deleted
ViewName	Identifies, by name, the updatable view that contains the data that is to be deleted
Condition	Identifies the search criterion that is to be used to locate one or more specific rows that are to be deleted; this condition is coded like the WHERE clause in a SELECT statement
CursorName	Identifies, by name, the cursor that is currently positioned on the row whose values are to be deleted

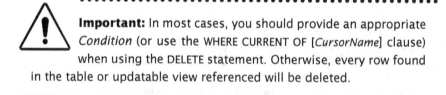

Important: In most cases, you should provide an appropriate *Condition* (or use the WHERE CURRENT OF [*CursorName*] clause) when using the DELETE statement. Otherwise, every row found in the table or updatable view referenced will be deleted.

Thus, to remove every record for company ACME, INC. from a base table named SALES that has the following characteristics:

Column Name	Data Type
ORDERNO	CHAR(10)
COMPANY	CHAR(20)
PURCHASEDATE	DATE
SALESPERSON	INTEGER

you would execute a DELETE statement that looks like this:

```
DELETE FROM sales
  WHERE company = 'ACME, INC.'
```

On the other hand, to remove every record from the SALES table used in the previous example for which no salesperson has been assigned, you would execute a DELETE statement that looks more like this:

```
DELETE FROM sales
  WHERE salesperson IS NULL
```

As with update operations, delete operations can be conducted in one of two ways: by performing a *searched delete* or by performing a *positioned delete*. To perform a positioned delete operation, a cursor must be created, opened, and then positioned on the row that is to be deleted. Then, a DELETE statement that contains a WHERE CURRENT OF [*CursorName*] clause must be executed to remove the row the cursor is currently positioned on. Like positioned update operations, positioned delete operations work with a single row at a time and are typically used in applications.

A Word About the TRUNCATE Statement

Although the DELETE statement is typically used to delete individual rows, it can be used to remove every record from a table. However, such delete operations can have unwanted side effects. For one thing, every time a row is deleted from a table, a record about the deletion is written to a transaction log file. Thus, the removal of every row in a table can cause a large number of log records to be generated, particularly if the table being emptied contains hundreds of thousands of rows.

Consequently, if circular logging is used or you have a limited amount of log space available, the influx of log records that is generated can cause a "log full" condition to occur. This, in turn, can cause the delete operation and any concurrently running transactions or operations to fail. Similarly, if any DELETE triggers have been defined on the table being emptied, those triggers can be fired multiple times. And depending on how the triggers were defined, other tables can be flooded with unnecessary information.

A better alternative to using the DELETE statement to empty a table of its contents is to use the TRUNCATE statement instead. Truncate operations do not generate transaction log records. And they give you more control over any DELETE triggers that may have been defined. The basic syntax for the TRUNCATE statement is:

```
TRUNCATE <TABLE> [TableName]
  <[DROP | REUSE] STORAGE>
  <IGNORE DELETE TRIGGERS | RESTRICT WHEN DELETE TRIGGERS>
```

where:

TableName   Identifies, by name, the table that is to be emptied of its contents

If the DROP STORAGE clause is specified with the TRUNCATE statement used, storage space that has been allocated for the table will be released and made available to the operating system. If the REUSE STORAGE clause is used instead, storage space for the table is merely emptied, and the space remains available for the table's future needs.

If the IGNORE DELETE TRIGGERS clause is specified with the TRUNCATE statement used, DELETE triggers defined on the table will not fire as the data in the table is being deleted. However, if the RESTRICT WHEN DELETE TRIGGERS clause is used, the system catalog will be examined to determine whether DELETE triggers on the table have been created. And if one or more triggers are found, the truncate operation will end and an error will be returned. (In this case, the table's storage remains intact and its records are left untouched.)

So, to remove every record from the SALES table presented earlier without firing any DELETE triggers that might have been created on the table, you could execute a TRUNCATE statement that looks like this:

```
TRUNCATE FROM sales
   IGNORE DELETE TRIGGERS
```

The SELECT Statement

Most databases are not used strictly as a place for archiving data. Therefore, at some point, the need to retrieve specific pieces of information (data) from a database will arise. The operation used to retrieve data from a database is called a *query* (because the database is usually searched to find the answer to some question), and the results returned are typically expressed either as a single data value or as multiple rows of data, otherwise known as a *result data set*, or simply *result set*. (If no values that correspond to the query specification are located, an empty result data set is returned to the user or application.)

All queries begin with a SELECT statement, which is a powerful SQL statement that can be used to construct a wide variety of queries containing an infinite number of variations. And because it is recursive, a single SELECT statement can derive its output from a successive number of nested SELECT statements, known as *subqueries*. (Earlier, you saw how to use a SELECT statement to provide data to INSERT and UPDATE statements. You can use a SELECT statement to provide input to other SELECT statements in a similar manner.) In its simplest form, the syntax for the SELECT statement is:

```
SELECT * FROM [TableName | ViewName]
```

where:

TableName	Identifies, by name, the table to retrieve data from
ViewName	Identifies, by name, the view to retrieve data from

Therefore, to construct a query that will retrieve all values currently stored in the DEPARTMENT table presented earlier, you would create a SELECT statement that looks like this:

```
SELECT * FROM department
```

And assuming the DEPARTMENT table is populated with the data shown in Table 5.1, when this query is executed, you should get a result data set that looks like this:

```
DEPTNO DEPTNAME             MGRID

------ -------------------- -----------

A01    ADMINISTRATION       1000
B01    PLANNING             1002
C01    DEVELOPMENT          1007
D01    PERSONNEL            1008
E01    OPERATIONS              -
F01    SUPPORT                 -


   6 record(s) selected.
```

Table 5.1: Data stored in the DEPARTMENT table		
DEPTNO	DEPTNAME	MGRID
A01	ADMINISTRATION	1000
B01	PLANNING	1001
C01	DEVELOPMENT	1007
D01	PERSONNEL	1008
E01	OPERATIONS	(NULL)
F01	SUPPORT	(NULL)

A Closer Look at the SELECT Statement and Its Clauses

You just saw how to retrieve every value stored in a table (or the underlying table of a view). But what if you want to retrieve just the values stored in two columns of a table? Or you want to arrange the data retrieved alphabetically in ascending order? (Data is stored in a table in no particular order, and unless otherwise specified, a query will return data in the order in which it is found.) To perform these types of operations, you will need to use a more advanced form of the SELECT statement to construct the query needed. The syntax used to construct advanced queries looks like this:

```
SELECT <ALL | DISTINCT>
  [* | [[Expression] <<AS> [NewColumnName]>, ...]
  FROM [TableName | ViewName <<AS> [CorrelationName]>, ...]
  <WhereClause>
  <GroupByClause>
  <HavingClause>
  <OrderByClause>
  <FetchFirstClause>
  <IsolationClause>
```

where:

Expression	Identifies one or more valid SQL language elements (such as column names or functions) that values are to be returned for when the SELECT statement is executed

NewColumnName	Identifies a column name to use in place of the column name that will be returned, by default, in the result data set produced by the SELECT statement
TableName	Identifies, by name, one or more tables to retrieve data from
ViewName	Identifies, by name, one or more views to retrieve data from
CorrelationName	Identifies a shorthand name that can be used to reference the table(s) or view(s) specified, in any of the SELECT statement clauses
WhereClause	Specifies a WHERE clause that is to be used with the SELECT statement
GroupByClause	Specifies a GROUP BY clause that is to be used with the SELECT statement
HavingClause	Specifies a HAVING clause that is to be used with the SELECT statement
OrderByClause	Specifies an ORDER BY clause that is to be used with the SELECT statement
FetchFirstClause	Specifies a FETCH FIRST clause that is to be used with the SELECT statement
IsolationClause	Specifies the isolation level under which the SELECT statement is to be run

If the DISTINCT clause is specified with the SELECT statement used, duplicate rows will be eliminated from the result data set returned. (Two rows are considered duplicates of one another if the value of every column of the first row is identical to the value of the corresponding column of the second row. For the purpose of determining whether two rows are identical, NULL values are considered equal.) However, if the ALL clause is specified or if neither clause is specified, duplicate rows will be returned. (If neither clause is specified, the ALL clause is used by default.) It is important to note that you cannot use the DISTINCT clause if you know that the result data set produced will contain BLOB, CLOB, DBCLOB, or XML data.

Thus, to retrieve just the first and last name of all employees found in the EMPLOYEE table presented earlier, you could execute a SELECT statement that looks like this:

```
SELECT fname, lname FROM employee
```

If the EMPLOYEE table is populated with the data shown in Table 5.2, when this statement is executed, you should get a result data set that looks like this:

```
FNAME       LNAME

----------  ----------

JAMES       DEAN

MARILYN     MONROE

HUMPHREY    BOGART

INGRID      BERGMAN

JAMES       CAGNEY

WILLIAM     HOLDEN

JACK        LEMMON

WALTER      MATTHAU

KATHARINE   HEPBURN

AVA         GARDNER


  10 record(s) selected.
```

Table 5.2: Data stored in the EMPLOYEE table							
EMPNO	FNAME	LNAME	SEX	HIREDATE	TITLE	DEPT	SALARY
1000	JAMES	DEAN	M	04/10/2002	PRESIDENT	A01	158096.00
1001	MARILYN	MONROE	F	05/10/2008	SYSTEMS ENGINEER	B01	103675.00
1002	HUMPHREY	BOGART	M	09/10/2006	DATABASE ADMINISTRATOR	C01	88192.00
1003	INGRID	BERGMAN	F	02/14/2001	PROGRAMMER/ ANALYST	C01	79475.00
1004	JAMES	CAGNEY	M	10/01/2004	TECHNICIAN I	E01	105787.00
1005	WILLIAM	HOLDEN	M	01/01/2012	TECHNICIAN I	F01	64428.00
1006	JACK	LEMMON	M	07/04/2007	TECHNICIAN II	E01	51584.00
1007	WALTER	MATTHAU	M	10/12/2003	DATABASE ADMINISTRATOR	F01	66943.00
1008	KATHARINE	HEPBURN	F	03/15/2002	MANAGER	C01	48903.00
1009	AVA	GARDNER	F	06/06/1999	ENGINEER	B01	59081.00

On the other hand, to retrieve just the first and last name of all employees from the EMPLOYEE table, *and* change the names of the FNAME and LNAME columns in the result data set produced to FIRST_NAME and LAST_NAME, respectively, you would need to execute a SELECT statement that looks more like this:

```
SELECT fname AS first_name,
       lname AS last_name
  FROM employee
```

And when this statement is executed, you should get a result data set that looks like this:

```
FIRST_NAME LAST_NAME
---------- ----------
JAMES      DEAN
MARILYN    MONROE
HUMPHREY   BOGART
INGRID     BERGMAN
JAMES      CAGNEY
WILLIAM    HOLDEN
JACK       LEMMON
WALTER     MATTHAU
KATHARINE  HEPBURN
AVA        GARDNER

  10 record(s) selected.
```

You could produce the same result data set by executing a query that looks almost identical to the previous query, but that uses the correlation name E to refer to columns found in the EMPLOYEE table. The altered the SELECT statement will look something like this:

```
SELECT e.fname AS first_name,
       e.lname AS last_name
  FROM employee AS e
```

As you can see, the columns named FNAME and LNAME are qualified with the correlation name E, which is then assigned to the EMPLOYEE table in the FROM clause of the SELECT statement used. With this particular example, the use of a correlation name and a qualifier is unnecessary because data is being retrieved from a single table (which guarantees that columns have unique names).

However, if data is retrieved from two or more tables *and* if one or more columns in those tables have identical names, a correlation name and qualifier is needed to tell DB2 which table to get data from for a particular column. For example, suppose the DEPTNO column in the DEPARTMENT table presented earlier was named DEPT. To retrieve data from both this table and the EMPLOYEE table presented earlier, *and* to ensure that the DEPT values retrieved came from the EMPLOYEE table (instead of from the DEPARTMENT table), you would need to construct a SELECT statement that looks something like this:

```
SELECT e.lname, e.dept, d.deptname
  FROM employee AS e, department AS d
  WHERE e.dept = d.dept
```

Here, the correlation names E and D, along with their corresponding qualifiers, tell DB2 when to retrieve data from the EMPLOYEE (E) table and when to retrieve it from the DEPARTMENT (D) table.

Other SELECT Statement Clauses

If you look at the syntax for the advanced form of the SELECT statement that was presented earlier, you will notice that a single SELECT statement can contain up to eight additional clauses:

- The DISTINCT clause
- The FROM clause
- The WHERE clause
- The GROUP BY clause
- The HAVING clause
- The ORDER BY clause
- The FETCH FIRST clause
- The isolation clause

(Incidentally, DB2 processes these clauses in the order that they are listed.) With the exception of the isolation clause, you can use each of these clauses to further control the size and contents of the result data sets produced in response to a query.

The Where Clause

The WHERE clause is used to tell DB2 *how* to select the rows that are to be returned in the result data set produced. When specified, the WHERE clause is followed by a *search condition*, which is nothing more than a simple test that, when applied to a row of data, will evaluate to TRUE, FALSE, or UNKNOWN. If the test evaluates to TRUE, the row is returned in the result data set produced; if the test evaluates to FALSE or UNKNOWN, the row is ignored.

The search condition itself consists of one or more predicates that make simple value comparisons. DB2 recognizes six common types of WHERE clause predicates; they are:

- Relational predicates
- BETWEEN
- LIKE
- IN
- EXISTS
- NULL

Each of these predicates can be used alone, or they can be combined, using parentheses or Boolean operators like AND and OR to create a WHERE clause that is quite complex.

Relational predicates

The *relational predicates* (or *comparison operators*) consist of a set of special operators that define a comparison relationship between the contents of a column and a constant value, the contents of two different columns (from the same or from different tables), or the results of some SQL expression and the results of another query (known as a *subquery*). The following comparison operators are available:

- = (Equal to)
- < (Less than)
- > (Greater than)
- <= (Less than or equal to)

- $>=$ (Greater than or equal to)
- $<>$ (Not equal to)

Furthermore, when any of these operators are used to define a comparison relationship between the results of an SQL expression and the results of a subquery, the qualifiers SOME, ANY, and ALL can be used to further control how rows are evaluated. When you use the qualifier SOME or ANY, the result of the comparison is considered TRUE if the relationship specified is true for at least one value returned by the subquery. If you use the qualifier ALL instead, the result of the comparison is considered TRUE only if the relationship is true for *every* value returned by the subquery.

Typically, relational predicates are used to include or exclude specific rows from the result data set produced. Therefore, to retrieve values from the EMPNO and SALARY columns of the EMPLOYEE table presented earlier and display information only for rows in which the value stored in the SALARY column is greater than $80,000.00, you would execute a SELECT statement that looks something like this:

```
SELECT empno, salary
  FROM employee
  WHERE salary > 80000.00
```

When this statement is executed, you should get a result data set that looks like this (provided the EMPLOYEE table is populated as shown in Table 5.2):

```
EMPNO        SALARY
-----------  ----------
       1000  158096.00
       1001  103675.00
       1002   88192.00
       1004  105787.00

   4 record(s) selected.
```

On the other hand, to retrieve values from the EMPNO, TITLE, HIREDATE, and SALARY columns of the EMPLOYEE table and display information only for employees who were hired before January 1, 2005, and whose salary is greater than $80,000.00 *or* who have the title of MANAGER, you would execute a SELECT statement that looks more like this:

```
SELECT empno, title, hiredate, salary
  FROM employee
  WHERE (hiredate < '2005-01-01' AND salary > 80000.00)
    OR (title = 'MANAGER')
```

This time, the result data set produced should look more like this (assuming the EMPLOYEE table is populated as shown in Table 5.2):

```
EMPNO        TITLE                        HIREDATE    SALARY

------------ ---------------------------- ----------- -----------
        1000 PRESIDENT                    04/10/2002  158096.00
        1004 TECHNICIAN I                 10/01/2004  105787.00
        1008 MANAGER                      03/15/2002   48903.00

  3 record(s) selected.
```

It is important to note that the data types of all items involved in a relational predicate comparison must be compatible or the comparison will fail. However, in many cases, you can use built-in functions provided with DB2 to make any data type conversions needed, as well as to perform other operations that might be necessary or desired. For example, if you wanted to find out how many employees were hired in the month of October, you could query the EMPLOYEE table presented earlier with a SELECT statement that looks like this:

```
SELECT COUNT(*) AS num_employees
  FROM employee
  WHERE MONTHNAME(hiredate) = 'October'
```

Here, the built-in function MONTHNAME() produces a mixed-case character string value (representing the name of the month) for the month portion of each date value stored in the HIREDATE column of the EMPLOYEE table. This string value is then compared with the string 'October' to determine which rows are to be included in the final count—the built-in function COUNT() totals the matching records found. Consequently, if this query is executed against the EMPLOYEE table presented earlier, a result data set that looks like this will be produced (provided the EMPLOYEE table is populated as shown in Table 5.2):

```
NUM_EMPLOYEES
-------------
            2

    1 record(s) selected.
```

The BETWEEN predicate

The BETWEEN predicate is used to define a comparison relationship in which the contents of a column or the results of some SQL expression are checked to determine whether they fall within a specified range of values. As with relational predicates, the BETWEEN predicate is used to include or exclude individual rows from the result data set produced.

Thus, to retrieve values from the LNAME and SALARY columns of the EMPLOYEE table presented earlier and display information only for rows where the value stored in the SALARY column is greater than or equal to $50,000.00 and less than or equal to $90,000.00, you could execute a SELECT statement that looks like this:

```
SELECT lname, salary
  FROM employee
  WHERE salary BETWEEN 50000.00 AND 90000.00
```

And when this statement is executed, you should get a result data set that looks like this (assuming the EMPLOYEE table is populated as shown in Table 5.2):

```
LNAME        SALARY

----------  ----------

BOGART       88192.00
BERGMAN      79475.00
HOLDEN       64428.00
LEMMON       51584.00
MATTHAU      66943.00
GARDNER      59081.00


  6 record(s) selected.
```

Using the NOT (negation) operator with the BETWEEN predicate (or with any predicate, for that matter) reverses the meaning of the predicate. Which means that, in the case of the BETWEEN predicate, the contents of a column or the results of an SQL expression are checked, and only values that fall *outside* the range specified are returned in the final result data set produced.

Therefore, to retrieve values from the LNAME and SALARY columns of the EMPLOYEE table presented earlier and display information only for rows where the value stored in the SALARY column is *less than or equal to* $50,000.00 and *greater than or equal to* $90,000.00, you would execute a SELECT statement that looks like this:

```
SELECT lname, salary
  FROM employee
  WHERE salary
    NOT BETWEEN 50000.00 AND 90000.00
```

And when this statement is executed, you should get a result data set that looks like this (provided the EMPLOYEE table is populated as shown in Table 5.2):

```
LNAME       SALARY

----------  ----------
DEAN         158096.00
MONROE       103675.00
CAGNEY       105787.00
HEPBURN       48903.00

  4 record(s) selected.
```

The LIKE predicate

The LIKE predicate is used to define a comparison relationship in which a character string value is checked to determine whether it contains a specific pattern of characters. The pattern of characters specified can consist of regular alphanumeric characters or a combination of alphanumeric characters and one or more of the following special metacharacters:

- The underscore character (_), which is treated as a wildcard character that stands for any single alphanumeric character
- The percent character (%), which is treated as a wildcard character that stands for any sequence of alphanumeric characters

Thus, to retrieve values from the EMPNO and LNAME columns of the EMPLOYEE table presented earlier and display information only for rows in which the value stored in the LNAME column begins with the letter M, you could execute a SELECT statement that looks like this:

```
SELECT empno, lname
  FROM employee
  WHERE lname LIKE 'M%'
```

When this statement is executed, you should get a result data set that looks like this (provided the EMPLOYEE table is populated as shown in Table 5.2):

```
EMPNO        LNAME
----------- ----------
       1001 MONROE
       1007 MATTHAU

   2 record(s) selected.
```

It is important to note that when using wildcard metacharacters, you must take care to ensure that they are placed in the appropriate location in the pattern string specified. For instance, specifying the character string pattern 'M%' (as in the previous example) will return only records for employees whose last name *begins with* the letter M. However, using the character string pattern '%M%' will return records for employees whose last name *contains* the character M (anywhere in the name). Consequently, had this character string pattern been used in the previous query, the result data set produced would have looked like this:

```
EMPNO        LNAME
----------- ----------
       1001 MONROE
       1003 BERGMAN
       1006 LEMMON
       1007 MATTHAU

   4 record(s) selected.
```

You must also be careful when using uppercase and lowercase characters in pattern strings. If the data being examined was stored in a case-sensitive manner, the characters used in the pattern string specified must *exactly* match the value being looked for. Otherwise, no matching records will be found.

• •

Important: Although the LIKE predicate provides a relatively easy way to search for character string values, it should be used with caution; the overhead involved in processing a LIKE predicate is very high and can be extremely resource-intensive.

• •

The IN predicate

The IN predicate is used to define a comparison relationship in which a value is checked to determine whether it matches a value found in a finite set of values. This finite set of values can consist of one or more literal values that are coded directly in the IN predicate, or it can comprise a set of non-null values that were produced by a subquery.

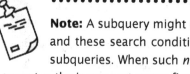

• •

Note: A subquery might contain search conditions of its own, and these search conditions might in turn include their own subqueries. When such *nested* subqueries are processed, DB2 executes the innermost query first and uses the results to execute the next outer query and so on until all nested queries have been processed.

• •

Therefore, to retrieve values from the EMPNO and DEPT columns of the EMPLOYEE table presented earlier and display information only for rows in which the value stored in the DEPT column is either 'B01' or 'C01', you could execute a SELECT statement that looks like this:

```
SELECT lname, dept
  FROM employee
  WHERE dept IN ('B01', 'C01')
```

And when this statement is executed, you should get a result data set that looks like this (assuming the EMPLOYEE table is populated as shown in Table 5.2):

```
LNAME        DEPT
----------   ----
MONROE       B01
BOGART       C01
BERGMAN      C01
HEPBURN      C01
GARDNER      B01

  5 record(s) selected.
```

On the other hand, to retrieve values from the LNAME and DEPT columns of the EMPLOYEE table and display information only for rows in which an employee works in a department that currently does not have a manager, you would execute a SELECT statement that looks more like this:

```
SELECT lname, dept
  FROM employee
  WHERE dept IN
    (SELECT deptno FROM department WHERE mgrid IS NULL)
```

And when this statement is executed, you should get a result data set that looks like this (provided the DEPARTMENT table is populated as shown in Table 5.1 and the EMPLOYEE table is populated as shown in Table 5.2):

```
LNAME        DEPT
----------   ----
CAGNEY       E01
HOLDEN       F01
LEMMON       E01
MATTHAU      F01

  4 record(s) selected.
```

In this example, the subquery "SELECT deptno FROM department WHERE mgrid IS NULL" produces a result data set that contains the values E01 and F01. The main query then checks each value found in the DEPT column of the EMPLOYEE table against the values returned by the subquery to see whether there is a match. If a match is found, the record is returned.

The EXISTS predicate

The EXISTS predicate is used to determine whether a particular value exists in a given result data set. Consequently, the EXISTS predicate is always followed by a subquery, and this predicate returns either TRUE or FALSE to indicate whether a specific value is found in the result data set produced by the subquery provided.

Consequently, to find out which values in the DEPTNO column of the DEPARTMENT table presented earlier are used in the DEPT column of the EMPLOYEE table (also presented earlier), you could execute a SELECT statement that looks like this:

```
SELECT deptno, deptname
  FROM department
  WHERE EXISTS
    (SELECT dept
       FROM employee
       WHERE dept = deptno)
```

When this statement is executed, you should get a result data set that looks like this (assuming the DEPARTMENT table is populated as shown in Table 5.1 and the EMPLOYEE table is populated as shown in Table 5.2):

```
DEPTNO DEPTNAME
------ --------------------
A01    ADMINISTRATION
B01    PLANNING
C01    DEVELOPMENT
E01    OPERATIONS
F01    SUPPORT

  5 record(s) selected.
```

In most situations, the EXISTS predicate is ANDed with other WHERE clause predicates to control final row selection.

The NULL predicate

The NULL predicate is used to determine whether a particular value is NULL. So, to retrieve values from the DEPTNO and DEPTNAME columns of the DEPARTMENT table presented earlier and display information only for rows in which the value stored in the MGRID column is NULL, you could execute a SELECT statement that looks like this:

```
SELECT deptno, deptname
  FROM department
  WHERE mgrid IS NULL
```

And when this statement is executed, you should get a result data set that looks like this (assuming the DEPARTMENT table is populated as shown in Table 5.1):

```
DEPTNO DEPTNAME

------ --------------------

E01    OPERATIONS
F01    SUPPORT


  2 record(s) selected.
```

On the other hand, to retrieve the same information for rows in which the value stored in the MGRID column is *not* NULL, you would execute a SELECT statement that looks more like this:

```
SELECT deptno, deptname
  FROM department
  WHERE mgrid IS NOT NULL
```

Now, when the SELECT statement is executed, you should get a result data set that looks like this:

```
DEPTNO DEPTNAME

------ --------------------

A01    ADMINISTRATION
B01    PLANNING
C01    DEVELOPMENT
D01    PERSONNEL


   4 record(s) selected.
```

When using the NULL predicate, it is important to keep in mind that NULL, zero (0), and blank ("") are three different values. NULL is a special marker that represents missing information, whereas zero and blank (or an empty string) are actual values that can be stored in a column to indicate a specific value or the lack thereof. Moreover, some columns accept NULL values while other columns do not, depending upon how they have been defined. So, before you execute a query that checks for NULL values, make sure a NULL value can be stored in the columns being queried.

The GROUP BY Clause

The GROUP BY clause is used to instruct DB2 on how to organize rows of data that are returned in a result data set. In its simplest form, the GROUP BY clause is followed by a *grouping expression*, which usually consists of one or more names that refer to columns in the result data set that is to be organized.

The GROUP BY clause is frequently used to group columns whose values are to be provided as input to aggregate functions such as AVG() and SUM(). For example, to obtain the average salary for each department found in the DEPT column of the EMPLOYEE table presented earlier (using salary information stored in the SALARY column), round the average salaries to two decimal points, and organize the information retrieved by department, you would execute a SELECT statement that looks like this:

```
SELECT dept,
       DECIMAL(AVG(salary),9,2) AS avg_salary
  FROM employee
  GROUP BY dept
```

And when this statement is executed, you should get a result data set that looks like this (provided the EMPLOYEE table is populated as shown in Table 5.2):

```
DEPT AVG_SALARY
---- -----------
A01     158096.00
B01      81378.00
C01      72190.00
E01      78685.50
F01      65685.50

  5 record(s) selected.
```

Here, each row returned in the result data set produced contains the department code for a particular department, along with the average salary for individuals who work in that department.

• •

Important: A common mistake that is often made with the GROUP BY clause is the addition of nonaggregate columns to the list of columns that are supplied as the grouping expression for the clause. Grouping is performed by combining all columns specified into a single concatenated key and breaking whenever that key value changes. Consequently, extraneous columns can cause unexpected breaks to occur.

• •

The GROUP BY ROLLUP Clause

The GROUP BY ROLLUP clause is used to analyze a collection of data in a single dimension, but at more than one level of detail. For example, you might group data by successively larger organizational units (such as team, department, and division) or by successively larger geographical units (such as city, county, state or province, and country).

Thus, if you were to change the GROUP BY clause used in the previous example to a GROUP BY ROLLUP clause, you would end up with a SELECT statement that looks like this:

```
SELECT dept,
       DECIMAL(AVG(salary),9,2) AS avg_salary
  FROM employee
  GROUP BY ROLLUP (dept)
```

And when this statement is executed, you should get a result data set that looks like this (assuming the EMPLOYEE table is populated as shown in Table 5.2):

```
DEPT AVG_SALARY
---- -----------
 -        82616.40
A01      158096.00
B01       81378.00
C01       72190.00
E01       78685.50
F01       65685.50

  6 record(s) selected.
```

Now, the result data set produced contains average salary information for all employees found in the EMPLOYEE table, regardless of which department they work in (the line in the result data set produced that has a NULL value for the DEPT column), as well as average salary information for each department found, rounded to two decimal points and organized by department.

This example contains only one grouping expression (the DEPT column) in the GROUP BY ROLLUP clause. However, multiple grouping expressions can be specified—for example, GROUP BY ROLLUP (dept, division). When multiple grouping expressions are supplied, DB2 groups the data by all expressions used, then by all but the last expression used, and so on until all grouping expressions have been processed. Then, it makes one final grouping that consists of the entire contents of the table or view. Consequently, when specifying multiple grouping expressions, it is important to ensure that the expressions provided are listed in the appropriate order; if one kind of group is logically contained inside another (for example, departments within a division), that group should be listed *after* the group it is logically contained in—for example, GROUP BY ROLLUP (city, state)—not before.

The GROUP BY CUBE Clause

The GROUP BY CUBE clause is used to analyze a collection of data by organizing it into groups, in multiple dimensions. For example, if you were to execute a SELECT statement that looks like this:

```
SELECT dept,
       sex,
       DECIMAL(AVG(salary),9,2) AS avg_salary
  FROM employee
  GROUP BY CUBE (dept, sex)
```

Assuming the EMPLOYEE table is populated as shown in Table 5.2 when this statement is executed, you should get a result data set that looks like this:

```
DEPT SEX AVG_SALARY
---- --- -----------
 -    F      72783.50
 -    M      89171.66
 -    -      82616.40
A01   -     158096.00
B01   -      81378.00
C01   -      72190.00
E01   -      78685.50
F01   -      65685.50
A01   M     158096.00
B01   F      81378.00
C01   F      64189.00
C01   M      88192.00
E01   M      78685.50
F01   M      65685.50

    14 record(s) selected.
```

Here, the result data set produced contains:

- Average salary information for all employees, regardless of the department they work in (the line in the result data set that has a NULL value for both the DEPT and the SEX columns)
- Average salary information for both male and female employees, regardless of the department they work in (lines in the result data set that have a NULL value for the DEPT column only)
- Average salary information for each department (lines in the result data set produced that have a NULL value for the SEX column only)
- Average salary information for both male and female employees, by department (lines in the result data set produced that have a value for every column)

In other words, the data in the result data set produced is grouped:

- By sex only
- By department only
- By sex and department
- As a single group that contains all sexes and all departments

In addition, the average salary information provided is rounded to two decimal points and the records returned are organized by department.

The term CUBE is intended to suggest that data is being analyzed in more than one dimension. In the previous example, you can see that data analysis was performed in two dimensions, which resulted in four types of groupings.

Suppose the following SELECT statement is executed:

```
SELECT dept,
       sex,
       title,
       DECIMAL(AVG(salary),9,2) AS avg_salary
  FROM employee
  GROUP BY CUBE (dept, sex, title)
```

In this case, data analysis will be performed in three dimensions (DEPT, SEX, and TITLE), and the data will be broken into eight types of groupings. In fact, you can determine the number of types of groupings a GROUP BY CUBE operation will produce by using the calculation 2^n, where n is the number of grouping expressions used in the GROUP BY CUBE clause.

The HAVING Clause

The HAVING clause is used to apply further selection criteria to columns that are referenced in a GROUP BY clause. Similar to the WHERE clause, the HAVING clause instructs DB2 on how to select rows that are to be returned in a result data set *from rows that have already been selected and grouped.*

Like the WHERE clause, the HAVING clause is followed by a search condition that acts as a simple test that, when applied to a row of data, evaluates to TRUE, FALSE, or UNKNOWN. If the test evaluates to TRUE, the row is returned in the result data set produced; if the test evaluates to FALSE or UNKNOWN, the row is ignored. Similarly, the search condition of a HAVING clause can utilize the same set of predicates that the WHERE clause recognizes.

Therefore, to obtain the average salary for each department in the DEPT column of the EMPLOYEE table presented earlier (using salary information stored in the SALARY column), round the average salaries to two decimal points and organize the information retrieved by department, and *display information only for rows in which the average salary is greater than $75,000.00*, you would execute a SELECT statement that looks like this:

```
SELECT dept,
        DECIMAL(AVG(salary),9,2) AS avg_salary
    FROM employee
    GROUP BY dept
    HAVING AVG(salary) > 75000
```

And when this statement is executed, you should get a result data set that looks like this (provided the EMPLOYEE table is populated as in Table 5.2):

```
DEPT AVG_SALARY

---- -----------

A01    158096.00
B01     81378.00
E01     78685.50


  3 record(s) selected.
```

The ORDER BY Clause

The ORDER BY clause is used to instruct DB2 on how to sort (order) the rows that are returned in a result data set. When specified, this clause is followed by the name (or position number) of one or more columns whose data values are to be sorted and a keyword that indicates whether the data is to be sorted in ascending (ASC) or descending (DESC) order. Multiple columns can be used and each column can be ordered in ascending or descending order, independently of the others. However, when multiple columns are specified, the order in which the columns are listed determines the order in which the requested sorts are performed. First, data is sorted for the first column specified (the *primary sort*), then the sorted data is sorted again for the next column specified, and so on until the data has been sorted for every column identified.

Thus, to retrieve values from the LNAME and DEPT columns of the EMPLOYEE table presented earlier and sort the information returned by department (DEPT) in ascending order, followed by last name (LNAME) in descending order, you could execute a SELECT statement that looks like this:

```
SELECT lname, dept
  FROM employee
  ORDER BY dept ASC, lname DESC
```

When this statement is executed, you should get a result data set that looks like this (assuming the EMPLOYEE table is populated as shown in Table 5.2):

```
LNAME        DEPT

----------   ----

DEAN         A01
MONROE       B01
GARDNER      B01
HEPBURN      C01
BOGART       C01
BERGMAN      C01
LEMMON       E01
CAGNEY       E01
MATTHAU      F01
HOLDEN       F01


  10 record(s) selected.
```

Using the ORDER BY clause is relatively easy if the result data set produced consists only of named columns. But what if you need to order the result data set according to data found in a column that cannot be specified by name (such as summary column)? In these situations, an integer value representing the column's position, as it appears in the result data set produced, can be used instead. (The first or leftmost column in a result data set is considered column 1, the next is column 2, and so on.) Consequently, the previous query could just have easily have been written as:

```
SELECT lname, dept
  FROM employee
  ORDER BY 2 ASC, 1 DESC
```

It is important to note that even though integer values are used primarily to refer to columns that cannot be specified by name, you can use them in place of any column, including columns you can reference by name.

The FETCH FIRST Clause
The FETCH FIRST clause is used to limit the number of rows that are returned in a result data set. When used, the FETCH FIRST clause must be followed by a positive integer value,

which in turn must be followed by the words ROWS ONLY. This informs DB2 that the user or application executing the query does not want to see more than *n* number of rows, regardless of how many rows might be returned if the FETCH FIRST clause were not used.

Therefore, to retrieve just the first five values from the EMPNO, LNAME, and DEPT columns of the EMPLOYEE table presented earlier, you would execute a SELECT statement that looks like this:

```
SELECT empno, lname, dept
  FROM employee
  FETCH FIRST 5 ROWS ONLY
```

And when this statement is executed, you should get a result data set that looks like this (provided the EMPLOYEE table is populated as shown in Table 5.2):

```
EMPNO        LNAME       DEPT
-----------  ----------  ----

       1000 DEAN         A01
       1001 MONROE       B01
       1002 BOGART       C01
       1003 BERGMAN      C01
       1004 CAGNEY       E01

  5 record(s) selected.
```

If you use other clauses to control the size and contents of the result data set produced *before* returning a specified number of rows, the actual values returned can differ, depending on where the FETCH FIRST clause appears. For example, if an ORDER BY clause were added to the query just executed, making it look like this:

```
SELECT empno, lname, dept
  FROM employee
  ORDER BY lname DESC
  FETCH FIRST 5 ROWS ONLY
```

The result data set produced would look something like this:

```
EMPNO        LNAME        DEPT
-----------  -----------  ----
      1001 MONROE        B01
      1007 MATTHAU       F01
      1006 LEMMON        E01
      1005 HOLDEN        F01
      1008 HEPBURN       C01

  5 record(s) selected.
```

Consequently, the FETCH FIRST clause can be used in conjunction with other clauses to control which rows are processed by other operations, such as updates and deletes, that obtain their values from a subquery.

The Isolation Clause

The isolation clause is used to specify the isolation level a query is to be run under, and in some cases, to suggest the type of lock DB2 should acquire and hold on the data being queried. (Isolation levels and locks are discussed in great detail in Chapter 7, "Data Concurrency.") The basic syntax for the isolation clause is:

```
WITH [RR <USE AND KEEP [SHARE | UPDATE | EXCLUSIVE] LOCKS> |
      RS <USE AND KEEP [SHARE | UPDATE | EXCLUSIVE] LOCKS> |
      CS |
      UR]
```

where:

RR	Indicates the query is to be run under the Repeatable Read isolation level
RS	Indicates the query is to be run under the Read Stability isolation level
CS	Indicates the query is to be run under the Cursor Stability isolation level

UR   Indicates the query is to be run under the Uncommitted Read isolation level

If the USE AND KEEP SHARE LOCKS clause is specified (along with RR or RS), concurrent processes will be allowed to acquire Share (S) or Update (U) locks on the data being queried; if the USE AND KEEP UPDATE LOCKS clause is specified, concurrent processes can obtain Share (S) locks on the data, but will be prevented from acquiring Update (U) or Exclusive (X) locks; and if the USE AND KEEP EXCLUSIVE LOCKS clause is specified, concurrent processes will not be allowed to acquire locks of any kind.

Thus, to retrieve values from the EMPNO, FNAME, and LNAME columns of the EMPLOYEE table presented earlier while running under the Repeatable Read (RR) isolation level, you could execute a SELECT statement that looks like this:

```
SELECT empno, fname, lname
  FROM employee
  WITH RR
```

A Word About Common Table Expressions

Common table expressions are used to construct temporary tables that reside in memory and that exist only for the life of the SQL statements that define them. (In fact, the table that is created for a common table expression can be referenced only by the SQL statement that created it.) Common table expressions are typically used:

- In place of a view when the creation of a view is undesirable, when the general use of a view is not required, and when positioned update or delete operations are not desired
- To enable grouping by a column that is derived from either a subquery or a scalar function that performs some external action
- When the desired result data set is based on host variables
- When the same result data set is to be used by several different queries
- When the results of a query must be derived using recursion

The syntax used to construct a common table expression is:

```
WITH [TableName]
  <([ColumnName], ...)>
  AS ([SELECTStatement])
```

where:

TableName	Identifies a unique name that is to be assigned to the temporary table that is to be created
ColumnName	Identifies one or more names that are to be assigned to columns that are to be part of the temporary table—each column name provided must be unique and unqualified; if you do not provide values for this parameter, names derived from the result data set produced by the *SELECTStatement* specified will be used by default; if you provide a list of column names, the number of column names supplied must match the number of columns that will be returned by the SELECT statement used to create the temporary table (if a common table expression is recursive, or if the result data set produced by the SELECT statement contains duplicate column names, column names *must* be specified)
SELECTStatement	Identifies a SELECT statement that, when executed, will produce the data values that are to be stored in the temporary table that is to be created (by retrieving them from other tables, views, or both)

So, if you wanted to create a common table expression that retrieves values from the LNAME, HIREDATE, and SEX columns of the EMPLOYEE table presented earlier, stores them in a temporary table (named EMP_INFO), and then queries the temporary table to obtain last name and hire date information for female employees, you could execute an SQL statement that looks like this:

```
WITH
  emp_info (lname, hiredate, sex)
    AS (SELECT lname, hiredate, sex FROM employee)
  SELECT lname, hiredate FROM emp_info WHERE sex = 'F'
```

And when this statement is executed, you should get a result data set that looks like this (provided the EMPLOYEE table is populated as shown in Table 5.2):

```
LNAME       HIREDATE

----------  ----------

MONROE      05/10/2008
BERGMAN     02/14/2001
HEPBURN     03/15/2002
GARDNER     06/06/1999


  4 record(s) selected.
```

Multiple common table expressions can be specified with a single WITH keyword/ statement, and each expression specified can be referenced, by name, in the FROM clause of subsequent common table expressions. However, if multiple table expressions are defined using a single WITH keyword/statement, the name you assign to each temporary table must be unique from all other table names used. It is also important to note that the name assigned to any temporary table created by a WITH keyword/statement will take precedence over any existing base tables, views, or aliases that have the same qualified name.

If the SELECT statement in a common table expression attempts to reference a table, view, or alias that exists outside the expression, it will actually be working with the temporary table that was created in the expression. (Existing tables, views, and aliases whose names match that of the temporary table are not altered but are simply inaccessible.)

A Word About CASE Expressions

One concise and efficient way to display compared values in a readable format is to use one or more SQL CASE expressions in the selection list of a query. Each CASE operation evaluates an expression and supplies a value, if a certain condition is met. CASE expressions can take one of two forms: *simple* or *searched.*

The basic syntax used to create a simple CASE expression is:

```
CASE [Expression1]
  [WHEN [Expression2] THEN [Result1], ...]
ELSE [Result2]
<END>
```

where:

Expression1	Identifies an expression or value that is to be compared against one or more *Expression2* expressions or values
Expression2	Identifies one or more expressions or values that, when compared with *Expression1*, evaluate to TRUE or FALSE
Result1	Identifies a value to use when a search condition evaluates to TRUE
Result2	Identifies a value to use when a search condition evaluates to FALSE

Thus, if you wanted to retrieve values from the EMPNO, LNAME, and DEPT columns of the EMPLOYEE table presented earlier, and you knew that the first character of each department code corresponds to a specific pay grade, you could use a simple CASE expression to convert the department codes found into a description of the pay grade that each employee has been assigned by executing a SELECT statement that looks like this:

```
SELECT empno, lname,
  CASE SUBSTR(dept,1,1)
    WHEN 'A' THEN 'GRADE-60'
    WHEN 'B' THEN 'GRADE-58'
    WHEN 'C' THEN 'GRADE-40'
    ELSE 'UNKNOWN GRADE'
  END AS pay_grade
  FROM employee
```

When this statement is executed, you should get a result data set that looks like this (assuming the EMPLOYEE table is populated as shown in Table 5.2):

```
EMPNO        LNAME       PAY_GRADE
-----------  ----------  --------------
       1000  DEAN        GRADE-60
       1001  MONROE      GRADE-58
       1002  BOGART      GRADE-40
       1003  BERGMAN     GRADE-40
       1004  CAGNEY      UNKNOWN GRADE
       1005  HOLDEN      UNKNOWN GRADE
       1006  LEMMON      UNKNOWN GRADE
       1007  MATTHAU     UNKNOWN GRADE
       1008  HEPBURN     GRADE-40
       1009  GARDNER     GRADE-58

  10 record(s) selected.
```

On the other hand, the basic syntax used to create a searched CASE expression is:

```
CASE
  [WHEN [SearchCondition] THEN [Result1], ...]
ELSE [Result2]
<END>
```

where:

SearchCondition	Identifies one or more logical conditions that evaluate to TRUE or FALSE
Result1	Identifies a value to use when the search condition specified evaluates to TRUE
Result2	Identifies a value to use when the search condition specified evaluates to FALSE

Therefore, to retrieve values from the TITLE and SALARY columns of the EMPLOYEE table presented earlier and calculate salary increases based on the job each employee performs, you could execute a SELECT statement that looks something like this:

```
SELECT title, salary AS old_salary,
  CASE
    WHEN title = 'PRESIDENT' THEN salary * 1.15
    WHEN title LIKE 'DATABASE%' THEN salary * 1.10
    WHEN title LIKE 'TECH%' THEN salary * 1.08
    ELSE salary * 1.05
  END AS new_salary
  FROM employee
```

And when this statement is executed, you should get a result data set that looks like this (provided the EMPLOYEE table is populated as shown in Table 5.2):

```
TITLE                         OLD_SALARY NEW_SALARY
----------------------------- ---------- -------------

PRESIDENT                     158096.00  181810.4000
SYSTEMS ENGINEER              103675.00  108858.7500
DATABASE ADMINISTRATOR         88192.00   97011.2000
PROGRAMMER/ANALYST             79475.00   83448.7500
TECHNICIAN I                  105787.00  114249.9600
TECHNICIAN I                   64428.00   69582.2400
TECHNICIAN II                  51584.00   55710.7200
DATABASE ADMINISTRATOR         66943.00   73637.3000
MANAGER                        48903.00   51348.1500
ENGINEER                       59081.00   62035.0500

  10 record(s) selected.
```

In this example, a searched CASE expression was used to perform the necessary calculations.

As you can see from the two previous examples, the value returned by a CASE expression is the value of the result-expression (*Result1*) that follows a condition that evaluates to TRUE. If no condition evaluates to TRUE and the ELSE keyword is provided, the CASE expression returns the value of the second result-expression (*Result2*). If, however, no condition evaluates to TRUE and the ELSE keyword is not provided, the result is assumed to be NULL.

It is important to note that when a condition evaluates to UNKNOWN (because a NULL value was returned), the CASE expression is considered not TRUE and therefore is treated the same as a CASE expression that evaluates to FALSE. It is also important to note that the data type of the search condition specified must be compatible with the data type of each result-expression returned.

Joining Tables

So far, the majority of the examples we have looked at have been focused on retrieving data from a single table. However, one of the more powerful features of the SELECT statement (and the feature that makes data normalization possible) is its ability to retrieve data from two or more tables by performing what is known as a *join operation*. In its simplest form, the syntax for a SELECT statement that performs a join operation is:

```
SELECT * FROM [TableName, ...]
```

where:

TableName   Identifies, by name, at least two tables that data is to be retrieved from

Thus, to retrieve values from all columns found in the EMPLOYEE and DEPARTMENT tables presented earlier, you would execute a SELECT statement that looks like this:

```
SELECT * FROM employee, department
```

When this statement is executed, the result data set produced will contain every possible combination of the rows found in both tables. This type of result data set is referred to as a *Cartesian product*. With Cartesian products, every row in the result data set produced consists of a row from the first table referenced concatenated with a row from the second table referenced, in turn concatenated with a row from the third table referenced, and so on. Therefore, the total number of rows returned is always the product of the number of rows in all tables referenced. For example, if the DEPARTMENT table is populated as shown in Table 5.1 (with 6 rows) and the EMPLOYEE table is populated as shown in Table 5.2 (with 10 rows), the query just presented will produce a result data set that consists of 60 rows (6 x 10 = 60).

●●

Important: Cartesian product joins should be used with extreme caution when working with large tables; a significant amount of resources can be required to perform such operations, and the operation itself can have a negative impact on performance.

●●

Because Cartesian products can generate large result data sets, they typically are not used very often. Instead, most join operations involve collecting data from two or more tables that have a specific column in common, and combining the results. This type of join is referred to as an *inner join*, and by far, inner joins are the simplest type of join operation to perform. Aside from Cartesian products and inner joins, one other type of join operation is possible—an *outer join*. And just as there is a difference between Cartesian products and inner joins, there is a significant difference between inner joins and outer joins.

Inner Joins

An inner join can be thought of as the cross product of two tables, in which every row in one table is paired with rows in another table that have matching values in one or more columns. Figure 5.1 depicts a conceptual view of an inner join operation; the shaded area in this illustration represents matching data found in both tables that was used to link the tables together.

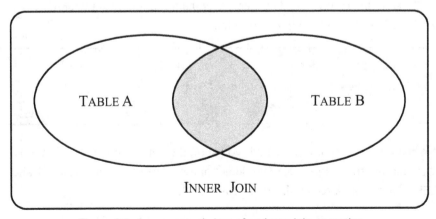

Figure 5.1: A conceptual view of an inner join operation

One way to perform an inner join is by executing a SELECT statement that looks like this:

```
SELECT
  [* | [[Expression] <<AS> [NewColumnName]>, ...]
  FROM [TableName <<AS> [CorrelationName]>, ...]
  [JoinCondition]
```

where:

Expression	Identifies one or more valid SQL language elements (typically column names) that values are to be returned for when the SELECT statement is executed
NewColumnName	Identifies a column name to use in place of the column name that will be returned, by default, in the result data set produced by the SELECT statement
TableName	Identifies, by name, two or more tables to retrieve data from
CorrelationName	Identifies a shorthand name that can be used to reference the tables specified in the *JoinCondition* provided
JoinCondition	Identifies the condition that is to be used to join the tables specified; typically, this is a WHERE clause in which the values of a column in one table are compared with the values of a similar column in another table

Therefore, to retrieve values from the LNAME and DEPTNAME columns of the EMPLOYEE and DEPARTMENT tables presented earlier, using a simple inner join operation, you could execute a SELECT statement that looks like this:

```
SELECT e.lname, d.deptname
  FROM employee AS e, department AS d
  WHERE e.dept = d.deptno
```

And when this statement is executed, you should get a result data set that looks like this (assuming the DEPARTMENT table is populated as shown in Table 5.1 and the EMPLOYEE table is populated as shown in Table 5.2):

```
LNAME       DEPTNAME

----------  --------------------

DEAN        ADMINISTRATION
MONROE      PLANNING
GARDNER     PLANNING
BOGART      DEVELOPMENT
HEPBURN     DEVELOPMENT
BERGMAN     DEVELOPMENT
CAGNEY      OPERATIONS
LEMMON      OPERATIONS
HOLDEN      SUPPORT
MATTHAU     SUPPORT


   10 record(s) selected.
```

The following SELECT statement syntax can be used to perform inner join operations as well:

```
SELECT
  [* | [[Expression] <<AS> [NewColumnName]>, ...]
  FROM [TableName1] <<AS> [CorrelationName1]>
  <INNER> JOIN
  [TableName2] <<AS> [CorrelationName2]>]
  ON [JoinCondition]
```

where:

Expression	Identifies one or more valid SQL language elements (typically column names) that values are to be returned for when the SELECT statement is executed
NewColumnName	Identifies a column name to use in place of the column name that will be returned, by default, in the result data set produced by the SELECT statement
TableName1	Identifies, by name, the first table to retrieve data from

CorrelationName1	Identifies a shorthand name that can be used to reference the first table specified (via the *TableName1* parameter) in the *JoinCondition* provided
TableName2	Identifies, by name, the second table to retrieve data from
CorrelationName2	Identifies a shorthand name that can be used to reference the second table specified (via the *TableName2* parameter) in the *JoinCondition* provided
JoinCondition	Identifies the condition that is to be used to join the two tables specified; typically, this is a WHERE clause in which the values of a column in one table are compared with the values of a similar column in the other table

Therefore, the inner join operation that was performed in the previous example could just as easily have been performed by executing a SELECT statement that looks like this:

```
SELECT e.lname, d.deptname
  FROM employee AS e INNER JOIN department AS d
  ON e.dept = d.deptno
```

Figure 5.2 illustrates how this inner join operation will look if the tables used (EMPLOYEE and DEPARTMENT) are defined and populated as depicted.

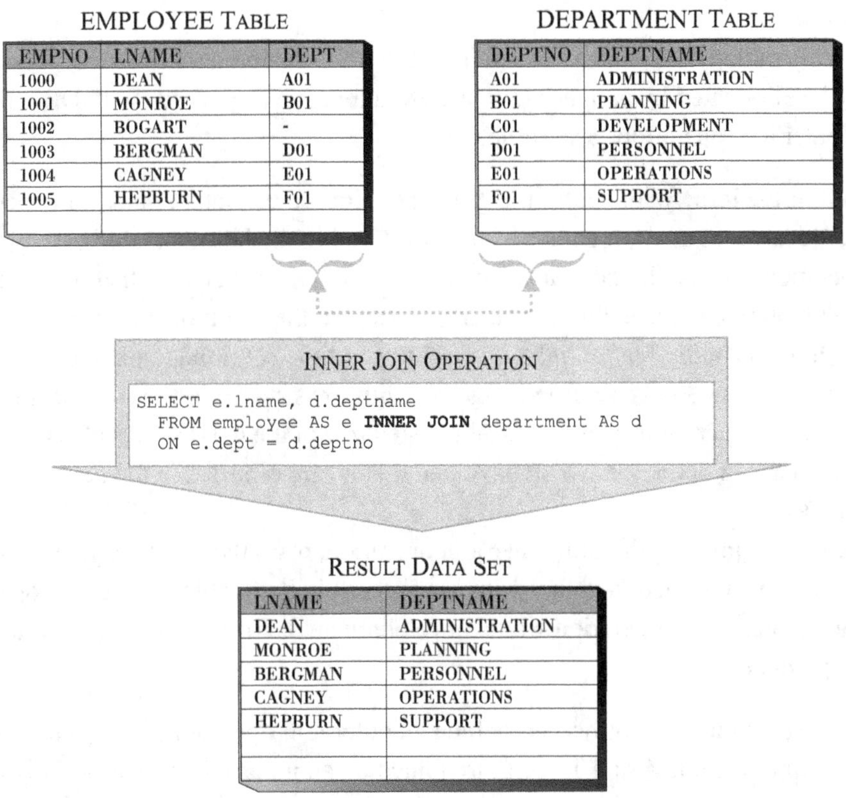

EMPLOYEE TABLE

EMPNO	LNAME	DEPT
1000	DEAN	A01
1001	MONROE	B01
1002	BOGART	-
1003	BERGMAN	D01
1004	CAGNEY	E01
1005	HEPBURN	F01

DEPARTMENT TABLE

DEPTNO	DEPTNAME
A01	ADMINISTRATION
B01	PLANNING
C01	DEVELOPMENT
D01	PERSONNEL
E01	OPERATIONS
F01	SUPPORT

INNER JOIN OPERATION

```
SELECT e.lname, d.deptname
   FROM employee AS e INNER JOIN department AS d
   ON e.dept = d.deptno
```

RESULT DATA SET

LNAME	DEPTNAME
DEAN	ADMINISTRATION
MONROE	PLANNING
BERGMAN	PERSONNEL
CAGNEY	OPERATIONS
HEPBURN	SUPPORT

Figure 5.2: A simple inner join operation

Inner joins work well as long as every row found in the first table has a corresponding row in the second table referenced. But when that is not the case, the result data set produced may be missing rows that exist in one or both of the tables being joined. For example, the result data set in Figure 5.2 does not contain records for BOGART (found in the EMPLOYEE table) and DEVELOPMENT (found in the DEPARTMENT table). That is because the value in the DEPT column of the BOGART record does not have a matching value in the DEPTNO column of the DEPARTMENT table. Similarly, the value in the DEPTNO column of the DEVELOPMENT record does not have a matching value in the DEPT column of the EMPLOYEE table. Consequently, to generate a result data set that contains one or both of these records, you will need to perform an outer join operation.

Outer Joins

Outer join operations are used when a join operation is desired and rows that would normally be eliminated by an inner join operation must be preserved. With DB2, three types of outer join operations are available:

- **Left outer join:** With a left outer join operation, rows that an inner join operation would have returned, together with rows stored in the leftmost table of the join operation (that is, the table listed *first* in the OUTER JOIN clause) that the inner join operation would have eliminated, are returned in the result data set produced.
- **Right outer join:** With a right outer join operation, rows that an inner join operation would have returned, together with rows stored in the rightmost table of the join operation (that is, the table listed *last* in the OUTER JOIN clause) that the inner join operation would have eliminated, are returned in the result data set produced.
- **Full outer join:** With a full outer join operation, rows that an inner join operation would have returned, together with rows stored in both tables of the join operation that the inner join operation would have eliminated, are returned in the result data set produced.

To understand the basic principles behind an outer join operation, it helps to look at an example. Suppose Table A and Table B are joined by an inner join operation. Any row in either table that does not have a matching row in the other table (based on the rules of the join condition) is eliminated from the result data set produced.

In contrast, if Table A and Table B are joined with an outer join, any row in either table that does not contain a matching row in the other table can be included in the result data set produced (exactly once). Thus, an outer join operation adds nonmatching rows to the final result data set produced, whereas an inner join operation excludes them. A left outer join of Table A with Table B preserves all nonmatching rows found in Table A; a right outer join of Table A with Table B preserves all nonmatching rows found in Table B; and a full outer join preserves all nonmatching rows found in both Table A *and* Table B. Figure 5.3 depicts a conceptual view of each of these join operations. The shaded areas represent the data that will be returned in the result data set produced by each type of outer join.

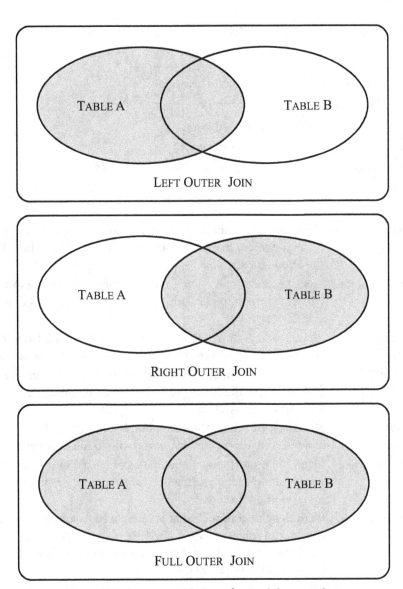

Figure 5.3: A conceptual view of outer join operations

The following syntax is used to perform an outer join operation:

```
SELECT
  [* | [[Expression] <<AS> [NewColumnName]>, ...]
  FROM [TableName1] <<AS> [CorrelationName1]>
  [LEFT | RIGHT | FULL] OUTER JOIN
  [TableName2] <<AS> [CorrelationName2]>]
  ON [JoinCondition]
```

where:

Expression	Identifies one or more valid SQL language elements (typically column names) that values are to be returned for when the SELECT statement is executed
NewColumnName	Identifies a column name to use in place of the column name that will be returned, by default, in the result data set produced by the SELECT statement
TableName1	Identifies, by name, the first table to retrieve data from; this table is considered the *leftmost* table in the outer join operation
CorrelationName1	Identifies a shorthand name that can be used to reference the first table specified (via the *TableName1* parameter), in the *JoinCondition* provided
TableName2	Identifies, by name, the second table to retrieve data from; this table is considered the *rightmost* table in the outer join operation
CorrelationName2	Identifies a shorthand name that can be used to reference the second table specified (via the *TableName2* parameter), in the *JoinCondition* provided
JoinCondition	Identifies the condition that is to be used to join the two tables specified; typically, this is a WHERE clause in which the values of a column in one table are compared with the values of a similar column in the other table

Thus, you can perform a simple left outer join operation by executing a SELECT statement that looks like this:

```
SELECT e.lname, d.deptname
  FROM employee AS e LEFT OUTER JOIN department AS d
  ON e.dept = d.deptno
```

Figure 5.4 illustrates how such a join operation will look if the tables used (EMPLOYEE and DEPARTMENT) are defined and populated as depicted.

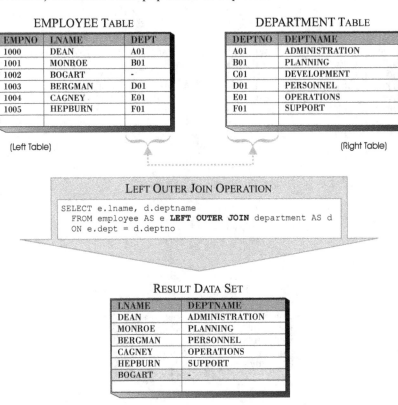

Figure 5.4: A simple left outer join operation

Here, the employee record for BOGART is included in the result data set produced, even though the DEPT column value for this record does not have a matching value in the DEPTNO column of the DEPARTMENT table. However, the record for the DEVELOPMENT department is excluded because the DEPTNO column of this record does not have a matching value in the DEPT column of the EMPLOYEE table.

In contrast, you can conduct a simple right outer join operation by executing a SELECT statement that looks like this:

```
SELECT e.lname, d.deptname
  FROM employee AS e RIGHT OUTER JOIN department AS d
  ON e.dept = d.deptno
```

Figure 5.5 illustrates how this type of a join operation will look if the tables used (EMPLOYEE and DEPARTMENT) are defined and populated as depicted.

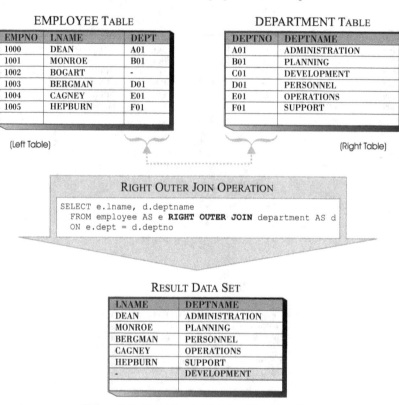

Figure 5.5: A simple right outer join operation

Now, the result data set produced includes the record for the DEVELOPMENT department, even though the value in the DEPTNO column this record does not have a matching value in the DEPT column of the EMPLOYEE table. However, the employee record for BOGART is excluded because the DEPT column of this record does not have a matching value in the DEPTNO column of the DEPARTMENT table.

Finally, a simple full outer join operation can be conducted by executing a SELECT statement that looks like this:

```
SELECT e.lname, d.deptname
  FROM employee AS e FULL OUTER JOIN department AS d
  ON e.dept = d.deptno
```

Figure 5.6 illustrates how such a join operation will look if the tables used (EMPLOYEE and DEPARTMENT) are defined and populated as depicted.

EMPLOYEE TABLE

EMPNO	LNAME	DEPT
1000	DEAN	A01
1001	MONROE	B01
1002	BOGART	-
1003	BERGMAN	D01
1004	CAGNEY	E01
1005	HEPBURN	F01

DEPARTMENT TABLE

DEPTNO	DEPTNAME
A01	ADMINISTRATION
B01	PLANNING
C01	DEVELOPMENT
D01	PERSONNEL
E01	OPERATIONS
F01	SUPPORT

(Left Table)   (Right Table)

FULL OUTER JOIN OPERATION

```
SELECT e.lname, d.deptname
   FROM employee AS e FULL OUTER JOIN department AS d
   ON e.dept = d.deptno
```

RESULT DATA SET

LNAME	DEPTNAME
DEAN	ADMINISTRATION
MONROE	PLANNING
BERGMAN	PERSONNEL
CAGNEY	OPERATIONS
HEPBURN	SUPPORT
-	DEVELOPMENT
BOGART	-

Figure 5.6: A simple full outer join operation

Here, the result data set produced includes records for both BOGART and DEVELOPMENT, even though the DEPT column value for the BOGART record does not have a matching value in the DEPTNO column of the DEPARTMENT table, and the value in the DEPTNO column for the DEVELOPMENT record does not have a matching value in the DEPT column of the EMPLOYEE table.

Using a Set Operator to Combine the Results of Two or More Queries

While a join operation can be used to retrieve data from two or more dissimilar tables, a special operator known as a *set operator* can be used to query two tables that have similar definitions. Essentially, a set operator combines the output from two or more individual queries to produce a single result data set. Consequently, set operators require that the tables being queried have the same number of columns, and that each of these columns have the same data types assigned to them.

The following set operators are available with DB2:

- **UNION**: The UNION set operator combines the result data sets produced by two individual queries and removes any duplicate rows found. Figure 5.7 illustrates how a simple UNION operation works.

CAKES TABLE

TYPE	INGREDIENT
CHOCOLATE	SUGAR
CHEESECAKE	SUGAR
CHOCOLATE	FLOUR
POUND	SALT
FRUIT	BUTTER
POUND	BUTTER

COOKIES TABLE

TYPE	INGREDIENT
SUGAR	SUGAR
GINGER SNAP	SUGAR
OATMEAL	SALT
SUGAR	VANILLA
OATMEAL	FLOUR

UNION OPERATION

```
SELECT ingredient FROM cakes
UNION
SELECT ingredient FROM cookies
ORDER BY ingredient
```

RESULT DATA SET

INGREDIENT
BUTTER
FLOUR
SALT
SUGAR
VANILLA

Figure 5.7: A simple UNION operation

- **UNION ALL**: The UNION ALL set operator combines the result data sets produced by two individual queries, while retaining all duplicate records found. Figure 5.8 illustrates how a simple UNION ALL operation works.

CAKES TABLE

TYPE	INGREDIENT
CHOCOLATE	SUGAR
CHEESECAKE	SUGAR
CHOCOLATE	FLOUR
POUND	SALT
FRUIT	BUTTER
POUND	BUTTER

COOKIES TABLE

TYPE	INGREDIENT
SUGAR	SUGAR
GINGER SNAP	SUGAR
OATMEAL	SALT
SUGAR	VANILLA
OATMEAL	FLOUR

UNION ALL OPERATION

```
SELECT ingredient FROM cakes
UNION ALL
SELECT ingredient FROM cookies
ORDER BY ingredient
```

RESULT DATA SET

INGREDIENT
BUTTER
BUTTER
FLOUR
FLOUR
SALT
SALT
SUGAR
SUGAR
SUGAR
SUGAR
VANILLA

Figure 5.8: A simple UNION ALL *operation*

- **INTERSECT**: The INTERSECT set operator combines the result data sets produced by two individual queries, removes all duplicate rows found, and then removes all records in the first result data set that do not have a matching record in the second result data set, leaving just the records that are found in both result data sets. Figure 5.9 illustrates how a simple INTERSECT operation works.

CAKES TABLE

TYPE	INGREDIENT
CHOCOLATE	SUGAR
CHEESECAKE	SUGAR
CHOCOLATE	FLOUR
POUND	SALT
FRUIT	BUTTER
POUND	BUTTER

COOKIES TABLE

TYPE	INGREDIENT
SUGAR	SUGAR
GINGER SNAP	SUGAR
OATMEAL	SALT
SUGAR	VANILLA
OATMEAL	FLOUR

INTERSECT OPERATION

```
SELECT ingredient FROM cakes
INTERSECT
SELECT ingredient FROM cookies
ORDER BY ingredient
```

RESULT DATA SET

INGREDIENT
FLOUR
SALT
SUGAR

Figure 5.9: A simple INTERSECT *operation*

- **INTERSECT ALL**: The INTERSECT ALL set operator combines the result data sets produced by two individual queries (retaining all duplicate rows found), and removes all records in the first result data set that do not have a matching record in the second result data set, leaving just the records that are found in both result data sets. Figure 5.10 illustrates how a simple INTERSECT ALL operation works.

CAKES TABLE

TYPE	INGREDIENT
CHOCOLATE	SUGAR
CHEESECAKE	SUGAR
CHOCOLATE	FLOUR
POUND	SALT
FRUIT	BUTTER
POUND	BUTTER

COOKIES TABLE

TYPE	INGREDIENT
SUGAR	SUGAR
GINGER SNAP	SUGAR
OATMEAL	SALT
SUGAR	VANILLA
OATMEAL	FLOUR

INTERSECT ALL OPERATION

```
SELECT ingredient FROM cakes
INTERSECT ALL
SELECT ingredient FROM cookies
ORDER BY ingredient
```

RESULT DATA SET

INGREDIENT
FLOUR
SALT
SUGAR
SUGAR

Figure 5.10: A simple INTERSECT ALL *operation*

- **EXCEPT**: The EXCEPT set operator combines the result data sets produced by two individual queries, removes all duplicate rows found, and then removes all records in the first result data set that have a matching record in the second result data set, leaving just the records not found in both result data sets. Figure 5.11 illustrates how a simple EXCEPT operation works.

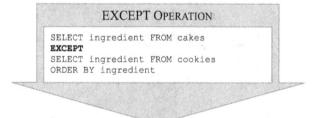

CAKES TABLE

TYPE	INGREDIENT
CHOCOLATE	SUGAR
CHEESECAKE	SUGAR
CHOCOLATE	FLOUR
POUND	SALT
FRUIT	BUTTER
POUND	BUTTER

COOKIES TABLE

TYPE	INGREDIENT
SUGAR	SUGAR
GINGER SNAP	SUGAR
OATMEAL	SALT
SUGAR	VANILLA
OATMEAL	FLOUR

EXCEPT OPERATION

```
SELECT ingredient FROM cakes
EXCEPT
SELECT ingredient FROM cookies
ORDER BY ingredient
```

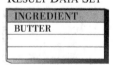

RESULT DATA SET

INGREDIENT
BUTTER

Figure 5.11: A simple EXCEPT *operation*

- **EXCEPT ALL:** The EXCEPT ALL set operator combines the result data sets produced by two individual queries (retaining all duplicate rows found), and removes all records in the first result data set that have a matching record in the second result data set, leaving just the records not found in both result data sets. Figure 5.12 illustrates how a simple EXCEPT ALL operation works.

CAKES TABLE

TYPE	INGREDIENT
CHOCOLATE	SUGAR
CHEESECAKE	SUGAR
CHOCOLATE	FLOUR
POUND	SALT
FRUIT	BUTTER
POUND	BUTTER

COOKIES TABLE

TYPE	INGREDIENT
SUGAR	SUGAR
GINGER SNAP	SUGAR
OATMEAL	SALT
SUGAR	VANILLA
OATMEAL	FLOUR

EXCEPT ALL OPERATION

```
SELECT ingredient FROM cakes
EXCEPT ALL
SELECT ingredient FROM cookies
ORDER BY ingredient
```

RESULT DATA SET

INGREDIENT
BUTTER
BUTTER

Figure 5.12: A simple EXCEPT ALL operation

It is important to note that, unlike when the UNION, UNION ALL, INTERSECT, and INTERSECT ALL set operators are used, the order in which queries are combined when the EXCEPT or EXCEPT ALL set operators are used is essential. Reversing the order of the queries when using the EXCEPT or EXCEPT ALL set operators will produce a very different result data set. Figure 5.13 illustrates how the EXCEPT operation presented earlier will produce a completely different result data set if the order of the queries specified are reversed.

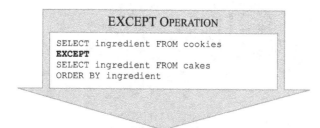

COOKIES TABLE

TYPE	INGREDIENT
SUGAR	SUGAR
GINGER SNAP	SUGAR
OATMEAL	SALT
SUGAR	VANILLA
OATMEAL	FLOUR

CAKES TABLE

TYPE	INGREDIENT
CHOCOLATE	SUGAR
CHEESECAKE	SUGAR
CHOCOLATE	FLOUR
POUND	SALT
FRUIT	BUTTER
POUND	BUTTER

EXCEPT OPERATION

```
SELECT ingredient FROM cookies
EXCEPT
SELECT ingredient FROM cakes
ORDER BY ingredient
```

RESULT DATA SET

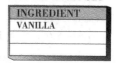

INGREDIENT
VANILLA

Figure 5.13: A simple EXCEPT operation with the order of the queries reversed

So, when might you want to combine the results of two queries using a set operator? Suppose your company keeps employee expense account information in a table whose contents are archived at the end of each fiscal year. (When a new fiscal year begins, expenditures for that year are recorded in a new table.) Now suppose, for tax purposes, you need a record of all employees' expenses for the past two years.

To obtain this information, each archived table must be queried, and the results must be combined. You can do this in a number of ways, but the easiest way by far is to query both archived tables and combine the results using the UNION set operator.

Using a Cursor to Obtain Results from a Result Data Set

Earlier, I mentioned that you can execute SQL statements interactively using tools such as Data Studio and the DB2 CLP. I have also pointed out that SQL statements can be embedded in high-level programming language source code files. However, the way in which a query is executed from within an application program is significantly different from the way in which it is executed from Data Studio or the CLP.

When a SELECT statement is executed from within an application program, DB2 uses a mechanism known as a *cursor* to retrieve data values from the result data set produced. The name *cursor* probably originated from the blinking cursor found on early computer screens. And just as that cursor indicated the current position on the screen, a DB2 cursor points to the current position in a result data set (that is, the current row). Depending upon how it is defined, a cursor can fall under one of the following categories:

- **Read-only:** Cursors that have been constructed in such a way that rows in the result data set they are associated with can be read but not modified or deleted; a cursor is considered read-only if it is based on a read-only SELECT statement (the statement "SELECT deptno FROM department" is an example of a SELECT statement that is considered read-only)
- **Updatable:** Cursors that have been constructed in such a way that rows in the result data set they are associated with can be modified or deleted; a cursor is considered updatable if the FOR UPDATE clause was specified when the cursor was created and if only one table was referenced in the SELECT statement that was used to create it
- **Ambiguous:** Cursors that have been constructed in such a way that it is impossible to tell whether they are meant to be read-only or updatable (ambiguous cursors are treated as read-only cursors if the BLOCKING ALL option was specified at the time the application that created the cursor was precompiled or bound to a database; otherwise, they are considered updatable)

Regardless of which type of cursor you use, to incorporate a cursor into an application program, you must perform the following steps, in the order shown:

1. Declare (define) the cursor along with its type and associate it with a query (that is, a SELECT or VALUES statement).
2. Open the cursor. This will cause the corresponding query to be executed and a result data set to be produced.
3. Retrieve (fetch) each row in the result data set, one by one, until an "End of data" condition occurs—each time a row is retrieved (fetched), the cursor is automatically moved to the next row.
4. If appropriate, alter or delete the current row by executing an UPDATE ... WHERE CURRENT OF or a DELETE ... WHERE CURRENT OF statement (but only if the cursor is updatable).
5. Close the cursor. This will delete the result data set that was produced when the cursor was first opened.

With DB2 (as well as with most other relational database management systems), the following SQL statements are used to carry out these steps:

- DECLARE CURSOR
- OPEN
- FETCH
- CLOSE

The DECLARE CURSOR Statement

Before you can use a cursor in an application program, you must first create it and associate it with a SELECT statement that will be used to generate a result data set. This is done by executing a DECLARE CURSOR statement; the basic syntax for this statement is:

```
DECLARE CURSOR [CursorName]
  <[WITHOUT | WITH] HOLD>
  <WITHOUT RETURN | WITH RETURN <TO CLIENT | TO CALLER>>
  FOR [SELECTStatement <FOR READ ONLY | FOR FETCH ONLY |
    FOR UPDATE <OF [ColumnName, ...]>> | StatementName]
```

where:

CursorName   Identifies the name to assign to the cursor that is to be created

SELECTStatement	Identifies a SELECT statement that, when executed, will produce a result data set that will be associated with the cursor that is to be created
StatementName	Identifies a prepared SELECT statement that, when executed, will produce a result data set that will be associated with the cursor that is to be created—this SELECT statement can contain parameter markers; however, it must have been prepared with the PREPARE statement before it can be used to create a result data set for the cursor
ColumnName	Identifies the name of one or more columns found in the result data set produced whose values can be modified by performing a positioned update or positioned delete operation; each name provided must identify an existing column in the result data set produced

•••

Note: The clauses FOR READ ONLY, FOR FETCH ONLY, and FOR UPDATE <OF [*ColumnName*, ...]> are actually part of the SELECT statement used to build the result data set the cursor will be associated with; they are not part of the DECLARE CURSOR statement's syntax. The use (or lack) of these clauses determines whether the resulting cursor will be read-only, updatable, or ambiguous.

•••

If the WITH HOLD clause is specified with the DECLARE CURSOR statement used, after the cursor that was created is opened, it will remain open across transaction boundaries and must be explicitly closed. (When this clause is not used, the scope of the cursor is limited to the transaction in which it is defined, and the cursor will be closed automatically when the transaction that created it ends.)

If the WITH RETURN clause is specified, it is assumed that the cursor will be opened from a stored procedure, and once opened, the cursor will remain open when control is passed back to either the calling application (if the WITH RETURN TO CALLER clause was specified) or to the client application (if the WITH RETURN TO CLIENT clause was used).

Therefore, to create a read-only cursor named MY_CURSOR and associate it with a result data set that contains just the first and last name of all employees found the EMPLOYEE table presented earlier (when we began our discussion about the SELECT statement), you could execute a DECLARE CURSOR statement that looks like this:

```
DECLARE my_cursor CURSOR
SELECT fname, lname FROM employee
FOR READ ONLY
```

Multiple cursors can be declared (created) within a single application; however, each cursor that is defined within the same source code file must be assigned a unique name.

The OPEN Statement

When you define a cursor (using the DECLARE CURSOR statement), the result data set associated with that cursor is not actually produced until the cursor is opened. A cursor can be opened at any time (after it is defined) by executing the OPEN statement. The basic syntax for this statement is:

```
OPEN [CursorName]
  <USING [HostVariable], ... |
  USING DESCRIPTOR [DescriptorName]>
```

where:

CursorName	Identifies, by name, the cursor that is to be opened
HostVariable	Identifies one or more host variables that are to provide values for parameter markers that were coded in the prepared SELECT statement that, when executed, will produce a result data set that will be associated with the cursor; host variables and parameter markers provide dynamic information to the DB2 Optimizer when an SQL statement is executed
DescriptorName	Identifies an SQL Descriptor Area (SQLDA) data structure variable that contains descriptions of the host variables that are to be used to provide values for parameter markers that were coded in the prepared SELECT statement that, when executed, will produce a result data set that will be associated with the cursor

Thus, to open a predefined cursor named MY_CURSOR (which, in turn, causes the result data set that is associated with the cursor to be produced), you would execute an OPEN statement that looks like this:

```
OPEN my_cursor
```

On the other hand, to open a cursor named MY_CURSOR and provide values (using host variables named FIRSTNAME and LASTNAME) for two parameter markers that were coded in the SELECT statement that was prepared and then associated with the cursor being opened, you would execute an OPEN statement that looks more like this:

```
OPEN my_cursor USING :firstname, :lastname
```

It is important to note that once a cursor is opened, it can be in one of three positions: "Before a Row of Data," "On a Row of Data," or "After the Last Row of Data." A cursor positioned "Before a Row of Data" is placed immediately before the first row of data in the result data set, and data values stored in that row will be assigned to the appropriate host variables when the FETCH statement (which we will look at next) is executed.

Once a FETCH statement is executed, the cursor will be positioned "On a Row of Data," and subsequent executions of the FETCH statement will cause the cursor to move to the next row in the result data set (if one exists)—each time the cursor moves, data values stored in the new row are automatically transferred to the appropriate host variables. If a cursor is positioned on the last row of the result data set when the FETCH statement is executed, it is moved to the "After the Last Row of Data" position, the value +100 (which means NOT FOUND) is assigned to the *sqlcode* field of the current SQLCA data structure variable, and the value 02000 is assigned to the *sqlstate* field of the same variable. No data is copied to the associated host variables because the cursor no longer sits on a valid row.

The FETCH Statement

After a cursor has been opened, data stored in its associated result data set can be retrieved by repeatedly calling the FETCH statement. The basic syntax for this statement is:

```
FETCH <FROM> [CursorName] INTO [HostVariable, ...]
```

or

```
FETCH <FROM> [CursorName] USING DESCRIPTOR [DescriptorName]
```

where:

CursorName	Identifies, by name, the cursor data is to be retrieved from
HostVariable	Identifies one or more host variables that values obtained from the result data set associated with the specified cursor are to be copied to
DescriptorName	Identifies an SQLDA data structure variable that contains descriptions of each host variable that values obtained from the result data set associated with the specified cursor are to be copied to

So, to retrieve a record from the result data set associated with a cursor named MY_CURSOR and copy the values obtained to host variables named DEPTNO and DEPTNAME, you could execute a FETCH statement that looks like this:

```
FETCH FROM my_cursor CURSOR INTO :deptno, :deptname
```

The CLOSE Statement

After all the records stored in the result data set associated with a cursor have been retrieved, or when the result data set associated with a cursor is no longer needed, it can be destroyed (along with the cursor) by executing the CLOSE statement. The syntax for this statement is:

```
CLOSE [CursorName]
  <WITH RELEASE>
```

where:

CursorName	Identifies, by name, the cursor to close

If the WITH RELEASE clause is specified with the CLOSE statement used, an attempt will be made to release all locks that were acquired on behalf of the cursor. (It is important to note that not all of the locks acquired are necessarily released; some locks might be held for other operations or activities.)

Note: The WITH RELEASE clause is available only with DB2 for Linux, UNIX, and Windows; it cannot be used with DB2 for z/OS.

Thus, to close a cursor named MY_CURSOR and destroy its associated result data set, you would execute a CLOSE statement that looks like this:

```
CLOSE my_cursor
```

Putting It All Together

Now that we have seen how to use each of the cursor-processing SQL statements available, let us examine how they are typically coded in an Embedded SQL application. An application written in the C programming language that uses a cursor to obtain and print employee identification numbers and last names for all employees who have the title of "Database Administrator" might look something like this:

```c
#include <stdio.h>
#include <stdlib.h>
#include <sql.h>

void main()
{
    /* Include The SQLCA Data Structure Variable */
    EXEC SQL INCLUDE SQLCA;

    /* Declare The SQL Host Memory Variables */
    EXEC SQL BEGIN DECLARE SECTION;
        int    EmployeeNo = 0;
        char   LastName[12];
    EXEC SQL END DECLARE SECTION;
                                                  Continued
```

```
/* Connect To The TEST Database */
EXEC SQL CONNECT TO test USER db2admin USING ibmdb2;

/* Declare A Cursor */
EXEC SQL DECLARE c1 CURSOR FOR
    SELECT empno, lname
    FROM employee
    WHERE title = 'DATABASE ADMINISTRATOR';

/* Open The Cursor */
EXEC SQL OPEN c1;

/* Fetch The Records Returned (Into Host Variables) */
while (sqlca.sqlcode == SQL_RC_OK)
{
    /* Retrieve A Record */
    EXEC SQL FETCH c1
        INTO :EmployeeNo, :LastName;

    /* Print The Information Retrieved */
    if (sqlca.sqlcode == SQL_RC_OK)
        printf("%d, %s\n", EmployeeNo, LastName);
}

/* Close The Cursor */
EXEC SQL CLOSE c1;

/* Issue A COMMIT To Free All Locks */
EXEC SQL COMMIT;
```

Continued

```
    /* Disconnect From The TEST Database */
    EXEC SQL DISCONNECT CURRENT;

    /* Return Control To The Operating System */
    return;
}
```

Keep in mind that an application can use several cursors concurrently. However, each cursor used must have a unique name, along with its own set of DECLARE CURSOR, OPEN, FETCH, and CLOSE SQL statements.

Working with Temporal (Time Travel) Tables

In Chapter 4, "Working with Databases and Database Objects," we saw how temporal tables can be used to manage multiple versions of data, as well as track effective dates for data that is subject to changing business conditions. We also saw that three different types of temporal tables are available: system-period, application-period, and bitemporal (which is a combination of the other two).

For the most part, the syntax and semantics of the INSERT, UPDATE, and DELETE statements presented earlier remain the same when used in conjunction with temporal tables. Thus, to add a record to a system-period temporal table named POLICY that has the following characteristics:

Column Name	Data Type
POLICYNUM	INTEGER
TYPE	CHAR(10)
COVERAGE	INTEGER
DEDUCTIBLE	INTEGER
SYS_START	TIMESTAMP(12)
SYS_END	TIMESTAMP(12)
TRANS_START	TIMESTAMP(12)

you could execute an INSERT statement that looks like this:

```
INSERT INTO policy (policynum, type, coverage, deductible)
    VALUES (1001, 'HOME', 350000, 500)
```

And if you wanted to change a record stored in the POLICY table such that the deductible for policy number 1001 is increased from $500.00 to $2,000.00, you could execute an UPDATE statement that looks like this:

```
UPDATE policy
  SET deductible = 2000
  WHERE policynum = 1001
```

Similarly, to add a record to an application-period temporal table named LOAN that has the following characteristics:

Column Name	Data Type
ACCTNUM	INTEGER
PRINCIPAL	INTEGER
RATE	DOUBLE
BUS_START	DATE
BUS_END	DATE

you could execute an INSERT statement that looks like this:

```
INSERT INTO loan
    VALUES (1000, 30000, 6.25, '14-07-01', '18-07-01')
```

And to remove the record for account number 5000 from the LOAN table, you would execute a DELETE statement that looks like this:

```
DELETE FROM loan
    WHERE acctnum = 5000
```

One significant difference between performing update and delete operations on traditional tables and performing similar operations on application-period and bitemporal

temporal tables is that with these types of temporal tables, you have the ability to change the values of one or more columns *for a specific period of time*. This is done by including the FOR PORTION OF BUSINESS_TIME FROM ... TO ... clause with the UPDATE or DELETE statement used. For example, to modify the record for account number 1000 that is stored in the LOAN table presented earlier in such a way that the interest rate is reduced from 6.25 percent to 5 percent *for the first six months of the loan*, you would execute an UPDATE statement that looks like this:

```
UPDATE loan
  FOR PORTION OF BUSINESS_TIME
    FROM '2014-07-01' TO '2014-12-01'
  SET rate = 5.0
  WHERE policynum = 1000
```

(Notice that the FOR PORTION OF BUSINESS_TIME FROM ... TO ... clause in this example—otherwise known as the *temporal restriction*—appears after the table name and not as part of the WHERE clause.)

Querying System-Period Temporal Tables

As with the other DML statements, when the SELECT statement is used to query temporal tables, the syntax and semantics remains essentially the same. One significant difference, however, is that SELECT statements that query system-period temporal tables can contain one of the following system time-period specifications:

- **FOR SYSTEM_TIME AS OF [*Timestamp*]**: Lets you query data as of a specific point in time
- **FOR SYSTEM_TIME FROM [*Timestamp*] TO [*Timestamp*]**: Lets you query data from one point in time to another—DB2 uses an *inclusive-exclusive* approach for this time-period specification, which means that the period specified begins at the start time provided and ends just prior to the end time provided; thus, a time-period specification of January 1, 2014 to February 1, 2014 would indicate a range from 12:00 a.m. on January 1, 2014 until 11:59 p.m. on January 31, 2014; February 1, 2014 is not included in the range
- **FOR SYSTEM_TIME BETWEEN [*Timestamp*] AND [*Timestamp*]**: Lets you query data between a start time and an end time—DB2 uses an *inclusive-inclusive* approach

for this time-period specification, which means that the period begins at the start
time provided and ends at the end time provided

To see only data that is current, simply construct a SELECT statement that does not
contain one of these time-period specifications. For example, to find out what the
deductible is for policy number 1001 *right now*, you could query the POLICY table
presented earlier with a SELECT statement that looks like this:

```
SELECT deductible
  FROM policy
  WHERE policynum = 1001
```

However, to see historical data, you will need to include an appropriate system time-
period specification in your query. For example, to determine what the deductible *was* for
policy number 1001 *at 12:30 a.m. on July 24, 2014*, you would need to query the POLICY
table presented earlier with a SELECT statement that looks like this:

```
SELECT deductible
  FROM policy
  FOR SYSTEM_TIME AS OF TIMESTAMP('2014-07-24-12.30.00')
  WHERE policynum = 1001
```

To resolve this query, DB2 will transparently access the POLICY table's history
table to retrieve the information requested. (In Chapter 4, "Working with Databases
and Database Objects," we saw that each system-period temporal table must have a
corresponding history table. For the sake of this example, assume that the POLICY table
presented earlier has a history table named POLICY_HISTORY.) Note that the history
table itself is not referenced in the query; the FOR SYSTEM_TIME AS OF time-period
specification causes DB2 to automatically look in the associated history table for the
information being sought.

Querying Application-Period Temporal Tables

Querying application-period temporal tables is also relatively straightforward—if you
are not concerned with obtaining temporal information, the syntax and semantics of the

SELECT statement used remains essentially the same. However, if you want to retrieve past, current, or future data values, you will need to construct a SELECT statement that contains one of the following business time-period specifications:

- **FOR BUSINESS_TIME AS OF [*Timestamp*]**: Lets you query data as of a specific point in time
- **FOR BUSINESS_TIME FROM [*Timestamp*] TO [*Timestamp*]**: Lets you query data from one point in time to another—DB2 uses an *inclusive-exclusive* approach for this time-period specification, which means that the period specified begins at the start time provided and ends just prior to the end time provided
- **FOR BUSINESS_TIME BETWEEN [*Timestamp*] AND [*Timestamp*]**: Lets you query data between a start time and an end time—DB2 uses an *inclusive-inclusive* approach for this time-period specification, which means that the period begins at the start time provided and ends at the end time provided

To see how these time specifications work, consider a scenario in which the LOAN table presented earlier is populated as shown in Table 5.3.

Table 5.3: Data initially stored in the LOAN table				
ACCTNUM	PRINCIPAL	RATE	BUS_START	BUS_END
1000	30000	6.25	06/01/2014	12/30/9999
1001	350000	3.5	07/01/2014	12/30/9999

If the following UPDATE statement is used to reduce the interest rate on account number 1000 from 6.25 percent to 5 percent for the first six months of the loan:

```
UPDATE loan
  FOR PORTION OF BUSINESS_TIME
    FROM '2014-07-01' TO '2014-12-01'
  SET rate = 5.0
  WHERE policynum = 1000
```

the LOAN table presented earlier will be populated as shown in Table 5.4.

Table 5.4: Data stored in the LOAN table after updating the record for account number 1000				
ACCTNUM	PRINCIPAL	RATE	BUS_START	BUS_END
1000	30000	5.0	06/01/2014	12/01/2014
1000	30000	6.25	12/02/2014	12/30/9999
1001	350000	3.5	07/01/2014	12/30/9999

To see how many records exist in the LOAN table for account number 1000 after the desired change is made, you could execute a SELECT statement that looks like this:

```
SELECT COUNT(*) AS num_records
  FROM loan
  WHERE acctnum = 1000
```

Because this query does not contain a business time-period specification, when it is executed you should get a result data set that looks like this:

```
NUM_RECORDS
-----------
          2

1 record(s) selected.
```

Now, suppose you want to retrieve information about the loan for account number 1000 *as it will be structured on November 18, 2014*. To obtain this information, you will need to query the LOAN table presented earlier using a SELECT statement that looks something like this:

```
SELECT principal, DECIMAL(rate, 4, 2) AS rate
  FROM loan
  FOR BUSINESS_TIME AS OF '2014-11-18'
  WHERE acctnum = 1000
```

And when this statement is executed, you should get a result data set that looks like this (provided the LOAN table is populated as shown in Table 5.4):

```
PRINCIPAL   RATE
----------- ------
     30000   5.00

  1 record(s) selected.
```

Had you not provided the FOR BUSINESS_TIME AS OF '2014-11-18' business time-period specification with the SELECT statement used, the result data set produced would have looked like this:

```
PRINCIPAL   RATE
----------- ------
     30000   5.00
     30000   6.25

  2 record(s) selected.
```

Querying Bitemporal Temporal Tables

If you want to query a bitemporal temporal table, you have the option of constructing a SELECT statement that:

- Does not contain any time-period specifications
- Contains a system time-period specification only
- Contains a business time-period specification only
- Contains both a system time-period specification *and* a business time-period specification

Regardless of the option you choose, the syntax and semantics of the SELECT statement used will be the same as that used to query the other types of temporal tables. If appropriate, you can construct a SELECT statement that contains both a system time-period specification and a business time-period specification.

Working with XML Data

You may recall that in Chapter 2, "Planning," we saw that DB2's pureXML technology unlocks the latent potential of XML by providing simple, efficient access to XML data, while offering the same levels of security, integrity, and resiliency that has always been available for relational data. With pureXML, XML data is stored in a hierarchical structure that naturally reflects the structure of XML documents. The ability to store XML data in its native structure, along with innovative indexing techniques, means that DB2 can efficiently manage XML documents while eliminating the complex and time-consuming parsing that is typically required to store XML data in a relational database.

To store XML data in its native format, DB2 Version 9 for Linux, UNIX, and Windows introduced a new data type—the XML data type. As the name implies, this data type is used to define columns that will be used to store well-formed XML documents, which typically look something like this:

```
<?xml version="1.0" encoding="UTF-8" ?>
<customerinfo>
  <name>John Doe</name>
  <addr country="United States">
    <street>25 East Creek Drive</street>
    <city>Raleigh</city>
    <state-prov>North Carolina</state-prov>
    <zip-pcode>27603</zip-pcode>
  </addr>
  <phone type="work">919-555-1212</phone>
  <email>john.doe@xyz.com</email>
</customerinfo>
```

Most XML documents begin with an XML and version encoding declaration. In the preceding XML document, the XML version and encoding declaration is the line that looks like this:

```
<?xml version="1.0" encoding="UTF-8" ?>
```

This is normally followed by one or more *elements* and *attributes*. XML elements are enclosed with opening and closing tags and look something like this:

```
<name>John Doe</name>
<email>john.doe@xyz.com</email>
```

Important: Opening and closing tags are case-sensitive—the tag <Letter> is different from the tag <letter>. Therefore, opening and closing tags must be written using the same case.

Similar to XML elements, XML attributes describe XML elements or provide additional information about a particular element. XML attributes are always contained within the opening tag of an element, and attribute values are always enclosed with double quotation marks (""). The attributes found in the XML document just presented are:

```
<addr country="United States">
<phone type="work">919-555-1212</phone>
```

As with relational data, DML statements can be used to store, alter, and delete XML data, as well as retrieve XML data values from tables and views. Thus, to add a record containing the XML document presented earlier to a table named CUSTOMER that has the following characteristics:

Column Name	Data Type
CUSTID	INTEGER
CUSTINFO	XML

you could execute an INSERT statement that looks something like this:

```
INSERT INTO customer
  VALUES (10,
      '<?xml version="1.0" encoding="UTF-8" ?>
      <customerinfo>
      <name>John Doe</name>
      <addr country="United States">
        <street>25 East Creek Drive</street>
        <city>Raleigh</city>
        <state-prov>North Carolina</state-prov>
        <zip-pcode>27603</zip-pcode>
      </addr>
      <phone type="work">919-555-1212</phone>
      <email>john.doe@xyz.com</email>
    </customerinfo>')
```

And to update only the XML data portion of this record, you could execute an UPDATE
statement that looks like this:

```
UPDATE customer
  SET custinfo =
      '<?xml version="1.0" encoding="UTF-8" ?>
    <customerinfo>
      <name>Jane Doe</name>
      <addr country="Canada">
        <street>8200 Warden Avenue</street>
        <city>Markham</city>
        <state-prov>Ontario</state-prov>
        <zip-pcode> L6G 1C7</zip-pcode>
      </addr>
      <phone type="work">905-555-3434</phone>
      <email>jane.doe@xyz.com</email>
    </customerinfo>'
  WHERE CUSTID = 10
```

Finally, to delete this record from the CUSTOMER table, you would execute a DELETE statement that looks something like this:

```
DELETE FROM customer
WHERE
  XMLEXISTS('$info/customerinfo[name/text()="Jane Doe"]'
  PASSING custinfo AS "info")
```

So how do you retrieve XML data after it has been stored in a table? One way is by using SQL. The SQL:2003 and SQL:2006 language standards include a variety of functions and features for working with XML data. This functionality is commonly referred to as SQL/XML and some of the SQL/XML functions that are frequently used with DB2 are:

- **XMLPARSE()**: Parses a character string value and returns a well-formed XML document
- **XMLSERIALIZE()**: Converts a well-formed XML document into a character string or large object value
- **XMLTEXT()**: Returns an XML value with a single XQuery text node
- **XMLTABLE()**: Returns a result data set, in the form of a table, from an XQuery expression—the table returned can contain columns of any SQL data type, including XML; the structure of the table is defined by the COLUMNS clause of the XMLTABLE() function, and the data in the table can be used to populate other base tables
- **XMLEXISTS()**: Determines whether an XQuery expression returns a sequence of one or more items—the XMLEXISTS() predicate can be used in the WHERE clause of an UPDATE, DELETE, or SELECT statement to include or exclude specific rows from the operation being performed
- **XMLVALIDATE()**: Performs an XML schema validation operation
- **XMLQUERY()**: Returns an XML value from the evaluation of an XQuery expression

Using one or more of these SQL/XML functions, you can combine XPath expressions (a query language for selecting nodes from an XML document) with familiar SQL statements to retrieve information stored XML columns. You can also retrieve XML data using *XQuery*—a functional programming language designed by the World Wide

Web Consortium (W3C) to meet specific requirements for querying XML data. XQuery consists of several different kinds of expressions, which can be combined to create more sophisticated expressions than are available with XPath alone. Some of the most important XQuery expressions available include:

- **Path:** Expressions that are used to locate nodes, such as elements and attributes, from the tree structure of an XML document
- **FLWOR:** Expressions that are used to iterate over the items in a sequence and bind variables to intermediate query results (the acronym FLWOR—pronounced *flower*—is based on the keywords for, let, where, order by, and return)
- **Constructor:** Expressions that are used to create nodes, such as elements and attributes, which can then be used to build new XML documents within a query
- **Cast:** Expressions that are used to convert values from one data type to another
- **Arithmetic:** Expressions that are used to perform addition (+), subtraction (-), multiplication (*), division (div), integer division (idiv), and modulus (mod) operations
- **Comparison, logical, and conditional:** Expressions that are used to formulate predicates to search for specific information
- **Sequence:** Expressions that are used to construct and combine sequences
- **Transform:** Expressions that are used to update or transform existing XML documents

Of these, the FLWOR expression is one of the most powerful and therefore the most frequently used. (This expression is comparable to the SELECT-FROM-WHERE statement/ clause combination available with SQL.) The basic syntax for a FLWOR expression is:

```
XQUERY
  for $Variable1 IN Expression1
  let $Variable2 := Expression2
  where Expression3
  order by Expression4 [ASCENDING | DESCENDING]
  return Expression3
```

Thus, to retrieve customer names for all customers who reside in North Carolina from XML documents stored in the CUSTINFO column of the table named CUSTOMER presented earlier, you could execute an XQuery expression that looks something like this:

```
XQUERY
  for $info
  in db2-fn:xmlcolumn('CUSTOMER.CUSTINFO')/customerinfo
  where $info/addr/state-prov="North Carolina"
  return $info/name
```

Assuming the CUSTOMER table was populated by using the INSERT statement shown earlier, you should get a result data set that looks like this:

```
1
-------------------------------------------------------
<name>John Doe</name>
```

To remove the XML tags and return only the customer name, you would need to execute an XQuery expression that looks like this instead:

```
XQUERY
  for $info
  in db2-fn:xmlcolumn('CUSTOMER.CUSTINFO')/customerinfo
  where $info/addr/state-prov="North Carolina"
  return $info/name/text()
```

Consequently, the result data set produced when this XQuery expression is executed will look like this:

```
1
--------
John Doe
```

Working with User-Defined Functions (UDFs)

In Chapter 4, "Working with Databases and Database Objects," we saw that UDFs are special objects that can extend and enhance the built-in functions that are available with DB2. Unlike DB2's built-in functions, UDFs can take advantage of system calls and

DB2's administrative APIs (depending upon how they are constructed) to provide more synergy between applications, operating systems, and database environments. We also saw that several different types of UDFs can be created:

- **Sourced (or Template):** This function is based on another function (referred to as the *source function*) that already exists. Sourced functions can be columnar, scalar, or tabular in nature; they can also be designed to overload a specific operator such as +, -, *, and /. When a sourced function is invoked, all arguments passed to it are converted to the data types that the underlying source function expects, and the source function itself is invoked. Upon completion, the source function performs any conversions necessary on the results produced and returns them to the calling application.
- **SQL scalar:** This function's body is written entirely in SQL; an SQL scalar function returns a single value each time it is called.
- **SQL table:** This function's body is written entirely in SQL and SQL Procedural Language (SQL PL); an SQL table function returns a result data set, in the form of a table, each time it is called.
- **External Scalar:** This function—written in a high-level programming language such as C, C++, or Java—returns a single value each time it is called. The function itself resides in an external library and is registered in the database, along with any related attributes.
- **External Table:** This function—written in a high-level programming language— returns a result data set, in the form of a table, each time it is called. As with external scalar functions, the function itself resides in an external library and is registered in the database, along with any related attributes. External table functions can make almost any data source appear as a base table. Consequently, the result data set produced can be used in join operations, grouping operations, set operations, or any other operation that can be applied to a read-only view.
- **OLE DB External Table:** This function—written in a high-level programming language—can access data from an Object Linking and Embedding, Database (OLE DB) provider and return a result data set, in the form of a table, each time it is called. A generic built-in OLE DB consumer that is available with DB2 for Linux, UNIX, and Windows can be used to interface with any OLE DB provider; simply register an OLE DB table function with a database and

refer to the appropriate OLE DB provider as the data source—no additional programming is required.

Note: OLE DB external table functions are available with DB2 for Linux, UNIX, and Windows only; they cannot be created with DB2 for z/OS. To use OLE DB table functions with a DB2 for Linux, UNIX, and Windows database environment, you must install OLE DB 2.0 or later—which is available from Microsoft—on your database server. (Refer to your data source documentation for more information about the system requirements and OLE DB providers that are available for that data source.)

Creating SQL Scalar and SQL Table User-Defined Functions

UDFs are created (and registered with a database) with the CREATE FUNCTION statement. Several forms of this statement are available; the appropriate form to use is determined by the type of function you wish to create. The basic syntax for the form that is used to create an SQL function (either scalar or tabular) is:

```
CREATE FUNCTION [FunctionName]
  (<<ParameterName> [InputDataType], ...>)
  RETURNS [[OutputDataType]
  <LANGUAGE SQL>
  <SPECIFIC [SpecificName]>
  <DETERMINISTIC | NOT DETERMINISTIC>
  <EXTERNAL ACTION | NO EXTERNAL ACTION>
  <READS SQL DATA | CONTAINS SQL | MODIFIES SQL DATA>
  [SQLStatements] | RETURN [ReturnStatement]
```

or

```
CREATE FUNCTION [FunctionName]
  (<<ParameterName> [InputDataType], ...>)
  RETURNS TABLE ([ColumnName] [ColumnDataType], ...)
  <LANGUAGE SQL>
```

```
<SPECIFIC [SpecificName]>
<DETERMINISTIC | NOT DETERMINISTIC>
<EXTERNAL ACTION | NO EXTERNAL ACTION>
<CONTAINS SQL | READS SQL DATA | MODIFIES SQL DATA>
[SQLStatements] | RETURN [ReturnStatement]
```

where:

FunctionName	Identifies the name to assign to the function that is to be created
ParameterName	Identifies the name to assign to one or more function input parameters
InputDataType	Identifies the data type the function expects to receive for each input parameter specified (in the *ParameterName* parameter)
OutputDataType	Identifies the data type the function is expected to return
ColumnName	Identifies one or more names to assign to the column(s) the function is expected to return (if the function is designed to return a table)
ColumnDataType	Identifies the data type the function expects to return for each column specified (in the *ColumnName* parameter)
SpecificName	Identifies a specific name to assign to the function that is to be created; you can use this name to reference or delete (drop) the function, but not to invoke it
SQLStatements	Identifies one or more SQL statements that are to be executed when the function is invoked; together, these statements act as a single dynamic compound SQL statement—if two or more statements are used, they should be enclosed with the keywords BEGIN ATOMIC and END, and each statement must be terminated with a semicolon (;)
ReturnStatement	Identifies a RETURN statement that is to be used to return data to the user/application/statement that invoked the function

If the DETERMINISTIC clause is specified with the CREATE FUNCTION statement used, it is implied that the function will always return the same scalar value or table when it is called with the same parameter values. By contrast, if the NOT DETERMINISTIC clause is specified (or if neither clause is specified) it is assumed that the function can return different results each time it is called with the same set of values.

If the EXTERNAL ACTION clause is specified with the CREATE FUNCTION statement used, it is implied that the function will perform some type of action that will change the state of an object that DB2 does not manage (for example, appending data to an external file). If, however, the NO EXTERNAL ACTION clause is specified (or if neither clause is specified), it is assumed that no such actions will be performed.

The <CONTAINS SQL | READS SQL DATA | MODIFIES SQL DATA> clause identifies the types of SQL statements that can be coded in the body of the function. If you specify the CONTAINS SQL clause, the function cannot contain SQL statements that read or modify data. If you specify the READS SQL DATA clause, the function cannot contain SQL statements that modify data. And if you specify the MODIFIES SQL DATA clause, the function can contain SQL statements that both read and modify data.

Therefore, to create an SQL scalar function named CONVERT_CTOF() that accepts a temperature value in degrees Celsius as input and returns a corresponding temperature value in degrees Fahrenheit, you could execute a CREATE FUNCTION statement that looks something like this:

```
CREATE FUNCTION convert_ctof (temp_c FLOAT)
  RETURNS INTEGER
  LANGUAGE SQL
  SPECIFIC convert_temp
  DETERMINISTIC
  RETURN INT((temp_c * 1.8) + 32)
```

On the other hand, to create an SQL table function named DEPT_EMPLOYEES() that accepts a department code as input and returns a result data set, in the form of a table, that contains basic information about each employee who works in the department specified, you would execute a CREATE FUNCTION statement that looks more like this:

```
CREATE FUNCTION dept_employees (deptno CHAR(3))
  RETURNS TABLE (empno CHAR(6),
                 fname CHAR(10),
                 lname CHAR(10))
  LANGUAGE SQL
                                                Continued
```

```
SPECIFIC dept_employees
DETERMINISTIC
NO EXTERNAL ACTION
READS SQL DATA
BEGIN ATOMIC
  RETURN
    SELECT empno, fname, lname
      FROM employee AS e
        WHERE e.dept = dept_employees.deptno;
END
```

Invoking SQL Scalar and SQL Table User-Defined Functions

How a UDF is invoked depends, in part, on what it is designed to do. Scalar UDFs are typically invoked as an expression in the select list of a query, whereas table functions must be referenced in the FROM clause of a SELECT statement. For example, suppose you have a base table named CLIMATE that has the following characteristics:

Column Name	Data Type
REGION	CHAR(15)
AVG_TEMP_C	FLOAT

To use the SQL scalar function named CONVERT_CTOF() that was created earlier to convert values found in the AVG_TEMP_C column of this table from degrees Celsius to degrees Fahrenheit, you could execute a SELECT statement that looks like this:

```
SELECT region, convert_ctof(avg_temp_c) AS avg_temp_f
  FROM climate
```

When this statement is executed, the result data set produced should look something like this (assuming the values for AVG_TEMP_C were originally –11 and 36 degrees Celsius, respectively):

```
REGION            AVG_TEMP_F

---------------   -----------

North                    12
South                    96


   2 record(s) selected.
```

Or, if you want use the SQL table function named DEPT_EMPLOYEES() that was created earlier to obtain a list of employees who work in development (the department that has been assigned the code 'C01'), you would execute a SELECT statement that looks like this:

```
SELECT empno, fname, lname
   FROM TABLE(dept_employees('C01')) AS results
```

And when this statement is executed, you should get a result data set that looks like this (provided the EMPLOYEE table—which the DEPT_EMPLOYEES() function queries—is populated as shown in Table 5.2):

```
EMPNO   FNAME         LNAME

------  -----------   -----------

1002    HUMPHREY      BOGART
1003    INGRID        BERGMAN
1008    KATHARINE     HEPBURN


   3 record(s) selected.
```

Working with Stored Procedures

In Chapter 4, "Working with Databases and Database Objects," we saw that if an application contains transactions that perform a relatively large amount of database activity with little or no user interaction, those transactions can be stored separately on a database server in what are known as *stored procedures*. Stored procedures allow work that is done by one or more transactions to be encapsulated and stored in such a way that it can be executed directly at a server by *any* application or user who has been given the necessary authority.

Client/server applications that use stored procedures have the following advantages over client/server applications that do not:

- **Reduced network traffic:** Messages are not sent across the network for SQL statements coded in a stored procedure. Instead, only data that the client application requests is transferred.

- **Improved performance of server-intensive work:** Because less data must be sent across the network, and because processing occurs directly at the server, complex queries and other server-intensive work executes faster.

- **Ability to separate and reuse business logic:** When business rules are incorporated into stored procedures, the logic can be reused multiple times, simply by calling the procedure as needed. Consequently, the same business rule logic will be enforced across all applications. And because the logic used in a stored procedure can be modified independently, you can avoid having to recode applications when business rules change.

- **Ability to access features that exist only on the server:** Because stored procedures run directly on the database server workstation, they can exploit any extra memory, faster processors, and so forth that the database server might have. (Typically, database servers have more memory and multiple or faster processors than client workstations.) Additionally, stored procedures can take advantage of DB2's set of administrative APIs, which can only be run at the server. And, because stored procedures are not restricted to performing database-only activities, they can take advantage of any additional software that has been installed on the server.

Developing and Registering SQL Stored Procedures

Depending upon the DB2 Edition used (DB2 for Linux, UNIX, and Windows or DB2 for z/OS), up to three different types of stored procedures can be created:

- **SQL (or Native SQL):** A stored procedure whose body is written entirely in SQL or SQL PL

- **External SQL:** A stored procedure whose body is written entirely in SQL, but that is implemented as an external program (*this type of procedure is available with DB2 for z/OS only*)

- **External:** A stored procedure that is written in a high-level programming language such as Assembler, C, C++, COBOL, Java, REXX, or PL/I that resides in an external library that is accessible to DB2; external stored procedures must be registered in a database, along with all their related attributes, before they can be invoked

Regardless of whether stored procedures are written using SQL or a high-level programming language, they must perform the following tasks, in the order shown:

1. Accept any input parameter values the calling application supplies
2. Perform whatever processing is appropriate (typically, this involves executing one or more SQL statements within a single transaction)
3. Return output data (if data is to be returned) to the calling application—at a minimum, a stored procedure should return a value that indicates whether it executed successfully

Stored procedures are created by executing the CREATE PROCEDURE statement. Two forms of this statement are available (three, if you are using DB2 for z/OS), and the appropriate form to use is determined by the type of procedure that is to be created. The basic syntax for the form of the CREATE PROCEDURE statement that is used to create an SQL stored procedure looks something like this:

```
CREATE PROCEDURE [ProcedureName]
  <([ParameterType] [ParameterName] [DataType], ...)>
  <LANGUAGE SQL>
  <DYNAMIC RESULT SETS [0 | NumResultSets]>
  <DETERMINISTIC | NOT DETERMINISTIC>
  <CONTAINS SQL | READS SQL DATA | MODIFIES SQL DATA>
  [SQLStatements]
```

where:

ProcedureName	Identifies the name to assign to the procedure that is to be created
ParameterType	Indicates whether the parameter specified (in the *ParameterName* parameter) is an input parameter (IN), an output parameter (OUT), or both an input and an output parameter (INOUT)—*INOUT cannot*

	be used if the SQL procedure is being created for a DB2 for z/OS database
ParameterName	Identifies the name to assign to one or more procedure parameters
DataType	Identifies the data type of the parameter specified (in the *ParameterName* parameter)
NumResultSets	Identifies the number of result data sets the procedure returns (if any)
SQLStatements	Identifies one or more SQL statements (or SQL PL statements) that are to be executed when the function is invoked; together, these statements act as a single dynamic compound SQL statement—if two or more statements are used, they should be enclosed with the keywords BEGIN ATOMIC and END, and each statement must be terminated with a semicolon (;)

Many of the clauses that are used with this form of the CREATE PROCEDURE statement are similar to the clauses that are available with the CREATE FUNCTION statement. For instance, the DETERMINISTIC clause indicates that the procedure will always return the same value (or table) when it is called with the same parameter values. And the <CONTAINS SQL | READS SQL DATA | MODIFIES SQL DATA> clause identifies the types of SQL statements that can be coded in the body of the procedure. (If you specify the CONTAINS SQL clause, the procedure cannot contain SQL statements that read or modify data; if you designate the READS SQL DATA clause, the procedure cannot contain SQL statements that modify data; and if you specify the MODIFIES SQL DATA clause, the procedure can contain SQL statements that both read and modify data.)

Thus, to create an SQL procedure named HIGH_EARNERS() that returns a list of employees whose salary exceeds the average salary, along with the average employee salary (in the form of a result data set), you could execute a CREATE PROCEDURE statement that looks something like this:

```
CREATE PROCEDURE high_earners
    (OUT avgSalary INTEGER)
  LANGUAGE SQL
  DYNAMIC RESULT SETS 1
  NOT DETERMINISTIC
  READS SQL DATA
```

Continued

```
BEGIN
  DECLARE c1 CURSOR WITH RETURN FOR
    SELECT fname, lname, salary
      FROM employee
      WHERE salary > avgSalary
      ORDER BY salary DESC;

  DECLARE EXIT HANDLER FOR NOT FOUND
    SET avgSalary = 9999;

  SET avgSalary = 0;
  SELECT AVG(salary) INTO avgSalary
    FROM employee;

  OPEN c1;
END
```

When this statement particular CREATE PROCEDURE statement is executed, the SQL procedure produced will return an integer value (in an output parameter called AVGSALARY) and a result data set that contains the first name, last name, and salary of each employee whose salary is higher than the average salary. This is done by:

1. Specifying the DYNAMIC RESULT SETS 1 clause with the CREATE PROCEDURE statement used to indicate that the SQL procedure being created is to return a single result data set

2. Defining a cursor within the procedure body (and specifying the WITH RETURN FOR clause in the DECLARE CURSOR statement used) so a result data set can be returned

3. Querying the EMPLOYEE table using the AVG() scalar function to obtain average salary information

4. Opening the cursor (which causes the query that obtains employee salary information to be executed and a result data set to be produced)

5. Returning the average salary to the calling statement (in the output parameter named AVGSALARY) and leaving the cursor that was created open so the data in the result data set produced can be accessed by the calling application

Calling a Stored Procedure

Once a stored procedure has been created and registered with a database (via the CREATE PROCEDURE statement), it can be invoked from an interactive utility such as the DB2 CLP, from an application, or from another stored procedure. Stored procedures are invoked by executing the CALL statement; the basic syntax for this statement is:

CALL ()

or

CALL [*ProcedureName*]
  ([*InputParameter*] | [*OutputParameter*] | DEFAULT | NULL, ...)

where:

ProcedureName	Identifies, by name, the stored procedure that is to be invoked
InputParameter	Identifies one or more values (or host variables containing values) that are to be passed to the stored procedure as input parameters
OutputParameter	Identifies one or more host variables or parameter markers that are to receive values that will be returned as output from the stored procedure

Like other dynamic SQL statements that can be prepared and executed at runtime, CALL statements can contain parameter markers in place of constants and expressions. Parameter markers are represented by the question mark character (?) and indicate the position in an SQL statement where the current value of one or more host variables (or elements of an SQLDA data structure variable) are to be substituted when the statement is executed. Parameter markers are typically used where a host variable would be referenced if the SQL statement being executed were static.

Thus, you can invoke the SQL procedure named HIGH_EARNERS() that was created earlier, by connecting to the appropriate database and executing a CALL statement, from the DB2 CLP, that looks something like this:

```
CALL high_earners(?)
```

And when this statement is executed, you should get a result data set that looks like this (provided the EMPLOYEE table—which is queried by the HIGH_EARNERS procedure—is populated as shown in Table 5.2):

```
Value of output parameters
---------------------------
Parameter Name   : AVGSALARY
Parameter Value  : 82616



Result set 1
---------------


FNAME       LNAME       SALARY
----------  ----------  ----------
JAMES       DEAN          158096.00
JAMES       CAGNEY        105787.00
MARILYN     MONROE        103675.00
HUMPHREY    BOGART         88192.00

4 record(s) selected.
Return Status = 0
```

To invoke the same procedure from an Embedded SQL application, you could execute a static CALL statement that looks more like this:

```
CALL high_earners(:avgSalary)
```

Here, :avgSalary is the name of a host variable that has been defined with an appropriate data type (for example, double avgSalary = 0;).

And finally, the HIGH_EARNERS() SQL procedure could be invoked from within another SQL procedure by coding a DECLARE statement and a CALL statement in the body of the procedure that looks something like this:

```
DECLARE v_avgsalary INTEGER;
...
CALL high_earners(v_avgsalary);
```

Transactions and Transaction Boundaries

A *transaction* (also known as a *unit of work*) is a sequence of one or more SQL operations that are grouped as a single unit, usually within an application process. Such a unit is considered *atomic* (from the Greek word meaning "not able to be cut," because it is indivisible—either all of a transaction's work is carried out, or none of its work is carried out.

A given transaction can perform any number of SQL operations, depending upon what is considered a single step within a company's business logic. With that said, it is important to note that the longer a transaction is—that is, the more SQL operations a transaction contains—the more problematic it can be to manage. This is especially true if multiple transactions must run concurrently.

The initiation and termination of a single transaction defines points of consistency within a database (we will take a closer look at data consistency in Chapter 7, "Data Concurrency"). Consequently, either the effects of all operations performed within a transaction are applied to the database and made permanent (committed), or they are backed out (rolled back) and the database is returned to the state it was in immediately before the transaction was initiated. (Any data pages that were copied to a buffer pool on behalf of a transaction will remain in the buffer pool until their storage space is needed— at that time, they will be removed.)

Normally, a transaction is initiated the first time an SQL statement is executed after a connection to a database has been established, or when a new SQL statement is executed after a running transaction ends. Once transactions are initiated, they can be implicitly terminated using a feature known as *automatic commit* (in which case, each executable SQL statement is treated as a single transaction, and changes made by that statement are either applied to the database or discarded, depending on whether the statement executed successfully). Transactions can also be explicitly terminated by executing either a COMMIT or a ROLLBACK statement. The basic syntax for these two statements is:

```
COMMIT <WORK>
```

and

```
ROLLBACK <WORK>
```

When the COMMIT statement is used to terminate a transaction, all changes made to the database since the transaction began are made permanent. When the ROLLBACK statement is used instead, all changes made are backed out, and the database is returned to the state it was in just before the transaction was started. (In either case, any locks that were acquired on behalf of the terminating transaction are released.) Figure 5.14 shows what happens when a COMMIT statement is used to terminate a transaction. Figure 5.15 illustrates what happens when a ROLLBACK statement is used to end a transaction instead.

EMPLOYEE TABLE

(Before the transaction)

EMPNO	LNAME	DEPT
1000	DEAN	A01
1001	MONROE	B01
1002	BOGART	-
1003	BERGMAN	D01

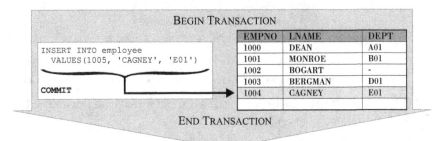

BEGIN TRANSACTION

```
INSERT INTO employee
  VALUES(1005, 'CAGNEY', 'E01')
```

```
COMMIT
```

EMPNO	LNAME	DEPT
1000	DEAN	A01
1001	MONROE	B01
1002	BOGART	-
1003	BERGMAN	D01
1004	CAGNEY	E01

END TRANSACTION

EMPLOYEE TABLE

(After the transaction)

EMPNO	LNAME	DEPT
1000	DEAN	A01
1001	MONROE	B01
1002	BOGART	-
1003	BERGMAN	D01
1004	CAGNEY	E01

Figure 5.14: What happens when the COMMIT statement is used to terminate a transaction

EMPLOYEE TABLE

(Before the transaction)

EMPNO	LNAME	DEPT
1000	DEAN	A01
1001	MONROE	B01
1002	BOGART	-
1003	BERGMAN	D01

BEGIN TRANSACTION

```
INSERT INTO employee
  VALUES(1005, 'CAGNEY', 'E01')
```

ROLLBACK

EMPNO	LNAME	DEPT
1000	DEAN	A01
1001	MONROE	B01
1002	BOGART	-
1003	BERGMAN	D01
1004	CAGNEY	E01

END TRANSACTION

EMPLOYEE TABLE

(After the transaction)

EMPNO	LNAME	DEPT
1000	DEAN	A01
1001	MONROE	B01
1002	BOGART	-
1003	BERGMAN	D01

Figure 5.15: What happens when the ROLLBACK statement is used to terminate a transaction

Important: COMMIT and ROLLBACK statements are not allowed in the body of an SQL UDF.

It is important to remember that commit and rollback operations have an effect only on the changes that are made within the transaction they terminate. So to evaluate the effects of a series of transactions, you must be able to identify where each transaction begins, as well as when and how each transaction ends. The effects of a series of transactions can be seen in Figure 5.16.

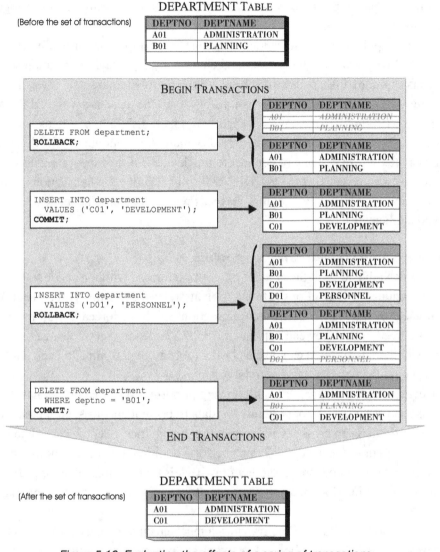

Figure 5.16: Evaluating the effects of a series of transactions

Uncommitted changes made by a transaction are usually inaccessible to other users and applications (there are exceptions, which we will look at in Chapter 7, "Data Concurrency") and can be backed out at any time. However, once a transaction's changes have been committed, they become accessible to all other users and applications—the only way to remove such changes is by performing an update, delete, or truncate operation. So what happens if a system failure occurs before a transaction's changes can be committed?

If a user or application's connection is broken (for example, because of a network failure), DB2 will back out all uncommitted changes by replaying information stored in the transaction log files, and the database will be returned to the state it was in immediately before the transaction began. If, however, the database or the DB2 Database Manager stops abruptly (for example, because of a hard disk failure or a loss of power), the next time the database is restarted (which will occur automatically the next time a user attempts to activate or connect to the database if the *autorestart* database configuration parameter is set to ON), DB2 will roll back all open transactions it finds in the transaction log files. Only after this succeeds will the database be made accessible to users and applications.

Transaction Management with Savepoints

Often, it is desirable to limit the amount of work performed within a single transaction so that locks acquired on behalf of the transaction are released in a timely manner. (When locks are held by one transaction, other transactions might be forced to wait for those locks to be freed before they can continue.) And if a large number of changes are made within a single transaction, it can take a considerable amount of time to back out those changes should the transaction need to be rolled back.

However, using several small transactions to perform a single large task has its drawbacks as well. First, the opportunity for data to become inconsistent increases if business rules have to cross several transaction boundaries. Second, each time a COMMIT statement is executed, DB2 must perform additional work to commit the current transaction and start a new one. (Another drawback is that portions of an operation might be committed and therefore become visible to other applications before the operation can complete.)

To get around these issues, DB2 provides a mechanism known as a *savepoint* that can be used to break the work being done by a single large transaction into one or more smaller subsets. By using savepoints, an application avoids the exposure to "dirty data" that might occur when multiple commits are performed, while maintaining granular control over long-running operations. You can use as many savepoints as you desire within a single transaction, provided you do not nest them.

Savepoints are created by executing the SAVEPOINT statement. The basic syntax for this statement is:

```
SAVEPOINT [SavepointName]
  <UNIQUE>
  ON ROLLBACK RETAIN CURSORS
  <ON ROLLBACK RETAIN LOCKS>
```

where:

SavepointName   Identifies the name to assign to the savepoint that is to be created

If the UNIQUE clause is specified with the SAVEPOINT statement used, the name assigned to the savepoint will be unique and cannot be reused as long as the savepoint remains active. If the ON ROLLBACK RETAIN LOCKS clause is specified with the SAVEPOINT statement used, any locks that are acquired after the savepoint is created are not tracked and, therefore, will not be released if the transaction is rolled back to the savepoint. The ON ROLLBACK RETAIN CURSORS clause indicates that any cursors that are opened after the savepoint is created will not be tracked and, therefore, will not be closed if the transaction is rolled back to the savepoint.

Thus, to create a savepoint named MY_SP, you would execute a SAVEPOINT statement that looks like this:

```
SAVEPOINT my_sp ON ROLLBACK RETAIN CURSORS
```

Once created, a savepoint can be used in conjunction with a special form of the ROLLBACK statement to return a database to the state it was in at the time the savepoint was created. The syntax for this form of the ROLLBACK statement is:

```
ROLLBACK <WORK> TO SAVEPOINT <SavepointName>
```

where:

SavepointName   Specifies, by name, the savepoint to roll back operations
                    performed against the database to

Figure 5.17 shows an example of how this form of the ROLLBACK statement is used, together with the SAVEPOINT statement, to break the work being performed by a single transaction into one or more subsets.

DEPARTMENT TABLE

(Before the transaction)

DEPTNO	DEPTNAME
A01	ADMINISTRATION
B01	PLANNING

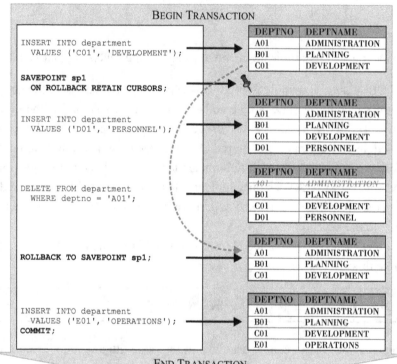

BEGIN TRANSACTION

```
INSERT INTO department
  VALUES ('C01', 'DEVELOPMENT');
```

DEPTNO	DEPTNAME
A01	ADMINISTRATION
B01	PLANNING
C01	DEVELOPMENT

```
SAVEPOINT sp1
  ON ROLLBACK RETAIN CURSORS;
```

DEPTNO	DEPTNAME
A01	ADMINISTRATION
B01	PLANNING
C01	DEVELOPMENT
D01	PERSONNEL

```
INSERT INTO department
  VALUES ('D01', 'PERSONNEL');
```

DEPTNO	DEPTNAME
~~A01~~	~~ADMINISTRATION~~
B01	PLANNING
C01	DEVELOPMENT
D01	PERSONNEL

```
DELETE FROM department
  WHERE deptno = 'A01';
```

DEPTNO	DEPTNAME
A01	ADMINISTRATION
B01	PLANNING
C01	DEVELOPMENT

```
ROLLBACK TO SAVEPOINT sp1;
```

DEPTNO	DEPTNAME
A01	ADMINISTRATION
B01	PLANNING
C01	DEVELOPMENT
E01	OPERATIONS

```
INSERT INTO department
  VALUES ('E01', 'OPERATIONS');
COMMIT;
```

END TRANSACTION

DEPARTMENT TABLE

(After the set of transactions)

DEPTNO	DEPTNAME
A01	ADMINISTRATION
B01	PLANNING
C01	DEVELOPMENT
E01	OPERATIONS

Figure 5.17: Using savepoints with the ROLLBACK statement to provide granular control over a long-running transaction

When a savepoint is no longer needed, you can delete (release) it by executing the RELEASE statement. The syntax for this statement is:

```
RELEASE <TO> SAVEPOINT <SavepointName>
```

where:

SavepointName   Identifies, by name, the savepoint that is to be deleted (released)

So, to delete a savepoint named MY_SP, you could execute a RELEASE statement that looks like this:

```
RELEASE SAVEPOINT my_sp
```

Once a savepoint is created, all subsequent SQL statements that are executed in a transaction are automatically associated with that savepoint until it is deleted—either explicitly by executing the RELEASE statement or implicitly by terminating the transaction the savepoint was created in. However, when a ROLLBACK TO SAVEPOINT statement is executed, the savepoint specified is not automatically deleted as part of the rollback operation.

Consequently, you can use multiple ROLLBACK statements to return a database to the state it was in at the time a particular savepoint was established. And if multiple savepoints are created, it is possible to roll back to any one of those savepoints, regardless of the order in which they were defined. (In other words, you are not required to roll back to every savepoint that exists, successively, in the opposite order in which they were defined.)

6

Working with DB2 Tables, Views, and Indexes

Twenty-two percent (22%) of the *DB2 10.1 Fundamentals* certification exam (Exam 610) is designed to test your ability to identify the data types and constraints that are available with DB2, as well as your ability to identify the characteristics of schemas, tables, indexes, and views. The questions that make up this portion of the exam are intended to evaluate the following:

- Your knowledge of the built-in data types that are available with DB2 (including Oracle compatibility data types)
- Your ability to identify the appropriate data type to use for a given situation
- Your knowledge of the various methods of data constraint that are available with DB2
- Your ability to identify when and how to use NOT NULL constraints, default constraints, UNIQUE constraints, CHECK constraints, and referential integrity constraints
- Your ability to create and modify both a base table and a temporary table
- Your ability to identify the characteristics of a table, view, or index
- Your knowledge of how to use schemas
- Your ability to identify how triggers are created and when they should be used

This chapter introduces you to the various data types and constraints that are available with DB2, and it shows you how to create new tables, indexes, and views. In this chapter, you will learn about the built-in data types that can be used to store different kinds of information in a DB2 database, and you will be shown how NOT NULL, default, UNIQUE, CHECK, and referential integrity constraints can be used to provide the logic needed to enforce certain business rules. You will also discover how to create and modify tables, as well as how to identify the characteristics of tables, views, and indexes. Finally, you will learn how schemas are used, and you will be shown how to create and use triggers to both automate data processing and supplement any constraints that may exist.

DB2's Data Types

If you stop to think about it, most "data" you encounter daily falls into several distinct categories. For example, the money you buy coffee with and the change you get back are numerical in nature; the email messages you receive and the replies you send consist of strings of alphanumeric characters; and many things you do such as waking up, going to the office, returning home, and going to bed revolve around time. This holds true for database data as well. Consequently, data stored in a database can be categorized according to its *data type*.

To ensure that data is stored as efficiently as possible, DB2 comes equipped with a wide variety of built-in data types, which are classified according to the kind of data they have been designed to hold:

- Numeric values
- Characters and character strings
- Dates and times
- Large objects
- Extensible Markup Language (XML) documents

In the event that none of the built-in data types meet your needs, DB2 also gives you the ability to create your own "user-defined" data types, which in turn can be used to store complex, nontraditional data that might be found in an intricate computing environment.

Numeric Data Types

As the name implies, numeric data types are used to store numerical values—specifically, numerical values that have a *sign* and a *precision*. The sign is considered positive if the value is greater than or equal to zero and negative if the value is anything else; the precision is the actual number of digits needed to properly display the value. Numeric data is stored by using a fixed amount of storage space, and the amount of space required increases as the precision of the number rises. The numeric data types that are available with DB2 include:

- **Small integer:** This data type is used to store numeric values that have a precision of five or fewer digits. The range for small integer values is –32,768 to 32,767, and 2 bytes of space is needed for every small integer value stored. (Positive numbers have one less value in their range because they start at the value 0; negative numbers start at –1.) The keyword SMALLINT denotes the small integer data type.
- **Integer:** This data type is used to store numeric values that have a precision of 10 digits. The range for integer values is –2,147,483,648 to 2,147,483,647, and 4 bytes of space is required for every integer value stored. The keywords INTEGER and INT denote the integer data type.
- **Big integer:** This data type is used to store numeric values that have a precision of 19 digits. The range for big integer values is –9,223,372,036,854,775,808 to 9,223,372,036,854,775,807, and 8 bytes of space is needed for every big integer value stored. The keyword BIGINT denotes the big integer data type. (This data type is typically used on systems that provide native support for 64-bit integers. On such systems, processing large numbers that have been stored as big integers is much more efficient and results in more precise calculations.)
- **Decimal:** This data type is used to store numeric values that contain both whole and fractional parts separated by a decimal point. Both the precision and the *scale* of the value determine the exact location of the decimal point. (The scale is the number of digits used by the fractional part of the number). The keywords DECIMAL, DEC, NUMERIC, and NUM (*DB2 for Linux, UNIX, and Windows only*) denote the decimal data type.

    The amount of space required to store a decimal value can be determined by solving the following equation: *Precision ÷ 2* (truncated) *+ 1 = Bytes required*. (For example, the value 67.12345 has a precision of 7, $7 ÷ 2 = 3$, and $3 + 1 = 4$; therefore, 4 bytes are required to store the value 67.12345.) The maximum precision allowed for decimal values is 31 digits, and the scale must be a positive number that is less than the precision. If no scale or precision is specified, a scale of 5 and a precision of 0 are used by default—in other words, DECIMAL(5,0).

- **Single-precision floating-point:** This data type is used to store a 32-bit approximation of a real number. This number can be zero, or it can fall within the range of $-3.402E^{+38}$ to $-1.175E^{-37}$ or $1.175E^{-37}$ to $3.402E^{+38}$. Each single-precision floating-point value can be up to 24 digits in length, and 4 bytes of space are needed for every value stored. The keywords REAL and FLOAT denote the single-precision floating-point data type.

- **Double-precision floating-point:** This data type is used to store a 64-bit approximation of a real number. This number can be zero, or it can fall within the range of $-1.79769E^{+308}$ to $-2.225E^{-307}$ or $2.225E^{-307}$ to $1.79769E^{+308}$. Each double-precision floating-point value can be up to 53 digits in length, and 8 bytes of space are needed for each value stored. The terms DOUBLE, DOUBLE PRECISION, and FLOAT denote the double-precision floating-point data type.

- **Decimal floating-point:** This data type is used to store floating-point numbers with a decimal point (as defined in the IEEE 754-2008 Standard for Binary Floating-Point Arithmetic) that have a precision of 16 or 34 digits and an exponent range of $10E^{-383}$ to $10E^{+384}$ or $10E^{-6143}$ to $10E^{+6144}$, respectively.

  In addition to finite numbers, the decimal floating-point data type can be used to store any of the following named decimal floating-point special values:

  » *Infinity*—a value that represents a number whose magnitude is infinitely large
  » *Quiet NaN*—a value that represents undefined results and does not cause an invalid number warning (NaN stand for *Not a Number*)
  » *Signaling NaN*—a value that represents undefined results and causes an invalid number warning if used in any numeric operation

  When a number has one of these special values, its coefficient and exponent are undefined—the sign of an infinity value is significant because it is possible to have positive or negative infinity. The sign of a NaN value has no meaning for arithmetic operations. The term DECFLOAT is used to denote the decimal floating-point data type.

Character String Data Types

Character string data types are used to store values composed of one or more alphanumeric characters—together, these characters can form a word, a sentence, a paragraph, or a complete document. A variety of character string data types are available, and deciding which type to use for a given situation depends primarily upon the storage requirements of the data value you want to store. Character string data types include:

- **Fixed-length character string:** This data type is used to store character string values that are between 1 and 254 characters in length. The amount of space required to store a fixed-length character string value can be determined by solving the following equation: (*Number of characters* × *1*) = *Bytes required*. A fixed amount of storage space is allocated, even if all the space is not needed—short strings are padded with blanks. The keywords CHARACTER and CHAR denote the fixed-length character string data type.

- **Fixed-length binary string** (*DB2 for z/OS only*)**:** This data type is used to store binary string values that are between 1 and 255 bytes long. The amount of space required to store a fixed-length binary string value can be determined by solving the following equation: (*Number of bytes* × *1*) = *Bytes required*. A fixed amount of storage space is allocated, even if all the space is not needed—short strings are padded with blanks. The keyword BINARY denotes the fixed-length binary string data type.

- **Varying-length character string:** This data type is used to store character string values that are up to 32,672 characters in length—the table space page size used governs the actual length allowed. For tables residing in table spaces that use 4 KB pages, varying-length character string values can be no more than 4,092 characters in length; for tables in table spaces that use 8 KB pages, varying-length character string values can be no more than 8,188 characters in length; and so on. The amount of space required to store a varying-length character string value can be determined by solving the following equation: (*Number of characters* × *1*) + *4* = *Bytes required*. Only the amount of storage space actually needed, plus 4 bytes for an "*end-of-string*" marker, is allocated—short strings are not padded with blanks. The keywords CHARACTER VARYING, CHAR VARYING, and VARCHAR denote the varying-length character string data type.

- **Varying-length binary string** (*DB2 for z/OS only*): This data type is used to store binary string values that are up to 32,704 bytes long—the actual length allowed is determined by the record size allowed, which is governed by the table space page size used. The amount of space required to store a varying-length binary string value can be determined by solving the following equation: (*Number of bytes* ×

1) + 2 = Bytes required. Only the amount of storage space actually needed, plus 2 bytes for an *end-of-string* marker, is allocated—short strings are not padded with blanks. The keywords BINARY VARYING and VARBINARY denote the varying-length character string data type.

- **Fixed-length double-byte character string:** This data type is used to store double-byte character set (DBCS) character string values that are up to 127 characters in length. (Most Asian character sets are double-byte character sets.) The amount of space required to store a fixed-length double-byte character string value can be determined by solving the following equation: *(Number of characters × 2) = Bytes required.* A fixed amount of storage space is allocated, even if all the space is not needed—short strings are padded with blanks. The term GRAPHIC denotes the fixed-length double-byte character string data type.

- **Varying-length double-byte character string:** This data type is used to store DBCS character string values that are up to 16,336 characters in length. Again, the table space page size used governs the actual length allowed. For tables residing in table spaces that use 4 KB pages, varying-length double-byte character string values can be no more than 2,046 characters in length; for tables that reside in a table spaces that use 8 KB pages, varying-length double-byte character string values can be no more than 4,094 characters in length; and so on. The amount of space required to store a varying-length double-byte character string value can be determined by solving the following equation: *(Number of characters × 2) + 4 = Bytes required.* The keyword VARGRAPHIC denotes the varying-length double-byte character string data type.

- **National fixed-length character string** (*DB2 for Linux, UNIX, and Windows only*)**:** This data type is used to store a sequence of bytes, up to 127 bytes in length, in a Unicode database that uses UTF-16BE encoding. The amount of space required to store a national fixed-length character string value can be determined by solving the following equation: *(Number of characters × 2) = Bytes required.* The keywords NATIONAL CHARACTER, NATIONAL CHAR, and NCHAR denote the national fixed-length character string data type.

- **National varying-length character string** (*DB2 for Linux, UNIX, and Windows only*)**:** This data type is used to store a sequence of bytes, up to 16,336 bytes in length, in a Unicode database that uses UTF-16BE encoding. Once again, the table space page size used governs the actual length allowed. For tables that reside in table spaces that use 4 KB pages, national varying-length character string values cannot be more than 2,046 characters in length; for tables that reside in a table spaces that use 8 KB pages, national varying-length character string values cannot be more than 4,094 characters in length; and so on. The amount of space required to store a national varying-length character string value can be determined by solving the following equation: (*Number of characters* × 2) + 4 = *Bytes required*. The keywords NATIONAL CHARACTER VARYING, NATIONAL CHAR VARYING, NCHAR VARYING, and NVARCHAR denote the national varying-length character string data type.

Date and Time Data Types

As the name implies, date and time data types are used to store values that represent dates and times. From a user perspective, such values appear to be character strings; however, they are actually stored as binary packed strings. Date/time data types include:

- **Date:** This data type is used to store three-part values (year, month, and day) that represent calendar dates. The range for the year portion is 0001 to 9999; the month portion is 1 to 12; and the day portion is 1 to 28, 29, 30, or 31, depending upon the month value specified and whether the year value corresponds to a leap year. Externally, date values appear to be fixed-length character string values that are 10 characters in length. However, only 4 bytes of space are needed for each date value stored. The keyword DATE denotes the date data type.
- **Time:** This data type is used to store three-part values (hours, minutes, and seconds) that represent time based on a 24-hour clock. The range for the hours portion is 0 to 24, the minutes portion is 0 to 59, and the seconds portion is 0 to 59. Externally, time values appear to be fixed-length character string values that are eight characters in length. However, only 3 bytes of space are required for each time value stored. The keyword TIME denotes the time data type.
- **Timestamp:** This data type is used to store six- or seven-part values (year, month, day, hours, minutes, seconds, and microseconds) that represent a specific calendar date and time (again, using a 24-hour clock). The range for the year portion is 0001 to 9999; the month portion is 1 to 12; the day portion is 1 to 28, 29, 30, or 31, depending upon the month value specified and whether the year specified is a leap year; the hours portion is 0 to 24; the minutes portion is 0 to 59; the seconds portion is 0 to 59; and the microseconds portion is 0 to 999,999,999,999. (The number of digits used in the fractional seconds portion can be anywhere from 0 to 12; however, the default is 6.)

Externally, timestamp values appear to be fixed-length character string values that are up to 32 characters in length, and in the United States, this string is normally displayed using the format *YYYY-MM-DD-HH.MM.SS.NNNNNN*, which translates to Year-Month-Day-Hour.Minute.Second.Microseconds, where four digits are used to present the year, six digits are used to present the microseconds (by default), and two digits are used to present each of the remaining elements. However, the internal representation of a timestamp requires between 7 and 13 bytes of storage. The keyword TIMESTAMP denotes the timestamp data type.

Because the representation of date and time values varies throughout the world, the actual string format used to present a date or time value is dependent upon the territory code that has been assigned to the database being used. Table 6.1 shows the date and time string formats that are currently available with DB2.

Table 6.1: Date and time formats currently available with DB2			
Format Name	**Abbreviation**	**Date String Format**	**Time String Format**
International Standards Organization	ISO	YYYY-MM-DD*	HH.MM.SS†
IBM USA Standard	USA	MM/DD/YYYY*	HH:MM AM or PM†
IBM European Standard	EUR	DD.MM.YYYY*	HH.MM.SS†
Japanese Industrial Standard	JIS	YYYY-MM-DD*	HH:MM:SS†
Site Specific	LOC	Based on database territory and the application's country code	Based on database territory and the application's country code
* For date formats: YYYY = Year, MM = Month, and DD = Day † For time formats: HH = Hour, MM = Minute, and SS = Seconds Adapted from Tables 1 and 2, found under Datetime Values in the IBM DB2 10.1 Information Center for Linux, UNIX, and Windows (publib.boulder.ibm.com/infocenter/db2luw/v10r1/topic/com.ibm.db2.luw.sql.ref.doc/doc/r0008474.html).			

Large Object Data Types

Large object (LOB) data types are used to store large, unstructured data values. LOB data types include:

- **Binary large object:** This data type is used to store binary data values (such as documents, graphic images, pictures, audio, and video) that are up to 2 GB in size—the actual amount of space set aside to store a binary large object value is determined by the length specification provided when a column with this data type is defined. For example, 800 bytes of storage space will be allocated for a column that is given a BINARY LARGE OBJECT(800) definition. The keywords BINARY LARGE OBJECT and BLOB denote the binary large object data type.

- **Character large object:** This data type is used to store single-byte character set (SBCS) or multibyte character set (MBCS) character string values that are between 32,700 and 2,147,483,647 characters in length—the actual amount of space set aside to store a character large object value is determined by the length specification provided when a column with this data type is defined. For example, 800 bytes of storage space will be allocated for a column that is given a CHARACTER LARGE OBJECT(800) definition. The keywords CHARACTER LARGE OBJECT, CHAR LARGE OBJECT, and CLOB denote the character large object data type.

- **Double-byte character large object:** This data type is used to store DBCS character string values that are between 16,350 and 1,073,741,823 characters in length—the actual amount of space set aside to store a double-byte character large object value is determined by the length specification provided when a column with this data type is defined. For example, 800 bytes of storage space will be allocated for a column that is given a DBCLOB(400) definition. The keyword DBCLOB denotes the double-byte character large object data type.

- **National character large object** (*DB2 for Linux, UNIX, and Windows only*): This data type is used to store a sequence of characters—between 16,350 and 1,073,741,823 bytes in length—in a Unicode database that uses UTF-16BE encoding. The actual amount of space set aside to store a national character large object value is determined by the length specification provided when a column with this data type is defined. For example, 800 bytes of storage space will be allocated for a column that is given a NATIONAL CHARACTER LARGE OBJECT(400) definition. The keyword NATIONAL CHARACTER LARGE OBJECT, NCHAR LARGE OBJECT, and NCLOB denote the national character large object data type.

The Extensible Markup Language (XML) Data Type

XML is a simple, yet flexible text-based format that provides a neutral way to exchange data between different devices, systems, and applications—XML data is maintained in a self-describing format that is hierarchical in nature. As the name implies, the **Extensible Markup Language Document** data type is used to store XML documents *in their native format*. In fact, only well-formed XML documents can be stored in columns that have been assigned the Extensible Markup Language data type. (XML values are processed in an internal representation that is not comparable to any string value; however, you can use the XMLSERIALIZE() function to transform an XML value into a serialized string that represents an XML document. Similarly, you can use the XMLPARSE() function to transform a string value that represents an XML document into an XML value.) The amount of space needed to store an XML document varies and is determined, in part, by the size and characteristics of the XML document being stored. (By default, XML data is stored in an XML storage object that is separate from the table's relational storage location.) The keyword XML denotes the Extensible Markup Language Document data type.

A Word About the Oracle Compatibility Data Types

DB2 10.1 for Linux, UNIX, and Windows contains a number of features that can greatly reduce the time and effort required to enable existing applications that were written for other relational database products, such as Oracle and Sybase, to execute in a DB2 environment. Some of these features are enabled by default, and others must be explicitly "turned on" (by assigning the appropriate value to the DB2_COMPATIBILITY_VECTOR registry variable). For instance, to use the DB2 compatibility features that exist for applications that have been developed for an Oracle database, you must assign the value ORA to the DB2_COMPATIBILITY_VECTOR registry variable. And in the case of Oracle, when features that provide compatibility are explicitly enabled, some additional Oracle-specific data types are made available for use. These data types are:

- **DATE as TIMESTAMP(0):** This data type provides support for applications that use the Oracle DATE data type. (The Oracle DATE data type is a datetime data type that is used to store date values that contain both date and time information—for example, '2014-07-04-10.45.05'.)
- **NUMBER:** This data type provides support for applications that use the Oracle NUMBER data type. (The Oracle NUMBER data type is a numeric data type that is used to store both fixed and floating-point numbers with up to 38 significant digits—the numeric value stored in a NUMBER data type can be zero, or it can fall within the range of $-1.0E^{-130}$ to $9.99E^{+125}$ or $1.0E^{-130}$ to $9.99E^{+125}$.)
- **VARCHAR2:** This data type provides support for applications that use the Oracle VARCHAR2 data type. (The Oracle VARCHAR2 data type is a variable-length character string data type that is used to store character string values that are up to 4,000 characters in length.)

- **NVARCHAR2**: This data type provides support for applications that use the Oracle NVARCHAR2 data type. (The Oracle NVARCHAR2 data type is a national variable-length character string data type that is used to store a sequence of bytes, up to 4,000 bytes in length, in a Unicode database that uses AL16UTF16 or UTF8 encoding.)

User-Defined Data Types

In Chapter 4, "Working with Databases and Database Objects," we saw that user-defined data types (UDTs) are data types that are explicitly created by a database user. Depending upon the edition used (DB2 for Linux, UNIX, and Windows or DB2 for z/OS), up to two different types of UDTs are available: *distinct* and *structured*. A distinct data type is a UDT that shares a common representation with one of the built-in data types available with DB2. A structured data type is a UDT that consists of a sequence of named attributes, each of which have a name and data type of their own. (*Structured types are available with DB2 for Linux, UNIX, and Windows only.*)

UDTs are subject to strong data typing, which means that even though they might share the same representation as other built-in or user-defined data types, the value of one UDT is compatible only with values of that same data type (or of other user-defined data types within the same structured data type hierarchy). As a result, you cannot use UDTs as arguments for most built-in functions. However, as we saw in Chapter 4, "Working with Databases and Database Objects," it is possible to create UDFs and operators that duplicate the functionality provided by many of the built-in functions available.

Understanding Data Constraints

Often, data must adhere to a set of business rules and restrictions. (For example, many companies have a specific format and numbering sequence they use when generating purchase order numbers.) And, in many cases, the logic required to enforce these rules and restrictions is woven into applications that interact with one or more databases. However, the logic needed to enforce business rules can often be placed directly in a database—by means of one or more *data constraints*. Data constraints are special rules that govern how new data values can be added to a table, as well as how existing values can be altered once they have been stored. The following types of data constraints are available with DB2:

- NOT NULL constraints
- Default constraints

- UNIQUE constraints
- CHECK constraints
- Referential integrity constraints
- Informational constraints

Any of these constraints can be defined during the table creation process. Or they can be added to existing tables by using various forms of the ALTER TABLE statement.

NOT NULL *Constraints*

With DB2, NULL values (not to be confused with empty strings) represent missing or unknown data and states. Consequently, by default, every column in a table will accept a NULL value—this allows records to be added to a table when all the information associated with a particular record is not known. However, there may be times when this behavior is unacceptable. For example, people hired in the United States usually must provide their Social Security number for state and federal tax purposes. Therefore, you probably do not want to allow NULL Social Security number values to be entered in a table that is used to keep track of employee information.

In these types of situations, the NOT NULL constraint can be used to ensure that a particular column in a table is never assigned a NULL value. Once a NOT NULL constraint has been defined for a column, any operation that attempts to place a NULL value in that column will fail. Figure 6.1 illustrates how the NOT NULL constraint is enforced.

Because NOT NULL constraints are associated with specific columns in a table, they are usually defined during the table creation process.

Default *Constraints*

Just as there may be times when you want to prevent NULL values from being stored, there might be instances when you would like the system to provide a default value for you. For example, you may want to automatically assign the current date to a particular column each time a new record is added to a table. This is where default constraints come in.

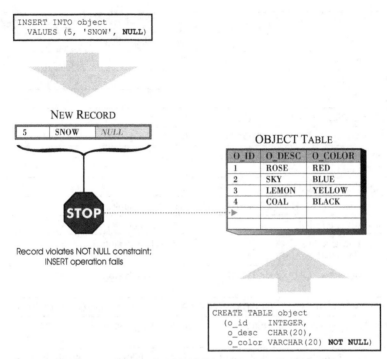

Figure 6.1: How the NOT NULL constraint is enforced

A default constraint ensures that a particular column in a table will be assigned a predefined default value if no value for that column is provided when a new record is added to the table. This default value can be NULL (provided a NOT NULL constraint has not been defined for the column), a user-supplied value that is compatible with the column's data type, or a value that DB2 supplies. Table 6.2 shows the default values that DB2 can furnish for each of the built-in data types available.

Table 6.2: DB2-supplied default values	
Column Data Type	**Default Value Provided**
Small integer (SMALLINT)	0
Integer (INTEGER or INT)	0
Big integer (BIGINT)	0
Decimal (DECIMAL, DEC, NUMERIC, or NUM)	0
Single-precision floating-point (REAL or FLOAT)	0
Double-precision floating-point (DOUBLE, DOUBLE PRECISION, or FLOAT)	0
Decimal floating-point (DECFLOAT)	0
Fixed-length character string (CHARACTER or CHAR)	A string of blank characters
Fixed-length binary string (BINARY)	A string of blank characters
Varying-length character string (CHARACTER VARYING, CHAR VARYING, or VARCHAR)	A zero-length string
Varying-length binary string (BINARY VARYING, or VARBINARY)	A zero-length string
Fixed-length double-byte character string (GRAPHIC)	A string of double-byte blank characters
Varying-length double-byte character string (VARGRAPHIC)	A zero-length string
National fixed-length character string (NATIONAL CHARACTER, NATIONAL CHAR, or NCHAR)	A string of double-byte blank characters
National varying-length character string (NATIONAL CHARACTER VARYING, NATIONAL CHAR VARYING, NCHAR VARYING, or NVARCHAR)	A zero-length string
Date (DATE)	The system date at the time the record is added to the table; when a date column is added to an existing table, existing rows are assigned the date January 01, 0001
Time (TIME)	The system time at the time the record is added to the table; when a time column is added to an existing table, existing rows are assigned the time 00:00:00
Timestamp (TIMESTAMP)	The system date and time (including microseconds) at the time the record is added to the table; when a timestamp column is added to an existing table, existing rows are assigned a timestamp that corresponds to January 01, 0001, 00:00:00.000000
Binary large object (BINARY LARGE OBJECT or BLOB)	A zero-length string
Character large object (CHARACTER LARGE OBJECT, CHAR LARGE OBJECT, or CLOB)	A zero-length string
Double-byte character large object (DBCLOB)	A zero-length string

Table 6.2: DB2-supplied default values (continued)	
Column Data Type	Default Value Provided
National character large object (NATIONAL CHARACTER LARGE OBJECT, NCHAR LARGE OBJECT, or NCLOB)	A zero-length string
XML document (XML)	Not applicable
Any distinct user-defined data type	The default value provided for the built-in data type that the distinct user-defined data type is based on, typecast to the distinct user-defined data type

Figure 6.2 illustrates how a default constraint is applied.

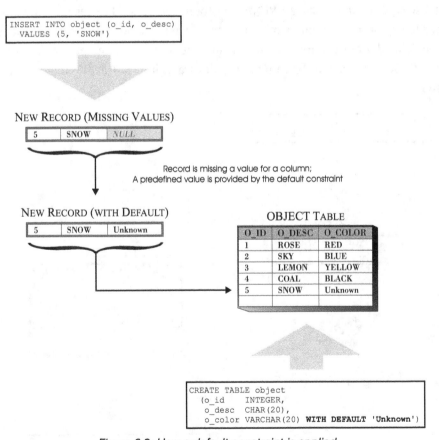

Figure 6.2: How a default constraint is applied

As with NOT NULL constraints, default constraints are associated with a specific column in a table and are normally defined during the table creation process.

UNIQUE Constraints

By default, records that are added to a table can have the same value assigned to any of their columns, any number of times. And, as long as the records stored in the table do not contain information that should never be duplicated, this kind of behavior is acceptable. However, sometimes certain pieces of information that are stored in a record should be unique. For example, if an employee identification number is assigned to every individual who works for a particular company, each number should probably be used only once— all sorts of problems can arise if two or more employees are assigned the same employee identification number.

In these types of situations, a UNIQUE constraint can be used to ensure that values assigned to one or more columns of a table are always unique. After a UNIQUE constraint has been defined for one or more columns, any operation that attempts to place duplicate values in those columns will fail. Figure 6.3 illustrates how a UNIQUE constraint is enforced.

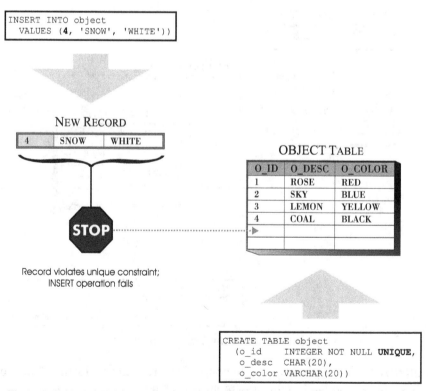

Figure 6.3: How a UNIQUE constraint can prevent the duplication of data values

Unlike NOT NULL and default constraints, which can be associated only with single columns, UNIQUE constraints can be associated with individual columns *or* a group of columns. However, each column in a table can participate in only one UNIQUE constraint, regardless of how the columns are grouped. As with the other constraints, a table can have any number of UNIQUE constraints defined, but *a table cannot have more than one UNIQUE constraint defined on the same set of columns*. UNIQUE constraints are typically defined during the table creation process.

Regardless of when a UNIQUE constraint is defined, at the time you create such a constraint, the DB2 Database Manager checks to see whether an index for the columns the UNIQUE constraint refers to already exists. If it finds an appropriate index, that index is marked as being "unique and system-required"; if not, a new index is created and given similar characteristics (unique and system-required). In either case, the index is then used to enforce uniqueness in the columns the constraint was defined for. (Because UNIQUE constraints are enforced by indexes, all the limitations that apply to indexes—such as no more than 16 columns with a combined length of 255 bytes allowed, and none of the columns used can have a large object data type—apply to UNIQUE constraints.)

Note: Although a unique, system-required index is used to enforce a UNIQUE constraint, a distinction exists between defining a UNIQUE constraint and creating a unique index. While both enforce uniqueness, a unique index will accept one (and only one) NULL value and generally cannot be used in a referential integrity constraint. A UNIQUE constraint, however, does not allow NULL values (thus, every column that is part of a UNIQUE constraint must also be assigned a NOT NULL constraint) and can participate in a referential integrity constraint.

A *primary key* is a special form of a UNIQUE constraint that uniquely defines the characteristics of each row in a table. The most significant difference between a primary key and a UNIQUE constraint is that only one primary key is allowed per table, whereas a single table can contain multiple UNIQUE constraints. As with UNIQUE constraints, primary keys can be used to define a referential integrity constraint (which we will look at shortly).

• •

Note: If you define a unique index for one or more columns in a table, and you later create a primary key for the same set of columns, the existing index will be converted to a unique, system-required index that is used to enforce the primary key constraint. When such an event takes place, a warning that looks something like this will be generated:

SQL0598W Existing index "nnn.nnn" is used as the index for the primary key or a unique key. SQLSTATE=01550

• •

Check Constraints

Sometimes, it is desirable to control which values will be accepted for a particular column (and which values will be denied). For instance, a company might decide that the lowest salary a nonexempt employee can receive is the federal minimum wage; consequently, salary values that are stored in the company's payroll database can never be lower than the current federal minimum wage. In such situations, the logic needed to determine whether a particular value is acceptable can be incorporated into the application that is used to add data to the database. Or, that logic can be included in the definition of the column that is to hold the data using what is known as a CHECK constraint. A CHECK constraint (also referred to as a *table check constraint*) can be used to ensure that a particular column in a table is never assigned an unacceptable value. After a CHECK constraint has been defined for a particular column, any operation that attempts to place a value into that column that does not meet a specific set of criteria will fail.

CHECK constraints consist of one or more predicates (connected by the keywords AND or OR) that collectively are known as a *check condition*. Each time an operation inserts a value into (or changes a value in) a column that has CHECK constraint defined for it, that value is compared with the corresponding check condition, and the result of the comparison is returned as TRUE, FALSE, or Unknown. If the result returned is TRUE, the value is deemed acceptable and is added to the database; if the result returned is FALSE or Unknown, the operation fails and changes made by the operation are backed out (rolled back). Unlike with other roll back situations, the transaction that initiated the operation is not terminated, and other operations within that transaction are not affected. Figure 6.4 illustrates just one example of how a CHECK constraint can be used.

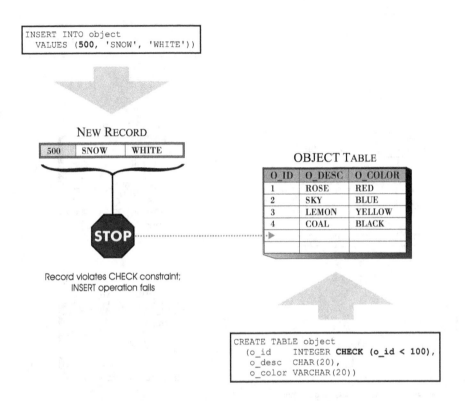

Figure 6.4: How to use a CHECK *constraint to control which values a column accepts*

As with NOT NULL and default constraints, CHECK constraints are associated with a specific column in a table and are typically defined during the table creation process.

Referential Integrity Constraints

If you have had the opportunity to work with any relational database management system in the past, you are probably aware that data normalization is a technique that is used to ensure that the same data values are not stored in multiple locations—that there is only one way to get to a single fact. Data normalization is possible because two or more individual tables can have some type of relationship with one another, and as we saw in Chapter 5, "Working with DB2 Data Using SQL," information stored in related tables can be combined by using a join operation. And when data is normalized, referential integrity constraints (also known as *referential constraints* and *foreign key constraints*) can be used to define *required* relationships between select columns and tables. Figure 6.5 shows a simple referential integrity constraint (and how such a constraint might be enforced).

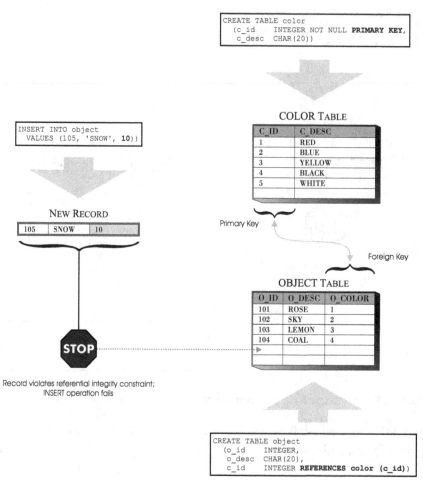

Figure 6.5: How a referential integrity constraint is used to define a relationship between two tables

In this example, a table named COLOR is used to store a numerical code and a corresponding description for several different colors, and a table named OBJECT is used to store predominant color information for a few basic objects. Because every object must be assigned a color value, a referential constraint can be used to ensure that every record that resides in the OBJECT table has a corresponding record in the COLOR table. The relationship between these two tables is established by comparing values that are to be added to the C_ID column of the OBJECT table (known as the *foreign key* of the *child table*) with values that currently exist for the C_ID column of the COLOR table (known as the *parent key* of the *parent table*).

In this scenario, a single column defines the parent and foreign keys of the referential integrity constraint. However, as with UNIQUE constraints, multiple columns can be used to define both parent and foreign keys.

> **Note:** The names of the columns you use to create the foreign key of a referential constraint do not have to be the same as the names of the columns that were used to create the primary key. Nevertheless, the data types of the columns that make up the primary and foreign keys of a referential constraint must be identical, and the number of columns used in both keys must be the same.

As you can see, referential constraints are much more complex than the other constraints we have looked at. In fact, referential constraints can be so complex that a set of special terms is used to identify the individual components that can make up a single referential constraint. You have already seen some of them; Table 6.3 contains the complete list.

Table 6.3: Referential integrity constraint terminology	
Term	**Meaning**
Unique key	A column or set of columns in which every row of values is different from the values of all other rows
Primary key	A special key that that uniquely defines the characteristics of each row in a table (and does not accept NULL values); a single primary key can be used in multiple referential constraints
Parent key	A primary key or unique key in a parent table that is referenced by a foreign key in a referential constraint
Parent table	A table that contains a parent key of a referential constraint; a table can be both a parent table and a child table of any number of referential constraints
Parent row	A row in a parent table that has at least one matching row in a child (dependent) table
Foreign key	A column or set of columns in a child table whose values must match those of a parent key in a parent table; a foreign key must reference a primary key, but only one primary key can be referenced
Child (or dependent) table	A table containing at least one foreign key that references a parent key in a referential constraint; a table can be both a child table and a parent table of any number of referential constraints
Child (or dependent) row	A row in a child table that has at least one matching row in a parent table

Table 6.3: Referential integrity constraint terminology (continued)	
Term	Meaning
Descendant table	A child table or a descendant of a child table
Descendant row	A child row or a descendant of a child row
Referential cycle	A set of referential constraints defined in such a way that each table in the set is a descendent of itself
Self-referencing table	A table that is both a parent and a child in the same referential constraint; such a constraint is known as a self-referencing constraint
Self-referencing row	A row that is a parent of itself

The primary reason for using referential constraints is to guarantee that data integrity is maintained whenever one table references another. As long as a referential constraint is in place, DB2 ensures that for every row in a child table that has a value in a foreign key column, a corresponding row in the associated parent table exists. So what happens when someone attempts to manipulate data in a way that will violate a referential constraint? To answer this question, let us first look at what can compromise data integrity if the checks and balances a referential constraint provides are not in place:

- An insert operation can add a value to a column in a child table that does not have a matching value in the associated parent table. (For instance, using the example in Figure 6.5, a value could be added to the O_COLOR column of the OBJECT table that does not exist in the C_ID column of the COLOR table.)
- An update operation can change an existing value in a child table such that it no longer has a matching value in the associated parent table. (For example, a value could be changed in the O_COLOR column of the OBJECT table in such a way that it no longer has a corresponding value in the C_ID column of the COLOR table.)

- An update operation can change an existing value in a parent table, leaving rows in a child table with values that no longer match those in the parent table. (For example, a value could be changed in the C_ID column of the COLOR table, leaving records in the OBJECT table with values in the O_COLOR column that no longer have a matching value in the COLOR table.)
- A delete operation can remove a value from a parent table, leaving rows in a child table with values that no longer match those in the parent table. (For example, a record could be removed from the COLOR table, leaving records in the OBJECT table with values in the O_COLOR column that no longer have a matching value in the C_ID column of the COLOR table.)

DB2 can prevent these types of operations from being performed on tables that are part of a referential constraint. Or it can attempt to carry out these actions in a way that will safeguard data integrity by using a special set of rules—an *Insert Rule*, an *Update Rule*, and a *Delete Rule*—to control the behavior. Each referential constraint has its own Insert, Update, and Delete Rule, and the way in which two of these rules will be enforced can be controlled during the referential constraint creation process.

The Insert Rule for referential constraints

The Insert Rule for referential constraints guarantees that a value can never be inserted into the foreign key of a child table unless a matching value exists in the parent key of the associated parent table. Consequently, any attempt to insert a record into a child table that violates this rule will result in an error. In contrast, no checking is performed when records are inserted into the parent key of the parent table. Figure 6.6 illustrates how a row that conforms to the Insert Rule for a referential constraint is successfully added to a child table. Figure 6.7 shows how a row that violates the Insert Rule will cause an insert operation to fail.

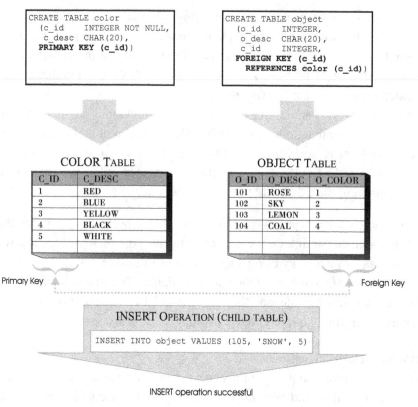

```
CREATE TABLE color
   (c_id    INTEGER NOT NULL,
    c_desc  CHAR(20),
    PRIMARY KEY (c_id))
```

```
CREATE TABLE object
   (o_id    INTEGER,
    o_desc  CHAR(20),
    c_id    INTEGER,
    FOREIGN KEY (c_id)
      REFERENCES color (c_id))
```

COLOR TABLE

C_ID	C_DESC
1	RED
2	BLUE
3	YELLOW
4	BLACK
5	WHITE

OBJECT TABLE

O_ID	O_DESC	O_COLOR
101	ROSE	1
102	SKY	2
103	LEMON	3
104	COAL	4

Primary Key   Foreign Key

INSERT OPERATION (CHILD TABLE)

```
INSERT INTO object VALUES (105, 'SNOW', 5)
```

INSERT operation successful

COLOR TABLE

C_ID	C_DESC
1	RED
2	BLUE
3	YELLOW
4	BLACK
5	WHITE

OBJECT TABLE

O_ID	O_DESC	O_COLOR
101	ROSE	1
102	SKY	2
103	LEMON	3
104	COAL	4
105	SNOW	5

Figure 6.6: An insert operation that conforms to the Insert Rule of a referential constraint

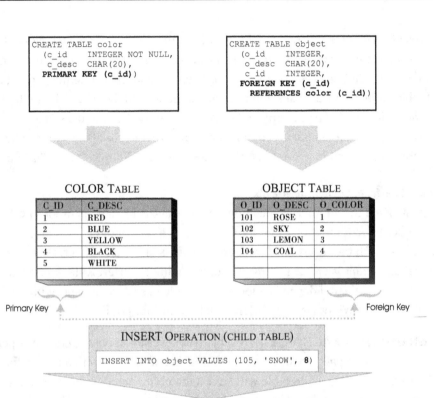

```
CREATE TABLE color
  (c_id    INTEGER NOT NULL,
   c_desc  CHAR(20),
   PRIMARY KEY (c_id))
```

```
CREATE TABLE object
  (o_id    INTEGER,
   o_desc  CHAR(20),
   c_id    INTEGER,
   FOREIGN KEY (c_id)
     REFERENCES color (c_id))
```

COLOR TABLE

C_ID	C_DESC
1	RED
2	BLUE
3	YELLOW
4	BLACK
5	WHITE

OBJECT TABLE

O_ID	O_DESC	O_COLOR
101	ROSE	1
102	SKY	2
103	LEMON	3
104	COAL	4

Primary Key

Foreign Key

INSERT OPERATION (CHILD TABLE)

```
INSERT INTO object VALUES (105, 'SNOW', 8)
```

STOP

The value **8** does not exist in the primary key;
INSERT operation fails

COLOR TABLE

C_ID	C_DESC
1	RED
2	BLUE
3	YELLOW
4	BLACK
5	WHITE

OBJECT TABLE

O_ID	O_DESC	O_COLOR
101	ROSE	1
102	SKY	2
103	LEMON	3
104	COAL	4

Figure 6.7: An insert operation that violates the Insert Rule of a referential constraint

An Insert Rule for a referential constraint is automatically created whenever a referential constraint is created, *and its behavior cannot be altered.* Therefore, once a referential constraint has been defined, records must be inserted into the parent key of the parent table *before* records that reference the parent key can be inserted into the foreign key of the child table. (For example, when populating the COLOR and OBJECT tables depicted in Figures 6.6 and 6.7, you must first add a record for a new color to the COLOR table before you can add a record that references the new color to the OBJECT table.)

The Update Rule for referential constraints

The Update Rule for referential constraints controls how update operations performed against either table (parent or child) participating in a referential constraint are to be processed. As with the Insert Rule, an Update Rule is automatically created when a referential constraint is created. However, unlike with the Insert Rule, *how* a particular Update Rule is evaluated depends upon how the rule has been defined. With DB2 for Linux, UNIX, and Windows, two different definitions are possible:

- **ON UPDATE NO ACTION**: Ensures that whenever an update operation is performed on either table participating in a referential constraint, the value for the foreign key of each row in the child table will have a matching value in the parent key of the associated parent table. *However, the value may or may not be the same as it was before the update operation was performed.* This type of Update Rule is enforced only after all other constraints, including other referential constraints, have been enforced.

- **ON UPDATE RESTRICT**: Ensures that whenever an update operation is performed on the parent table of a referential constraint, the value for the foreign key of each row in the child table will have the same matching value in the parent key of the parent table that it had before the update operation was performed. This type of Update Rule is enforced before all other constraints, including other referential constraints, are enforced.

•••

Note: The definitions for the Update Rule of a referential constraint are available with DB2 for Linux, UNIX, and Windows only. They cannot be used with DB2 for z/OS.

•••

Figure 6.8 illustrates how the Update Rule is enforced when the ON UPDATE NO ACTION definition is used. Figure 6.9 shows how the Update Rule is enforced when the ON UPDATE RESTRICT definition is used instead.

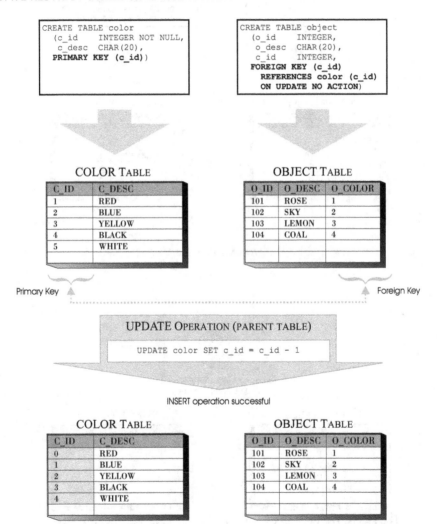

Figure 6.8: How an ON UPDATE NO ACTION *Update Rule of a referential constraint is enforced*

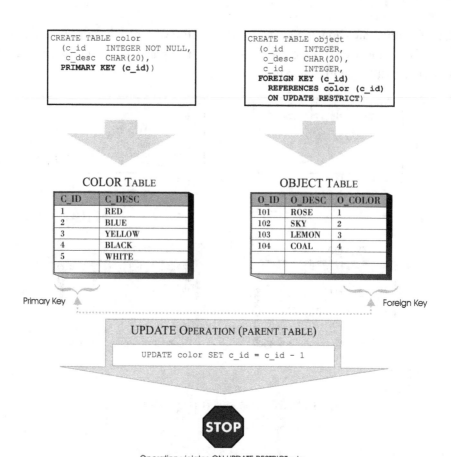

Figure 6.9: How an ON UPDATE RESTRICT Update Rule of a referential constraint is enforced

If you do not provide an Update Rule definition when you create a referential constraint, the ON UPDATE NO ACTION definition is used by default. Regardless of which definition is used, if an update operation violates the Update Rule's condition, the operation will fail, an error will be returned, and any changes that you made to either table participating in the referential constraint will be backed out of the database.

The Delete Rule for referential constraints

The Delete Rule for referential constraints controls how delete operations performed against the parent table in a referential constraint are to be processed. As with the Update Rule, *how* a particular Delete Rule is evaluated depends upon the way in which the rule has been defined. Four different definitions are possible:

- **ON DELETE CASCADE**: Ensures that whenever a row is deleted from the parent table of a referential constraint, all records in the child table with matching foreign key values are deleted as well
- **ON DELETE SET NULL**: Ensures that whenever a row is deleted from the parent table of a referential constraint, all records in the child table with matching foreign key values are altered such that the foreign key columns are set to NULL—provided the columns that make up the foreign key are nullable (that is, they do not have a NOT NULL constraint associated with them); other values for the dependent row are not affected
- **ON DELETE NO ACTION**: Ensures that whenever a delete operation is performed on the parent table of a referential constraint, each row in the child table will have the same value for its foreign key that it had before the delete operation was performed; this type of Delete Rule is enforced only after all other constraints, including other referential constraints, have been enforced
- **ON DELETE RESTRICT**: Ensures that whenever a delete operation is performed on the parent table of a referential constraint, each row in the child table will have the same value for its foreign key that it had before the delete operation was performed; this type of Delete Rule is enforced before all other constraints, including other referential constraints, are enforced

Figure 6.10 illustrates how the Delete Rule is enforced when the ON DELETE CASCADE definition is used. Figure 6.11 shows how the Delete Rule is enforced when the ON DELETE SET NULL definition is used instead.

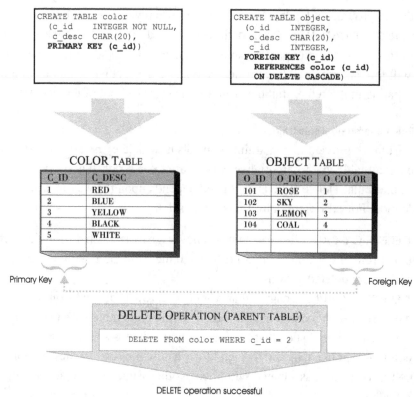

Figure 6.10: How an ON DELETE CASCADE *Delete Rule of a referential constraint is enforced*

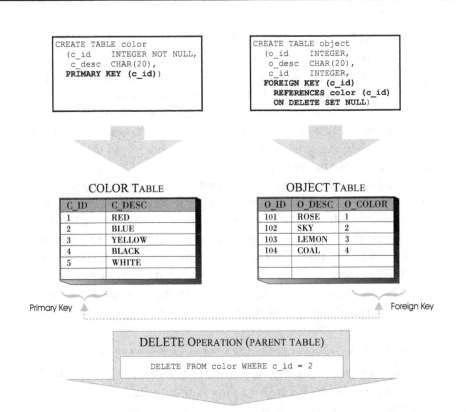

Figure 6.11: How an ON DELETE SET NULL *Delete Rule of a referential constraint is enforced*

• •

Note: If the ON DELETE CASCADE Delete Rule definition is specified at the time a referential constraint is created, the child table participating in the constraint is said to be *delete-connected* to the parent table. And if the deletion of a parent row in a parent table causes one or more dependent rows to be deleted from an associated child table, the delete operation is said to have been *propagated* to the child table.

Because a delete-connected child table can also be the parent table in another referential constraint, a delete operation that is propagated to one child table can, in turn, be propagated to another child table, and so on. Thus, the deletion of a single parent row can result in the deletion of several hundred rows from any number of tables, depending upon how tables in a database are delete-connected. Consequently, you should use the ON DELETE CASCADE Delete Rule definition with extreme caution when a hierarchy of referential constraints is spread throughout a database.

• •

Figure 6.12 illustrates how the Delete Rule is enforced when the ON DELETE NO ACTION definition is used. And Figure 6.13 shows how the Delete Rule is enforced when the ON DELETE RESTRICT definition is used.

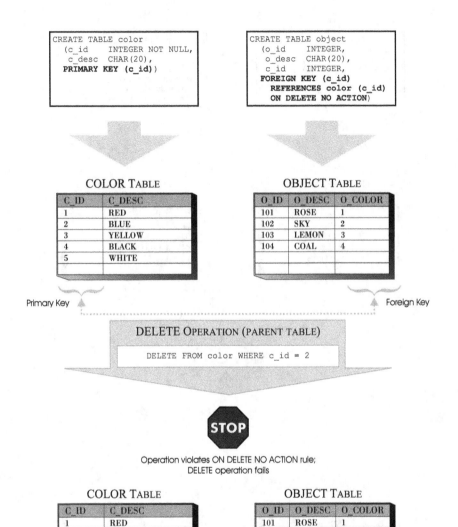

Figure 6.12: How an ON DELETE NO ACTION *Delete Rule of a referential constraint is enforced*

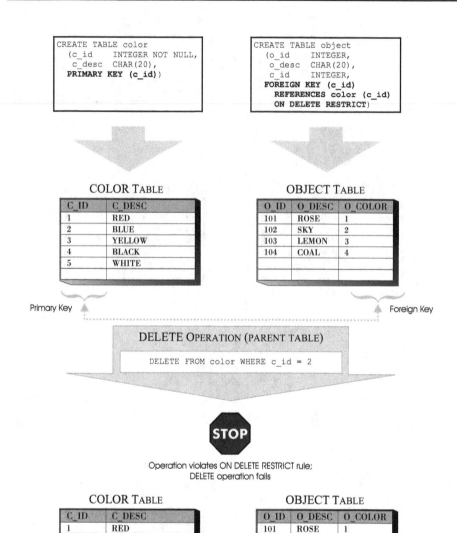

Figure 6.13: How an ON DELETE RESTRICT *Delete Rule of a referential constraint is enforced*

If a table participates in only one referential constraint (as in the previous examples), the behavior of the ON DELETE NO ACTION and the ON DELETE RESTRICT definition is essentially the same—delete operations that violate either Delete Rule will fail, and data will remain unchanged because there are no other constraints to consider. However, that is not the case when a table participates in multiple referential constraints; here, the behavior can differ because of *when* each Delete Rule is enforced. For example, the scenario depicted in Figure 6.14 illustrates how the ON DELETE NO ACTION Delete Rule will allow a delete operation to be performed.

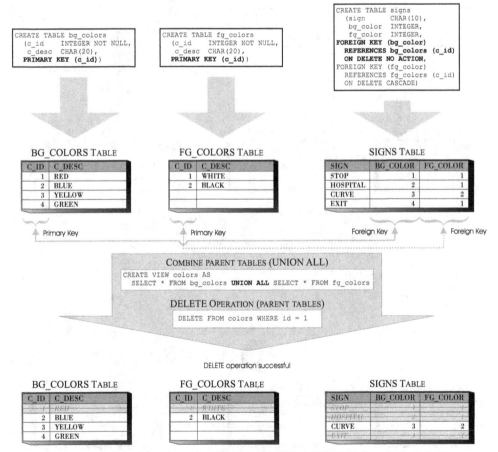

Figure 6.14: Example where the ON DELETE NO ACTION *Delete Rule definition allows data in tables to be deleted*

In this example, the referential constraint with the ON DELETE NO ACTION Delete Rule definition is enforced only *after* the referential constraint with the ON DELETE CASCADE Delete Rule is processed, allowing the deletion of records from all tables participating in both referential constraints. Had the ON DELETE RESTRICT Delete Rule definition been used in the previous example instead, the referential constraint with that Delete Rule would have been enforced first and the second delete operation would have failed. Figure 6.15 illustrates this behavior.

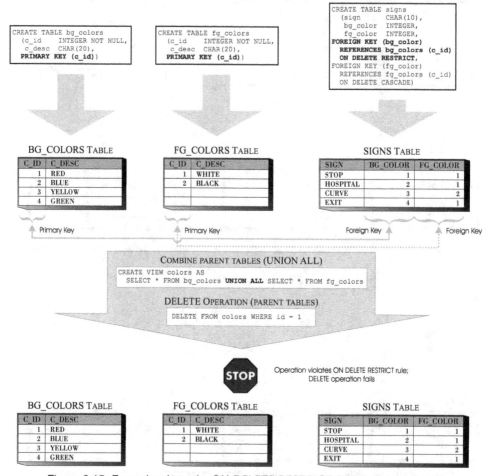

Figure 6.15: Example where the ON DELETE RESTRICT *Delete Rule definition prevents data in tables from being deleted*

As with Insert and Update Rules, a Delete Rule is automatically created when a referential constraint is created. If you do not provide a Delete Rule definition, the ON DELETE NO ACTION definition is used by default. And regardless of which definition is used, if a delete operation violates the Delete Rule's condition, the operation will fail, an error will be returned, and any changes that were made to either table participating in the referential constraint will be backed out of the database.

Informational Constraints

By default, whenever you add, modify, and in some cases delete data from a DB2 database, the DB2 Database Manager automatically enforces any constraints that have been defined. Consequently, if a large number of constraints have been defined, a significant amount of overhead may be required to enforce those constraints, especially when large amounts of data are bulk-loaded into a table that participates in several different constraints. Therefore, if an application already contains the logic needed to apply the business rules and restrictions required, there may not be any advantage to creating a set of similar data constraints that do essentially the same thing. There is, however, a very good reason to create a set of similar *informational constraints*—such constraints can often improve query performance.

Informational constraints tell DB2 which business rules data conforms to, but unlike other constraints, they are not enforced. So why is it important that DB2 know this information? Because if DB2 is aware of constraints that are being enforced at the application level, the DB2 Optimizer can use this information to choose an optimum access plan to use when retrieving data from the database.

Informational constraints are defined by appending the keywords NOT ENFORCED ENABLE QUERY OPTIMIZATION to a CHECK or referential constraint definition. Figure 6.16 illustrates how to create a simple informational constraint, as well as how a record that violates an informational constraint will be inserted into a table because such a constraint is not enforced.

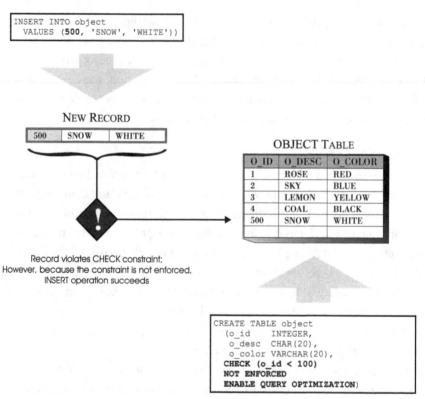

Figure 6.16: A simple informational constraint

Note: With DB2 for Linux, UNIX, and Windows, the keywords NOT ENFORCED ENABLE QUERY OPTIMIZATION can be added to both CHECK and referential constraint definitions; with DB2 for z/OS, these keywords can be used only when defining referential constraints.

It is important to note that because the DB2 Optimizer evaluates informational constraints when selecting an access plan to use to resolve a query, records that have been inserted into a table that violate an informational constraint may not be returned by some queries. For example, if the following query is executed against the OBJECT table shown in Figure 6.16:

```
SELECT * FROM object
  WHERE o_id > 100
```

the following results will be returned:

```
O_ID         O_DESC                O_COLOR
-----------  --------------------  --------------------


   0 record(s) selected.
```

That is because the DB2 Optimizer assumes that no records exist in the OBJECT
table that have an O_ID value that is greater than 100. (The DB2 Optimizer makes this
assumption based on information it received from the informational constraint that was
defined.) However, if the following query is executed instead:

```
SELECT * FROM object
```

the results produced will look like this:

```
O_ID         O_DESC                O_COLOR
-----------  --------------------  --------------------
          1  ROSE                  RED
          2  SKY                   BLUE
          3  LEMON                 YELLOW
          4  COAL                  BLACK
        500  SNOW                  WHITE

   5 record(s) selected.
```

Why? Because in this case, the DB2 Optimizer probably chose a simple table scan to
resolve the query. As a result, information provided by the informational constraint did
not play a part in the access plan chosen.

Creating Tables

In Chapter 4, "Working with Databases and Database Objects," we saw that tables act as the main repository in a DB2 database. We also saw that tables present data as a collection of unordered rows with a fixed number of columns, that each column contains values of the same data type, and that each row contains a set of values for one or more of the columns available. As with many of the other database objects available, tables can be created from within Data Studio. Tables can also be created by executing the CREATE TABLE statement. However, this statement is probably the most complex SQL statement available. Consequently, its syntax can be very intimidating.

Fortunately, you do not have to know all the nuances of the CREATE TABLE statement to pass the *DB2 10.1 Fundamentals* certification exam (Exam 610). Still, you do need to know the basics. Therefore, the bulk of this section is devoted to the CREATE TABLE statement syntax you need to be familiar with to answer questions on the *DB2 10.1 Fundamentals* exam that address this particular topic. With that said, let us begin by looking at a very basic form of the CREATE TABLE statement. In its simplest form, the syntax for the CREATE TABLE statement looks like this:

```
CREATE TABLE [TableName] ( [Element], ...)
  <IN [TablespaceName]>
```

where:

TableName	Identifies the name to assign to the table that is to be created; the table name specified must be unique within the schema the table is to be defined in
Element	Identifies one or more columns, UNIQUE constraints, CHECK constraints, referential constraints, informational constraints, and/or a primary key constraint to include in the table definition; the syntax used to define each of these elements varies according to the element specified
TablespaceName	Identifies, by name, the table space the table is to be stored in

The basic syntax used to define a column element is:

```
[ColumnName] [DataType]
<NOT NULL>
<WITH DEFAULT <[DefaultValue] | NULL>>
```

```
<UniqueConstraint>
<CheckConstraint>
<RIConstraint>
```

where:

ColumnName	Identifies the name to assign to the column; the name specified must be unique
DataType	Identifies the data type (built-in or user-defined) to assign to the column; the data type specified determines the kind of data values that can be stored in the column—Table 6.4 contains a list of valid built-in data type definitions
DefaultValue	Identifies the default value to provide for the column if no value for the column is supplied when a new record is inserted into the table
UniqueConstraint	Identifies a UNIQUE or primary key constraint that is to be associated with the column
CheckConstraint	Identifies a CHECK constraint that is to be associated with the column
RIConstraint	Identifies a referential integrity constraint that is to be associated with the column

Table 6.4: Built-in data type definitions to use with the CREATE TABLE statement

Data Type	Definition(s)
Small integer	SMALLINT
Integer	INTEGER INT
Big integer	BIGINT
Decimal	DECIMAL(*Precision, Scale*) DEC(*Precision, Scale*) NUMERIC(*Precision, Scale*) NUM(*Precision, Scale*) where *Precision* is any number between 1 and 31, and *Scale* is any number between 0 and *Precision*
Single-precision floating-point	REAL FLOAT(*Precision*) where *Precision* is any number between 1 and 24

Table 6.4: Built-in data type definitions to use with the CREATE TABLE statement (continued)	
Data Type	**Definition(s)**
Double-precision floating-point	DOUBLE DOUBLE PRECISION FLOAT(*Precision*) where *Precision* is any number between 25 and 53
Decimal floating-point	DECFLOAT(*Precision*) where *Precision* is either 16 or 34
Fixed-length character string	CHARACTER(*Length*) <FOR BIT DATA> CHAR(*Length*) <FOR BIT DATA> where *Length* is any number between 1 and 254 (see footnote for the meaning of the FOR BIT DATA clause)
Fixed-length binary string (DB2 for z/OS only)	BINARY(*Length*) where *Length* is any number between 1 and 255
Varying-length character string	CHARACTER VARYING(*MaxLength*) <FOR BIT DATA> CHAR VARYING(*MaxLength*) <FOR BIT DATA> VARCHAR(*MaxLength*) <FOR BIT DATA> where *MaxLength* is any number between 1 and 32,672 (see footnote for the meaning of the FOR BIT DATA clause)
Varying-length binary string (DB2 for z/OS only)	BINARY VARYING(*MaxLength*) VARBINARY(*MaxLength*) where *MaxLength* is any number between 1 and 32,704
Fixed-length double-byte character string	GRAPHIC(*Length*) where *Length* is any number between 1 and 127
Varying-length double-byte character string	VARGRAPHIC(*MaxLength*) where *MaxLength* is any number between 1 and 16,336
National fixed-length character string (DB2 for Linux, UNIX, and Windows only)	NATIONAL CHARACTER(*Length*) NATIONAL CHAR(*Length*) NCHAR(*Length*) where *Length* is any number between 1 and 127
National varying-length character string (DB2 for Linux, UNIX, and Windows only)	NATIONAL CHARACTER VARYING(*MaxLength*) NATIONAL CHAR VARYING(*MaxLength*) NCHAR VARYING(*MaxLength*) NVARCHAR(*MaxLength*) where *MaxLength* is any number between 1 and 16,336
Date	DATE
Time	TIME

Table 6.4: Built-in data type definitions to use with the CREATE TABLE statement (continued)	
Data Type	**Definition(s)**
Timestamp	TIMESTAMP TIMESTAMP(*Precision*) where *Precision* is any number between 0 and 12
Binary large object	BINARY LARGE OBJECT(*Length* <K | M | G>) BLOB(*Length* <K | M | G>) where *Length* is any number between 1 and 2,147,483,647; if K (for kilobyte) is specified, *Length* is any number between 1 and 2,097,152; if M (for megabyte) is specified, *Length* is any number between 1 and 2,048; and if G (for gigabyte) is specified, *Length* is any number between 1 and 2
Character large object	CHARACTER LARGE OBJECT(*Length* <K | M | G>) CHAR LARGE OBJECT(*Length* <K | M | G>) CLOB(*Length* <K | M | G>) where *Length* is any number between 1 and 2,147,483,647; if K (for kilobyte) is specified, *Length* is any number between 1 and 2,097,152; if M (for megabyte) is specified, *Length* is any number between 1 and 2,048; and if G (for gigabyte) is specified, *Length* is any number between 1 and 2
Double-byte character large object	DBCLOB(*Length* <K | M | G>) where *Length* is any number between 1 and 1,073,741,823; if K (for kilobyte) is specified, *Length* is any number between 1 and 1,048,576; if M (for megabyte) is specified, *Length* is any number between 1 and 1,024; and if G (for gigabyte) is specified, *Length* is must be 1
National character large object (DB2 for Linux, UNIX, and Windows only)	NATIONAL CHARACTER LARGE OBJECT(*Length* <K | M | G>) NCHAR LARGE OBJECT(*Length* <K | M | G>) NCLOB(*Length* <K | M | G>) where *Length* is any number between 1 and 1,073,741,823; if K (for kilobyte) is specified, *Length* is any number between 1 and 1,048,576; if M (for megabyte) is specified, *Length* is any number between 1 and 1,024; and if G (for gigabyte) is specified, *Length* is must be 1
XML document	XML
Note: If the FOR BIT DATA option is used with a character string data type definition, the contents of the column the data type is assigned to will be treated as binary data. This means that code page conversions are not performed if data in the column is exchanged between other systems, and that all comparisons are done in binary, regardless of the collating sequence used.	

The syntax used to create a UNIQUE or primary key constraint as part of a column definition is:

```
<CONSTRAINT [ConstraintName]> [UNIQUE | PRIMARY KEY]
```

where:

ConstraintName   Identifies the name to assign to the constraint; the name specified
                      must be unique

The syntax used to create a CHECK constraint as part of a column definition is:

```
<CONSTRAINT [ConstraintName]> CHECK ([CheckCondition])
```

where:

ConstraintName   Identifies the name to assign to the constraint; the name specified
                      must be unique
CheckCondition   Identifies a condition or test that must evaluate to TRUE before a
                      value can be stored in the associated column

And finally, the syntax used to create a referential constraint as part of a column definition is:

```
<CONSTRAINT [ConstraintName]>
REFERENCES [PKTableName] <([PKColumnName], ...)>
<ON UPDATE [NO ACTION | RESTRICT]>
<ON DELETE [CASCADE | SET NULL | NO ACTION | RESTRICT]>
<ENFORCED | NOT ENFORCED>
<[ENABLE | DISABLE] QUERY OPTIMIZATION>
```

where:

ConstraintName   Identifies the name to assign to the constraint; the name specified
                      must be unique
PKTableName   Identifies, by name, the parent table that is to participate in the
                      referential constraint
PKColumnName   Identifies one or more columns that comprise the parent key of the
                      parent table that is to participate in the referential constraint

As mentioned earlier, if the NOT ENFORCED clause is specified as part of a constraint's definition, the constraint will not be enforced—it will become an informational constraint instead. If the ENABLE QUERY OPTIMIZATION clause is specified, the DB2 Optimizer will evaluate the information the constraint provides when deciding which data access plan to use to resolve a query.

Therefore, to create a table named EMPLOYEES that contains three columns, two of which are named EMPID and NAME that will be used to store integer data and one that is named DEPT that will be used to store fixed-length character string data, you could execute a CREATE TABLE statement that looks something like this:

```
CREATE TABLE employees
  (empid  INTEGER,
   name   CHAR(50),
   dept   INTEGER)
```

On the other hand, to create a table named EMPLOYEES that has the same columns, but that also has both a NOT NULL constraint and a primary key constraint associated with the EMPID column, you would execute a CREATE TABLE statement that looks more like this:

```
CREATE TABLE employees
  (empid  INTEGER NOT NULL PRIMARY KEY,
   name   CHAR(50),
   dept   INTEGER)
```

Or, to create a similar table, but have the DEPT column participate in a referential constraint with a column named DEPTID that resides in another table named DEPARTMENT, you would execute a CREATE TABLE statement that looks like this:

```
CREATE TABLE employees
  (empid INTEGER,
   name  CHAR(50),
   dept  INTEGER REFERENCES department (deptid))
```

And finally, to create a similar table that has an informational constraint associated with the DEPT column, you would execute a CREATE TABLE statement that looks like this:

```
CREATE TABLE employees
  (empid INTEGER,
   name  CHAR(50),
   dept  INTEGER REFERENCES department (deptid)
          NOT ENFORCED
          ENABLE QUERY OPTIMIZATION)
```

As these examples show, a UNIQUE constraint, CHECK constraint, referential constraint, or informational constraint can be associated with a particular column as part of that column's definition. But what if you need to define a referential constraint that encompasses more than one column? Or you want to separate constraint definitions from column definitions to make it easier for other DBAs to maintain your DDL? In both cases, you can define a constraint as separate element, rather than as an extension to a column definition.

The syntax used to define a UNIQUE or primary key constraint as an individual element is:

```
<CONSTRAINT [ConstraintName]> [UNIQUE | PRIMARY KEY]
  ([ColumnName], ...)
```

where:

ConstraintName	Identifies the name to assign to the constraint; the name specified must be unique
ColumnName	Identifies one or more columns that are to be part of the UNIQUE or primary key constraint

The syntax used to create a CHECK constraint as an individual element is identical to the syntax that is used to create a CHECK constraint as part of a column definition:

```
<CONSTRAINT [ConstraintName]> CHECK ( [CheckCondition] )
```

where:

ConstraintName	Identifies the name to assign to the constraint; the name specified must be unique
CheckCondition	Identifies a condition or test that must evaluate to TRUE before a value can be stored in the associated column

And finally, the syntax used to create a referential constraint as an individual element is:

```
<CONSTRAINT [ConstraintName]>
FOREIGN KEY ([ColumnName], ...)
REFERENCES [PKTableName] <([PKColumnName], ...)>
<ON UPDATE [NO ACTION | RESTRICT]>
<ON DELETE [CASCADE | SET NULL | NO ACTION | RESTRICT]>
<ENFORCED | NOT ENFORCED>
<[ENABLE | DISABLE] QUERY OPTIMIZATION>
```

where:

ConstraintName	Identifies the name to assign to the constraint; the name specified must be unique
ColumnName	Identifies one or more columns that are to be part of the foreign key of the referential constraint
PKTableName	Identifies, by name, the parent table that is to participate in the referential constraint
PKColumnName	Identifies one or more columns that comprise the parent key of the parent table that is to participate in the referential constraint

Thus, a table that was created by executing a CREATE TABLE statement that looks like this:

```
CREATE TABLE employees
  (empid INTEGER,
   name  CHAR(50),
   dept  INTEGER REFERENCES department (deptid))
```

could also be created by executing a CREATE TABLE statement that looks like this:

```
CREATE TABLE employees
  (empid INTEGER,
   name  CHAR(50),
   dept  INTEGER,
   FOREIGN KEY (dept) REFERENCES department (deptid))
```

Creating Tables with Identity Columns

Often, base tables are designed in such a way that a single column is used to store a unique identifier that represents an individual record (or row). And frequently, this identifier is a number that is sequentially incremented each time a new record is added to the table. You can generate numbers for these types of columns by using a trigger (which we looked at in Chapter 4, "Working with Databases and Database Objects"), or DB2 can generate them automatically—provided the column is defined as an *identity column.*

Identity columns are created by specifying the GENERATED...AS IDENTITY clause, along with one or more identity column attributes, as part of a column's definition. The syntax used to create an identity column is:

```
[ColumnName] [DataType]
GENERATED <ALWAYS | BY DEFAULT> AS IDENTITY
<(
   <START WITH [1 | StartingValue]>
   <INCREMENT BY [1 | IncrementValue]>
   <NO MINVALUE | MINVALUE [MinValue]>
   <NO MAXVALUE | MAXVALUE [MaxValue]>
   <NO CYCLE | CYCLE>
   <CACHE 20 | NO CACHE | CACHE [CacheSize]>
   <NO ORDER | ORDER>
)>
```

where:

ColumnName   Identifies the name to assign to the column; the name specified must be unique

DataType	Identifies the data type (built-in or user-defined) to assign to the identity column; the data type specified must be a numeric data type with a scale of 0; therefore, only the following values are valid: SMALLINT, INTEGER, BIGINT, DECIMAL, NUMERIC, or a user-defined data type that is based on one of these data types
StartingValue	Identifies the first value that is to be assigned to the identity column
IncrementValue	Identifies the interval that is to be used to calculate each consecutive value that is to be assigned to the identity column
MinValue	Identifies the smallest value that can be assigned to the identity column
MaxValue	Identifies the largest value that can be assigned to the identity column
CacheSize	Identifies the number of values of the identity sequence that are to be generated at one time and kept in memory

If the CYCLE clause is specified as part of an identity column's definition, values will continue to be generated for the column after any minimum or maximum value specified has been reached. (After an ascending identity column reaches the maximum value allowed, a new minimum value is generated and the cycle begins again; after a descending identity column reaches the minimum value allowed, a new maximum value is generated and the cycle repeats itself.)

Thus, to create a table named EMPLOYEES that contains a simple identity column that DB2 will always generate a value for, you could execute a CREATE TABLE statement that looks something like this:

```
CREATE TABLE employees
  (empid INTEGER GENERATED ALWAYS AS IDENTITY,
   name  CHAR(50),
   dept  INTEGER)
```

It is important to note that after this table is created, if you attempt to execute an SQL statement that looks like this:

```
INSERT INTO employees VALUES (1, 'SCHIEFER', 50)
```

you will receive an error message that looks like this:

```
SQL0798N  A value cannot be specified for column "EMPID" which
is defined as GENERATED ALWAYS. SQLSTATE=428C9
```

That is because the GENERATED ALWAYS AS IDENTITY clause implies that DB2 will always be responsible for providing values for the EMPID column of the EMPLOYEES table.

On the other hand, to create a table named EMPLOYEES that contains an identity column that DB2 will generate a value for *if no value is explicitly provided*, you would execute a CREATE TABLE statement that looks more like this:

```
CREATE TABLE employees
  (empid INTEGER GENERATED BY DEFAULT AS IDENTITY,
   name  CHAR(50),
   dept  INTEGER)
```

Here, the INSERT statement shown in the previous example will succeed because the GENERATED BY DEFAULT AS IDENTITY clause instructs DB2 to supply a value for the EMPID column only when no value is explicitly provided for that column.

• •

Note: A table can have only one identity column, all identity columns are implicitly assigned a NOT NULL constraint, and identity columns are not allowed to have a default constraint assigned to them.

• •

Creating Tables That Are Similar to Existing Tables

At times, it might be desirable to create a new, empty table that has the same attributes as an existing table (for example, when a history table for a system-period temporal table is needed). One way to create a new, empty table that is similar to another is by executing a CREATE TABLE statement that is identical to the statement that was used to create the original table. (Of course, the name assigned to new table will have to be changed.) Another way is to execute a special form of CREATE TABLE that was designed specifically with this purpose in mind. The syntax for this form of the CREATE TABLE statement is:

```
CREATE TABLE [TableName] LIKE [SourceTable]
<[INCLUDING | EXCLUDING] COLUMN DEFAULTS>
<[INCLUDING | EXCLUDING] IDENTITY COLUMN ATTRIBUTES>
```

where:

TableName	Identifies the name to assign to the table that is to be created; the table name specified must be unique within the schema the table is to be defined in
SourceTable	Identifies, by name, an existing table whose structure and attributes are to be used to define the table that is to be created

Thus, to create an empty table named 2ND_QTR_SALES that has the exact same structure as an existing table named 1ST_QTR_SALES, you would execute a CREATE TABLE statement that looks like this:

```
CREATE TABLE 2nd_qtr_sales LIKE 1st_qtr_sales
```

When this form of the CREATE TABLE statement is executed, the table that is created will have the same number of columns as the source table used, and these columns will have the same names, data types, and nullability characteristics as those of the source table. If the EXCLUDING COLUMN DEFAULTS clause is not specified, any default constraints that have been defined for the source table will be copied to the new table as well. Similarly, if the EXCLUDING IDENTITY COLUMN ATTRIBUTES clause is not specified, any identity column attributes that have been defined for the source will be copied to the target table. However, no other attributes of the source table will be duplicated. Thus, the target table will not contain any UNIQUE constraints, CHECK constraints, referential integrity constraints, triggers, or indexes that have been defined for the source table. (If the target table needs these characteristics, you must create them separately after the target table has been created.)

A Quick Word About Schemas

In Chapter 4, "Working with Databases and Database Objects," we saw that schemas are objects that are used to logically classify and group other objects (such as tables, indexes, and views) in a database. Schemas also make it possible to create a large number of objects in a database without encountering namespace collisions. Many of the objects in a DB2 database are named using a two-part naming convention—the first (leftmost) part of the name is the *schema name* or *qualifier*, and the second (rightmost) part is the user-supplied object name. Syntactically, these two parts are concatenated and separated by a period (for example, HR.EMPLOYEES).

When select data objects (that is, table spaces, tables, indexes, distinct data types, functions, stored procedures, and triggers) are created, they are automatically assigned to a schema, based upon the qualifier that was provided as part of the user-supplied object name. If a schema name or qualifier is not provided as part of an object's name, the object is automatically assigned to a default schema, which is determined by examining the value found in a special register. With DB2 for Linux, UNIX, and Windows, this special register is the CURRENT SCHEMA (or CURRENT_SCHEMA) special register; with DB2 for z/OS, the CURRENT SQLID (or CURRENT_SQLID) special register is used instead.

By default, the value assigned to these special registers is the authorization ID of the current session user. However, this value can be changed using the SET SCHEMA (DB2 for Linux, UNIX, and Windows) or the SET CURRENT SQLID (DB2 for z/OS) statement. Thus, if you were to log on to a DB2 server with the user ID "db2inst1" and execute a CREATE TABLE statement that looks like this:

```
CREATE TABLE employees
  (empid INTEGER GENERATED BY DEFAULT AS IDENTITY,
   name  CHAR(50),
   dept  INTEGER)
```

a table named DB2INST1.EMPLOYEES will be created—because a qualifier was not provided with the table name specified, the authentication ID that the CREATE TABLE statement was executed under (which in this case is "db2inst1"), is used as the qualifier by default.

Examples of the CREATE TABLE Statement

Now that you have seen the basic syntax for the CREATE TABLE statement and some very simple examples of how this statement can be used, let us look at some more-complex CREATE TABLE statement examples and examine the characteristics of the tables that would be produced if each of these statements were to be executed.

Example 1

If the following CREATE TABLE statement is executed:

```
CREATE TABLE project
  (projno    CHAR(6) NOT NULL,
   projname  VARCHAR(24) NOT NULL,
   deptno    SMALLINT,
   budget    DECIMAL(6,2),
   startdate DATE,
   enddate   DATE)
```

a table named PROJECT will be created as follows:

- The first column will be named PROJNO and can be used to store fixed-length character string data that is six characters in length (for example, 'PROJ01' or 'PROJ02').
- The second column will be named PROJNAME and can be used to store variable-length character string data up to 24 characters in length (for example, 'DB2 Benchmarks Tool' or 'Auto-Configuration Tool').
- The third column will be named DEPTNO and can be used to store numeric values in the range of $-32,768$ to $+32,767$.
- The fourth column will be named BUDGET and can be used to store numerical values that contain both whole and fractional parts. Up to six numbers—four for the whole number part and two for the fractional part—can be stored (for example, 1500.00 or 2000.50).
- The fifth column will be named STARTDATE and can be used to store date values.
- The sixth column will be named ENDDATE and can also be used to store date values.
- The table will be created in a schema that has the name of the authorization ID of the individual who created it (because a schema name was not provided and this is the default schema name used).
- The table will be created in the table space USERSPACE1 (because a table space was not specified and this is the default table space used).

- Whenever data is added to the table, values must be provided for both the PROJNO and the PROJNAME columns. (NULL values are not allowed because a NOT NULL constraint was defined for both of these columns.)

Example 2

If the following CREATE TABLE statement is executed:

```
CREATE TABLE central.sales
  (po_number INTEGER NOT NULL CONSTRAINT uc1 UNIQUE,
   date      DATE NOT NULL WITH DEFAULT),
   office    CHAR(128) NOT NULL WITH DEFAULT 'Dallas',
   amt       DECIMAL(10,2) NOT NULL CHECK (amt > 99.99)
   IN my_space
```

a table named SALES will be created as follows:

- The first column will be named PO_NUMBER (for Purchase Order Number) and can be used to store numeric values in the range of –2,147,483,648 to 2,147,483,647.
- The second column will be named DATE and can be used to store date values.
- The third column will be named OFFICE and can be used to store fixed-length character string data up to 128 characters in length (for example, 'Kansas City' or 'Dallas').
- The fourth column will be named AMT (for Amount) and can be used to store numerical values that contain both whole and fractional parts. Up to 10 numbers— eight for the whole number part and two for the fractional part—can be stored (for example, 20000000.50).
- The table will be created in a schema named CENTRAL.
- The table will be created in a table space named MY_SPACE.
- Whenever data is added to the table, values must be provided for the PO_NUMBER and the AMT columns. (NULL values are not allowed in any column because a NOT NULL constraint was defined for every column; however, because default values can be provided by DB2 for the DATE and OFFICE columns, values do not have to be supplied for those two columns.)
- Every value provided for the PO_NUMBER column must be unique (because a UNIQUE constraint named UC1 was defined for this column).

- An index was automatically created for the PO_NUMBER column (because a UNIQUE constraint named UC1 was defined for this column). As data is added to the table, values provided for the PO_NUMBER column are added to the index, and the entries in the index are sorted in ascending order.
- If a value is not provided for the DATE column when a row is inserted into the table, the system date at the time the row is inserted will be written to the column by default (because a default constraint was defined for this column).
- If a value is not provided for the OFFICE column, the value 'Dallas' will be written to the column by default (because a default constraint was defined for this column).
- Every value provided for the AMT column must be greater than or equal to 100.00 (because a CHECK constraint was defined for this column).

Example 3

If the following CREATE TABLE statements are executed in the order shown:

```
CREATE TABLE payroll.employees
  (empid      INTEGER NOT NULL PRIMARY KEY,
   emp_fname CHAR(30),
   emp_lname CHAR(30))


CREATE TABLE payroll.paychecks
  (empid        INTEGER,
   weeknumber CHAR(2),
   pay_amt      DECIMAL(6,2),
   CONSTRAINT fkconst FOREIGN KEY (empid)
     REFERENCES employee(empid) ON DELETE CASCADE,
   CONSTRAINT chk1 CHECK (pay_amt > 0 AND weeknumber
     BETWEEN 1 AND 52))
```

first, a table named EMPLOYEES will be created as follows:

- The first column will be named EMPID (for Employee ID) and can be used to store numeric values in the range of –2,147,483,648 to 2,147,483,647.

- The second column will be named EMP_FNAME (for Employee First Name) and can be used to store fixed-length character string data up to 30 characters in length (for example, 'Bob' or 'Mark').
- The third column will be named EMP_LNAME (for Employee Last Name) and can be used to store fixed-length character string data up to 30 characters in length (for example, 'Jancer' or 'Hayakawa').
- The table will be created in a schema named PAYROLL.
- The table will be created in the table space USERSPACE1 (because a table space was not specified and this is the default table space used).
- Whenever data is added to the table, values must be provided for the EMPID column. (NULL values are not allowed because a NOT NULL constraint was defined for this column.)
- Every value provided for the EMPID column must be unique (because a primary key constraint was defined for this column).
- An index was automatically created for the EMPID column (because a primary key constraint was defined for this column). As data is added to the table, values provided for the EMPID column are added to the index, and the entries in the index are sorted in ascending order.

Then, a table named PAYCHECKS will be created, as follows:

- The first column will be named EMPID and can be used to store numeric values in the range of –2,147,483,648 to 2,147,483,647.
- The second column will be named WEEKNUMBER and can be used to store fixed-length character string data up to two characters in length (for example, '1' or '35').
- The third column will be named PAY_AMT and can be used to store numerical values that contain both whole and fractional parts. Up to six numbers—four for the whole number part and two for the fractional part—can be stored (for example, 2000.50).
- The table will be created in a schema named PAYROLL.
- The table will be created in the table space USERSPACE1 (because a table space was not specified and this is the default table space used).
- Every value entered in the EMPID column must have a matching value in the EMPID column of the EMPLOYEES table (because a referential constraint has been defined in which the EMPID column of the EMPLOYEES table is the parent key and the EMPID

column of the PAYCHECKS table is the foreign key—this referential constraint is named FKCONST).

- Whenever a row is deleted from the EMPLOYEES table, rows in the PAYCHECKS table that have a value in the EMPID column that matches the primary key value of the deleted row are also removed (because the ON DELETE CASCADE Delete Rule was specified for the FKCONST referential constraint).
- Every value provided for the PAY_AMT column must be greater than 0 (because a CHECK constraint named CHK1 was defined for both the PAY_AMT and WEEKNUMBER columns).
- Every value provided for the WEEKNUMBER column must be greater than or equal to 1 and less than or equal to 52 (again, because a CHECK constraint named CHK1 was defined for both the PAY_AMT and WEEKNUMBER columns).

Example 4

If the following CREATE TABLE statement is executed:

```
CREATE TABLE employees
  (empid      SMALLINT NOT NULL
                GENERATED BY DEFAULT AS IDENTITY,
   firstname VARCHAR(30) NOT NULL,
   lastname  VARCHAR(30) NOT NULL,
   deptid    CHAR(3),
   edlevel   CHAR(1) CHECK (edlevel IN ('C', 'H', 'N')),
  CONSTRAINT emp_pk PRIMARY KEY (empid),
  CONSTRAINT emp_dept_fk FOREIGN KEY (deptid)
    REFERENCES department (deptno))
```

a table named EMPLOYEES will be created as follows:

- The first column will be named EMPID (for Employee ID) and can be used to store numeric values in the range of –32,768 to +32,767.
- The second column will be named FIRSTNAME and can be used to store variable length character string data up to 30 characters in length (for example, 'Melanie' or 'Susan').

- The third column will be named LASTNAME and can be used to store variable length character string data up to 30 characters in length (for example, 'Stopfer' or 'Weaver').
- The fourth column will be named DEPTID and can be used to store fixed-length character string data up to three characters in length (for example, '1' or '352').
- The fifth column will be named EDLEVEL and can be used to store fixed-length character string data that is only one character in length (for example, 'C' or 'H').
- The table will be created in a schema that has the name of the authorization ID of the individual who created it (because a schema name was not provided and this is the default schema name used).
- The table will be created in the table space USERSPACE1 (because a table space was not specified and this is the default table space used).
- Whenever data is added to the table, DB2 will automatically assign a unique numeric value to the EMPID column, unless the user provides a value for this column (because the EMPID column is an identity column that was defined with the GENERATED BY DEFAULT AS IDENTITY clause). If the user does provide a value for the EMPID column, it cannot be the value NULL. (NULL values are not allowed because a NOT NULL constraint was defined for this column.)
- Whenever data is added to the table, values must be provided for both the FIRSTNAME and the LASTNAME columns. (NULL values are not allowed because a NOT NULL constraint was defined for both of these columns.)
- Only the values 'C', 'H', or 'N' can be stored in the EDLEVEL column (because a CHECK constraint was defined for this column).
- Every value provided for the EMPID column must be unique (because a primary key constraint named EMP_PK was defined for this column).
- An index was automatically created for the EMPID column (because a primary key constraint named EMP_PK was defined for this column). As data is added to the table, values provided for the EMPID column are added to the index, and the entries in the index are sorted in ascending order.
- Every value entered in the DEPTID column must have a matching value in the DEPTNO column of a table named DEPARTMENT (because a referential constraint has been defined in which the DEPTNO column of the DEPARTMENT table is the parent key and the DEPTID column of the EMPLOYEES table is the foreign key—this referential constraint is named EMP_DEPT_FK).

Example 5

If the following CREATE TABLE statement is executed:

```
CREATE TABLE stock.activity
  (activityno SMALLINT NOT NULL
              GENERATED BY DEFAULT AS IDENTITY
              (START WITH 10 INCREMENT BY 10),
   actkwd     CHAR(6) NOT NULL,
   actdesc    VARCHAR(40) NOT NULL,
  UNIQUE (activityno))
```

a table named ACTIVITY will be created as follows:

- The first column will be named ACTIVITYNO (for Activity Number) and can be used to store numeric values in the range of –32,768 to +32,767.
- The second column will be named ACTKWD (for Activity Keyword) and can be used to store fixed-length character string data up to six characters in length (for example, 'Sell' or 'Buy').
- The third column will be named ACTDESC (for Activity Description) and can be used to store variable-length character string data up to 40 characters in length (for example, 'Sell 1000 shares of IBM' or 'Buy 250 shares of EMC').
- The table will be created in a schema named STOCK.
- The table will be created in the table space USERSPACE1 (because a table space was not specified and this is the default table space used).
- Whenever data is added to the table, DB2 will automatically assign a unique numeric value to the ACTIVITYNO column, unless the user provides a value for this column (because the ACTIVITY column is an identity column that was defined with the GENERATED BY DEFAULT AS IDENTITY clause). If the user does not provide a value, the first value generated will be the number 10, and subsequent generated values will be incremented by 10. If the user does provide a value for the EMPID column, it cannot be the value NULL. (NULL values are not allowed because a NOT NULL constraint was defined for this column.)
- Whenever data is added to the table, values must be provided for the ACTKWD and the ACTDESC columns. (NULL values are not allowed these columns because a NOT NULL constraint was defined for each column.)

- Every value provided for the ACTIVITYNO column must be unique (because a UNIQUE constraint was defined for this column).
- An index was automatically created for the ACTIVITYNO column (because a UNIQUE constraint was defined for this column). As data is added to the table, values provided for the ACTIVITYNO column are added to the index, and the entries in the index are sorted in ascending order.

Example 6

If the following CREATE TABLE statement is executed:

```
CREATE TABLE self_reference
  (idcol1 SMALLINT NOT NULL PRIMARY KEY,
   idcol2 SAMLLINT,
   CONSTRAINT fkconst FOREIGN KEY (idcol2)
     REFERENCES self_reference(idcol1))
```

a table named SELF_REFERENCE will be created as follows:

- The first column will be named IDCOL1 and can be used to store numeric values in the range of –32,768 to +32,767.
- The second column will be named IDCOL2 and can be used to store numeric values in the range of –32,768 to +32,767.
- The table will be created in a schema that has the name of the authorization ID of the individual who created it (because a schema name was not provided and this is the default schema name used).
- The table will be created in the table space USERSPACE1 (because a table space was not specified and this is the default table space used).
- Every value provided for the IDCOL1 column must be unique (because a primary key constraint was defined for this column).
- An index was automatically created for the IDCOL1 column (because a primary key constraint was defined for this column). As data is added to the table, values provided for the IDCOL1 column are added to the index, and the entries in the index are sorted in ascending order.
- Every value entered in the IDCOL2 column must have a matching value in the IDCOL1 column of the table (because a referential constraint has been defined in

which the IDCOL1 column of the table is the parent key and the IDCOL2 column of the same table is the foreign key—this referential constraint is named FKCONST).

Altering Tables

Over time, it may become necessary for a table to hold additional data values either that did not exist or that were not considered at the time the table was created. Or, character data that was originally thought to be one size may have turned out to be larger than anticipated. These are just a couple of reasons why it can become necessary to modify an existing table's definition. When only a small amount of data is stored in a table and the table has few or no dependencies, it can be relatively easy to save the associated data, drop the existing table, create a new table with the appropriate modifications, populate it with the previously saved data, and redefine any necessary dependencies. But how can you make such modifications to a table that holds a large volume of data or has numerous dependency relationships?

Select properties of an existing table can be modified and additional columns and constraints can be added or removed by executing the ALTER TABLE statement. Like the CREATE TABLE statement, the ALTER TABLE statement can be quite complex. However, in its simplest form, the syntax for the ALTER TABLE statement looks like this:

```
ALTER TABLE [TableName] ADD ([Element], ...)
```

or

```
ALTER TABLE [TableName]
  ALTER COLUMN [ColumnName]
  SET DATA TYPE [DataType]
```

or

```
ALTER TABLE [TableName]
  DROP [COLUMN [ColumnName] <CASCADE | RESTRICT> |
    PRIMARY KEY |
    UNIQUE [ConstraintName] |
    CHECK [ConstraintName] |
    FOREIGN KEY [ConstraintName]]
```

where:

TableName	Identifies, by name, the table whose definition is to be altered
Element	Identifies one or more columns, UNIQUE constraints, CHECK constraints, referential integrity constraints, and/or a primary key constraint that are to be added to the existing table's definition; the syntax used to define each of these elements varies according to the element specified
ColumnName	Identifies, by name, an existing column whose data type is to be changed *or* that is to be removed from the table's definition
DataType	Identifies the new data type (built-in or user-defined) that is to be assigned to the column—Table 6.4 contains a list of valid built-in data type definitions
ConstraintName	Identifies, by name, an existing UNIQUE, CHECK, referential integrity, or primary key constraint that is to be removed from the table's definition

The syntax used to define a column element is the same as that used to define a column element with the CREATE TABLE statement. Likewise, the syntax used to define UNIQUE constraints, CHECK constraints, referential integrity constraints, informational constraints, and primary key constraints as individual elements is the same as that used to define each of these constraints.

Therefore, if a table named EMPLOYEES was created with a CREATE TABLE statement that looks something this:

```
CREATE TABLE employees
   (empid  INTEGER,
    name   CHAR(50),
    dept   INTEGER)
```

you could add a column named HIRE_DATE that will be used to store date values to this table by executing an ALTER TABLE statement that looks like this:

```
ALTER TABLE employees
   ADD COLUMN hire_date  DATE
```

On the other hand, to change the data type associated with the column named NAME (in the same EMPLOYEES table) from a fixed-length character string data type that can hold up to 50 bytes (CHAR(50)) to a varying-length character string data type that can hold up to 60 bytes (VARCHAR(60)), you would execute an ALTER TABLE statement that looks more like this:

```
ALTER TABLE employees
    ALTER COLUMN name SET DATA TYPE VARCHAR(60)
```

As we saw in Chapter 3, "Security," the ALTER TABLE statement can also be used to activate row access control and column access control for a given table. In these cases, the ALTER TABLE statement must be executed with either the ACTIVATE ROW ACCESS CONTROL or the ACTIVATE COLUMN ACCESS CONTROL clause specified.

A Closer Look at Temporary Tables

In Chapter 4, "Working with Databases and Database Objects," we saw that, along with base tables, another type of table that is commonly used is a *temporary table*. Unlike base tables, which act as a long-term repository for data, temporary tables serve as temporary work areas. Temporary tables are often used for recording the results of data manipulation or for storing intermediate results of a subquery (when this information will not fit in the memory available). With DB2 10 and 10.1, two types of temporary tables are available: *declared temporary tables* and *created temporary tables.*

Unlike base tables, whose definitions are stored in the system catalog of the database they belong to, declared temporary tables are not persistent and can only be used by the application that creates them—and only for the life of that application. When the application that creates a declared temporary table disconnects from the database (or is terminated, either on purpose or prematurely), the table's rows are deleted, and the table is implicitly dropped. Another significant difference between the two centers around naming conventions: base table names must be unique within a schema, but because each application that defines a temporary table has its own instance of that table, multiple applications can create declared temporary tables that have the same name.

Similar to declared temporary tables, created temporary tables are used by applications to temporarily store the results of data manipulation. But whereas information about declared temporary tables is not stored in the system catalog, information about created temporary tables *is*. Thus, created temporary tables are persistent and can be shared with other applications, across different connections, and across transaction boundaries. (Declared temporary tables, on the other hand, must be defined in every session where they are used.) Table 6.5 lists other important distinctions between base tables, declared temporary tables, and created temporary tables.

Table 6.5: Important distinctions between base tables, declared temporary tables, and created temporary tables			
Area of Distinction	**Base Tables**	**Declared Temporary Tables**	**Created Temporary Tables**
Creation	Created with the CREATE TABLE statement.	Created with the DECLARE GLOBAL TEMPORARY TABLE statement.	Created with the CREATE GLOBAL TEMPORARY TABLE statement.
Schema qualifier	The name of the table can be qualified. If the table name is not explicitly qualified, it is implicitly qualified using the current value of the CURRENT SCHEMA (DB2 for Linux, UNIX, and Windows) or the CURRENT SQLID (DB2 for z/OS) special register.	The name of the table can be qualified. If the table name is explicitly qualified, the name SESSION must be used as the qualifier; if the table name is not explicitly qualified, SESSION is implicitly used as the qualifier.	The name of the table can be qualified; if the table name is not explicitly qualified, it is implicitly qualified using the current value of the CURRENT SCHEMA (DB2 for Linux, UNIX, and Windows) or the CURRENT SQLID (DB2 for z/OS) special register.
System catalog storage	A description of the table is stored in the system catalog.	A description of the table is not stored in the system catalog.	A description of the table is stored in the system catalog.
Persistence/ability to share table description	The table description is persistent and shareable across different connections.	The table description is not persistent beyond the life of the connection that was used to declare the table. Furthermore, the description is known only to that connection. Thus, each connection can have its own description of the same declared temporary table.	The table description is persistent and shareable across different connections.

Table 6.5: Important distinctions between base tables, declared temporary tables, and created temporary tables (continued)

Area of Distinction	Base Tables	Declared Temporary Tables	Created Temporary Tables
Table instantiation	The CREATE TABLE statement creates one empty instance of the table, and all connections use that instance of the table.	The DECLARE GLOBAL TEMPORARY TABLE statement creates an empty instance of the table for the connection. Each connection that declares the table has its own unique instance of the table, and the instance is not persistent beyond the life of the connection.	The CREATE GLOBAL TEMPORARY TABLE statement does not create an instance of the table. The first implicit or explicit reference to the table in an OPEN, SELECT, INSERT, UPDATE, or DELETE statement that is executed by any program using the connection creates an empty instance of the given table. Each connection that references the table has its own unique instance of the table, and the instance is not persistent beyond the life of the connection.
Ability to share data	The table and data are persistent.	The table and its data are not persistent beyond the life of the connection it was created under.	The table and its data are not persistent beyond the life of the connection it was created under.
References to the table during connections	References to the table name in multiple connections refer to the same single persistent table description and to the same instance at the current server.	References to the table name in multiple connections refer to a distinct description and instance of the table for each connection at the current server.	References to the table name in multiple connections refer to the same single persistent table description, but to a distinct instance of the table for each connection at the current server.

Table 6.5: Important distinctions between base tables, declared temporary tables, and created temporary tables (continued)			
Area of Distinction	**Base Tables**	**Declared Temporary Tables**	**Created Temporary Tables**
Table privileges and authorization	The owner implicitly has all table privileges on the table and the authority to drop the table. The owner's table privileges can be granted and revoked, either individually or with the ALL clause. Another authorization ID can access the table only if it has been granted appropriate privileges for the table.	PUBLIC implicitly has all table privileges on the table without GRANT authority and also has the authority to drop the table. These table privileges cannot be granted or revoked. Any authorization ID can access the table without requiring a grant of any privileges for the table.	The owner implicitly has all table privileges on the table and the authority to drop the table. The owner's table privileges can be granted and revoked, either individually or with the ALL clause. Another authorization ID can access the table only if it has been granted appropriate privileges for the table.
Indexes and other SQL statement support	Indexes and SQL statements that modify data (INSERT, UPDATE, DELETE, and so on) are supported.	Indexes and SQL statements that modify data (INSERT, UPDATE, DELETE, and so on) are supported.	Indexes and SQL statements that modify data (INSERT, UPDATE, DELETE, and so on) are supported.
Locking, logging, and recovery	Locking, logging, and recovery apply.	Locking and recovery do not apply; logging applies only when LOGGED is explicitly or implicitly specified. The ability to undo recovery (rolling back changes to a savepoint or the most recent commit point) is supported when LOGGED is explicitly or implicitly specified.	Locking and recovery do not apply; logging applies when LOGGED is explicitly specified. The ability to undo recovery (rolling back changes to a savepoint or the most recent commit point) is supported when LOGGED is explicitly or implicitly specified.
Adapted from Tables 1 found under **Distinctions between DB2 base tables and temporary tables** in the IBM DB2 10.1 Information Center for Linux, UNIX, and Windows *(pic.dhe.ibm.com/infocenter/db2luw/v10r1/topic/com.ibm.db2.luw.admin.dbobj.doc/doc/r0054491.html)* and the IBM Information Management Software for z/OS Solutions Information Center (*publib.boulder.ibm.com/infocenter/dzichelp/v2r2/topic/com.ibm.db2z10.doc.admin/src/tpc/db2z_tabletypedistinctions.htm*)			

It is important to note that to construct a declared or created temporary table, you must first create a user temporary table space. That is because declared and created temporary tables can be stored only in user temporary table spaces. And a user temporary table space is not created by default as part of the database creation process.

A Closer Look at Views

In Chapter 4, "Working with Databases and Database Objects," we saw that views can provide a different way of describing and looking at data stored in one or more base tables. Essentially, a view is a named specification of a result table that is populated whenever the view is referenced in an SQL statement. (Each time a view is referenced, a query is executed, and the results are retrieved from the underlying table and returned in a table-like format.)

Like base tables, views can be thought of as having columns and rows. And in most cases, data can be manipulated using a view just as it can be manipulated using a table. (In other words, you can use views to insert, update, and delete data values.)

As with tables, views can be created via Data Studio or by executing the CREATE VIEW statement. The basic syntax for this statement is:

```
CREATE VIEW [ViewName]
  <([ColumnName], ...)>
  AS [SELECTStatement]
  <WITH <LOCAL | CASCADED> CHECK OPTION>
```

where:

ViewName	Identifies the name to assign to the view that is to be created; the view name specified must be unique within the schema the view is to be defined in
ColumnName	Identifies, by name, one or more columns that are to be included in the view—if a list of column names is provided, the number of column names supplied must match the number of columns that will be returned by the SELECT statement used to create the view; if a list of column names is not provided, the view will inherit the names that are assigned to the columns returned by the SELECT statement used
SELECTStatement	Identifies a SELECT statement that, when executed, will produce the data values that are to be used to populate the view (by retrieving them from other tables, views, or both)

Therefore, to create a view named DEPT_VIEW that references specific data values stored in a table named DEPARTMENT, you could execute a CREATE VIEW statement that looks something like this:

```
CREATE VIEW dept_view
  AS SELECT (dept_no, dept_name, dept_size)
  FROM department
  WHERE dept_size > 25
```

The resulting view will contain department number (DEPT_NO), department name (DEPT_NAME), and department size (DEPT_SIZE) information for every department that has more than 25 people assigned to it.

If the WITH <LOCAL> CHECK OPTION clause is specified with the CREATE VIEW statement used, all insert and update operations that are performed against the resulting view will be checked to ensure that the rows being added or modified conform to the view's definition. What does that mean? Suppose you created a view named CHOICE_OBJECTS (that is based on the OBJECTS table that was used in some of the earlier examples) by executing a CREATE VIEW statement that looks like this:

```
CREATE VIEW choice_objects
  AS SELECT * FROM object
  WHERE o_id < 100
  WITH LOCAL CHECK OPTION
```

Now, suppose a user tries to add a new record to this view, using an INSERT statement that looks like this:

```
INSERT INTO choice_objects
  VALUES (500, 'SNOW', 'WHITE')
```

The insert operation will fail because the record violates the view's definition. (The value specified for the O_ID column is greater than 100.) Figure 6.17 illustrates this scenario.

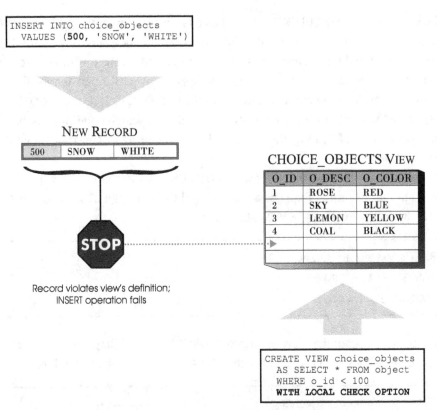

Figure 6.17: How the WITH LOCAL CHECK OPTION *clause ensures that rows being added or modified via a view conform to the view's definition*

Had the WITH LOCAL CHECK OPTION clause not been specified when the CHOICE_ OBJECTS view was created, the insert operation would have been successful. However, the record that was added would not have been visible to the view. So essentially, the WITH LOCAL CHECK OPTION clause guarantees that an insert or update operation performed against a view will not create a record that the view will never see.

Note: Views created with the WITH LOCAL CHECK OPTION clause are referred to as *symmetric views* because every record that can be inserted into them can also be retrieved from them.

If the WITH CASCADED CHECK OPTION clause is specified with the CREATE VIEW statement used, the resulting view will inherit the search conditions of the parent view (that the view is based upon), and it will treat those conditions as one or more constraints that are to be used to validate insert and update operations performed against the view. Any child view of the view that is created with the WITH CASCADED CHECK OPTION clause specified will inherit those constraints as well; the search conditions of both parent and child views are ANDed together to form the complete set of constraints that data must adhere to.

To better understand how the WITH CASCADED CHECK OPTION clause works, let us look at another example. Suppose a view named CHOICE_OBJECTS was created by executing the following CREATE VIEW statement:

```
CREATE VIEW choice_objects
  AS SELECT * FROM object
  WHERE o_id < 100
```

Now, suppose a second a view named RED_OBJECTS (which happens to be a child of the CHOICE_OBJECTS view) is created with a CREATE VIEW statement that looks like this:

```
CREATE VIEW red_objects
  AS SELECT * FROM choice_objects
  WHERE o_color = 'RED'
  WITH CASCADED CHECK OPTION
```

If a user attempts to add a new record to the RED_OBJECTS view using an INSERT statement that looks like this:

```
INSERT INTO red_objects
  VALUES (500, 'CHERRY', 'RED')
```

the insert operation will fail because the record violates the *parent* view's definition— the value specified for the O_ID column is greater than 100. Figure 6.18 illustrates this scenario.

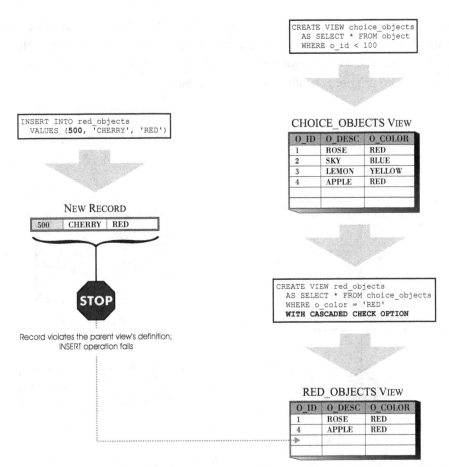

```
CREATE VIEW choice_objects
   AS SELECT * FROM object
   WHERE o_id < 100
```

```
INSERT INTO red_objects
   VALUES (500, 'CHERRY', 'RED')
```

CHOICE_OBJECTS VIEW

O_ID	O_DESC	O_COLOR
1	ROSE	RED
2	SKY	BLUE
3	LEMON	YELLOW
4	APPLE	RED

NEW RECORD

500	CHERRY	RED

```
CREATE VIEW red_objects
   AS SELECT * FROM choice_objects
   WHERE o_color = 'RED'
   WITH CASCADED CHECK OPTION
```

STOP

Record violates the parent view's definition;
INSERT operation fails

RED_OBJECTS VIEW

O_ID	O_DESC	O_COLOR
1	ROSE	RED
4	APPLE	RED

Figure 6.18: How the WITH CASCADED CHECK OPTION *clause ensures that rows being added or modified via a child view conform to the parent view's definition*

It is important to note that when a view is created with the WITH CASCADED CHECK OPTION clause, all insert and update operations performed against the view will be checked to ensure that the rows being added or modified conform to both the view's definition *and the parent view's definition*. Consequently, if a user tries to add a new record to the RED_OBJECTS view that was created in the previous example using an INSERT statement that looks like this:

```
INSERT INTO red_objects
   VALUES (500, 'SNOW', 'WHITE')
```

the insert operation will fail because the record violates both the view's definition and the parent view's definition—the value specified for the O_ID column is greater than 100 (parent view's definition) and the value provided for the O_COLOR column is not 'RED' (view's definition). Figure 6.19 illustrates this behavior.

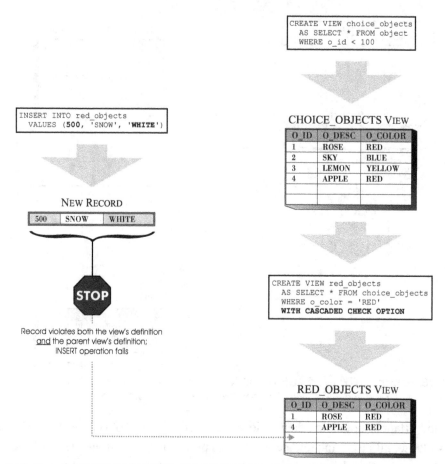

Figure 6.19: How the WITH CASCADED CHECK OPTION *clause ensures that rows being added or modified via a child view conform to both the child and the parent view's definition*

A Closer Look at Indexes

In Chapter 4, "Working with Databases and Database Objects," we saw that an index is an object that contains pointers to rows (in a table) that are logically ordered according to the values of one or more columns (known as *key columns* or *keys*). Indexes are important because:

- They provide a fast, efficient method for locating specific rows of data in large tables
- They provide a logical ordering of the rows in a table
- They can enforce the uniqueness of records in a table
- They can force a table to use *clustering* storage, which causes the rows of a table to be physically arranged according to the ordering of their key column values

Although some indexes are created implicitly to provide support for a unique constraint or primary key, most indexes are explicitly created using either Data Studio or the CREATE INDEX statement. The basic syntax for the CREATE INDEX statement is:

```
CREATE <UNIQUE> INDEX [IndexName]
ON [TableName] ([PriColumnName] <ASC | DESC>, ...)
<INCLUDE ([SecColumnName], ... )>
<CLUSTER>
<PCTFREE [10 | PercentFree]>
```

where:

IndexName	Identifies the name to assign to the index that is to be created; the index name specified must be unique within the schema the index is to be defined in
TableName	Identifies, by name, the table that the index is to be created for (and associated with)
PriColumnName	Identifies, by name, one or more primary columns that are to be part of the key for the index—if the index is a unique index, the combined values of each primary column specified will be used to enforce data uniqueness in the associated base table

> *SecColumnName*   Identifies, by name, one or more secondary columns whose values are to be stored with the values of the primary columns, but that are not part of the index key—if the index is a unique index, the values of each secondary column specified will not be used to enforce data uniqueness
>
> *PercentFree*   Specifies the percentage of each index page to leave as free space as the index is populated

If the INCLUDE clause is specified with the CREATE INDEX statement used, data from the secondary columns specified will be appended to the index's key values. By storing this information in the index (along with key values), you can improve the performance of some queries—if all the data needed to resolve a particular query can be obtained by accessing the index only, data does not have to be retrieved from the associated base table. (If the data needed to resolve a particular query does not reside solely in an index, both the index and the associated table must be accessed.)

Thus, to create an index named EMPNO_IDX for a base table named EMPLOYEES whose key consists of a column named EMPNO and that includes data from a column named LASTNAME, you would execute a CREATE INDEX statement that looks something like this:

```
CREATE UNIQUE INDEX empno_idx
  ON employees(empno) INCLUDE (lastname)
```

If the UNIQUE clause is specified with the CREATE INDEX statement used, the resulting index will be a *unique index* and, as we saw earlier, it will be used to ensure that the associated table does not contain duplicate occurrences of the same values in the columns that make up the index key. If the base table the index is to be created for already contains data, uniqueness is checked and enforced at the time DB2 attempts to create the index, and if records with duplicate index key values are found, the index will not be created. On the other hand, if no duplicates exist, the index will be created and uniqueness will be enforced whenever insert and update operations are performed against the associated table. (Any time uniqueness of the index key is compromised, the insert or update operation will fail and an error will be generated.)

Important: If the INCLUDE clause is specified with the CREATE INDEX statement used, the UNIQUE clause must be provided.

Thus, to create a unique index named EMPNO_IDX for a base table named EMPLOYEES whose key consists of a column named EMPNO, you would execute a CREATE INDEX statement that looks like this:

```
CREATE UNIQUE INDEX empno_idx
    ON employees(empno)
```

Note: If you decide to create an index to support a UNIQUE constraint (rather than have DB2 automatically create one for you), the index must be created with the UNIQUE clause specified.

If the CLUSTER clause is specified with the CREATE INDEX statement used, the resulting index will be a *clustering index,* which as we saw in Chapter 4, "Working with Databases and Database Objects," is a special index that attempts to physically store records for a table on a page that contains other records with similar index key values. (If no space is available on that page, DB2 will attempt to store the record in a nearby page.) A clustering index usually increases performance by decreasing the amount of I/O that is needed to access data. A table can have only one clustering index.

Therefore, to create a clustering index named EMPNO_CIDX for a base table named EMPLOYEES whose key consists of a column named EMPNO, you would execute a CREATE INDEX statement that looks like this:

```
CREATE UNIQUE INDEX empno_cidx
    ON employees(empno)
    CLUSTER
```

When creating a clustering index, the CREATE INDEX statement's PCTFREE clause can be used to control how much space is reserved for future insert and update operations. A higher PCTFREE value (the default is 10 percent) can reduce the likelihood that index page splits will occur when records are added to an index.

> **Note:** Over time, update operations can cause rows to change page locations, thereby reducing the degree of clustering that exists between an index and its data pages. Reorganizing a table (with the REORG utility) by the clustering index will return the index to its original level of clustering.

You can create any number of indexes for a table by using a wide variety of column combinations. However, as we saw in Chapter 4, "Working with Databases and Database Objects," every index comes at a price. Because indexes store key column and row pointer information, additional storage space is needed for each index used. Furthermore, write performance is negatively affected—every time a transaction performs an insert, update, or delete operation against a table with indexes, each index affected must be updated to reflect the changes made. Because of this, indexes should only be created when there is a clear performance advantage to having them.

Indexes are typically used to improve query performance. Therefore, tables that are used for data mining, business intelligence, business warehousing, and other applications that execute many (and often complex) queries but that rarely modify data are prime candidates for indexes. Conversely, tables in Online Transaction Processing (OLTP) environments or environments where data throughput is high should use indexes sparingly or avoid them altogether.

A Closer Look at Triggers

In Chapter 4, "Working with Databases and Database Objects," we saw that a trigger is an object that is used to define a set of actions that are to be executed whenever a transaction performs an insert, update, or delete operation against a table or updatable view. Like constraints, triggers are often used to enforce data integrity and business rules. Unlike constraints, triggers can also be used to automatically update other tables, generate or transform values for inserted or updated rows, and invoke functions to perform tasks such as issuing errors or alerts.

Before you can create a trigger, you must identify the following components:

- **Subject table/view:** The table or view that the trigger is to be associated with
- **Trigger event:** An SQL operation that, when performed against the subject table or view, will cause the trigger to be activated (*fired*); the trigger event can be an insert operation, an update operation, a delete operation, or a merge operation that inserts, updates, or deletes data
- **Trigger activation time:** Indicates whether the trigger should be fired *before*, *after*, or *instead of* the trigger event (a BEFORE trigger is fired before the trigger event occurs and can see new data values that are about to be inserted into the subject table; an AFTER trigger is fired after the trigger event occurs and can see data values that have already been inserted into the subject table; and an INSTEAD OF trigger is executed against the subject view, in place of the trigger event)
- **Set of affected rows:** The rows of the subject table or view that are being added, updated, or removed
- **Triggered action:** An optional search condition and a set of SQL statements that are executed when the trigger is fired—if a search condition is specified, the SQL statements are executed only if the search condition evaluates to TRUE
- **Trigger granularity:** Specifies whether the triggered action is to be executed once, when the trigger event takes place, or once for every row that the trigger event affects

After the appropriate trigger components have been identified, a trigger can be created by executing the CREATE TRIGGER statement. The basic syntax for this statement is:

```
CREATE TRIGGER [TriggerName]
[NO CASCADE BEFORE | AFTER | INSTEAD OF]
[INSERT | UPDATE <OF [ColumnName], ... > | DELETE]
ON [TableName | ViewName]
<REFERENCING [Reference]>
FOR EACH [ROW | STATEMENT]
<WHEN ( [SearchCondition] )>
[TriggeredAction]
```

where:

TriggerName	Identifies the name to assign to the trigger that is to be created; the trigger name specified must be unique within the schema the trigger is to be defined in
ColumnName	Identifies, by name, one or more columns in the subject table or view whose values must be updated before the triggered action (*TriggeredAction*) will be performed
TableName	Identifies, by name, the subject table of the BEFORE or AFTER trigger that is to be created
ViewName	Identifies, by name, the subject view of the INSTEAD OF trigger that is to be created
Reference	Identifies one or more transition variables or transition tables that the triggered action (*TriggeredAction*) will use; the syntax used to create transition variables and transition tables is:

```
<OLD <AS> [CorrelationName]>
<NEW <AS> [CorrelationName]>
<OLD TABLE <AS> [Identifier]>
<NEW TABLE <AS> [Identifier]>
```

where:

CorrelationName	Identifies a shorthand name that can be used to reference a specific row in the subject table of the trigger, either before the triggered action (OLD <AS>) altered the row or after the triggered action (NEW <AS>) modified it
Identifier	Identifies a shorthand name that can be used to identify a temporary table that contains a set of rows found in the subject table of the trigger, either before the triggered action (OLD TABLE <AS>) altered the rows or after the triggered action (NEW TABLE <AS>) modified them
SearchCondition	Identifies a search condition that, when evaluated, will return TRUE, FALSE, or Unknown; this condition determines whether or not the triggered action (*TriggeredAction*) is to be performed

TriggeredAction   Identifies one or more SQL statements or SQL Procedural Language (SQL PL) statements that are to be executed when the trigger is fired; together, these statements act as a single dynamic compound SQL statement—if two or more statements are used, they should be enclosed with the keywords BEGIN ATOMIC and END, and each statement must be terminated with a semicolon (;)

As you can see from the CREATE TRIGGER statement syntax, SQL statements that are to be executed when a trigger is fired (that is, the triggered action) can reference specific values within the set of affected rows using what are known as *transition variables*. Transition variables inherit the names of the columns in the subject table and are defined with the REFERENCING [*Reference*] clause of the CREATE TRIGGER statement. The OLD <AS> keywords indicate that a particular transition variable refers to the original value (as it existed before the trigger event was executed), and the NEW <AS> keywords denote that the variable refers to the new value (after the trigger event has completed).

If it is necessary to access the entire set of affected rows, *transition tables* can be used in lieu of transition variables. Like transition variables, transition tables inherit the names of the columns of the subject table and are defined with the REFERENCING [*Reference*] clause. In this case, the OLD TABLE <AS> keywords indicate that the set of affected rows refer to the original records, whereas the NEW TABLE <AS> keywords denote that the set of affected rows refer to new records.

The type of SQL operation that causes a trigger to fire determines which transition variables and/or tables can be defined. For example, if the trigger event is an insert operation, only NEW transition variables and tables can be defined (because no original state of the record being inserted exists, there are no old values). If the trigger event is a delete operation, only OLD transition variables and tables can be defined (because no new values are available with delete operations). However, if the trigger event is an update operation, *both* OLD and NEW transition variables and tables can be defined. In addition, transition variables can only be specified for triggers whose granularity is FOR EACH ROW. Transition tables, however, can be specified for triggers whose granularity is FOR EACH ROW or FOR EACH STATEMENT.

Consequently, if you have a base table named EMPLOYEES that has the following characteristics:

Column Name	Data Type
EMPID	CHAR(3)
FIRSTNAME	VARCHAR(20)
LASTNAME	VARCHAR(20)
SALARY	DECIMAL(10, 2)
BONUS	DECIMAL(8, 2)

and you want to create a trigger that will recalculate an employee's annual bonus any time his or her salary changes, you could execute a CREATE TRIGGER statement that looks something like this:

```
CREATE TRIGGER calc_bonus
  NO CASCADE BEFORE
  UPDATE OF salary
  ON employees
  REFERENCING NEW AS n
  FOR EACH ROW
  SET n.bonus = n.salary * .025
```

Earlier, we saw that there are essentially three different ways a trigger can be fired: before the trigger event takes place, after the trigger event completes, or in place of the trigger event. For this reason, triggers are often referred to as being BEFORE triggers, AFTER triggers, or INSTEAD OF triggers.

As the name implies, a BEFORE trigger is fired for every row in the set of affected rows *before* the trigger event takes place. Consequently, BEFORE triggers are often used to validate input data, to automatically generate values for newly inserted rows, and to prevent certain types of trigger events from being performed.

For example, to prevent users from changing the employee ID assigned to an individual after a record for that individual is stored in the EMPLOYEES table presented earlier, you might create a BEFORE trigger that enforces this behavior by executing a CREATE TRIGGER statement that looks something like this:

```
CREATE TRIGGER block_empid_updates
  NO CASCADE BEFORE
  UPDATE OF empid
  ON employees
  FOR EACH ROW
  SIGNAL SQLSTATE '75001'
  SET MESSAGE_TEXT = 'Updates of EMPID column not allowed!'
```

On the other hand, an AFTER trigger is fired *after* the trigger event has been successfully executed. Because of this, AFTER triggers are often used to insert, update, or delete data in the same or in other tables; to check data against other data values in the same or in other tables; or to invoke UDFs that perform nondatabase operations. For example, suppose you have a base table named SALES that has the following characteristics:

Column Name	Data Type
INVOICE	INTEGER
AMOUNT	DECIMAL(10, 2)
SALES_DATE	DATE
SHIP_DATE	DATE
BILL_DATE	DATE

Now, assume that business rules dictate that any time a user inserts a record into the SALES table, the current date is to be recorded as the sales date, a shipping date is to be scheduled three days out, and billing is to occur 30 days from the date of the sale. You could create three AFTER triggers to enforce these business rules by executing a set of CREATE TRIGGER statements that look like this:

```
CREATE TRIGGER calc_sales_date
  AFTER
  INSERT ON sales
  REFERENCING NEW AS n
                                                    Continued
```

```
  FOR EACH ROW
  UPDATE sales SET sales_date = CURRENT DATE
    WHERE invoice = n.invoice


CREATE TRIGGER calc_ship_date
  AFTER
  INSERT ON sales
  REFERENCING NEW AS n
  FOR EACH ROW
  UPDATE sales SET ship_date = CURRENT DATE + 3 DAYS
    WHERE invoice = n.invoice


CREATE TRIGGER calc_bill_date
  AFTER
  INSERT ON sales
  REFERENCING NEW AS n
  FOR EACH ROW
  UPDATE sales SET bill_date = CURRENT DATE + 30 DAYS
    WHERE invoice = n.invoice
```

Notice that in this scenario, three triggers were created: one to generate a sales date, one to generate a shipping date, and one to generate a billing date. If necessary, several different triggers can be created for a single table. However, when multiple triggers are needed, the order in which they are defined can be important. That is because triggers are fired in the order in which they are created.

Thus, in the previous example, each time a new record is inserted into the SALES table, the CALC_SALES_DATE trigger will be fired first, followed by the CALC_SHIP_DATE trigger, followed by the CALC_BILL_DATE trigger. (It is easy to see the problems that could arise had these three triggers been defined in the opposite order.) If, for some reason, one trigger fails, the firing of the others will not be affected.

Unlike BEFORE and AFTER triggers, which are fired whenever a specific trigger event is performed against a subject table, INSTEAD OF triggers are fired only when specific trigger events are performed against a subject view. Consequently, INSTEAD OF triggers are often used to force applications to use views as the only interface for performing insert, update, delete, and query operations. However, to use a view in this manner, it must not have been defined with a WITH CHECK OPTION specified.

Thus, if you were to create an updateable view for the EMPLOYEES table presented earlier by executing a CREATE VIEW statement that looks like this:

```
CREATE VIEW emp_info AS
  SELECT * FROM employees
```

assuming all data entry is to be performed by using the EMP_INFO view just created, you can prevent users from changing the employee ID assigned to an individual after a record for that individual has been stored in the EMPLOYEES table by creating an INSTEAD OF trigger with a CREATE TRIGGER statement that looks something like this:

```
CREATE TRIGGER empv_update
  INSTEAD OF
  UPDATE ON emp_info
  REFERENCING NEW AS n OLD AS o
  FOR EACH ROW
  BEGIN ATOMIC
    VALUES(CASE WHEN n.empid = o.empid THEN 0
           ELSE RAISE_ERROR('75001', 'No EMPID changes!')
           END);
    UPDATE employees AS e
    SET (firstname, lastname, salary, bonus)
      = (n.firstname, n.lastname, n.salary, n.bonus)
    WHERE n.empid = e.empid;
  END
```

It is important to note that once a trigger is created, it cannot be altered. Therefore, if you create a trigger and later discover that you need to change its behavior, you must drop the existing trigger and then recreate it with the changes desired.

7

Data Concurrency

Thirteen percent (13%) of the *DB2 10.1 Fundamentals* certification exam (Exam 610) is designed to test your knowledge of the mechanisms DB2 uses to allow multiple users and applications to interact with a database simultaneously, without adversely affecting data consistency. The questions that make up this portion of the exam are designed to evaluate the following:

- Your ability to identify the appropriate isolation level to use for a given situation
- Your ability to identify the characteristics of DB2 locks
- Your ability to list objects that locks can be acquired for
- Your ability to identify factors that can influence locking

This chapter introduces you to the concept of data consistency and to the two important mechanisms DB2 uses to maintain data consistency in both single-user and multiuser database environments: *isolation levels* and *locks*. In this chapter, you will learn what isolation levels are, which isolation levels are available, and how to use isolation levels to keep transactions from interfering with each other in a multiuser environment. You will also discover how DB2 provides concurrency control through the use of locking, which types of locks are available, how to acquire locks, and which factors can influence locking performance.

Understanding Data Consistency

To understand how DB2 attempts to maintain data consistency in both single and multiuser environments, you must first know what data consistency is. In addition, you should be able to identify the types of events that can leave a database in an inconsistent state. So just what is data consistency? The best way to answer that question is by looking at an example.

Suppose a company that owns a chain of hardware stores uses a database to keep track of, among other things, the inventory at each store. Consequently, the database contains inventory tables for every store in the chain, and whenever a particular store receives or sells merchandise, its designated inventory table is updated. Now suppose a case of hammers is physically moved from one store (which has plenty of hammers in stock) to another (which has just run out).

To reflect this inventory move, a user must increase the hammer count value stored in the receiving store's inventory table and decrease the hammer count value stored in the donating store's table. If, however, a user raises the hammer count value in the receiving store's table, but fails to lower the value in the donating store's table, the data in the database will be inconsistent—the total hammer count for the entire chain is no longer accurate (nor is the hammer count for the donating store).

In single-user environments, a database can become inconsistent if a user fails to make all the necessary changes (as in the previous example), if the database system crashes while a user or application is in the middle of making modifications, or if an application terminates prematurely. In multiuser environments, inconsistency can also occur when several users or applications attempt to access the same data *at the same time*. For example, in the previous scenario, if one user is updating both stores' inventory tables to show that a case of hammers was physically moved from one store to another, and another user queries the database to obtain the hammer count value for the receiving store *before* the update has been committed, the query will erroneously indicate that no more hammers are available. (Reacting to this misinformation, the second user might then place an order for more hammers when no more hammers are needed.)

Transactions, Isolation Levels, and Locks

The primary mechanism that DB2 uses to keep data consistent is the *transaction*. In Chapter 5, "Working with DB2 Data Using SQL," we saw that a transaction (also referred to as a *unit of work*) is a recoverable sequence of one or more SQL operations that are grouped as a single unit, usually within an application. The initiation and termination of a transaction defines points of consistency within a database; either the effects of all operations performed within a transaction are applied to the database and made permanent (committed), or they are backed out (rolled back) and the database is returned to its previous state.

In single-user environments, transactions are run serially and do not have to contend with other concurrently running transactions. But in multiuser environments, transactions are often run simultaneously. As a result, each transaction can potentially interfere with any other running transaction—the amount of interference allowed is controlled through the use of another mechanism, the *isolation level*.

Transactions that have the potential to interfere with one another are said to be *interleaved*, or *parallel*, whereas transactions that are completely isolated from one another are deemed *serializable*, which means that the results of running them simultaneously are the same as the results of running them serially (one after another). Ideally, every transaction should be serializable. Why?

Suppose a salesperson and an accountant are working with the same database simultaneously. Now assume the salesperson enters an order for Company X (to generate a quote) but does not commit the entry. At the same time, the accountant queries the database for a list of all unpaid orders, retrieves the new order for Company X, and generates a bill. Now imagine that the individual the salesperson is working with at Company X decides not to place the order. The salesperson rolls back the transaction since the order was not placed, and information about the order is removed from the database. However, one week later, Company X receives a bill for the order. Had the salesperson's transaction and the accountant's transaction been completely isolated from each other (that is, serialized), this situation would not have occurred—either the salesperson's transaction would have finished before the accountant's transaction began or vice versa. In either case, Company X would not have received a bill.

When transactions are not serializable, four types of phenomena can occur:

- **Lost updates:** Occurs when two transactions read the same data and both attempt to update that data at the same time, resulting in the loss of one of the updates—for example, Transaction 1 and Transaction 2 read the same row of data and calculate new values for that row based upon the values read; if Transaction 1 updates the row with its new value, and Transaction 2 then updates the same row, Transaction 1's update will be lost

- **Dirty reads:** Occurs when a transaction reads data that has not yet been committed—for example, Transaction 1 modifies a row of data, and Transaction 2 reads the modified row before the change is committed; if Transaction 1 rolls back the change, Transaction 2 will have read data that never really existed
- **Nonrepeatable reads:** Occurs when a transaction reads the same row of data twice and retrieves different results each time—for example, Transaction 1 reads a row of data, and then Transaction 2 modifies or deletes that row and commits the change; when Transaction 1 attempts to reread the row, it will retrieve different data values (if the row was updated) or discover that the row no longer exists (if the row was deleted)
- **Phantoms:** Occurs when a row of data matches some search criteria but is not seen initially—for example, Transaction 1 retrieves a set of rows that satisfies some search criteria, and Transaction 2 inserts a new row that matches the search criteria of Transaction 1's query; if Transaction 1 re-executes the query that produced the original set of rows, a different set of rows will be returned (the new row that Transaction 2 added will now be included in the set of rows produced)

Isolation Levels

Because different users and applications might attempt to access or modify data stored in a DB2 database at the same time, DB2 must be able to allow transactions to run simultaneously while ensuring that data integrity is never compromised. The simultaneous sharing of database resources by multiple users and applications is known as *concurrency*, and one way that DB2 enforces concurrency is through the use of isolation levels. As the name implies, isolation levels determine how DB2 *"isolates"* data that is accessed or modified by one transaction from other transactions that happen to be running at the same time. With DB2 10.1, the following isolation levels are recognized and supported:

- Repeatable Read
- Read Stability
- Cursor Stability
- Uncommitted Read

Table 7.1 shows the various phenomena that can occur when each of these isolation levels is used.

Table 7.1: DB2 isolation levels and the phenomena that can occur when each is used				
Isolation Level	**Phenomena**			
	Lost Updates	**Dirty Reads**	**Nonrepeatable Reads**	**Phantoms**
Repeatable Read	No	No	No	No
Read Stability	No	No	No	Yes
Cursor Stability	No	No	Yes	Yes
Uncommitted Read	No	Yes	Yes	Yes

The Repeatable Read (RR) isolation level

The Repeatable Read isolation level is the most restrictive isolation level available. It completely isolates the effects of one transaction from the effects of other concurrently running transactions. Thus, lost updates, dirty reads, nonrepeatable reads, and phantoms cannot occur.

With the Repeatable Read isolation level, every row that is referenced *in any manner* by the owning transaction is locked for the life of that transaction. (The transaction that has a resource associated with it is said to *hold* or *own* the lock on the resource.) Consequently, if the same query (SELECT statement) is issued multiple times within the same transaction, the result data sets produced are guaranteed to be identical. In fact, transactions running under the Repeatable Read isolation level can retrieve the same set of rows any number of times and perform any number of operations on them until terminated (by either a COMMIT or a ROLLBACK operation). However, other transactions are prohibited from performing insert, update, or delete operations that will alter rows that the owning transaction has accessed as long as that transaction remains active.

To ensure that other transactions do not adversely affect the data being accessed by a transaction running under the Repeatable Read isolation level, every row that the owning transaction references is locked—not just the rows that are actually retrieved or modified. Thus, if a transaction scans 1,000 rows to retrieve 10, locks are acquired and held on all 1,000 rows scanned—not on just the 10 rows retrieved.

> **Note:** With the Repeatable Read isolation level, if an entire table or view is scanned in response to a query, the entire table or all rows the view references are locked. This greatly reduces concurrency, especially when large tables and views are used.

So how does this isolation level work in a real-world situation? Suppose you own a small motel and use a DB2 database to keep track of reservation and room rate information. You also have a web-based application that allows individuals to reserve rooms on a first-come, first-served basis. If your reservation application runs under the Repeatable Read isolation level, a customer scanning the database for a list of available rooms for a given date range will prevent other customers from making or canceling reservations that would cause the list to change if it were to be generated again (by executing the same query—assuming, of course, that the query is executed from the same transaction).

Similarly, your motel's manager cannot change the room rate for any room records that were scanned in response to the first customer's query. However, other customers *can* make or cancel room reservations for rooms whose records were not scanned when the first customer's query was executed. Likewise, your manager can change room rates for any room whose record was not read when the list of available rooms was produced. (Anyone attempting to make or cancel room reservations or change room rates for rooms whose records were scanned in response to the first customer's query will be forced to wait until the first customer's transaction is terminated.) Figure 7.1 illustrates this behavior.

The Read Stability (RS) isolation level

The Read Stability isolation level is not quite as restrictive as the Repeatable Read isolation level. Therefore, it does not completely isolate one transaction from the effects of other concurrently running transactions. Specifically, when this isolation level is used, lost updates, dirty reads, and nonrepeatable reads cannot occur, but phantoms can and might be seen. That is because when the Read Stability isolation level is used, only rows that the owning transaction retrieves or modifies are locked. So, if a transaction scans 1,000 rows to retrieve 10, locks are acquired and held on just the 10 rows retrieved, not on the 1,000 rows that were scanned. Because fewer locks are acquired, more transactions can run concurrently. However, if the owning transaction executes the same query more than once, the result data set produced may be different each time.

As with the Repeatable Read isolation level, transactions running under the Read Stability isolation level can retrieve a set of rows and perform any number of operations

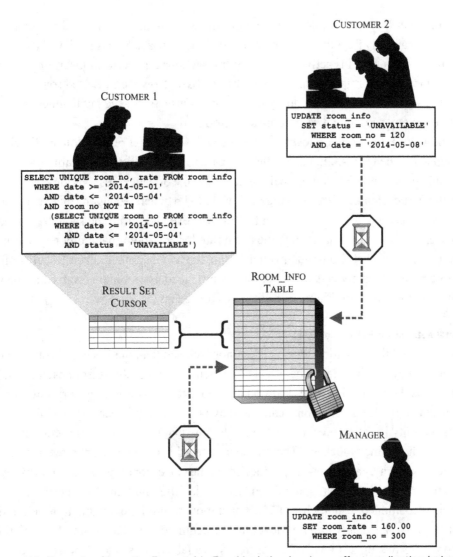

Figure 7.1: Example of how the Repeatable Read isolation level can affect application behavior

on them. Other transactions, however, are prohibited from performing update and delete operations that will affect the set of rows the owning transaction has retrieved (for as long as the transaction remains active). But other transactions *can* perform insert operations against other tables or updatable views in the database. However, inserted rows that match the selection criteria of a query the owning transaction issued will appear as phantoms in any subsequent result data sets produced.

So how does this isolation level change the way your motel reservation application works? Now, when a customer scans the database to obtain a list of available rooms for a given date range, other customers will be able to make or cancel reservations that might cause the first customer's list to change if it were to be generated again (by executing the same query—assuming, of course, that the query is executed from the same transaction). Likewise, your manager can change the room rate for any room that did not appear in the first customer's list. Consequently, each time the first customer generates a list of available rooms for a given date range, the list produced may contain rooms and room rates not previously seen. Figure 7.2 illustrates this behavior.

The Cursor Stability (CS) Isolation level

The Cursor Stability isolation level is even more relaxed than the Read Stability isolation level in the way that it isolates the effects of concurrent transactions from each other. When this isolation level is used, lost updates and dirty reads cannot occur; however, nonrepeatable reads and phantoms can and may be seen. That is because, when the Cursor Stability isolation level is used, only the row that the owning transaction is currently referencing is locked. (The moment a record is retrieved from a result data set, a pointer—known as a *cursor*—is positioned on the corresponding row in the underlying table, and that is the row that gets locked. This lock will remain in effect until the cursor is repositioned, usually by a FETCH operation, or until the owning transaction is terminated.) Because only one row-level lock is acquired, the Cursor Stability isolation level provides the highest level of concurrency available. Consequently, this is the isolation level that DB2 uses by default.

When a transaction using the Cursor Stability isolation level retrieves a row from a table (by means of a cursor), no other transaction is allowed to update or delete that row *as long*

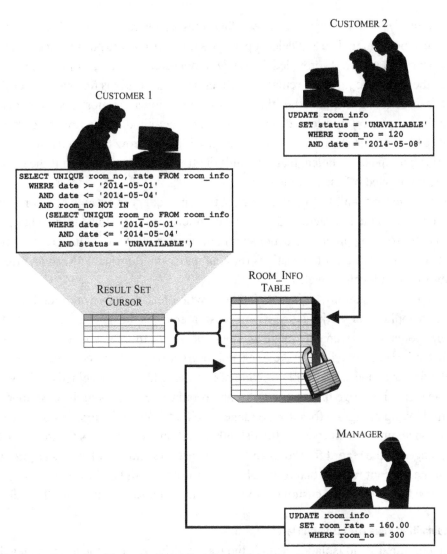

Figure 7.2: Example of how the Read Stability isolation level can affect application behavior

as the cursor is positioned on it. However, other transactions can add new rows to the table, and they can perform update and delete operations on rows that are positioned on either side of the cursor (locked row)—provided the row was not accessed by way of an index.

After the lock is acquired, it remains in effect until the cursor is repositioned or the owning transaction is terminated. If the cursor is repositioned, in most cases the lock held on the current row is released, and a new lock is acquired on the row the cursor is moved to. If, however, the owning transaction modifies any row that it retrieves, no other transaction can update or delete that row until the transaction ends—even if the cursor is subsequently moved off the modified row.

With the Cursor Stability isolation level, if the same query is executed two or more times within the same transaction, the results produced can vary. In addition, changes made to other rows by other transactions will not be seen until those changes have been committed. (This is true for transactions running under the Repeatable Read and Read Stability isolation levels as well.)

Once again, consider how this isolation level will affect the way your motel reservation application works. Now, when a customer scans the database for a list of available rooms for a given date range and then views information about the first room in the list, other customers can make or cancel reservations for any room *except* the room the first customer is currently looking at (for the date range specified). Likewise, your manager can change the room rate for any room *except* the room the customer is currently looking at (again, for the date range specified). When the first customer views information about the next room in the list, other customers, as well as the manager, can make changes to the record for the room the first customer was just looking at (provided the customer did not reserve that room). However, no one will be allowed to change the record for the room the first customer is viewing now. Figure 7.3 illustrates this behavior.

The Uncommitted Read (UR) isolation level

The Uncommitted Read isolation level is the least restrictive of all the isolation levels available. With this isolation level, the effects of one transaction are typically *not* isolated from the effects of other concurrently running transactions. Consequently, dirty reads, nonrepeatable reads, and phantoms can and often do occur. That is because when the Uncommitted Read isolation level is used, the rows that a transaction retrieves are locked only if that transaction attempts to modify the data stored in them. Or if another

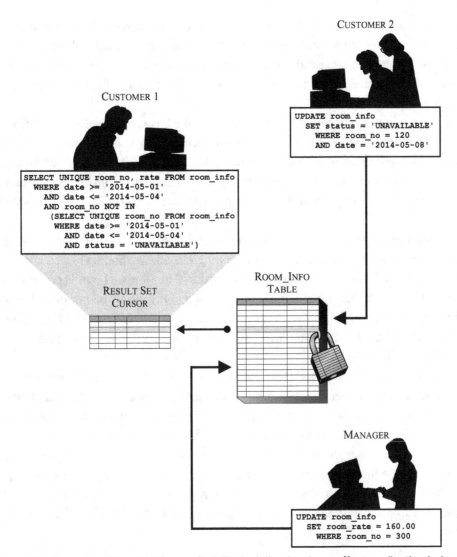

Figure 7.3: Example of how the Cursor Stability isolation level can affect application behavior

transaction attempts to drop or alter the underlying table the rows were retrieved from. Because rows usually remain unlocked when the Uncommitted Read isolation level is used, this isolation level is typically employed when transactions access read-only tables and views or when transactions for which the retrieval of uncommitted data will have no adverse effect are executed.

As the name implies, transactions running under the Uncommitted Read isolation level can see changes made to rows by other transactions *before those changes have been committed.* However, that is not the case when other transactions create tables, indexes, and views. In such situations, the transaction creating the objects must be committed *before* transactions running under the Uncommitted Read isolation level will be able to see or access them.

The same applies when a transaction deletes (or drops) existing tables, indexes, or views. Transactions running under the Uncommitted Read isolation level will not learn that these objects no longer exist until the transaction that dropped them is committed. (It is important to note that when a transaction running under the Uncommitted Read isolation level uses an updatable cursor, the transaction will behave as if it is running under the Cursor Stability isolation level, and the constraints of the Cursor Stability isolation level will apply.)

So how does the Uncommitted Read isolation level affect your motel reservation application? Now when a customer scans the database to obtain a list of available rooms for a given date range, other customers can make or cancel reservations for any room in the motel, including the room the first customer is currently looking at. Likewise, your manager can change the room rates for any room in the motel, over any date range. (Unfortunately, the first customer might be prevented from reserving a room that appears to have been taken but is actually available. Or that customer might reserve a room at one rate, only to discover that the original price has changed.) Figure 7.4 illustrates this behavior.

Choosing the Proper Isolation Level

In addition to controlling the level at which DB2 provides transaction concurrency, the isolation level used determines how well concurrently running transactions will perform—typically, the more restrictive the isolation level, the less concurrency is possible. So how do you decide which isolation level to use? The best way is to identify

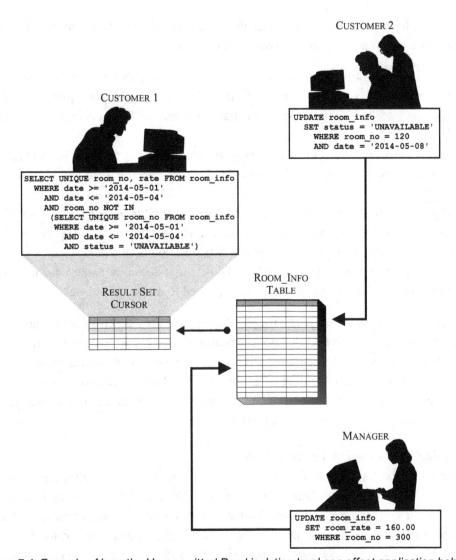

Figure 7.4: Example of how the Uncommitted Read isolation level can affect application behavior

the types of phenomena that are unacceptable, and then select an isolation level that will prevent those phenomena from occurring. For example:

- If you are executing large queries, and you want to prevent other concurrently running transactions from making changes that might cause your queries to return different results if they are run more than once, use the Repeatable Read isolation level.
- If you want some level of concurrency, yet you also want qualified rows to remain stable for the duration of an individual transaction, use the Read Stability isolation level.
- If you want the greatest amount of concurrency possible, yet you do not want queries to see uncommitted data, use the Cursor Stability isolation level.
- If you are executing queries on read-only tables, views, and databases, *or* you want the greatest amount of concurrency possible and it does not matter whether queries return uncommitted data, use the Uncommitted Read isolation level.

Keep in mind that choosing the wrong isolation level for a given situation can have a significant negative effect on both concurrency and performance (performance for some applications can be degraded as they wait for locks on resources to be released). Therefore, when deciding on an isolation level to use, consider your database environment as a whole. Then, make your decision according to the way most applications will need to interact with your data.

Specifying the Isolation Level to Use

Although isolation levels control concurrency at the transaction level, they are set at the application level (or sometimes at the SQL statement level). Therefore, in most cases, the isolation level that a particular application uses is applied to every transaction the application executes. (It is important to note that an application can be constructed in several parts, and that each part can be assigned a different isolation level. In this case, the isolation level that is assigned to a part determines which isolation level each transaction within that part will use.)

With Embedded SQL applications, the isolation level to use is specified at precompile time or when an application is bound to a database (if deferred binding is used). Here, the isolation level is set with the ISOLATION [RR | RS | CS | UR] option of the PRECOMPILE and BIND commands. With Call Level Interface (CLI) and Open Database Connectivity (ODBC) applications, the isolation level is set at application run time by calling the SQLSetConnectAttr() function with the SQL_ATTR_TXN_ISOLATION connection attribute specified. (Alternatively, the desired isolation level can be set by assigning a value to the TXNISOLATION keyword in the *db2cli.ini* configuration file. However, this approach does not provide the flexibility of using different isolation levels for different transactions that the first approach offers.) Finally, with Java Database Connectivity (JDBC) and SQL for Java (SQLJ) applications, the isolation level is set at application run time by calling the setTransactionIsolation() method that resides within DB2's java.sql connection interface.

As mentioned earlier, when the isolation level for a particular application is not explicitly set (by using one of the methods just outlined), DB2 uses the Cursor Stability isolation level by default. This holds true for DB2 commands, SQL statements, and scripts that are executed from the DB2 Command Line Processor (CLP), as well for Embedded SQL, CLI/ODBC, JDBC, and SQLJ applications. Therefore, not only can you control the isolation level that an application uses, but you can also control the isolation level that will be used when operations are performed from the DB2 CLP. Here, the isolation level used can be controlled by executing the CHANGE ISOLATION LEVEL command just before a connection to a database is established.

With DB2 Version 8.1 and later, it is possible to override the default isolation level (or the isolation level specified for a particular application) when individual queries are executed. This is done by appending the clause WITH [RR | RS | CS | UR] to a SELECT statement—the clause itself indicates that the associated SELECT statement is to be executed using the Repeatable Read (RR), Read Stability (RS), Cursor Stability (CS), or Uncommitted Read (UR) isolation level. Thus, if you want to obtain a list of all employees who work in a specific department, *and* you want to run the query that will produce this list under the Repeatable Read isolation level, you can simply execute a SELECT statement that looks something like this:

```
SELECT lastname FROM employee WHERE workdept = 'E11'
   WITH RR
```

So if you have an application that needs to run in a less-restrictive isolation level the majority of the time (to support maximum concurrency), but that contains one or two queries that must not see certain types of phenomena, you can use a combination of application-level and SQL statement-level isolation levels to meet your objective.

Locks

The one commonality among the isolation levels just described (with the exception of Uncommitted Read) is that they all acquire one or more *locks*. But just what is a lock? A lock is a mechanism that is used to associate a data resource with a single transaction, for the sole purpose of controlling how other transactions interact with that resource while it is associated with the transaction that has it locked.

Essentially, locks in a database environment serve the same purpose as they do for a house or car: they determine who can and cannot gain access, in this case, to a particular resource, which can be one or more table spaces, tables, or rows. DB2 imposes locks to prohibit other transactions from making data modifications that might adversely affect the owning transaction.

When an owning transaction is terminated (by a COMMIT or ROLLBACK operation), any changes that have been made to the locked resource are either made permanent or backed out, and all locks on the resource that were acquired on behalf of the owning transaction are released. Once unlocked, a resource can be relocked and manipulated by another transaction. Figure 7.5 illustrates the basic principles of transaction/resource locking.

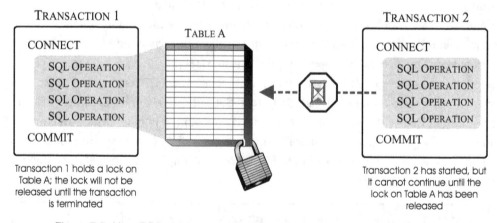

TRANSACTION 1

TABLE A

TRANSACTION 2

CONNECT

SQL OPERATION
SQL OPERATION
SQL OPERATION
SQL OPERATION

COMMIT

CONNECT

SQL OPERATION
SQL OPERATION
SQL OPERATION
SQL OPERATION

COMMIT

Transaction 1 holds a lock on Table A; the lock will not be released until the transaction is terminated

Transaction 2 has started, but it cannot continue until the lock on Table A has been released

Figure 7.5: How DB2 prevents uncontrolled concurrent access to a resource through the use of locks

Lock Attributes and Lock States

Locks used by DB2 have the following basic attributes:

- **Object:** Identifies the data resource that is being locked; DB2 implicitly acquires locks on data resources (specifically, table spaces, tables, and rows) whenever they are needed
- **Size:** Identifies the physical size of the data resource that is being locked (in other words, how much data is being locked); a lock does not always have to control an entire data resource—for example, rather than giving a transaction exclusive control over an entire table, DB2 can elect to give a transaction exclusive control over just one or two rows within a table
- **Duration:** Identifies the length of time a lock is held; the isolation level used has a significant effect on the duration of a lock—for example, the lock acquired for a Repeatable Read transaction that accesses 500 rows is likely to have a long duration if all 500 rows are to be updated; on the other hand, the lock acquired for a Cursor Stability transaction is likely to have a much shorter duration
- **State** (or **Mode**): Identifies the type of access that is allowed for both the lock owner and other concurrent users of the locked data resource. Table 7.2 shows the various lock states available (along with their effects) in order of increasing control over resources

Table 7.2: Lock States (Modes) available with DB2 10.1

Lock State (Mode)	Platform	Applicable Objects	Lock Owner Access	Concurrent Transaction Access
Intent None (IN)	DB2 for Linux, UNIX, and Windows	Table spaces, blocks, tables, data partitions	Lock owner can read all data, including uncommitted data, stored in the locked resource; however, lock owner cannot modify data stored in the resource. Intent None locks are typically acquired for read-only transactions that have no intention of modifying data (thus, additional locks will not be acquired on the transaction's behalf).	Other transactions can read and modify data stored in the locked resource; however, they cannot delete data stored in the resource.
Intent Share (IS)	DB2 for Linux, UNIX, and Windows; DB2 for z/OS	Table spaces, blocks, tables, data partitions	Lock owner can read all data (excluding uncommitted data) stored in the locked resource; however, lock owner cannot modify data stored in the resource. Intent Share locks are typically acquired for transactions that do not convey the intent to modify data (transactions that do not contain SELECT FOR UPDATE, UPDATE WHERE, or INSERT statements).	Other transactions can read and modify data stored in the locked resource.
Intent Exclusive (IX)	DB2 for Linux, UNIX, and Windows; DB2 for z/OS	Table spaces, blocks, tables, data partitions	Lock owner can read and modify data stored in the locked resource. Intent Exclusive locks are typically acquired for transactions that convey the intent to modify data (transactions that contain SELECT FOR UPDATE, UPDATE WHERE, or INSERT statements).	Other transactions can read and modify data stored in the locked resource.
Scan Share (NS)	DB2 for Linux, UNIX, and Windows	Rows	Lock owner can read all data (excluding uncommitted data) stored in the locked resource; however, lock owner cannot modify data stored in the resource. Scan Share locks are typically acquired in place of a Share (S) lock for transactions that are running under the Read Stability or Cursor Stability isolation level.	Other transactions can read all data (excluding uncommitted data) stored in the locked resource; however, they cannot modify data stored in the resource.

Table 7.2: Lock States (Modes) available with DB2 10.1 (continued)				
Lock State (Mode)	**Platform**	**Applicable Objects**	**Lock Owner Access**	**Concurrent Transaction Access**
Next Key Weak Exclusive (NW)	DB2 for Linux, UNIX, and Windows	Rows	Lock owner can read all data (excluding uncommitted data) stored in the locked resource; however, lock owner cannot modify data stored in the resource. Next Key Weak Exclusive locks are typically acquired on the next available row in a table whenever a row is inserted into an index. This occurs only if the next row is currently locked by a scan that was performed under the Repeatable Read isolation level.	Other transactions can read all data (excluding uncommitted data) stored in the locked resource; however, they cannot modify data stored in the resource.
Share (S)	DB2 for Linux, UNIX, and Windows; DB2 for z/OS	Blocks, tables, rows, data partitions	Lock owner can read all data (excluding uncommitted data) stored in the locked resource; however, lock owner cannot modify data stored in the resource. Share locks are typically acquired for transactions that do not convey the intent to modify data that are running under the Repeatable Read isolation level. (Transactions that contain SELECT FOR UPDATE, UPDATE WHERE, or INSERT statements convey the intent to modify data.)	Other transactions can read all data (excluding uncommitted data) stored in the locked resource; however, they cannot modify data stored in the resource.
Share With Intent Exclusive (SIX)	DB2 for Linux, UNIX, and Windows; DB2 for z/OS	Blocks, tables, data partitions	Lock owner can read and modify data stored in the locked resource. Share With Intent Exclusive locks are typically acquired when a transaction holding a Share (S) lock on a resource attempts to acquire an Intent Exclusive (IX) lock on the same resource (or vice versa).	Other transactions can read all data (excluding uncommitted data) stored in the locked resource; however, they cannot modify data stored in the resource.

Table 7.2: Lock States (Modes) available with DB2 10.1 (continued)

Lock State (Mode)	Platform	Applicable Objects	Lock Owner Access	Concurrent Transaction Access
Update (U)	DB2 for Linux, UNIX, and Windows; DB2 for z/OS	Blocks, tables, rows, data partitions	Lock owner can modify all data (excluding uncommitted data) stored in the locked resource; however, lock owner cannot read data stored in the resource. Update locks are typically acquired for transactions that modify data with INSERT, UPDATE, or DELETE statements.	Other transactions can read all data (excluding uncommitted data) stored in the locked resource; however, they cannot modify data stored in the resource.
Exclusive (X)	DB2 for Linux, UNIX, and Windows; DB2 for z/OS	Blocks, tables, rows, data partitions, buffer pools	Lock owner can both read and modify data stored in the locked resource. Exclusive locks are typically acquired for transactions that retrieve data with SELECT statements and then modify the data retrieved with INSERT, UPDATE, or DELETE statements. (Transactions that only retrieve data with SELECT statements do not require an Exclusive lock.)	Transactions using the Uncommitted Read isolation level can read all data, including uncommitted data, stored in the locked resource; however, they cannot modify data stored in the resource. All other transactions can neither read nor modify data stored in the locked resource.
Super Exclusive (Z)	DB2 for Linux, UNIX, and Windows	Table spaces, blocks, tables, data partitions	Lock owner can read and modify data stored in the locked resource. Super Exclusive locks are typically acquired on a table whenever the lock owner attempts to alter the table, drop the table, create an index for the table, drop an index that has already been defined for the table, or reorganize the contents of the table (while the table is offline) by running the REORG utility.	Other transactions can neither read nor modify data stored in the locked resource.

Adapted from Table 1 under *Lock attributes* in the *IBM DB2 10.1 Information Center for Linux, UNIX, and Windows.* (publib.boulder.ibm.com/infocenter/db2luw/v10r1/topic/com.ibm.db2.luw.admin.perf.doc/doc/c0005270.html)

How Locks Are Acquired

Except for occasions when the Uncommitted Read isolation level is used, it is never necessary for a transaction to explicitly request a lock. That is because DB2 automatically acquires locks as they are needed, and after they are acquired, locks remain under DB2's control until they are released. By default, DB2 always attempts to acquire row-level locks. However, you can control whether DB2 will attempt to acquire row-level locks or table-level locks on behalf of transactions working with a specific table by executing a special form of the ALTER TABLE statement. This form of the ALTER TABLE statement has the following syntax:

```
ALTER TABLE [TableName] LOCKSIZE [ROW | TABLE]
```

where:

TableName   Identifies, by name, an existing table to lock at the locking level specified

•••

Note: This form of the ALTER TABLE statement is available with DB2 for Linux, UNIX, and Windows only; it cannot be used with DB2 for z/OS.

•••

For example, if the following SQL statement is executed:

```
ALTER TABLE employee LOCKSIZE ROW
```

DB2 will automatically acquire row-level locks for every transaction that accesses a table named EMPLOYEE. (This is the default behavior.) If the following SQL statement is executed instead:

```
ALTER TABLE employee LOCKSIZE TABLE
```

DB2 will attempt to acquire table-level locks for every transaction that accesses the EMPLOYEE table.

But what if you do not want every transaction that works with a particular table to acquire table-level locks? What if, instead, you want one or two specific transactions to acquire table-level locks, and all other transactions to acquire row-level locks when working with that table? In this case, you can simply leave the default locking behavior alone (so that row-level locking is applied) and use the LOCK TABLE statement to acquire a table-level lock on the table for select transactions. The syntax for the LOCK TABLE statement is:

```
LOCK TABLE [TableName] IN [SHARE | EXCLUSIVE] MODE
```

where:

TableName   Identifies, by name, the table to lock

As you can see, the LOCK TABLE statement allows a transaction to acquire a table-level lock on a particular table in one of two modes: SHARE or EXCLUSIVE. If a table is locked in SHARE mode, a table-level Share (S) lock is acquired on behalf of the requesting transaction, and other concurrent transactions can read, but not change, data stored in the locked table. However, if a table is locked in EXCLUSIVE mode, a table-level Exclusive (X) lock is acquired instead, and other concurrent transactions cannot perform any type of operation against the table as long as it remains locked.

For example, if the following SQL statement is executed:

```
LOCK TABLE employee IN SHARE MODE
```

a table-level Share (S) lock will be acquired on a table named EMPLOYEE on behalf of the current transaction (provided no other transaction holds a lock on this table), and any other concurrently running transactions will be allowed to read, but not change, data stored in the table.

On the other hand, if the following SQL statement is executed instead:

```
LOCK TABLE employee IN EXCLUSIVE MODE
```

a table-level Exclusive (X) lock will be acquired for the EMPLOYEE table, and no other transaction will be allowed to read or modify data stored in this table until the transaction that executed the LOCK TABLE statement is either committed or rolled back.

When deciding whether to use row-level locks or table-level locks, keep in mind that any time a transaction holds a lock on a particular resource, other transactions can be denied access to that resource until the owning transaction is terminated. Therefore, row-level locks are usually better than table-level locks because they restrict access to a much smaller resource. However, because each lock acquired requires some amount of storage space (to hold) and some degree of processing time (to manage), there is usually considerably less overhead involved when a single table-level lock is used instead of multiple row-level locks.

To a certain extent, you can use the LOCK TABLE statement (and with DB2 for Linux, UNIX, and Windows, the ALTER TABLE statement) to control lock granularity (that is, whether row-level locking or table-level locking will be used) at both the global level (ALTER TABLE) and the transaction level (LOCK TABLE). So when is it more desirable to control granularity at the global level rather than at the transaction level? It all depends.

Suppose you have a read-only lookup table that multiple concurrent transactions must access. Forcing DB2 to acquire table-level Share (S) locks globally on behalf of each transaction that attempts to access this table might improve performance, because doing so will greatly reduce the locking overhead required. However, for a table that needs to be accessed frequently by read-only transactions and periodically by a single transaction that performs some type of maintenance, forcing DB2 to acquire a table-level Exclusive (X) lock only for the maintenance transaction is probably better than forcing DB2 to acquire a table-level Exclusive (X) lock for every transaction that attempts to access the table. In this case, if DB2 acquires a table-level Exclusive (X) lock at the instance level, the read-only transactions will be locked out of the table only when the maintenance transaction runs. In all other situations, these transactions will be able to access the table concurrently without requiring a lot of locking overhead.

Which Locks Are Acquired?

Although you can control whether DB2 will acquire row-level locks or table-level locks for a particular transaction, you cannot control what type of lock will be acquired. Instead, DB2 implicitly makes that decision by analyzing the transaction to determine the type of processing it has been designed to perform. To decide which particular type of lock a given situation needs, DB2 places all transactions into one of four categories:

- Read-Only
- Intent-to-Change
- Change
- Cursor-Controlled

The characteristics used to assign transactions to these categories, along with the types of locks that are typically acquired for each, can be seen in Table 7.3.

Table 7.3: Types of transactions available and their associated locks		
Type of Transaction	**Description**	**Locks Typically Acquired**
Read-Only	Transactions that contain SELECT statements (which are intrinsically read-only), SELECT statements that have the FOR READ ONLY clause specified, or SQL statements that are ambiguous but are presumed to be read-only because of the BLOCKING option that was specified as part of the precompile and/or bind process	Intent Share (IS) and/or Share (S) locks
Intent-to-Change	Transactions that contain SELECT statements that have the FOR UPDATE clause specified, or SQL statements that are ambiguous but are presumed to be intended for change because of the way they are interpreted by the SQL precompiler	Intent Exclusive (IX), Share (S), Update (U), and Exclusive (X) locks
Change	Transactions that contain INSERT, UPDATE, or DELETE statements, but not UPDATE WHERE CURRENT OF or DELETE WHERE CURRENT OF statements	Intent Exclusive (IX) and/or Exclusive (X) locks
Cursor-Controlled	Transactions that contain UPDATE WHERE CURRENT OF or DELETE WHERE CURRENT OF statements	Intent Exclusive (IX) and/or Exclusive (X) locks

It is important to keep in mind that in some cases, a single transaction will consist of multiple transaction types. For example, a transaction that contains an SQL statement that performs an INSERT operation against a table using the results of a subquery consists of two different types of processing: Read-Only and Change. Here, locks needed for the resources referenced in the subquery are determined using the rules for Read-Only transactions, and the locks required for the target table of the INSERT operation are determined using the rules for Change transactions.

Lock Avoidance

Before DB2 Version 9.7, if the Cursor Stability isolation level was used and a row was locked on behalf of a transaction, DB2 would block attempts by other concurrently running transactions to modify the locked row. Furthermore, if the transaction holding the lock changed the locked row in any way, other SQL statements in concurrent transactions could not access the row (unless they were running under the Uncommitted Read isolation level) until the transaction that made the change was terminated. (In other words, writers would block readers, and in some situations readers could block writers.) In either case, concurrent transactions that needed to access a locked row were forced to wait for the lock to be released before they could continue processing. This, in turn, would often cause undesired behavior to occur.

With DB2 Version 9.5 several lock avoidance techniques were introduced to help eliminate some of the locking overhead that is required for the Cursor Stability isolation level. Essentially, these techniques allow scan operations to execute without locking rows when the data and pages being accessed are known to have been committed. For example, consider the following query:

```
SELECT COUNT(*) FROM sales
```

Prior to DB2 Version 9.5, when such a query was executed, the first row in the table specified would be locked, a count would be taken, and the lock would be released. Then, the second row in the table would be locked, the count would be updated, and the lock would be released. And this process would continue until the query had counted all the rows in the table. With DB2 Version 9.5 and later, the same query will scan the table specified and count the rows, but intermittent locks are no longer acquired and released— provided DB2 can determine that the rows have been committed without having to acquire locks.

Essentially, lock avoidance allows DB2 to determine whether the data needed has been committed, and if that is indeed the case, locks are not acquired. With DB2 Versions 9.7 and 10.1, lock avoidance works for any read-only SQL statement executed under the Cursor Stability isolation level that is using cursor blocking. (Cursor blocking is a technique that reduces overhead by having DB2 retrieve a block of rows, rather than a single row, in one operation.)

Currently Committed Semantics

With DB2 Version 9.7, a new implementation of the Cursor Stability isolation level was introduced that incorporates Currently Committed (CC) semantics to further prevent writers from blocking readers. The intent is to provide a Cursor Stability isolation level that avoids lock waits without violating ANSI standards for Cursor Stability isolation level semantics. (With earlier versions of DB2 for Linux, UNIX, and Windows, the following registry variables can be used to delay or avoid acquiring locks in certain circumstances:

- **DB2_SKIPINSERTED**: Allows Cursor Stability/Read Stability scans to skip uncommitted inserted rows
- **DB2_SKIPDELETED**: Allows Cursor Stability/Read Stability scans to skip uncommitted deleted rows and index keys
- **DB2_EVALUNCOMMITTED**: Allows Cursor Stability/Read Stability scans to apply and perform query predicate evaluation on uncommitted data; also permits such scans to skip uncommitted deleted rows—in effect, scans are treated as an Uncommitted Read operation until a qualifying row is found, at which time DB2 might acquire a lock to ensure that only committed data is processed or returned

However, the use of these registry variables violates the ANSI standard for Cursor Stability isolation level semantics.)

When the lock avoidance techniques that were introduced in DB2 9.5 are used, a read-only transaction operating under Currently Committed semantics will not acquire a lock as long as DB2 can determine that the data needed has been committed. (Transactions performing read and write operations avoid lock waits on uncommitted inserts, and transactions performing read-only operations end up trading a lock wait for a log read when they encounter uncommitted updates or deletes from concurrent transactions.)

If DB2 is unable to determine whether a row has been committed, it will try to acquire a lock on the row in question on behalf of the transaction—if a lock can be acquired, processing will continue using traditional Cursor Stability isolation level behavior. If, however, a lock cannot be acquired (because another transaction holds an Exclusive lock on the row) DB2 will examine the lock the other transaction is holding to obtain information about the row that contains the data needed. In this case, each lock can contain one of the following:

- **No information:** Indicates that the row is locked but nothing has been done to it (that is, no uncommitted changes are in-flight)
- **An Uncommitted Insert identifier:** Indicates that the row is a newly inserted row that has not yet been committed
- **Log information:** Indicates that the row contains uncommitted data; in this case, the log information identifies the log record that corresponds to the first time the row was modified by the transaction that currently holds the lock on the row

If the lock contains no information, the row is treated as if the desired lock were acquired. If the lock has an Uncommitted Insert identifier, the row is skipped because this identifier represents a row that has not yet been committed. And if the lock contains log information, this information is used to return the "currently committed" version of the row (that is, the row as it existed before changes were initiated) from a log record that is stored in either the log buffer or a transaction log file. (DB2 uses the Log Sequence Number, or LSN, to directly access the appropriate log record; all data row and index entries have a "flags" byte that contains a "Possibly UNCommitted"—or PUNC—bit. If the PUNC bit is not set, the data row/index entry is guaranteed to be committed. Otherwise, the commit status is unknown. Data pages contain a "pageLSN" that identifies the LSN of the log record that corresponds to the last modification made to the page. If the pageLSN is older than the database's "commitLSN" or a table's "readLSN", then the row/key is guaranteed to be committed. Otherwise, the commit status is unknown.)

Figure 7.6 illustrates how a SELECT statement running under the Cursor Stability isolation level with Currently Committed semantics enabled will retrieve records when another transaction is making changes to the records simultaneously. In this example, Transaction 1 executed three DML statements, which caused log information to be written to the log buffer and an uncommitted insert identifier to be written to the lock list for the SALES_REP table. When Transaction 2 queried the SALES_REP table, Currently Committed semantics allowed data for locked rows to be read from log records that contained information about previously committed transactions; the query did not return the record for the uncommitted insert.

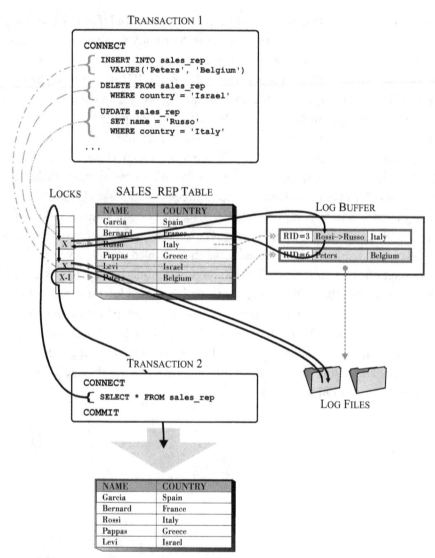

Figure 7.6: Example of how a query running under the Cursor Stability isolation level with Currently Committed semantics enabled will retrieve records

It is important to note that Currently Committed semantics can apply to SQL statements that are executed under both the Read Stability (RS) and the Cursor Stability (CS) isolation levels. However, under the Read Stability isolation level, Currently Committed semantics provides only DB2_SKIPINSERTED behavior, which is the capability to no longer incur lock waits for uncommitted inserted rows.

Enabling Currently Committed Semantics Behavior

By default, Currently Committed semantics are enabled for new databases that are created with DB2 9.7 and later. To use Currently Committed semantics for existing databases that are upgraded from earlier releases of DB2, you must assign either the value ON or the value AVAILABLE to the *cur_commit* database configuration parameter of the converted database.

If the *cur_commit* database configuration parameter is set to ON, Currently Committed semantics are applied database-wide for both the Read Stability and Cursor Stability isolation levels. If this configuration parameter is set to AVAILABLE instead, DB2 will store the appropriate information in locks and perform the extra logging overhead needed (to ensure that the logged data contains the full uncommitted version of the row being changed) to support Currently Committed semantics. However, Currently Committed semantics behavior will have to be enabled on an application-by-application basis. This is done either by binding an Embedded SQL application to the database using the CONCURRENTACCESSRESOLUTION USE CURRENTLY COMMITTED option, or by specifying the SQL_ATTR_CONCURRENT_ACCESS_RESOLUTION connection attribute with CLI/ODBC and Java applications.

It is important to note that the use of Currently Committed semantics will result in an increase in the amount of log space needed for update operations that are performed against tables that have been defined as DATA CAPTURE NONE. This additional space is used to log the first update of a data row by an active transaction; it is this data that is used to retrieve the currently committed image of the row.

Locks and Performance

Because DB2 implicitly acquires locks as they are needed, aside from using the LOCK TABLE statement (and with DB2 for Linux, UNIX, and Windows, the ALTER TABLE statement) to force DB2 to acquire table-level locks, locking is pretty much out of your control. However, there are several factors that can influence how locking affects performance that you should be aware of. They are:

- Lock compatibility
- Lock conversion
- Lock escalation
- Lock waits and timeouts
- Deadlocks

Knowing what these factors are and understanding how they affect performance can assist you in designing applications that work well in multiuser database environments.

Lock compatibility

If the state of a lock that one transaction places on a data resource is such that another transaction can place another lock on the same resource before the first lock is released, the locks are said to be *compatible*. And any time one transaction holds a lock on a data resource and another transaction attempts to acquire a lock on the same resource, DB2 will examine each lock's state to determine whether they are compatible. Table 7.4 contains a lock compatibility matrix that identifies which locks are compatible and which are not.

Table 7.4: Lock compatibility matrix										
	Lock Requested by Second Transaction									
Lock State	**IN**	**IS**	**NS**	**S**	**IX**	**SIX**	**U**	**X**	**Z**	**NW**
IN	Yes	Yes	Yes	Yes	Yes	Yes	Yes	Yes	No	Yes
IS	Yes	Yes	Yes	Yes	Yes	Yes	Yes	No	No	No
NS	Yes	Yes	Yes	Yes	No	No	Yes	No	No	Yes
S	Yes	Yes	Yes	Yes	No	No	Yes	No	No	No
IX	Yes	Yes	No	No	Yes	No	No	No	No	No
SIX	Yes	Yes	No	No	No	No	No	No	No	No
U	Yes	Yes	Yes	Yes	No	No	No	No	No	No
X	Yes	No	No	No	No	No	No	No	No	No
Z	No	No	No	No	No	No	No	No	No	No
NW	Yes	No	Yes	No	No	No	No	No	No	No

Lock Held by First Transaction

Yes   *Locks are compatible; therefore, the lock request is granted immediately.*

No   *Locks are not compatible; therefore, the requesting transaction must wait for the held lock to be released or for a lock timeout to occur before the lock request can be granted.*

Lock States:

IN	*Intent None*	*SIX*	*Share With Intent Exclusive*
IS	*Intent Share*	*U*	*Update*
NS	*Scan Share*	*X*	*Exclusive*
S	*Share*	*Z*	*Super Exclusive*
IX	*Intent Exclusive*	*NW*	*Next Key Weak Exclusive*

Adapted from Table 1 under **Lock type compatibility** *in the* IBM DB2 10.1 Information Center for Linux, UNIX, and Windows (publib.boulder.ibm.com/infocenter/db2luw/v10r1/topic/com.ibm.db2.luw.admin.perf.doc/doc/r0005274.html).

Lock conversion/promotion

If a transaction that is holding a lock on a resource needs to acquire a more restrictive lock on that resource, rather than releasing the old lock and acquiring a new one, DB2 will attempt to change the state of the lock being held to the more restrictive state. The action of changing the state of an existing lock is known as *lock conversion* (DB2 for Linux, UNIX, and Windows) or *lock promotion* (DB2 for z/OS). Lock conversion/ promotion occurs because a transaction is allowed to hold only one lock on any given resource. Figure 7.7 illustrates how lock conversion/promotion works.

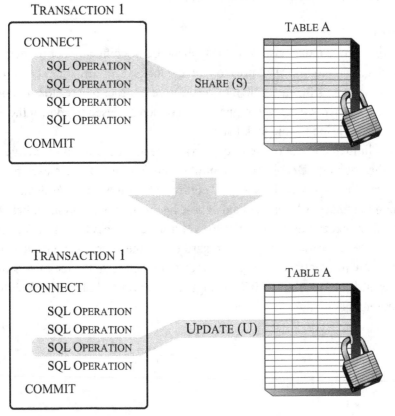

Figure 7.7: Lock conversion/promotion changing a lock being held—a Share (S) lock—to a more restrictive state—an Update (U) lock

Normally, lock conversion/promotion is performed on row-level locks, and the process is fairly straightforward. For example, if an Update (U) lock is held and an Exclusive (X) lock is needed, the Update (U) lock will be converted/promoted to an Exclusive (X) lock.

However, that is not always the case when it comes to Share (S) and Intent Exclusive (IX) locks. Because neither lock is considered more restrictive than the other, if one of these locks is held and the other is requested, the lock that is held is converted/promoted to a Share With Intent Exclusive (SIX) lock.

With all other locks, the state of the current lock is changed to the lock state being requested—provided the requested lock state is a more restrictive state. (Lock conversion/ promotion occurs only if the lock held can increase its restriction.) After a lock has been converted, it stays at the highest level attained until the transaction holding the lock is terminated, at which point the lock is released.

Lock escalation

When a connection to a database is first established, a specific amount of memory is set aside to hold a structure that DB2 uses to manage locks. This structure, known as the *lock list*, is where locks that are held by every active transaction are stored after they are acquired. (The *locklist* database configuration parameter is used to control the amount of memory that is set aside for the lock list.)

Because a limited amount of memory is available and because every active transaction must share this memory, DB2 imposes a limit on the amount of space each transaction can consume in the lock list. (This limit is controlled via the *maxlocks* database configuration parameter.) To prevent a database agent (that is working on behalf of a transaction) from exceeding its lock list space limits, a process known as *lock escalation* is performed whenever too many locks (regardless of their type) have been acquired on behalf of a single transaction. During lock escalation, space in the lock list is freed by replacing several row-level locks with a single table-level lock. Figure 7.8 shows how lock escalation works.

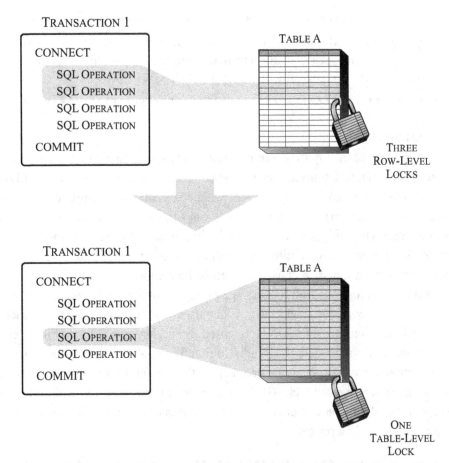

Figure 7.8: Lock escalation replaces several individual row-level locks with a single table-level lock

So just how does lock escalation work? When a transaction requests a lock and a database's lock list is full, one of the tables associated with the transaction requesting the lock is selected, a table-level lock for that table is acquired on behalf of the transaction, and all row-level locks for that table are released to create space in the lock list. The table-level lock is then added to the lock list, and if the lock list still lacks the storage space needed to acquire the requested lock, another table is selected and the process is repeated until enough free space is made available. Only then will the requested lock be acquired (at which point, the transaction will be allowed to continue). If, however, the lock list space needed is still unavailable (after all the transaction's row-level locks have been escalated), an error is generated, all database changes made by the transaction are rolled back, and the transaction is gracefully terminated.

Note: Use of the LOCK TABLE statement does not prevent normal lock escalation from occurring. However, it can reduce the frequency at which lock escalations take place.

Lock waits and timeouts

As you have already seen, any time a transaction holds a lock on a particular resource, other concurrently running transactions can be denied access to that resource until the transaction holding the lock is terminated (in which case, all locks acquired on behalf of the transaction are released). Consequently, without some sort of lock timeout mechanism in place, one transaction might wait indefinitely for a lock that is held by another transaction. And unfortunately, if either transaction were to be terminated prematurely by another user or application, data consistency could be compromised.

To prevent such situations from occurring, an important feature known as *lock timeout detection* has been incorporated into DB2. When used, this feature prevents transactions from waiting indefinitely for a lock to be released. By assigning a value to the *locktimeout* parameter in the appropriate database configuration file, you can control when lock timeout detection occurs. This parameter specifies the amount of time that any transaction will wait to obtain a requested lock—if the desired lock is not acquired within the time interval specified, all database changes made by the transaction are rolled back, and the transaction is gracefully terminated.

Note: By default, the *locktimeout* configuration is set to -1, which means that transactions will wait indefinitely to acquire the locks they need. However, in many cases, it is recommend that you change this value to something else. In addition, applications should be written such that they capture any timeout (or deadlock) SQL return code returned by DB2 and respond appropriately.

Deadlocks

Often, the problem of one transaction waiting indefinitely for a lock can be avoided by using Currently Committed semantics and by defining a lock timeout period. However, that is not the case when lock contention results in a situation known as a *deadlock*. The best way to illustrate what a deadlock is and how it can occur is by looking at example.

Suppose Transaction 1 acquires an Exclusive (X) lock on Table A, and Transaction 2 acquires an Exclusive (X) lock on Table B. Now, suppose Transaction 1 attempts to acquire an Exclusive (X) lock on Table B, and Transaction 2 attempts to acquire an Exclusive (X) lock on Table A. You have already seen that processing by both transactions will be suspended until their second lock request is granted. However, neither lock request can be granted until one of the owning transactions releases the lock it currently holds (by performing a commit or rollback operation), and neither transaction can perform a commit or rollback operation because they both are waiting to acquire locks. As a result, a deadlock situation has occurred. Figure 7.9 illustrates this scenario.

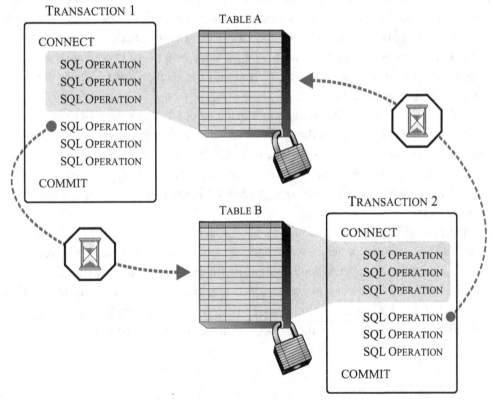

Figure 7.9: Example of a deadlock situation—Transaction 1 is waiting for Transaction 2 to release its lock on Table B, and Transaction 2 is waiting for Transaction 1 to release its lock on Table A; however, neither transaction can release its respective lock because each transaction is waiting to acquire the other lock it has requested.

A deadlock is more precisely referred to as a *deadlock cycle* because the transactions involved form a circle of wait states—each transaction in the circle waits for a lock held by another transaction in the circle to be released (see Figure 7.9). When a deadlock cycle occurs, all transactions involved will wait indefinitely for a lock unless some outside agent steps in to break the cycle. With DB2, this agent is a background process known as the *deadlock detector*, and its sole responsibility is to locate and resolve any deadlocks found in the locking subsystem.

Each database has its own deadlock detector, which is activated as part of the database initialization process. Once the deadlock detector is activated, it stays "asleep" most of the time but "wakes up" at preset intervals and examines the locking subsystem to determine whether a deadlock situation exists. Normally, the deadlock detector wakes up, finds that there are no deadlocks present in the locking subsystem, and goes back to sleep.

However, if the deadlock detector discovers a deadlock cycle, it randomly selects one of the transactions involved to roll back and terminate. The transaction chosen (referred to as the *victim process*) is then sent an SQL error code, and every lock the transaction had acquired is released. The remaining transactions can then proceed because the deadlock cycle has been broken.

It is possible, but very unlikely, that more than one deadlock cycle exists in a database's locking subsystem. In the event several deadlock cycles exist, the detector locates each one and terminates one of the offending transactions in the same manner until all deadlock cycles have been broken. Eventually, the deadlock detector goes back to sleep, only to wake up at the next predefined interval and examine the locking subsystem again.

Although most deadlock cycles involve two or more resources, a special type of deadlock, known as a *conversion deadlock*, can occur on an individual resource. Conversion deadlocks happen when two or more transactions that already hold compatible locks on an object request new, incompatible locks on that same object. This typically takes place when two or more concurrent transactions search for rows in a table via an index scan, and then try to modify one or more of the rows retrieved.

DB2 10.1 Fundamentals Exam (Exam 610) Objectives

The *DB2 10.1 Fundamentals* exam (Exam 610) consists of 69 questions, and candidates have 90 minutes to complete the exam. A score of 66 percent or higher is required to pass.

The primary objectives the *DB2 10.1 Fundamentals* exam (Exam 610) is designed to cover are as follows:

Planning (10%)

- Knowledge of DB2 products (DB2 for LUW vs. DB2 for z/OS vs. DB2 pureScale—at a high-level; how each product differs and what they do)
- Knowledge of database workloads (OLTP vs. warehousing; appropriate DB2 product to use for each)
- Knowledge of nonrelational data concepts (XML data, LOB data)

Security (15%)

- Knowledge of restricting data access
- Knowledge of different privileges and authorities

- Given a DCL SQL statement, ability to identify results (GRANT, REVOKE, CONNECT statements)
- Knowledge of Row and Column Access Control (RCAC)
- Knowledge of roles and trusted contexts

Working with Databases and Database Objects (20%)

- Ability to create and connect to DB2 servers and databases (requirements to give ability to connect)
- Ability to identify DB2 objects
- Knowledge of basic characteristics and properties of DB2 objects
- Given a DDL SQL statement, ability to identify results (ability to create DB2 objects)
- Knowledge of temporal (time travel) tables—system-period, application-period, and bitemporal; ability to create temporal tables (greater precision timestamps)

Working with DB2 Data Using SQL (20%)

- Ability to use SQL to SELECT data from tables
- Ability to use SQL to SORT or GROUP data
- Ability to use SQL to INSERT, UPDATE, or DELETE data
- Knowledge of transactions and transaction boundaries (COMMIT, ROLLBACK, and SAVEPOINT)
- Ability to create and call an SQL stored procedure or a user-defined function (understanding of passing parameters and retrieving results)
- Given an XQuery statement, knowledge to identify results
- Knowledge of temporal (time travel) tables; ability to query system-period, application-period, and bitemporal tables

Working with DB2 Tables, Views, and Indexes (22%)

- Ability to demonstrate usage of DB2 data types (traditional data types, XML data types, Oracle compatibility data types)
- Given a situation, ability to create a temporary table
- Knowledge to identify when referential integrity should be used
- Knowledge to identify methods of data constraint
- Knowledge to identify characteristics of a table, view or index

- Knowledge to identify when triggers should be used
- Knowledge of schemas

Data Concurrency (13%)

- Knowledge to identify factors that influence locking
- Ability to list objects on which locks can be obtained (LOCK TABLE)
- Knowledge to identify characteristics of DB2 locks (common locks shared across platforms)
- Given a situation, knowledge to identify the isolation levels that should be used (knowledge of Currently Committed semantics)

B

Practice Questions

Welcome to the section that really makes this book unique. In my opinion, one of the best ways to prepare for the *DB2 10.1 Fundamentals* certification exam (Exam 610) is by answering practice questions that are similar to, and are presented in the same format as, the questions you will see when you take the actual exam. In this last part of the book, you will find 150 practice questions, as well as comprehensive answers for each question. (It's not enough to know *which* answer is correct; it's also important to know *why* a particular answer is correct—and why the other choices are wrong!)

All of the questions presented here were developed using copious notes that were taken during the exam development process. (As a member of the team that developed the *DB2 10.1 Fundamentals* certification exam, I had the opportunity to see every question that was created for this exam!) I trust you will find these practice questions helpful.

Roger E. Sanders

Planning

Question 1

A database will be used primarily to identify sales patterns for products sold within the last three years and to summarize sales by region, on a quarterly basis. Which type of system is needed?

○ A. Analytical
○ B. DB2 pureScale
○ C. Data warehouse
○ D. Online transaction processing (OLTP)

Question 2

Which product can be used to tune performance for a single query?

○ A. IBM Data Studio
○ B. IBM Control Center
○ C. IBM Data Administrator
○ D. IBM Workload Manager

Question 3

Which two DB2 products are suitable for very large data warehouse applications? (Choose two.)

☐ A. DB2 for i
☐ B. DB2 for AIX
☐ C. DB2 for z/OS
☐ D. DB2 pureScale
☐ E. DB2 Express-C

Question 4

What is the DB2 Workload Manager (WLM) used for?

- ○ A. To identify, diagnose, solve, and prevent performance problems in DB2 products and associated applications.
- ○ B. To customize execution environments for the purpose of controlling system resources so that one department or service class does not overwhelm the system.
- ○ C. To respond to significant changes in a database's workload by dynamically distributing available memory resources among several different database memory consumers.
- ○ D. To improve the performance of applications that require frequent, but relatively transient, simultaneous user connections by allocating host database resources only for the duration of an SQL transaction.

Question 5

Which of the following is NOT a characteristic of a data warehouse?

- ○ A. Sub-second response time
- ○ B. Voluminous historical data
- ○ C. Heterogeneous data sources
- ○ D. Summarized queries that perform aggregations and joins

Question 6

Which statement about the DB2 pureScale feature is NOT true?

- ○ A. The DB2 pureScale feature provides a database cluster solution for non-mainframe platforms.
- ○ B. The DB2 pureScale feature is only available as part of DB2 Advanced Enterprise Server Edition.
- ○ C. The DB2 pureScale feature can only work with the General Parallel File System (GPFS) file system.
- ○ D. The DB2 pureScale feature is best suited for online transaction processing (OLTP) workloads.

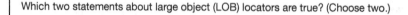

Question 7

Which two statements about large object (LOB) locators are true? (Choose two.)

- ☐ A. A LOB locator represents a value for a LOB resource that is stored in a database.
- ☐ B. A LOB locator is a simple token value that is used to refer to a much bigger LOB value.
- ☐ C. A LOB locator is a special data type that is used to store LOB data in external binary files.
- ☐ D. A LOB locator represents a value for a LOB resource that is stored in an external binary file.
- ☐ E. A LOB locator is a mechanism that acts similar to an index in the way that it organizes LOB values so they can be quickly located in response to a query.

Question 8

Which type of database workload typically involves making changes to a small number of records within a single transaction?

- ○ A. Decision support
- ○ B. Data warehousing
- ○ C. Online analytical processing (OLAP)
- ○ D. Online transaction processing (OLTP)

Question 9

Which of the following is NOT a characteristic of an OLTP database?

- ○ A. Current data
- ○ B. Frequent updates
- ○ C. Granular transactions
- ○ D. Optimized for queries

Question 10

Which two platforms support DB2 10.1 pureScale environments? (Choose two.)

☐ A. IBM mainframes running z/OS
☐ B. IBM p Series servers running AIX
☐ C. IBM p Series servers running Linux
☐ D. IBM x Series servers running Linux
☐ E. IBM x Series servers running a supported version of Windows

Question 11

Which tool can analyze and provide recommendations for tuning individual queries?

○ A. IBM InfoSphere Data Architect
○ B. IBM InfoSphere Optim Query Tuner
○ C. IBM InfoSphere Optim pureQuery Runtime
○ D. IBM InfoSphere Optim Performance Manager Extended Edition

Question 12

Which SQL statement will create a table named EMPLOYEE that can be used to store XML data?

○ A. CREATE TABLE employee (empid INT, resume XML)
○ B. CREATE TABLE employee (empid INT, resume XML(2000))
○ C. CREATE TABLE employee (empid INT, resume CLOB AS XML)
○ D. CREATE TABLE employee (empid INT, resume CLOB USING XML)

Question 13

Which DB2 product provides a complete data warehousing solution that contains components that facilitate data warehouse construction and administration?

- ○ A. DB2 pureScale Feature
- ○ B. DB2 Workload Manager
- ○ C. IBM InfoSphere Warehouse
- ○ D. Database Partitioning Feature

Question 14

Which statement about IBM Data Studio is NOT true?

- ○ A. The IBM Data Studio administration client can be installed on servers running Red Hat Linux, SUSE Linux, Windows, and AIX.
- ○ B. IBM Data Studio replaces the DB2 Control Center as the standard GUI interface for DB2 database administration and application development.
- ○ C. IBM Data Studio is an Eclipse-based, integrated development environment (IDE) that can be used to perform instance and database administration.
- ○ D. IBM Data Studio allows users to connect to a DB2 database using a wizard; however, users are required to provide login credentials before a connection will be established.

Question 15

Which statement about inline large objects (LOBs) is NOT true?

- ○ A. When a table contains columns with inline LOBs, fewer rows can fit on a page.
- ○ B. Inline LOBs are created by appending the INLINE LENGTH clause to a LOB column's definition.
- ○ C. Because DML operations against inline LOBs are never logged, their use can reduce logging overhead.
- ○ D. Inline LOBs improve query performance by storing LOB data in the same data pages as the rest of a table's rows, rather than in a separate LOB storage object.

Security

Question 16

A user named USER1 has been granted DATAACCESS authority for a database named PAYROLL. What is user USER1 allowed to do?

○ A. Implicitly create a new schema in the PAYROLL database.
○ B. Grant and revoke privileges on objects that reside in the PAYROLL database.
○ C. Retrieve and change data stored in user tables, views, and materialized query tables.
○ D. Create database objects, issue database-specific DB2 commands, and run DB2 utilities that do not change data.

Question 17

Which attribute is NOT needed to define a trusted context?

○ A. A system authorization ID
○ B. A data stream encryption value
○ C. A system authorization password
○ D. The IP address or domain name of an incoming connection

Question 18

Which SQL statement will take the ability to run an Embedded SQL application named PERF_REVIEW that calls a package named CORP.CALC_BONUS away from a user named USER1?

○ A. REVOKE EXECUTE ON APPLICATION perf_review FROM user1
○ B. REVOKE EXECUTE ON PACKAGE corp.calc_bonus FROM user1
○ C. REVOKE EXECUTE ON APPLICATION perf_review PACKAGE corp.calc_bonus FROM user1
○ D. REVOKE EXECUTE ON APPLICATION perf_review USING PACKAGE corp.calc_bonus FROM user1

Question 19

If a user is given SELECT privilege on a table named EMPLOYEES, which two actions are they allowed to perform? (Choose two.)

☐ A. Add data to the EMPLOYEE table.
☐ B. Create a view on the EMPLOYEE table.
☐ C. Retrieve data from the EMPLOYEE table.
☐ D. Create an index for the EMPLOYEE table.
☐ E. Change the definition for the EMPLOYEE table.

Question 20

Which SQL statement will allow a user named USER1 to both remove records from a table named SALES and give the ability to remove records from the SALES table to others?

○ A. GRANT DELETE ON TABLE sales TO user1 WITH GRANT OPTION
○ B. GRANT REMOVE ON TABLE sales TO user1 WITH GRANT OPTION
○ C. GRANT DELETE ON TABLE sales TO user1 WITH GRANT PRIVILEGES
○ D. GRANT REMOVE ON TABLE sales TO user1 WITH GRANT PRIVILEGES

Question 21

If a user is granted the BIND privilege, what are they allowed to do?

○ A. Create a new package.
○ B. Bind or rebind (recreate) a specific package.
○ C. Register user-defined functions (UDFs) and procedures.
○ D. Associate user-defined functions (UDFs) and procedures with specific database objects.

Question 22

Which statement about Security Administrator (SECADM) authority is true?

○ A. Users with SECADM authority are not allowed to access data stored in system catalog tables and views.
○ B. Only users with SECADM authority are allowed to grant and revoke SECADM authority to/from others.
○ C. When a user with SECADM authority creates a database, that user is automatically granted DBADM authority for that database.
○ D. With DB2 for z/OS, SYSADM authority and SECADM authority are combined under SYSADM authority and cannot be separated.

Question 23

Which statement about trusted contexts is true?

○ A. Trusted context objects can only be defined by someone with SYSADM or SECADM authority.
○ B. An authorization ID, IP address, encryption value, and authentication type must be identified before a trusted context can be defined.
○ C. After a trusted connection is established, if a switch request is made with an authorization ID that is not allowed on the connection, the connection is placed in the "Unconnected" state.
○ D. If a trusted context is assigned to a role, any authorization ID that uses the trusted context will acquire the authorities and privileges that have been assigned to the role; any authorities or privileges that have been granted to the authorization ID are ignored.

Question 24

If a user has ACCESSCTRL authority, which two authorities and/or privileges are they allowed to grant to others? (Choose two.)

☐ A. SYSADM
☐ B. SECADM
☐ C. EXECUTE
☐ D. CREATETAB
☐ E. ACCESSCTRL

Question 25

Which of the following is used to group a collection of privileges together so that they can be simultaneously granted to and revoked from multiple users?

- ○ A. Role
- ○ B. Catalog
- ○ C. Function
- ○ D. Collection

Question 26

Which method for restricting data access relies on the server or the local DB2 subsystem to prevent unauthorized users from accessing data stored in a database?

- ○ A. Privileges
- ○ B. Authentication
- ○ C. Label-based access control
- ○ D. Row and column access control

Question 27

When is an SQL search condition used to limit access to data in a table?

- ○ A. When mandatory access control (MAC) is used to protect the table.
- ○ B. When label-based access control (LBAC) is used to protect the table.
- ○ C. When discretionary access control (DAC) is used to protect the table.
- ○ D. When row and column access control (RCAC) is used to protect the table.

Question 28

Which SQL statement will give user USER1 the ability to create tables in a table space named USERSPACE2?

○ A. GRANT USE OF TABLESPACE userspace2 TO user1
○ B. GRANT ALTER ON TABLESPACE userspace2 TO user1
○ C. GRANT USAGE OF TABLESPACE userspace2 TO user1
○ D. GRANT CREATETAB ON TABLESPACE userspace2 TO user1

Question 29

Which SQL statement will give user USER1 the ability to assign a comment to a table named MYTABLE?

○ A. GRANT ALTER ON TABLE mytable TO user1
○ B. GRANT USAGE ON TABLE mytable TO user1
○ C. GRANT INSERT ON TABLE mytable TO user1
○ D. GRANT UPDATE ON TABLE mytable TO user1

Question 30

Which privileges are needed to invoke an SQL stored procedure that queries a table?

○ A. CALL privilege on the procedure; SELECT privilege on the table.
○ B. EXECUTE privilege on the procedure; SELECT privilege on the table.
○ C. CALL privilege on the procedure; REFERENCES privilege on the table.
○ D. EXECUTE privilege on the procedure; REFERENCES privilege on the table.

Question 31

Which privilege allows a user to use the PREVIOUS VALUE and NEXT VALUE sequence expressions?

○ A. USE
○ B. ALTER
○ C. USAGE
○ D. EXECUTE

Question 32

A table named CUSTOMER was created as follows:

```
CREATE TABLE customer
   (cust_id    INTEGER NOT NULL PRIMARY KEY,
    f_name     VARCHAR(30),
    l_name     VARCHAR(40),
    cc_number  NUMERIC(16,0) NOT NULL)
```

Which two actions will prevent unauthorized users from accessing credit card number (CC_NUMBER) information? (Choose two.)

☐ A. Assign the CC_NUMBER column to a restricted role that only authorized users are allowed to access.

☐ B. Only grant ACCESSCTRL authority for the CC_NUMBER column to users who need to access credit card number information.

☐ C. Alter the table definition so that CC_NUMBER data is stored in a separate schema that only authorized users are allowed to access.

☐ D. Create a view for the CUSTOMER table that does not contain the CC_NUMBER column and require unauthorized users to use the view.

☐ E. Create a column mask for the CC_NUMBER column with the ENABLE option specified and alter the CUSTOMER table to activate column access control.

Question 33

Which authority is needed to create and drop databases?

○ A. DBADM
○ B. DBCTRL
○ C. SYSCTRL
○ D. SYSMAINT

Question 34

Which statement regarding label-based access control (LBAC) is true?

○ A. Two types of security label components are supported: array and tree.

○ B. Every LBAC-protected table must have only one security policy associated with it.

○ C. To configure a table for row-level LBAC protection, you must include the SECURED WITH clause with each column's definition.

○ D. To configure a table for column-level LBAC protection, you must include a column with the DB2SECURITYLABEL data type in the table's definition.

Question 35

Which method for restricting data access relies on an SQL CASE expression to control the conditions under which a user can access values for a column?

○ A. Authority

○ B. Authentication

○ C. Label-based access control

○ D. Row and column access control

Question 36

Which two statements about Row and Column Access Control (RCAC) are valid? (Choose two.)

❏ A. A column mask's access control rule is defined by an SQL search condition.

❏ B. A column mask's access control rule is defined by an SQL CASE expression.

❏ C. A row permission's access control rule is defined by an SQL search condition.

❏ D. A row permission's access control rule is defined by an SQL CASE expression.

❏ E. A column mask's access control rule is defined by a SECURED WITH clause of a CREATE TABLE or ALTER TABLE statement.

Question 37

Which privilege is needed to invoke a stored procedure?

- ○ A. USE
- ○ B. CALL
- ○ C. USAGE
- ○ D. EXECUTE

Working with Databases and Database Objects

Question 38

Which statement about views is NOT true?

- ○ A. A view can be defined as being updatable or read-only.
- ○ B. Views obtain their data from the table(s) or view(s) they are based on.
- ○ C. A view can be used to limit a user's ability to retrieve data from a table.
- ○ D. The SQL statement provided as part of a view's definition determines what data is presented when the view is referenced.

Question 39

If the following SQL statement is executed:

```
CREATE DISTINCT TYPE pound_sterling AS DECIMAL (9,2)
   WITH COMPARISONS
```

Which event will NOT happen?

- ○ A. A user-defined data type that can be used to store numerical data as British currency will be created.
- ○ B. Six comparison functions will be created so that POUND_STERLING values can be compared to each other.
- ○ C. Two casting functions will be created so that POUND_STERLING values can be converted to DECIMAL values, and vice versa.
- ○ D. A compatibility function will be created so all of DB2's built-in functions that accept DECIMAL values as input can be used with POUND_STERLING data.

Question 40

If the following SQL statements are executed:

```
CREATE TABLE sales(
    order_num       INTEGER NOT NULL,
    customer_name   VARCHAR(50),
    amount_due      DECIMAL(6,2));

CREATE UNIQUE INDEX idx_ordernum ON sales(order_num);
```

Which two statements are true? (Choose two.)

☐ A. Every ORDER_NUM value must be unique.
☐ B. Duplicate ORDER_NUM values are allowed.
☐ C. No other indexes can be created for the SALES table.
☐ D. A query will return rows from the SALES table in no specific order.
☐ E. Index IDX_ORDERNUM will serve as the primary key for the SALES table.

Question 41

What is the minimum product that is needed to give applications running on personal computers the ability to work with DB2 databases that reside on System z platforms, without using a gateway?

○ A. DB2 Connect Personal Edition
○ B. DB2 Connect Enterprise Edition
○ C. IBM DB2 Connect Unlimited Advanced Edition for System z
○ D. IBM DB2 Connect Unlimited Advanced Edition for System i

Question 42

Which action does NOT need to be performed to complete the definition of an application-period temporal table?

○ A. A business-time-begin column must be created for the table.
○ B. A business-time-end column must be created for the table.
○ C. A BUSINESS_TIME period must be specified in a CREATE or ALTER of the table.
○ D. A unique index must be created that prevents overlapping of the BUSINESS_ TIME period of the table.

Question 43

What are buffer pools used for?

○ A. To cache table and index data as it is read from disk.
○ B. To keep track of changes that are made to a database as they occur.
○ C. To control the amount of processor resources that SQL statements can consume.
○ D. To provide a layer of indirection between a data object and the storage where that object's data resides.

Question 44

Which statement regarding distributed requests is NOT true?

○ A. To implement distributed request functionality, all you need is a federated database and one or more remote data sources.
○ B. Distributed request functionality allows a UNION operation to be performed between a DB2 table and an Oracle view.
○ C. Distributed request functionality allows SQL operations to reference two or more databases or relational database management systems in a single statement.
○ D. DB2 Connect provides the ability to perform distributed requests across members of the DB2 Family, as well as across other relational database management systems.

Question 45

Which statement about indexes is NOT true?

○ A. An index can be used to enforce the uniqueness of records in a table.
○ B. Indexes provide a fast, efficient method for locating specific rows in a table.
○ C. When an index is created, metadata for the index is stored in the system catalog.
○ D. Indexes automatically provide both a logical and a physical ordering of the rows in a table.

Question 46

What are Materialized Query Tables (MQTs) used for?

○ A. To physically cluster data on more than one dimension, simultaneously.
○ B. To improve the execution performance of qualified SELECT statements.
○ C. To hold nonpersistent data temporarily, on behalf of a single application.
○ D. To track effective dates for data that is subject to changing business conditions.

Question 47

Which two actions must be performed to track changes made to a system-period temporal table over time? (Choose two.)

❑ A. A history table must be created with columns that are identical to those of the system-period temporal table.
❑ B. The system-period temporal table must be altered using the ADD VERSIONING clause to relate it to a history table.
❑ C. A primary key must be defined for the system-period temporal table that prevents overlapping of SYSTEM_TIME periods.
❑ D. A unique index must be defined on the transaction-start-id column of both the system-period temporal table and its associated history table.
❑ E. The system-period temporal table must be altered to add system-time-begin, system-time-end, transaction-start-id, and transaction-end-id columns.

Question 48

Which database object can be used to automatically generate a numeric value that is not tied to any specific column or table?

○ A. Alias
○ B. Schema
○ C. Package
○ D. Sequence

Question 49

Which column is NOT required as part of the table definition for a system-period temporal table?

O A. A row-begin column with a TIMESTAMP(12) data type
O B. A row-end column with a TIMESTAMP(12) data type
O C. A transaction-start-id column with a TIMESTAMP(12) data type
O D. A transaction-stop-id column with a TIMESTAMP(12) data type

Question 50

Which object can NOT be enabled for compression?

O A. Views
O B. Indexes
O C. Base tables
O D. Temporary tables

Question 51

What is a schema used for?

O A. To provide an alternate name for a table or view.
O B. To provide a logical grouping of database objects.
O C. To generate a series of numbers, in ascending or descending order.
O D. To provide an alternative way of describing data stored in one or more tables.

Question 52

Which view definition type is NOT supported?

O A. Insertable
O B. Updatable
O C. Read-only
O D. Write-only

Question 53

When should an application-period temporal table be used?

○ A. When you want to keep track of historical versions of a table's rows.
○ B. When you want to define specific time periods in which data is valid.
○ C. When you want to cluster data according to the time in which rows are inserted.
○ D. When you want to cluster data on more than one key or dimension, simultaneously.

Question 54

Which statement about buffer pools is NOT true?

○ A. Every table space must have a buffer pool assigned to it.
○ B. One buffer pool is created automatically as part of the database creation process.
○ C. Dirty pages are automatically removed from a buffer pool when they are written to storage.
○ D. Once a page has been copied to a buffer pool, it remains there until the space it occupies is needed.

Question 55

Which DB2 object can a view NOT be derived from?

○ A. Alias
○ B. View
○ C. Table
○ D. Procedure

Question 56

Which two expressions can be used with a sequence? (Choose two.)

☐ A. NEXT VALUE
☐ B. PRIOR VALUE
☐ C. CURRENT VALUE
☐ D. PREVIOUS VALUE
☐ E. SUBSEQUENT VALUE

Question 57

Which object is a distinct data type defined into?

○ A. Schema
○ B. Package
○ C. Database
○ D. Table space

Question 58

Which two objects can NOT be created in DB2? (Choose two.)

☐ A. Plan
☐ B. Trigger
☐ C. Scheme
☐ D. Function
☐ E. Sequence

Question 59

Which statement about Type 2 connections is true?

○ A. Type 2 connections cannot be used with DB2 for z/OS.
○ B. Type 2 connections are used by default with DB2 for Linux, UNIX, and Windows.
○ C. Type 2 connections allow applications to be connected to only one database at a time.
○ D. Type 2 connections allow applications to connect to and work with multiple DB2 databases simultaneously.

Question 60

Which two statements about bitemporal tables are valid? (Choose two.)

☐ A. Bitemporal tables are system tables and can only be queried by the table owner.
☐ B. When data in a bitemporal table is updated, a row is added to its associated history table.
☐ C. Creating a bitemporal table is similar to creating a base table except users must define a SYSTEM_TIME_PERIOD column.
☐ D. When querying a bitemporal table, you have the option of providing a system time-period specification, a business time-period specification, or both.
☐ E. Bitemporal tables must contain bitemporal-time-begin, bitemporal-time-end, and transaction-start-id columns, along with SYSTEM_TIME and BUSINESS_TIME periods.

Question 61

Which programming interface is widely used for database access because it allows applications to run, unchanged, on most hardware platforms?

○ A. ODBC
○ B. SQLJ
○ C. JDBC
○ D. OLE DB

Question 62

Which two types of temporal tables can be used to store time-sensitive data? (Choose two.)

- ❑ A. Bitemporal
- ❑ B. Time-period
- ❑ C. System-period
- ❑ D. Business-period
- ❑ E. Application-period

Question 63

In which of the following scenarios would a stored procedure be beneficial?

- ○ A. An application running on a remote client needs to track every modification made to a table that contains sensitive data.
- ○ B. An application running on a remote client needs to be able to convert degrees Celsius to degrees Fahrenheit and vice versa.
- ○ C. An application running on a remote client needs to ensure that every new employee that joins the company is assigned a unique, sequential employee number.
- ○ D. An application running on a remote client needs to collect input values from a user, perform a calculation using the values provided, and store the input data, along with the calculation results, in a base table.

Question 64

Given the following SQL statement:

```
CREATE ALIAS emp_info FOR employees
```

Which two objects can the name EMPLOYEES refer to? (Choose two.)

- ❑ A. A view
- ❑ B. An alias
- ❑ C. An index
- ❑ D. A sequence
- ❑ E. A procedure

Question 65

Which operation can NOT be performed by executing an ALTER SEQUENCE statement?

- O A. Change a sequence's data type.
- O B. Change whether a sequence cycles.
- O C. Establish new minimum and maximum sequence values.
- O D. Change the number of sequence numbers that are cached.

Question 66

Which object must exist before an index can be created?

- O A. View
- O B. Table
- O C. Schema
- O D. Sequence

Question 67

If the following SQL statement is executed:

```
CREATE DATABASE payroll
```

Which two statements are true? (Choose two.)

- ☐ A. The PAYROLL database will have a page size of 4 KB.
- ☐ B. The PAYROLL database will have a page size of 8 KB.
- ☐ C. The PAYROLL database will be an automatic storage database.
- ☐ D. The PAYROLL database will not be an automatic storage database.
- ☐ E. The PAYROLL database will be assigned the comment "PAYROLL DATABASE."

Working with DB2 Data Using SQL

Question 68

If the following result set is desired:

STATE	REGION	AVG_INCOME
MARYLAND	MID-ATLANTIC	86056.00
NEW JERSEY	NORTHEAST	85005.00
CONNECTICUT	NORTHEAST	84558.00
MASSACHUSETTS	NORTHEAST	82009.00
ALASKA	PACIFIC-ALASKA	79617.00

Which SQL statement must be executed?

O A. SELECT state, region, avg_income
           FROM census_data
           ORDER BY 3
           FETCH FIRST 5 ROWS

O B. SELECT state, region, avg_income
           FROM census_data
           ORDER BY 3
           FETCH FIRST 5 ROWS ONLY

O C. SELECT state, region, avg_income
           FROM census_data
           ORDER BY 3 DESC
           FETCH FIRST 5 ROWS

O D. SELECT state, region, avg_income
           FROM census_data
           ORDER BY 3 DESC
           FETCH FIRST 5 ROWS ONLY

Question 69

Which type of join will usually produce the smallest result set?

- ○ A. INNER JOIN
- ○ B. LEFT OUTER JOIN
- ○ C. RIGHT OUTER JOIN
- ○ D. FULL OUTER JOIN

Question 70

Which statement about SQL subqueries is NOT true?

- ○ A. A subquery can be used with an UPDATE statement to supply values for one or more columns that are to be updated.
- ○ B. A subquery can be used with an INSERT statement to retrieve values from one base table or view and copy them to another.
- ○ C. If a subquery is used with a DELETE statement and the result set produced is empty, every record will be deleted from the table specified.
- ○ D. If a subquery is used with an UPDATE statement and the result set produced contains multiple rows, the operation will fail and an error will be generated.

Question 71

Which statement about savepoints is NOT true?

- ○ A. You can use as many savepoints as you desire within a single unit of work, provided you do not nest them.
- ○ B. Savepoints provide a way to break the work being done by a single large transaction into one or more smaller subsets.
- ○ C. The COMMIT FROM SAVEPOINT statement is used to commit a subset of database changes that have been made within a unit of work.
- ○ D. The ROLLBACK TO SAVEPOINT statement is used to back out a subset of database changes that have been made within a unit of work.

Question 72

Which two statements about UPDATE processing are true? (Choose two.)

☐ A. A positioned UPDATE is used to modify one or more rows, and a searched UPDATE is used to modify exactly one row.

☐ B. A searched UPDATE is used to modify one or more rows, and a positioned UPDATE is used to modify exactly one row.

☐ C. When the UPDATE statement modifies parent key columns, the values of corresponding foreign key columns are modified as well.

☐ D. The UPDATE statement can be used to remove data from specified columns in the rows of a table, provided those columns are not nullable.

☐ E. The UPDATE statement can be used to modify the values of specified columns in the rows of a table, view, or underlying table(s) of a specified fullselect.

Question 73

A table named SALES has two columns: SALES_AMT and REGION_CD.
Which SQL statement will return the number of sales in each region, ordered by number of sales made?

○ A. SELECT sales_amt, COUNT(*)
      FROM sales
      ORDER BY 2

○ B. SELECT sales_amt, COUNT(*)
      FROM sales
      GROUP BY sales_amt
      ORDER BY 1

○ C. SELECT region_cd, COUNT(*)
      FROM sales
      GROUP BY region_cd
      ORDER BY COUNT(*)

○ D. SELECT region_cd, COUNT(*)
      FROM sales
      GROUP BY sales_amt
      ORDER BY COUNT(*)

Question 74

A user wants to retrieve records from a table named SALES that satisfy at least one of the following criteria:

- The sales date (SALESDATE) is after June 1, 2012, and the sales amount (AMT) is greater than $40.00.

- The sale was made in the hardware department.

Which SQL statement will accomplish this?

○ A. SELECT * FROM sales
       WHERE (salesdate > '2012-06-01' OR (amt > 40
       AND (dept = 'Hardware')

○ B. SELECT * FROM sales
       WHERE (salesdate > '2012-06-01') OR (amt > 40)
       OR (dept = 'Hardware')

○ C. SELECT * FROM sales
       WHERE (salesdate > '2012-06-01' AND amt > 40
       AND (dept = 'Hardware')

○ D. SELECT * FROM sales
       WHERE (salesdate > '2012-06-01' AND amt > 40)
       OR (dept = 'Hardware')

Question 75

Which two statements about INSERT operations are true? (Choose two.)

☐ A. The INSERT statement can be used to insert rows into a table, view, or table function.

☐ B. Inserted values must satisfy the conditions of any check constraints that have been defined on the table specified.

☐ C. The values provided in the VALUES clause of an INSERT statement are assigned to columns in the order in which they appear.

☐ D. If an INSERT statement omits any column from the inserted row that is defined as NULL or NOT NULL WITH DEFAULT, the statement will fail.

☐ E. If the underlying table of a view that is referenced by an INSERT statement has one or more unique indexes, each row inserted does not have to conform to the constraints imposed by those indexes.

Question 76

Which SQL statement should be used to select the minimum and maximum rainfall amounts (RAINFALL), by month (MONTH), from a table named WEATHER?

○ A. SELECT month, MIN(rainfall), MAX(rainfall)
       FROM weather
       ORDER BY month

○ B. SELECT month, MIN(rainfall), MAX(rainfall)
       FROM weather
       GROUP BY month

○ C. SELECT month, MIN(rainfall), MAX(rainfall)
       FROM weather
       GROUP BY month, MIN(rainfall), MAX(rainfall)

○ D. SELECT month, MIN(rainfall), MAX(rainfall)
       FROM weather
       ORDER BY month, MIN(rainfall), MAX(rainfall)

Question 77

An SQL function named REGIONAL_SALES was created as follows:

```
CREATE FUNCTION regional_sales()
    RETURNS TABLE (region_id  VARCHAR(20),
                   sales_amt   DECIMAL(8,2))
    READS SQL DATA
    BEGIN ATOMIC
    RETURN
        SELECT region, amt
        FROM sales
        ORDER BY region;
    END
```

Which two statements demonstrate the proper way to use this function in a query? (Choose two.)

☐ A. SELECT * FROM regional_sales()
☐ B. SELECT regional_sales (region_id, sales_amt)
☐ C. SELECT region_id, sales_amt FROM regional_sales()
☐ D. SELECT * FROM TABLE (regional_sales()) AS results
☐ E. SELECT region_id, sales_amt FROM TABLE (regional_sales()) AS results

Question 78

If the following SQL statement is executed:

```
SELECT dept, AVG(salary)
  FROM employee
  GROUP BY dept
  ORDER BY 2
```

What will be the results?

○ A. The department number and average salary for all employees will be retrieved from a table named EMPLOYEE, and the results will be arranged in descending order, by department.

○ B. The department number and average salary for all departments will be retrieved from a table named EMPLOYEE, and the results will be arranged in ascending order, by department.

○ C. The department number and average salary for all employees will be retrieved from a table named EMPLOYEE, and the results will be arranged in ascending order, by average departmental salary.

○ D. The department number and average salary for all departments will be retrieved from a table named EMPLOYEE, and the results will be arranged in descending order, by average departmental salary.

Question 79

If a table named SALES contains information about invoices that do not have a negative balance, which two SQL statements can be used to retrieve invoice numbers for invoices that are for less than $25,000.00? (Choose two.)

❏ A. SELECT invoice_num FROM sales WHERE amt < 25000

❏ B. SELECT invoice_num FROM sales WHERE amt < 25,000

❏ C. SELECT invoice_num FROM sales WHERE amt LESS THAN 25,000

❏ D. SELECT invoice_num FROM sales WHERE amt BETWEEN 0 AND 25000

❏ E. SELECT invoice_num FROM sales WHERE amt BETWEEN 0 AND 25,000

Question 80

An SQL function designed to convert miles to kilometers was created as follows:

```
CREATE FUNCTION mi_to_km (IN miles FLOAT)
    RETURNS FLOAT
    LANGUAGE SQL
    SPECIFIC convert_mtok
    READS SQL DATA
    RETURN FLOAT (miles * 1.60934)
```

How can this function be used to convert miles (MILES) values stored in a table named DISTANCES?

- ○ A. CALL mi_to_km (distances.miles)
- ○ B. CALL convert_mtok (distances.miles)
- ○ C. SELECT mi_to_km (miles) FROM distances
- ○ D. SELECT convert_mtok (miles) FROM distances

Question 81

Which two statements about system-period temporal tables are true? (Choose two.)

- ☐ A. They store user-based period information.
- ☐ B. They do not require a separate history table.
- ☐ C. They store system-based historical information.
- ☐ D. They can be queried without a time-period specification.
- ☐ E. They manage data based on time criteria specified by users or applications.

Question 82

A table named PARTS contains a record of every part that has been manufactured by a company. A user wishes to see the total number of parts that have been made by each craftsman employed at the company. Which SQL statement will produce the desired results?

○ A. SELECT name, COUNT(*) AS parts_made
       FROM parts
○ B. SELECT name, COUNT(*) AS parts_made
       FROM parts
       GROUP BY name
○ C. SELECT name, COUNT(DISTINCT name) AS parts_made
       FROM parts
○ D. SELECT DISTINCT name, COUNT(*) AS parts_made
       FROM parts
       GROUP BY parts_made

Question 83

Given an EMPLOYEES table and a DEPARTMENTS table, a user wants to produce a list of all departments and employees who work in them, including departments that no employees have been assigned to. Which SQL statement will produce the desired list?

○ A. SELECT employees.name, departments.deptname
       FROM employees
       INNER JOIN department ON employees.dept = departments.deptno
○ B. SELECT employees.name, departments.deptname
       FROM employees
       INNER JOIN department ON departments.deptno = employees.dept
○ C. SELECT employees.name, departments.deptname
       FROM employees
       LEFT OUTER JOIN departments ON
          employees.dept = departments.deptno
○ D. SELECT employees.name, departments.deptname
       FROM employees
       RIGHT OUTER JOIN departments ON
          employees.dept = departments.deptno

Question 84

Which statements are NOT allowed in the body of an SQL scalar user-defined function?

○ A. CALL statements
○ B. COMMIT statements
○ C. SQL CASE statements
○ D. SQL control statements

Question 85

A table named TABLE_A contains 200 rows and a user wants to update the 10 rows in this table with the lowest values in a column named COL1. Which SQL statement will produce the desired results?

○ A. UPDATE
  (SELECT * FROM table_a
    ORDER BY col1 ASC) AS temp
  SET col2 = 99
  FETCH FIRST 10 ROWS ONLY
○ B. UPDATE
  (SELECT * FROM table_a
    ORDER BY col1 DESC) AS temp
  SET col2 = 99
  FETCH FIRST 10 ROWS ONLY
○ C. UPDATE
  (SELECT * FROM table_a
    ORDER BY col1 ASC
    FETCH FIRST 10 ROWS ONLY) AS temp
  SET col2 = 99
○ D. UPDATE
  (SELECT * FROM table_a
    ORDER BY col1 DESC
    FETCH FIRST 10 ROWS ONLY) AS temp
  SET col2 = 99

Question 86

Which statement best describes a transaction?

O A. A transaction is a recoverable sequence of operations whose point of consistency is established only when a savepoint is created.

O B. A transaction is a recoverable sequence of operations whose point of consistency can be obtained by querying the system catalog tables.

O C. A transaction is a recoverable sequence of operations whose point of consistency is established when a database connection is established or a savepoint is created.

O D. A transaction is a recoverable sequence of operations whose point of consistency is established when an executable SQL statement is processed after a database connection has been established or a previous transaction has been terminated.

Question 87

A table named TABLE_A contains 200 rows and a user wants to delete the last 10 rows from this table. Which SQL statement will produce the desired results?

O A. DELETE FROM
    (SELECT * FROM table_a
     ORDER BY col1 ASC
     FETCH FIRST 10 ROWS ONLY) AS result

O B. DELETE FROM
    (SELECT * FROM table_a
     ORDER BY col1 DESC
     FETCH FIRST 10 ROWS ONLY) AS result

O C. DELETE FROM
    (SELECT * FROM table_a
     ORDER BY col1 ASC
     FETCH LAST 10 ROWS ONLY) AS result

O D. DELETE FROM
    (SELECT * FROM table_a
     ORDER BY col1 DESC
     FETCH LAST 10 ROWS ONLY) AS result

Question 88

Which clause could be added to the following SQL statement

```
SELECT student_id, enroll_date, gpa
    FROM students
```

to ensure that only information (STUDENT_ID, ENROLL_DATE, and GPA) for students who started school before 2012 and who have a GPA that is higher than 3.50 will be retrieved?

- O A. FOR enroll_date < '2012-01-01' OR gpa > 3.50
- O B. FOR enroll_date < '2012-01-01' AND gpa > 3.50
- O C. WHERE enroll_date < '2012-01-01' OR gpa > 3.50
- O D. WHERE enroll_date < '2012-01-01' AND gpa > 3.50

Question 89

Which statement correctly describes what a native SQL stored procedure is?

- O A. A procedure whose body is written entirely in SQL or SQL PL.
- O B. A procedure that is written in a high-level programming language such as Java or REXX.
- O C. A procedure whose body is written entirely in SQL, but that is implemented as an external program.
- O D. A procedure that accesses data using an Object Linking and Embedding, Database (OLE DB) provider.

Question 90

Given the following statements:

```
CREATE TABLE customer (custid INTEGER, custinfo XML);
INSERT INTO customer VALUES (100,
'<customerinfo>
  <name>ACME Manufacturing</name>
  <addr country="United States">
     <street>25 Elm Street</street>
  <city>Raleigh</city>
  <state>North Carolina</state>
  <zip>27603</zip>
   </addr>
</customerinfo>');
```

If the following XQuery statement is executed:

```
XQUERY
for $info in db2-fn:xmlcolumn('CUSTOMER.CUSTINFO')/customerinfo
return $info/name
```

What will be the result?

- ○ A. ACME Manufacturing
- ○ B. \<name>ACME Manufacturing\</name>
- ○ C. \<customerinfo>ACME Manufacturing\</customerinfo>
- ○ D. \<customerinfo>\<name>ACME Manufacturing\</name>\</customerinfo>

Question 91

Which two statements about roll back operations are correct? (Choose two.)

- ☐ A. When a ROLLBACK statement is executed, all locks held by the terminating transaction are released.
- ☐ B. When a ROLLBACK TO SAVEPOINT statement is executed, all locks acquired after the most recent savepoint are released.
- ☐ C. When a ROLLBACK statement is executed, all locks acquired for open cursors that were declared WITH HOLD are held.
- ☐ D. When a ROLLBACK TO SAVEPOINT statement is executed, all locks acquired up to the most recent savepoint are released.
- ☐ E. When a ROLLBACK TO SAVEPOINT statement is executed, a savepoint is not automatically deleted as part of the rollback operation.

Question 92

Which SQL statement illustrates the proper way to perform a positioned update operation on a table named SALES?

○ A. UPDATE sales SET amt = 102.45
○ B. UPDATE sales SET amt = 102.45 WHERE cust_id = '000290'
○ C. UPDATE sales SET amt = 102.45 WHERE CURRENT OF cursor1
○ D. UPDATE sales SET amt = 102.45 WHERE ROWID =
         (SELECT ROWID FROM sales WHERE cust_id = '000290')

Question 93

Which two statements about application-period temporal tables are true? (Choose two.)

☐ A. They are useful when one wants to keep user-based time period information.
☐ B. They consist of explicitly supplied timestamps and a separate associated history table.
☐ C. They are useful when one wants to keep both user-based and system-based time period information.
☐ D. They are based on explicitly supplied timestamps that define the time periods during which data is valid.
☐ E. They consist of a pair of columns with database-manager maintained values that indicate the period when a row is current.

Question 94

When should the TRUNCATE statement be used?

○ A. When you want to delete all rows from a table without generating log records.
○ B. When you want to delete select rows from a table without generating log records.
○ C. When you want to delete all rows from a table and fire any delete triggers that have been defined for the table.
○ D. When you want to delete select rows from a table and fire any delete triggers that have been defined for the table.

Question 95

Which two commands will terminate the current transaction and start a new transaction boundary? (Choose two.)

- ❏ A. COMMIT
- ❏ B. REFRESH
- ❏ C. RESTART
- ❏ D. CONNECT
- ❏ E. ROLLBACK

Question 96

Which SQL statement should be used to retrieve the minimum and maximum annual temperatures (TEMP) for each major city (CITY), sorted by city, from a table named WEATHER?

- ○ A. SELECT city, MIN(temp), MAX(temp)
       FROM weather
       ORDER BY city
- ○ B. SELECT city, MIN(temp), MAX(temp)
       FROM weather
       GROUP BY city
- ○ C. SELECT city, MIN(temp), MAX(temp)
       FROM weather
       GROUP BY city
       ORDER BY city
- ○ D. SELECT city, MIN(temp), MAX(temp)
       FROM weather
       GROUP BY MIN(temp), MAX(temp)
       ORDER BY city

Question 97

What is the XMLTABLE() function typically used for?

- ○ A. To convert a well-formed XML document into a table of character string values.
- ○ B. To obtain values from XML documents that are to be inserted into one or more tables.
- ○ C. To parse a character string value and return a table of well-formed XML documents.
- ○ D. To produce a temporary table whose columns are based on the elements found in a well-formed XML document.

Working with DB2 Tables, Views, and Indexes

Question 98

The following SQL statements were used to create a table and a unique index:

```
CREATE TABLE parts
    (part_cd   INTEGER NOT NULL,
     part_desc VARCHAR (20));

CREATE UNIQUE INDEX indx1 ON parts (part_cd);
```

If the following ALTER statement is executed later:

```
ALTER TABLE parts ADD PRIMARY KEY (part_cd);
```

Which two events will take place? (Choose two.)

- ☐ A. An error will be returned.
- ☐ B. A warning will be returned.
- ☐ C. Index INDX1 will become the index for the new primary key.
- ☐ D. Index INDX1 will be marked invalid and will be rebuilt the next time it is accessed.
- ☐ E. Index INDX1 will be dropped and a different index will be created for the primary key.

Question 99

Which statement about unique constraints is true?

○ A. A unique constraint can be used to ensure that a column will never be assigned a NULL value.

○ B. A unique constraint can be used to control which values will be accepted for a column in a table.

○ C. A unique constraint can be used to ensure that a column in a table will always be assigned a value.

○ D. A unique constraint can be used to ensure that a column in a table will never be assigned more than one NULL value.

Question 100

Which two statements regarding triggers are true? (Choose two.)

❏ A. The triggered action (body) of a trigger cannot contain executable code.

❏ B. Triggers cannot be modified; they must be dropped and recreated with new definitions.

❏ C. Adding a trigger to a table that already has rows in it will cause triggered actions to be fired.

❏ D. Triggers can only be fired one time per statement irrespective of the number of rows affected.

❏ E. Triggers perform actions in response to an event such as an INSERT, UPDATE, or DELETE operation on a table.

Question 101

Which statement about primary key constraints is true?

○ A. Each primary key must have at least one corresponding foreign key.
○ B. Before a primary key can be created, a unique constraint must exist on the primary key's key columns.
○ C. A range partition must be defined on the key columns found in a primary key, immediately after the key is created.
○ D. A "unique and system-required" index will be created, if one doesn't exist, for a primary key's columns at the time the key is created.

Question 102

The following SQL statement was used to create a table named PARTS:

```
CREATE TABLE parts (
    part_no       VARCHAR(10),
    description   VARCHAR(50))
```

If values stored in the DESCRIPTION column are less than 36 characters in length, which SQL statement will successfully decrease the size of the DESCRIPTION column?

○ A. ALTER TABLE parts RESIZE COLUMN description 40
○ B. ALTER TABLE parts ADJUST COLUMN description VARCHAR(40)
○ C. ALTER TABLE parts ALTER COLUMN description
        SET DATA TYPE VARCHAR(40)
○ D. ALTER TABLE parts ALTER COLUMN description
        ALTER DATA TYPE VARCHAR(40)

Question 103

A table named SALES was created and populated using the follow SQL statements:

```
CREATE TABLE sales (
   invoice_no    VARCHAR(10) NOT NULL,
   invoice_amt   DECIMAL(6,2) NOT NULL);
INSERT INTO sales VALUES ('2014-007', 102.90);
INSERT INTO sales VALUES ('2014-024', 82.50);
INSERT INTO sales VALUES (NULL, 224.37);
INSERT INTO sales VALUES ('', 0.0);
```

If the following query is executed:

```
SELECT count(*) FROM sales;
```

How many rows will be returned?

○ A. 1
○ B. 2
○ C. 3
○ D. 4

Question 104

When should an informational constraint be used?

○ A. When you want to ensure that a column will never be assigned a NULL value.
○ B. When you want to control which values can be assigned to a column in a table.
○ C. When you want to define a required relationship between select columns and tables.
○ D. When you want to tell the DB2 Optimizer that a parent-child relationship exists between two tables, but that the relationship is not enforced.

Question 105

What are two valid reasons for creating an index? (Choose two.)

- ☐ A. To allow queries to run more efficiently.
- ☐ B. To enforce CHECK and NOT NULL constraints.
- ☐ C. To order the columns of a table in ascending or descending sequence according to values in a row.
- ☐ D. To order the rows of a table in ascending or descending sequence according to the values in a column.
- ☐ E. To improve the performance of online transaction processing (OLTP) environments or environments where data throughput is high.

Question 106

Which data type can be used to store character string data in such a way that any comparisons of values that are made will be done so in binary format, regardless of the database collating sequence used?

- ○ A. BLOB(500)
- ○ B. VARCHAR(500)
- ○ C. CLOB(500) FOR BIT DATA
- ○ D. VARCHAR(500) FOR BIT DATA

Question 107

Which two events will cause a trigger to be fired? (Choose two.)

- ☐ A. Execution of an IMPORT command.
- ☐ B. Execution of an UPDATE statement.
- ☐ C. Execution of a TRUNCATE statement.
- ☐ D. Execution of an LOAD ... REPLACE command.
- ☐ E. Execution of an INSERT operation of a MERGE statement.

Question 108

A user wants to ensure that any rows that are inserted or updated with a view will conform to the view's definition. Which clause of the CREATE VIEW statement can be used to accomplish this goal?

- ○ A. RESTRICT
- ○ B. CASCADE
- ○ C. WITH CHECK OPTION
- ○ D. WITH CONTROL OPTION

Question 109

Which statement about the TIMESTAMP data type is NOT true?

- ○ A. By default, 6 digits are used to represent the fractional seconds portion of a TIMESTAMP value.
- ○ B. TIMESTAMP values are stored as fixed-length character string values that are 32 characters in length.
- ○ C. The TIMESTAMP data type is used to store six- or seven-part values that represent a specific calendar date and time.
- ○ D. The actual string format used to present a date or time value stored in a TIMESTAMP column is dependent upon the territory code that has been assigned to the database.

Question 110

Which of the following is the best statement to use to create a user-defined data type that will be used to store currency values?

- ○ A. CREATE DISTINCT TYPE currency AS BIGINT
- ○ B. CREATE DISTINCT TYPE currency AS DOUBLE
- ○ C. CREATE DISTINCT TYPE currency AS SMALLINT
- ○ D. CREATE DISTINCT TYPE currency AS NUMERIC(7,2)

Question 111

Which two statements about BEFORE triggers are true? (Choose two.)

☐ A. A BEFORE trigger can be used to automatically generate values for newly inserted rows.
☐ B. A BEFORE trigger can be used to insert, update, or delete data in the same or in different tables.
☐ C. A BEFORE trigger is fired for each row in the set of affected rows before the trigger event takes place.
☐ D. A BEFORE trigger can be used to check data against other data values in the same or in different tables.
☐ E. A BEFORE trigger is fired for each row in the set of affected rows in place of the trigger event.

Question 112

Which of the following is NOT a true statement about unique indexes and primary keys?

○ A. A table can have many unique indexes but only one primary key.
○ B. A primary key is a special form of a unique constraint; both use a unique index.
○ C. Unique indexes can be defined over one or more columns; primary keys can only be defined on a single column.
○ D. Unique indexes can be defined over one or more columns that allow null values; primary keys cannot contain null values.

Question 113

Which type of constraint can be used to provide a method of ensuring a column's values are within a specific range?

○ A. Check
○ B. Unique
○ C. Referential
○ D. Informational

Question 114

Which is NOT a valid reason for creating a view?

- ○ A. To restrict access to sensitive data.
- ○ B. To combine data from multiple tables.
- ○ C. To enable a single SQL statement to work with a variety of tables.
- ○ D. To provide an alternative way of describing data that exists in one or more base tables.

Question 115

If a user named USER1 executes the following statement:

```
CREATE FUNCTION conv_temp (IN temp_f FLOAT)
   RETURNS INTEGER
   RETURN INT((temp_f - 32) / 1.8)
```

What schema will the CONV_TEMP function be stored in?

- ○ A. USER1
- ○ B. SYSIBM
- ○ C. SYSFUN
- ○ D. SYSCAT

Question 116

Which two statements about referential integrity constraints are true? (Choose two.)

- ❑ A. A foreign key can reference multiple primary keys.
- ❑ B. A primary key can be referenced by only one foreign key.
- ❑ C. Primary keys and foreign keys are used to define relationships between two tables.
- ❑ D. A foreign key can be defined on an individual column or a set of columns in a table.
- ❑ E. Foreign keys are enforced during the execution of INSERT, UPDATE, DELETE, and SELECT statements.

Question 117

Which statement about foreign key constraints is NOT true?

O A. The columns used in a foreign key constraint must be defined as being NOT
       NULL.
O B. The columns of one foreign key constraint can be used in another foreign key
       constraint.
O C. The number and data types of foreign key constraint columns must match the
       parent key.
O D. To define a foreign key constraint there must be an associated primary key or
       unique key in the same or different table.

Question 118

What are two valid reasons for using the INCLUDE clause with a CREATE INDEX
statement? (Choose two.)

☐ A. To combine two or more indexes to create a single index.
☐ B. To append data from select columns to the index's key values.
☐ C. To identify one or more columns that are to serve as the index's key.
☐ D. To improve the performance of some queries by enabling index-only access.
☐ E. To control how much space is reserved for future insert and update
       operations.

Question 119

Which statement about the XML data type is true?

O A. The XML data type allows XML documents to be stored as character large
       object strings.
O B. The format used to present an XML value depends on the territory code that
       has been assigned to the database used.
O C. By default, the data for a column with an XML data type is stored in an XML
       storage object that is separate from the table.
O D. The amount of space set aside to store an XML value is determined by the
       length specification provided when an XML column is defined.

Question 120

Which type of trigger is used to perform insert, update, and delete operations against complex views?

- ○ A. AFTER
- ○ B. BEFORE
- ○ C. BETWEEN
- ○ D. INSTEAD OF

Question 121

Which two statements are true regarding constraints? (Choose two.)

- ☐ A. A table can only have one unique key constraint.
- ☐ B. A table can have multiple primary key constraints.
- ☐ C. Unique constraints ensure that a column in a table will never contain duplicate values.
- ☐ D. Informational constraints tell DB2 what rules the data conforms to, but the rules are not enforced.
- ☐ E. Foreign key constraints are enforced on the values within the rows of a table, or between the rows of two tables, by a unique index on the foreign key.

Question 122

What statement about triggers is NOT true?

- ○ A. Triggers can be fired just before an insert, update, or delete operation takes place.
- ○ B. Triggers can be fired immediately after an insert, update, or delete operation takes place.
- ○ C. BEFORE and AFTER triggers can be used with both tables and views; INSTEAD OF triggers can only be used with views.
- ○ D. Triggers can be used to automatically update other tables, generate or transform values for inserted or updated rows, and perform tasks such as issuing alerts.

Question 123

Which two statements about temporary tables are true? (Choose two.)

☐ A. A temporary table is best suited for clustering data according to the time in which rows are inserted.

☐ B. A temporary table is best suited for recording results from application data manipulation that is not required to be persistent.

☐ C. When an application using a temporary table disconnects from the database unexpectedly, the data in the table is deleted and the table is implicitly dropped.

☐ D. Three different types of temporary tables are available: declared global temporary tables, declared local temporary tables, and created global temporary tables.

☐ E. When an application using a temporary table disconnects from the database unexpectedly, the temporary table is converted to a base table and its data is retained.

Question 124

When does a view get populated?

○ A. When it is first created.

○ B. When it is referenced by an INSERT statement.

○ C. Any time it is referenced by an executable SQL statement.

○ D. The first time it is referenced by an executable SQL statement.

Question 125

When should the DECIMAL data type be used?

○ A. When you need to store a 32-bit approximation of a real number.

○ B. When you need to store numeric values that have a precision of 19 digits.

○ C. When you need to store data in a column that represents money and that accurately returns a two-position scale.

○ D. When you need to store data in a column that represents ID numbers that have a precision of five or fewer digits.

Question 126

If the following SQL statement was used to create a table named ITEMS:

```
CREATE TABLE items (
    item_no      VARCHAR(10),
    description  VARCHAR(50))
```

Which SQL statement will add a column named PRICE to the ITEMS table?

- ○ A. ALTER TABLE items
       ADD COLUMN price NUMERIC (6, 2)
- ○ B. ALTER TABLE items
       INSERT COLUMN price NUMERIC (6, 2)
- ○ C. ALTER TABLE items
       APPEND COLUMN price NUMERIC (6, 2)
- ○ D. ALTER TABLE items
       ATTACH COLUMN price NUMERIC (6, 2)

Question 127

Which statement about indexes is NOT true?

- ○ A. In order to support a unique constraint, an index must be defined with the UNIQUE attribute.
- ○ B. If an index is created with INCLUDE columns, it must be defined with the UNIQUE clause.
- ○ C. A clustering index usually increases performance by decreasing the amount of I/O that is needed to access data.
- ○ D. With clustering indexes, higher PCTFREE values will increase the likelihood that index page splits will occur when records are added to the index.

Question 128

A user wants to define a required relationship between two tables named DEPARTMENT and EMPLOYEE such that whenever a record is deleted from the DEPARTMENT table, any related records will be deleted from the EMPLOYEE table. What two things must the user do to accomplish this? (Choose two.)

☐ A. Create a primary key on the EMPLOYEE table.
☐ B. Create a primary key on the DEPARTMENT table.
☐ C. Create a foreign key on the DEPARTMENT table that references the EMPLOYEE table and adheres to the ON DELETE CASCADE rule.
☐ D. Create a foreign key on the EMPLOYEE table that references the DEPARTMENT table and adheres to the ON DELETE RESTRICT rule.
☐ E. Create a foreign key on the EMPLOYEE table that references the DEPARTMENT table and adheres to the ON DELETE CASCADE rule.

Question 129

What type of constraint can be used to ensure that the value of one column in a table is never less than the value of another column in the same table?

○ A. A check constraint
○ B. A unique constraint
○ C. An informational constraint
○ D. A referential integrity constraint

Question 130

Which two data types can only be used in databases that have been configured for Oracle compatibility? (Choose two.)

☐ A. NUMBER
☐ B. VARCHAR
☐ C. VARCHAR2
☐ D. NVARCHAR
☐ E. CHARACTER VARYING

Data Concurrency

Question 131

If a Share (S) lock is acquired, which statement is true?

O A. The lock owner and all concurrent applications are allowed to read, but not update, the locked data.
O B. The lock owner is allowed to read and update the locked data; all concurrent applications are only allowed to read the locked data.
O C. The lock owner is allowed to read and update the locked data; all concurrent applications can neither read nor update the locked data.
O D. The lock owner is allowed to update, but not read the locked data; all concurrent applications are allowed to read, but not update the locked data.

Question 132

An application acquired a Share (S) lock on a row in a table and now wishes to update the row. Which of the following statements is true?

O A. DB2 will convert the row-level Share (S) lock to a row-level Update (U) lock, automatically.
O B. DB2 will convert the row-level Share (S) lock to a table-level Update (U) lock, automatically.
O C. The application must release the row-level Share (S) lock it currently holds and acquire an Update (U) lock on the row.
O D. The application must release the row-level Share (S) lock it currently holds and acquire an Update (U) lock on the table.

Question 133

What is the primary reason for using Currently Committed semantics with the Cursor Stability (CS) isolation level?

O   A.   To prevent read-only transactions from seeing uncommitted data, even when they are running under the Uncommitted Read (UR) isolation level.

O   B.   To reduce the amount of log space needed to track data changes by automatically removing log records for transactions that have been committed.

O   C.   To reduce lock contention by allowing read transactions to access the most recently committed data rather than having to wait for locks to be released.

O   D.   To force DB2 to write all data changes to the database as soon as the DB2 Database Manager can make a determination that those changes will eventually be committed.

Question 134

Which statement about the Cursor Stability (CS) isolation level is NOT true?

O   A.   The Cursor Stability (CS) isolation level prevents lost updates and dirty reads.

O   B.   Unless otherwise specified, the Cursor Stability (CS) isolation level is used by default.

O   C.   The Cursor Stability (CS) isolation level offers the greatest protection of data, but provides the least amount of concurrency.

O   D.   When the Cursor Stability (CS) isolation level is used, if the same query is executed two or more times within the same transaction, the results produced may vary.

Question 135

If the following SQL statement is executed:

```
LOCK TABLE sales IN SHARE MODE
```

Which statement is true?

- ○ A. From now on, DB2 will attempt to acquire table-level Share (S) locks for every transaction that accesses the SALES table.
- ○ B. From now on, DB2 will attempt to acquire row-level Share (S) locks for every transaction that accesses the SALES table.
- ○ C. A table-level Share (S) lock was acquired on the SALES table and concurrent transactions are allowed to perform both read and write operations against the table.
- ○ D. A table-level Share (S) lock was acquired on the SALES table and concurrent transactions are prevented from performing anything other than read-only operations against the table.

Question 136

Which two terms are used to describe the act of changing the lock an application currently holds on a resource to a more restrictive lock? (Choose two.)

- ☐ A. Lock exchange
- ☐ B. Lock escalation
- ☐ C. Lock promotion
- ☐ D. Lock conversion
- ☐ E. Lock substitution

Question 137

Which type of lock is acquired for a transaction that intends to read or change data?

- ○ A. Intent None (IN)
- ○ B. Intent Share (IS)
- ○ C. Intent Exclusive (IX)
- ○ D. Share With Intent Exclusive (SIX)

Question 138

Which two statements about the Repeatable Read (RR) isolation level are true? (Choose two.)

☐ A. The Repeatable Read (RR) isolation level prevents lost updates, dirty reads, nonrepeatable reads, and phantoms.

☐ B. The Repeatable Read (RR) isolation level prevents lost updates, dirty reads, and nonrepeatable reads, but not phantoms.

☐ C. The Repeatable Read (RR) isolation level offers the greatest protection of data, but provides the least amount of concurrency.

☐ D. The Repeatable Read (RR) isolation level offers the lowest protection of data, but provides the greatest amount of concurrency.

☐ E. The Repeatable Read (RR) isolation level does not completely isolate one transaction from the effects of other concurrently running transactions.

Question 139

Application APP_A is performing updates to a table named TAB1 using the Cursor Stability (CS) isolation level.

Application APP_B is querying several tables, including table TAB1. If application APP_B is running under the Uncommitted Read (UR) isolation level, which statement is true?

○ A. Application APP_B will not be able to retrieve rows from table TAB1 until application APP_A has finished making updates.

○ B. Application APP_B will be able to retrieve all rows from table TAB1 without waiting for application APP_A to finish making updates.

○ C. Application APP_B will only be able to retrieve the row currently being updated by application APP_A from table TAB1, while application APP_A is running.

○ D. Application APP_B will be able to retrieve all rows from table TAB1 except the row currently being updated, without waiting for application APP_A to finish.

Question 140

Which two factors influence lock escalation? (Choose two.)

☐ A. Lock size
☐ B. Lock list size
☐ C. Lock mode needed
☐ D. Number of locks held
☐ E. Lock mode currently held

Question 141

Which statement correctly describes when a deadlock will occur?

○ A. When two or more transactions hold Exclusive (X) locks on related resources, simultaneously.
○ B. When two or more transactions are forced to wait for another transaction to be committed or rolled back.
○ C. When DB2 attempts to convert multiple row-level Share (S) locks to a single, table-level Exclusive (X) lock and the lock is unavailable.
○ D. When one transaction holds locks on resources another transaction needs and the other transaction holds locks on resources the first transaction needs.

Question 142

Which two factors influence lock conversion? (Choose two.)

☐ A. Lock size
☐ B. Lock list size
☐ C. Lock mode needed
☐ D. Number of locks held
☐ E. Lock mode currently held

Question 143

Which operation normally does NOT acquire an Intent Exclusive (IX) or Exclusive (X) lock?

○ A. DROP
○ B. SELECT
○ C. UPDATE
○ D. DELETE

Question 144

Which statement about deadlocks is NOT true?

○ A. Each database has its own deadlock detector, which is activated as part of the database initialization process.
○ B. If a deadlock is discovered, the deadlock detector rolls back and terminates all transactions involved in the cycle.
○ C. If a deadlock is discovered, the deadlock detector randomly selects a "victim" transaction to roll back and terminate.
○ D. When a deadlock occurs, all transactions involved will wait indefinitely for a lock until the deadlock detector breaks the cycle.

Question 145

A table contains a list of all seats available on an airplane, and each record in the table consists of a row number, a seat number, and whether or not the seat has been assigned. Ticket agents working at the check-in counter and at the gate frequently generate a list of unassigned seats for passengers that request a new seat assignment. What is the best isolation level to use to ensure that whenever any agent refreshes the list, it will only change if one or more previously unassigned seats have been assigned?

○ A. Read Stability
○ B. Cursor Stability
○ C. Repeatable Read
○ D. Uncommitted Read

Question 146

Which object will DB2 NOT place locks on to provide concurrency and prevent uncontrolled data access?

- ○ A. Rows
- ○ B. Tables
- ○ C. Buffer pools
- ○ D. Table spaces

Question 147

Which action will cause a lock being held by an application running under the Cursor Stability isolation level to be released?

- ○ A. Moving the cursor to another row.
- ○ B. Updating or deleting the row the cursor is currently positioned on.
- ○ C. Moving the cursor to a row that has been deleted by another application.
- ○ D. Moving the cursor to a row that is in the process of being updated by another application.

Question 148

Which statement correctly defines lock escalation?

- ○ A. Lock escalation is the term that is used to describe the act of exchanging one lock an application holds on a resource for a more restrictive lock on the same resource.
- ○ B. Lock escalation is the term that is used to describe the act of releasing a large number of row-level locks an applications holds on a single table to acquire a table-level lock.
- ○ C. Lock escalation is the term that is used to describe the process that is used to prevent one transaction from waiting indefinitely for another transaction to release a lock on a resource it needs.
- ○ D. Lock escalation is the term that is used to describe the process that is used to allow scan operations to execute without locking rows when the data being accessed is known to have been committed.

Question 149

Which option of the LOCK TABLE statement is used to prevent concurrent application processes from performing read and write operations against the table being locked?

○ A. SHARE MODE
○ B. UPDATE MODE
○ C. EXCLUSIVE MODE
○ D. SUPEREXCLUSIVE MODE

Question 150

If a transaction updating rows in a table is still active, which statement is true?

○ A. Only applications running under the Uncommitted Read (UR) isolation level are allowed to retrieve the updated rows.
○ B. Only applications running under the Repeatable Read (RR) isolation level are allowed to retrieve the updated rows.
○ C. Only applications running under the Read Stability (RS) or Cursor Stability (CS) isolation level are allowed to retrieve the updated rows.
○ D. Only applications running under the Cursor Stability (CS) or Uncommitted Read (UR) isolation level are allowed to retrieve the updated rows.

APPENDIX

Answers to Practice Questions

Planning

Question 1

The correct answer is **C**. Data warehouses are typically used to store and manage large volumes of data that is often historical in nature and that is used primarily for analysis. Thus, a data warehouse could be used to identify sales patterns for products sold within the past three years or to summarize sales by region, on a quarterly basis.

Online transaction processing (OLTP) systems (*Answer D*), on the other hand, are designed to support day-to-day, mission-critical business activities such as web-based order entry and stock trading.

IBM offers two solutions that are tailored specifically for one system workload type or the other: *InfoSphere Warehouse* for data warehouses and the *DB2 pureScale Feature* (*Answer B*) for OLTP workloads.

Analytical workloads (*Answer A*) are better handled by a specialized product known as DB2 for i and by IBM BLU Acceleration, which is currently available only with DB2 10.5 for Linux, UNIX, and Windows.

Question 2

The correct answer is **A**. IBM Data Studio is an Eclipse-based, integrated development environment (IDE) that can be used to perform instance and database administration, routine (SQL procedures, SQL functions, etc.) and application development, and performance-tuning tasks. It replaces the DB2 Control Center (*Answer B*) as the standard GUI tool for DB2 database administration and application development.

IBM Workload Manager, or WLM (*Answer D*) is a comprehensive workload management feature that can help identify, manage, and control database workloads to maximize database server throughput and resource utilization.

There is no such product as IBM Data Administrator (*Answer C*).

Question 3

The correct answers are **B** and **C**. DB2 for z/OS is a multiuser, full-function database management system that has been designed specifically for z/OS, IBM's flagship mainframe operating system. Tightly integrated with the IBM mainframe, DB2 for z/OS leverages the strengths of System z 64-bit architecture to provide, among other things, the ability to support complex data warehouses.

In addition to DB2 for z/OS, all of the DB2 Editions available *except* DB2 Express-C (*Answer E*) and DB2 Express Edition can be used to create data warehouse and OLTP environments. However, IBM offers two solutions that are tailored specifically for one workload type or the other: *InfoSphere Warehouse* for data warehousing workloads and the *DB2 pureScale Feature* (*Answer D*) for OLTP workloads.

DB2 for i (*Answer A*), formerly known as DB2 for i5/OS™, is an advanced, 64-bit Relational Database Management System that leverages the high performance, virtualization, and energy efficiency features of IBM's Power Systems; its self-managing attributes, security, and built-in analytical processing functions make DB2 for i an ideal database server for applications that are analytical in nature.

Question 4

The correct answer is **B**. DB2 Workload Manager (WLM) is a comprehensive workload management feature that can help identify, manage, and control database workloads to maximize database server throughput and resource utilization; with DB2 Workload Manager, it is possible to customize execution environments so that no single workload can control and consume all of the system resources available. (This prevents any one department or service class from overwhelming the system.)

IBM InfoSphere Optim Performance Manager Extended Edition can be used to identify, diagnose, solve, and prevent performance problems in DB2 products and associated applications (*Answer A*). The Self-Tuning Memory Manager (STMM) responds to significant changes in a database's workload by dynamically distributing available memory resources among several different database memory consumers (*Answer C*). And the Connection Concentrator improves the performance of applications that require frequent, but relatively transient, simultaneous user connections by allocating host database resources only for the duration of an SQL transaction (*Answer D*).

Question 5

The correct answer is **A**. OLTP systems are designed to support day-to-day, mission-critical business activities where subsecond end-user response time is frequently required.

In contrast, data warehousing involves storing and managing large volumes of data that is often historical in nature (*Answer B*) and that is used primarily for analysis. Workloads in a data warehouse environment often consist of bulk load operations, short-running simple queries, and long-running complex and multidimensional queries that perform aggregations, full-table scans, and multiple table joins (*Answer D*). Data warehouse workloads can also consist of random ad hoc queries, infrequent updates to data, or the execution of queries that access data stored in multiple, heterogeneous data sources (*Answer C*).

Question 6

The correct answer is **B**. The DB2 pureScale feature is included as part of DB2 Workgroup Server Edition (WSE), DB2 Enterprise Server Edition (ESE), and DB2 Advanced Enterprise Server Edition (AESE).

The DB2 pureScale Feature leverages IBM's System z Sysplex technology to bring active-active clustering services to DB2 for LUW database environments (*Answer A*). This technology enables a DB2 for LUW database to continuously process incoming requests, even if multiple system components fail simultaneously, which makes it ideal for OLTP workloads where high availability is crucial (*Answer D*).

The DB2 pureScale Feature is based on a "shared data" architecture: the DB2 engine runs on multiple servers or logical partitions (LPARs) as data "members," each member has its own set of buffer pools and log files (which are accessible to the other members), and each member has equal, shared access to the database's underlying storage. IBM's General Parallel File System (GPFS) makes shared storage access possible (*Answer C*). Cluster Caching Facility (CF) software provides global locking and buffer pool management and serves as the center of communication and coordination between all members. And integrated Cluster Services (CS) handles failure detection and provides recovery automation.

Question 7

The correct answers are **A** and **B**. A LOB locator is a mechanism that refers to a LOB value from within a transaction. It is *not* a data type (*Answer C*), nor is it a database object. Instead, it is a token value—in the form of a host variable—that is used to refer to a much bigger LOB value.

LOB locators *do not* store copies of LOB data—they store a description of a base LOB value, and the actual data that a LOB locator refers to is only materialized when it is assigned to a specific location, such as an application host variable or another table record (*Answer E*).

LOB data types—*not LOB locators*—are used to store binary data values *in a DB2 database* (*Answer D*).

Question 8

The correct answer is **D**. An online transaction processing (OLTP) environment often consists of hundreds to thousands of users issuing millions of transactions per day against databases that vary in size. Consequently, the volume of data affected may be very large, even though each transaction typically makes changes to only a small number of records.

Data warehousing (*Answer B*) involves storing and managing large volumes of data that is often historical in nature and that is used primarily for analysis. Consequently, data warehouses are frequently used in reporting, online analytical processing (OLAP) (*Answer C*), and decision support (*Answer A*) environments.

Question 9

The correct answer is **D**. Data warehouse workloads typically consist of bulk load operations, short-running queries, long-running complex queries, random queries, occasional updates to data, and the execution of online utilities. Therefore, data warehouses are optimized for queries.

Online transaction processing (OLTP) systems, on the other hand, are designed to support day-to-day, mission-critical business activities; OLTP environments typically support hundreds to thousands of users issuing millions of transactions per day (*Answer C*) against databases that vary in size. Response time requirements tend to be subsecond, and workloads tend to be a mix of real-time insert, update (*Answer B*), and delete operations against current—as opposed to historical—data (*Answer A*).

Question 10

The correct answers are **B** and **D**. DB2 pureScale (Version 10.1) can *only* be installed on IBM p Series or x Series servers that are running either the AIX (p Series) or the Linux (x Series) operating system.

DB2 pureScale *cannot* be installed on IBM mainframes running z/OS (*Answer A*), IBM p Series servers running Linux (*Answer C*), or IBM x Series servers running Windows (*Answer E*).

Question 11

The correct answer is **B**. IBM InfoSphere Optim Query Tuner, often referred to as the Query Tuner, can analyze and make recommendations on ways to tune existing queries, as well as provide expert advice on writing new queries.

IBM InfoSphere Data Architect offers a complete solution for designing, modeling, discovering, relating, and standardizing data assets (*Answer A*), IBM InfoSphere Optim pureQuery Runtime bridges the gap between data and Java technology by harnessing the power of SQL within an easy-to-use Java data access platform (*Answer C*), and IBM InfoSphere Optim Performance Manager Extended Edition can identify, diagnose, solve, and prevent performance problems in DB2 products and associated applications (*Answer D*).

Question 12

The correct answer is **A**. The DB2 pureXML feature offers a simple and efficient way to create a "hybrid" DB2 database that allows XML data to be stored in its native, hierarchical format. With pureXML, XML documents are stored in tables that contain one or more columns that have been defined with the XML data type.

Since the XML data type does not require a size specification (*Answer B*), and because "CLOB AS XML" (*Answer C*) and "CLOB USING XML" (*Answer D*) are not valid column definitions, the only CREATE TABLE statement shown that will execute successfully is:

```
CREATE TABLE employee (empid INT, resume XML)
```

Question 13

The correct answer is **C**. IBM InfoSphere Warehouse is a complete data warehousing solution that contains components that facilitate data warehouse construction and administration, as well as tools that enable embedded data mining and multidimensional online analytical processing (OLAP).

The DB2 pureScale Feature enables a DB2 for LUW database to continuously process incoming requests, even if multiple system components fail simultaneously, which makes it ideal for OLTP workloads where high availability is crucial (*Answer A*). DB2 Workload Manager (WLM) is a comprehensive workload management feature that can help identify, manage, and control database workloads to maximize database server throughput and resource utilization (*Answer B*). And the Data Partitioning Feature (DPF) provides the ability to divide very large databases into multiple parts (known as partitions) and store them across a cluster of inexpensive servers (*Answer D*).

Question 14

The correct answer is **A**. There are three different IBM Data Studio components to choose from: IBM Data Studio administration client, IBM Data Studio full client, and IBM Data Studio web console. All three components can be installed on servers running Red Hat Linux, SUSE Linux, and Windows; IBM Data Studio web console can be installed on servers running the AIX operating system as well. (*The IBM Data Studio administration client cannot be installed on AIX servers.*)

IBM Data Studio is an Eclipse-based, integrated development environment (IDE) that can be used to perform instance and database administration (*Answer C*), routine development, application development, and performance-tuning tasks—it replaces the DB2 Control Center as the standard GUI tool for DB2 database administration and application development (*Answer B*). Users coming from the DB2 Control Center should find IBM Data Studio intuitive and relatively easy to use. For instance, like the DB2 Control Center, IBM Data Studio allows users to connect to a DB2 database using a wizard (*Answer D*).

Question 15

The correct answer is **C**. By default, large object (LOB) data is stored in separate LOB storage objects and changes to LOB data are not recorded in transaction log files. However, LOBs that are relatively small can be stored in the same data pages as the rest of a table's rows—such LOBs are referred to as *inline LOBs*, and transactions that modify inline LOB data are always logged. Consequently, the use of inline LOBs can increase—*not reduce*—logging overhead.

Inline LOBs are created by appending the INLINE LENGTH clause to a LOB column's definition (*Answer B*), which can be specified via the CREATE TABLE or ALTER TABLE statement. Inline LOBs improve the performance of queries that access LOB data since no additional I/O is needed to access this type of data (*Answer D*). However, when a table has columns with inline LOBs in it, fewer rows will fit on a page (*Answer A*).

Security

Question 16

The correct answer is **C**. Data Access (DATAACCESS) authority provides select individuals with the ability to access and modify data stored in user tables, views, and materialized query tables. Users with this authority can also execute plans, packages, functions, and stored procedures.

Access Control (ACCESSCTRL) authority provides select individuals with the ability to grant and revoke privileges on objects that reside in a specific database (*Answer B*); Database Maintenance (DBMAINT) authority provides select individuals with the ability to create database objects, issue database-specific DB2 commands, and run DB2 utilities that do not change data (*Answer D*); and the IMPLICIT_SCHEMA database privilege allows a user to implicitly create a new schema in a specific database (*Answer A*).

Question 17

The correct answer is **C**. A system authorization password is *not* needed to define a trusted context.

However, the following information *is* required:

- A system authorization ID that represents the authorization ID that an incoming connection must use to be considered "trusted" (*Answer A*)

- The IP address, domain name, or security zone name an incoming connection must originate from to be considered "trusted" (*Answer D*)

- A data stream encryption value that represents the level of encryption that an incoming connection (if any) must use to be considered "trusted" (*Answer B*)

Question 18

The correct answer is **B**. The REVOKE statement is used to remove any authorities and privileges that have been granted to a user, group, or role. And package privileges control what users can and cannot do with a particular package. (A package is an object that contains information that DB2 uses to efficiently process SQL statements embedded in an application.) The following package privileges are available:

- **CONTROL**: Provides a user with all package privileges available; with this privilege, a user can remove (drop) a certain package from the database, as well as grant and revoke individual package privileges (with the exception of the CONTROL privilege) to/from others

- **BIND**: Allows a user to bind or rebind (recreate) a certain package, as well as add new versions of a package that has already been bound, to a database

- **COPY**: Allows a user to copy a certain package

- **EXECUTE**: Allows a user to execute or run a certain package

Since there are no "APPLICATION" database objects (or related privileges), (*Answers A, C, and D*), the only REVOKE statement shown that will execute successfully is:

```
REVOKE EXECUTE ON PACKAGE corp.calc_bonus FROM user1
```

Question 19

The correct answers are **B** and **C**. The SELECT table privilege allows a user to retrieve data from a certain table, as well as create a view that references the table.

The INSERT table privilege allows a user to add data to a certain table (*Answer A*); the INDEX table privilege allows a user to create an index for a certain table (*Answer D*); and the ALTER table privilege allows a user to change a certain table's definition and/or the comment associated with the table (*Answer E*).

Question 20

The correct answer is **A**. The GRANT statement is used to explicitly give authorities and privileges to others, and the DELETE table privilege allows a user to remove data from a certain table. If the WITH GRANT OPTION clause is specified with the GRANT statement used, the individual receiving the designated authorities and privileges will receive the ability to grant those authorities and privileges to others.

The GRANT statement does not have a WITH GRANT PRIVILEGES clause (*Answers C and D*), and there is no "REMOVE" table privilege (*Answers B and D*). Therefore, the only GRANT statement shown that will execute successfully is:

```
GRANT DELETE ON TABLE sales TO user1 WITH GRANT OPTION
```

Question 21

The correct answer is **B**. The BIND package privilege allows a user to bind or rebind (recreate) a certain package, as well as add new versions of a package that has already been bound, to a database.

The BINDADD table privilege allows a user to create packages in a certain database (*Answer A*), and the CREATE_EXTERNAL_ROUTINE table privilege allows a user to register user-defined functions (UDFs) and procedures (*Answer C*). There is no authority or privilege that allows a user to associate user-defined functions (UDFs) and procedures with specific database objects (*Answer D*).

Question 22

The correct answer is **B**. Only users with SECADM authority are allowed to grant and revoke SECADM authority to/from others.

Security Administrator (SECADM) authority provides select individuals with the ability to manage security-related database objects, such as those needed for RCAC and LBAC. Users who possess this authority can also grant and revoke database-level authorities and privileges, execute DB2's audit system routines, *and access data stored in system catalog tables and views* (*Answer A*). Individuals who possess SECADM authority *cannot* create databases (*Answer C*) or access user data.

With DB2 for z/OS, SYSADM authority and SECADM authority are combined (under SYSADM authority). To separate SECADM authority from SYSADM authority, you must set the SEPARATE_SECURITY system parameter on panel DSNTIPP1 to YES during installation or migration (*Answer D*).

Question 23

The correct answer is **C**. After an explicit trusted connection is established, an application can switch the connection's user to a different authorization ID. (Switching can occur with or without authenticating the new authorization ID, depending upon the definition of the trusted context object associated with the connection. If a switch request is made using an authorization ID that is not allowed, the explicit trusted connection is placed in an "unconnected" state.)

A trusted context is a database object that describes a trust relationship between a DB2 database and an external entity, like a web server or an application client. The following information is used to define a trusted context:

- A system authorization ID that represents the authorization ID that an incoming connection must use to be considered "trusted"
- The IP address, domain name, or security zone name an incoming connection must originate from to be considered "trusted"
- A data stream encryption value that represents the level of encryption that an incoming connection (if any) must use to be considered "trusted"

An authentication type is *not* needed to define a trusted context (*Answer B*).

Trusted context objects *can only be defined by someone with SECADM authority* (*Answer A*). DB2 for z/OS extends the trusted context concept to allow the assignment of a trusted context to a role. An authorization ID that uses such a trusted context can inherit the privileges assigned to the role, in addition to the authorities and privileges that have already been granted to that authorization ID (*Answer D*).

Question 24

The correct answers are **C** and **D**. Access Control (ACCESSCTRL) authority provides select individuals with the ability to grant and revoke privileges on objects that reside in a specific database. The CREATETAB privilege allows a user to create new tables in a certain database, while the EXECUTE privilege allows a user to invoke a certain UDF, stored procedure, or method.

System Administrator (SYSADM) authority (*Answer A*), Security Administrator (SECADM) authority (*Answer B*), and Access Control (ACCESSCTRL) authority (*Answer E*) are system-level and database-level authorities—not object privileges. Consequently, they can only be granted by someone with Security Administrator (SECADM) authority.

Question 25

The correct answer is **A**. A role is a database entity that is used to group two or more authorities or privileges (or a combination of authorities and privileges) together so they can be simultaneously granted or revoked.

The system catalog (or catalog) is a set of special tables that contain information about everything that has been defined for a database system that is under DB2's control (*Answer B*). Functions return a single value or a table and can be specified in an SQL statement wherever a regular expression or table can be used (*Answer C*). And a collection is an object that is used to logically classify and group packages (*Answer D*).

Question 26

The correct answer is **B**. The purpose of authentication is to verify that users really are who they say they are. And in most cases, an external security facility that is not part of DB2 is used to perform this task. This facility might be part of the operating system, or it can be a separate add-on product.

Privileges (*Answer A*) control what operations, if any, a user is allowed to perform against database objects. Label-based access control (*Answer C*) is a security feature that uses one or more security labels to control who has read access, who has write access, and who has both read and write access to individual rows and/or columns in a table. And row and column access control (*Answer D*) is a security feature that defines the rules and conditions under which a user, group, or role can access rows and columns of a table.

Question 27

The correct answer is **D**. Row and column access control is a security feature that defines the rules and conditions under which a user, group, or role can access rows and columns of a table. Data access is restricted based on individual user permissions, row permissions, and column masks. Written in the form of a query search condition, a row permission specifies the conditions under which a user, group, or role can access individual rows of data in a table. Written in the form of an SQL CASE expression, a column mask indicates the conditions under which a user, group, or role can access values for a column.

Trusted Computer System Evaluation Criteria (TCSEC) is a United States Government Department of Defense standard that sets basic requirements for assessing the effectiveness of computer security controls built into a computer system. Originally published in 1983, and updated in 1985, the TCSEC was replaced in 2005 with the development of the Common Criteria for Information Technology Security Evaluation (abbreviated as *Common Criteria* or *CC*). Today, Common Criteria is an international standard (ISO/IEC 15408) for computer security.

Both TCSEC and Common Criteria define two policies for securing data: Mandatory Access Control (*Answer A*), which enforces access control rules based directly on an individual's clearance, authorization for the information being sought, and the confidentiality level of the information being sought, and Discretionary Access Control (*Answer C*), which enforces a consistent set of rules for controlling and limiting access based on identified individuals who have been determined to have a "need to know" the information. DB2 enforces Discretionary Access Control through its use of authentication, authorizations, and privileges. Mandatory Access Control is implemented using label-based access control (*Answer B*), which is a security feature that uses one or more security labels to control who has read access, who has write access, and who has both read and write access to individual rows and/or columns in a table.

Question 28

The correct answer is **A**. The GRANT statement is used to explicitly give authorities and privileges to others, and the USE (or USE OF TABLESPACE) privilege controls what users can and cannot do with a particular table space.

Since the ALTER privilege (*Answer B*) and the CREATETAB privilege (*Answer D*) are table privileges—not table space privileges—and because the USAGE privilege (*Answer C*) is a sequence privilege, the only GRANT statement shown that can be used to achieve the desired objective is:

```
GRANT USE OF TABLESPACE userspace2 TO user1
```

Question 29

The correct answer is **A**. The GRANT statement is used to explicitly give authorities and privileges to others, and the ALTER table privilege allows a user to change a certain table's definition and/or the comment associated with the table, as well as create or drop a table constraint.

The INSERT table privilege (*Answer C*) allows a user to add data to a certain table; the UPDATE table privilege (*Answer D*) allows a user to modify data in a certain table; and the USAGE privilege (*Answer B*) is a sequence privilege—not a table privilege. Therefore, the only GRANT statement shown that can be used to achieve the desired objective is:

```
GRANT ALTER ON TABLE mytable TO user1
```

Question 30

The correct answer is **B**. The procedure/routine privilege controls what users can and cannot do with a particular stored procedure; only one procedure privilege exists—the EXECUTE privilege, which, when granted, allows a user to run a certain stored procedure. The SELECT table privilege, on the other hand, allows a user to retrieve data from (query) a certain table, as well as create a view that references the table.

The REFERENCES privilege (*Answers C and D*) allows a user to create and drop foreign key constraints that reference a certain table in a referential integrity constraint. And while there is a CALL SQL statement, there is no CALL privilege (*Answers A and C*).

Question 31

The correct answer is **C**. The USAGE sequence privilege allows a user to use the PREVIOUS VALUE and NEXT VALUE expressions that are associated with a certain sequence—the PREVIOUS VALUE expression returns the most recently generated value for the specified sequence; the NEXT VALUE expression returns the next value for the specified sequence.

The ALTER sequence privilege (*Answer B*) allows a user to perform administrative tasks on a certain sequence, such as restarting the sequence or changing the increment value for the sequence. The USE privilege (*Answer A*) is a table space privilege, and the EXECUTE privilege (*Answer D*) is a routine (user-defined function or stored procedure) privilege.

Question 32

The correct answers are **D** and **E**. Traditionally, if a database administrator needed to restrict access to specific columns or rows in a table, he or she relied on views. For example, if a table containing employee information held sensitive information such as Social Security numbers and salaries, access to that data might be restricted by creating a view that contained only the columns that held nonsensitive data. Then, only authorized users would be given access to the table, while everyone else would be required to work with the view.

Row and column access control (RCAC) eliminates the need to use views to restrict access to sensitive data, although views can still be used. With RCAC, all users access the same table, but data access is restricted based on individual user permissions, row permissions, and column masks. Written in the form of a query search condition, a row permission specifies the conditions under which a user, group, or role can access individual rows of data in a table; written in the form of an SQL CASE expression, a column mask indicates the conditions under which a user, group, or role can access values for a column.

There is no such thing as a "restricted" role (*Answer A*), and Access Control (ACCESSCTRL) authority (*Answer B*) provides select individuals with the ability to grant and revoke privileges on objects that reside in a specific database—it does not allow select users to retrieve data. Objects such as tables, views, and indexes can be stored in different schemas, but individual table columns cannot (*Answer C*). And even if they could, there is no privilege that can be used to prevent certain individuals from accessing objects that have been stored in a particular schema.

Question 33

The correct answer is **C**. System Control (SYSCTRL) authority provides select individuals with the ability to create and drop DB2 databases, use almost all of the DB2 utilities available, and execute the majority of the DB2 commands that exist.

Database Administrator (DBADM) authority (*Answer A*) provides select individuals with the ability to create database objects (such as tables, indexes, and views), issue database-specific DB2 commands, and execute built-in DB2 routines (with the exception of audit routines). Database Control (DBCTRL) authority (*Answer B*) provides select individuals with the ability to create database objects, issue database-specific DB2 commands, run DB2 utilities (including those that change data), and terminate any running utility except DIAGNOSE, REPORT, and STOSPACE. And System

Maintenance (SYSMAINT) authority (*Answer D*) provides select individuals with the ability to perform maintenance operations on an instance and any databases that fall under that instance's control.

Question 34

The correct answer is **B**. Every LBAC-protected table must have one (and only one) security policy associated with it. A table's security policy identifies the security label components that will be part of the policy, the rules to use when security label components are compared (at this time, only one set of rules is supported: DB2LBACRULES), and optional behaviors to use when data protected by the policy is accessed.

Three types of security label components can exist (*Answer A*):

- **SET**: A set is a collection of elements (character string values) where the order in which each element appears is not important.

- **ARRAY**: An array is an ordered set that can represent a simple hierarchy. With an array, the order in which the elements appear is important—the first element ranks higher than the second, the second ranks higher than the third, and so on.

- **TREE**: A tree represents a more complex hierarchy that can have multiple nodes and branches.

To configure a new table for *row-level* LBAC protection, you must associate a security policy with the table (using the SECURITY POLICY clause of the CREATE TABLE or ALTER TABLE statement) and *include a column with the DB2SECURITYLABEL data type in the table's definition*. To configure a table for *column-level* LBAC protection, you must associate a security policy with the table and *configure each of the table's columns for protection by adding the SECURED WITH clause to every column's definition*. (*Answers C and D are incorrect because they state just the opposite.*)

Question 35

The correct answer is **D**. Row and column access control (RCAC) is a security feature that defines the rules and conditions under which a user, group, or role can access rows and columns of a table. With RCAC, all users access the same table, but data access is restricted based on individual user permissions, row permissions, and column masks. Written in the form of a query search condition, a row permission specifies the conditions under which a user, group, or role can access individual rows of data in a table; written in the form of an SQL CASE expression, a column mask indicates the conditions under which a user, group, or role can access values for a column.

The purpose of authentication (*Answer B*) is to verify that users really are who they say they are. Authorities (*Answer A*) control what operations, if any, a user is allowed to perform against an instance or database. And label-based access control (*Answer C*) is a security feature that uses one or more security labels to control who has read access, who has write access, and who has both read and write access to individual rows and/or columns in a table. LBAC is implemented by assigning unique labels to users and data and allowing access only when assigned labels match.

Question 36

The correct answers are **B** and **C**. Row and column access control (RCAC) is a security feature that defines the rules and conditions under which a user, group, or role can access rows and columns of a table. With RCAC, all users access the same table, but data access is restricted based on individual user permissions, row permissions, and column masks. Written in the form of a search condition, a row permission specifies the conditions under which a user, group, or role can access individual rows of data in a table; written in the form of an SQL CASE expression, a column mask indicates the conditions under which a user, group, or role can access values for a column. (*Answers A and D are incorrect because they state just the opposite.*)

The SECURED WITH clause of the CREATE TABLE and ALTER TABLE statements (*Answer E*) is used to configure a table for column-level label-based access control (LBAC) protection—*not RCAC protection*.

Question 37

The correct answer is **D**. The procedure/routine privilege controls what users can and cannot do with a particular stored procedure. Only one procedure privilege exists—the EXECUTE privilege, which, when granted, allows a user to invoke a certain stored procedure.

The USE table space privilege (*Answer A*) allows a user to use a certain table space; the USAGE sequence privilege (*Answer C*) allows a user to use the PREVIOUS VALUE and NEXT VALUE expressions that are associated with a certain sequence. And while the CALL statement is used to invoke a procedure/routine, there is no CALL privilege (*Answer B*).

Working with Databases and Database Objects

Question 38

The correct answer is **A**. Views provide an alternative way of describing and presenting data stored in one or more tables. Whether a particular view can be used to insert, update, or delete data depends upon how the view was defined—views can be defined as being *insertable*, updatable, *deletable*, or read-only.

Although views look similar to base tables, they do not contain data. Instead, they obtain their data from the table(s) or view(s) they are based upon (*Answer B*). Views are frequently used to control access to sensitive data (*Answer C*). And the SQL query provided as part of a view's definition determines the data that is to be presented when a particular view is referenced (*Answer D*).

Question 39

The correct answer is **D**. Distinct types cannot be used as arguments for most built-in functions, and built-in data types cannot be used in arguments or operands that expect distinct data types. Instead, user-defined functions (UDFs) that provide similar functionality must be developed if that capability is needed.

A distinct data type is a user-defined data type (UDT) that is derived from one of the built-in data types available with DB2. When a distinct data type is created, by default, six comparison functions (named =, <>, <, <=, >, and >=) are also created—provided the distinct type is not based on a LOB data type (*Answer B*). These functions let you compare two values of the distinct data type in the same manner that you can compare two values of a built-in data type. In addition, two casting functions are generated that allow data to be converted between a distinct type and the built-in data type that the distinct type is based on (*Answer C*).

If the CREATE DISTINCT TYPE statement shown in the scenario presented is executed, a user-defined data type that can be used to store numerical data as British currency will be created (*Answer A*).

Question 40

The correct answers are **A** and **D**. An index is an object that contains pointers to rows in a table that are logically ordered according to the values of one or more columns, known as keys. And if an index is defined as being UNIQUE, rows in the table associated with the index are not allowed to have more than one occurrence of the same value in the set of columns that make up the index key. Because indexes do not physically change the order of records in a table, queries that do not take advantage of indexes will return rows from a table in no specific order.

A single table can contain a significant number of indexes (*Answer C*). Because the index shown in the scenario presented was defined as being UNIQUE, duplicate rows in the table associated with the index are *not* allowed (*Answer B*). And because the ORDER_NUM column was not defined as a primary key in the scenario presented, the index produced by the CREATE INDEX statement shown will *not* serve as the primary key index for the SALES table (*Answer E*).

Question 41

The correct answer is **A**. IBM DB2 Connect Personal Edition makes DB2 data stored on System z, System i, and IBM Power Systems servers directly available to desktop applications; it enables applications to work transparently with data stored on multiple systems *without using a gateway*.

IBM DB2 Connect Enterprise Edition (*Answer B*) connects LAN-based systems and desktop applications to System z, System i, and IBM Power Systems databases; host access can be consolidated through a gateway, making it easier to deploy web and multitier client/server applications.

IBM DB2 Connect Unlimited Advanced Edition for System z (*Answer C*) makes it easy to access, manage, and optimize the performance of enterprise information, wherever it resides. Because it is licensed for unlimited deployment on authorized servers, this edition is a cost-effective solution for organizations that use DB2 Connect extensively, especially where multiple applications are involved.

IBM DB2 Connect Unlimited Edition for System i (*Answer D*) integrates IBM System i data with client/server, web, mobile, and service-oriented architecture (SOA) applications; it delivers unified application development, integrated data, and pervasive data functionality to System i users.

Question 42

The correct answer is **D**. The creation of a unique primary key that is made up of an application-period temporal table's "business time begin" column, "business time end" column, and one other data column will ensure that no overlapping time periods exist for values in the data column specified. However, an application-period temporal table can be created without such a primary key.

Application-period temporal tables are created by executing a CREATE TABLE statement with the PERIOD BUSINESS_TIME clause specified (*Answer C*). In addition, the table definition provided must include "business time begin" (*Answer A*) and "business time end" (*Answer B*) columns, which are normally populated with user- or application-supplied values that indicate the time period in which a particular row is considered valid.

Question 43

The correct answer is **A**. A buffer pool is an object that is used to cache table and index pages when they are read from disk. The first time a row of data is accessed, a DB2 agent retrieves the page containing the row from storage and copies it to a buffer pool before passing it on to the user or application that requested it. (If an index was used to locate the row, the index page containing a pointer to the row is copied first; the pointer is then used to locate the data page containing the row, and that page is copied to the buffer pool as well.) This is done to improve performance—data that resides in a buffer pool can be accessed much faster than data stored on disk.

Transaction log files are used to keep track of changes that are made to a database as they occur (*Answer B*), the resource limit facility is used to control the amount of processor resources that SQL statements can consume (*Answer C*), and table spaces provide a layer of indirection between a data object (such as a table or an index) and the physical storage where that object's data resides (*Answer D*).

Question 44

The correct answer is **A**. To implement distributed request functionality, you need *a DB2 Connect instance*, a database that will serve as a federated database, and one or more remote data sources.

A distributed request is a distributed database function that lets applications/users perform SQL operations that reference two or more databases or RDBMSs within a single statement (*Answer C*). For example, a distributed request will allow a UNION operation to be performed between a DB2 table and an Oracle view (*Answer B*). DB2 Connect provides the ability to perform distributed requests across members of the DB2 Family, as well as across other relational database management systems (*Answer D*).

Question 45

The correct answer is **D**. An index is an object that contains pointers to rows in a table that are *logically* ordered according to the values of one or more columns (known as keys). Special indexes known as *clustering* indexes can cause the rows of a table to be physically arranged according to the ordering of their key column values, but such indexes are not created automatically.

Indexes can be used to enforce the uniqueness of records in a table (*Answer A*); if an index is defined as being UNIQUE, rows in the table associated with the index are not allowed to have more than one occurrence of the same value in the set of columns that make up the index key. Indexes provide a fast, efficient method for locating specific rows of data in large tables (*Answer B*). And when an index is first created, its characteristics (referred to as its metadata) are stored in one or more system catalog tables (*Answer C*).

Question 46

The correct answer is **B**. Materialized query tables (MQTs) derive their definitions from the results of a query (SELECT statement); their data consists of precomputed values taken from one or more tables the MQT is based upon. MQTs can greatly improve performance and response time for complex queries, particularly queries that aggregate data over one or more dimensions or that join data across multiple base tables.

Multidimensional clustering (MDC) tables—*not MQTs*—are physically clustered on more than one key or dimension simultaneously (*Answer A*). Declared global temporary tables are used to hold nonpersistent data temporarily, on behalf of a single application (*Answer C*). And application-period temporal tables are used to track effective dates for data that is subject to changing business conditions (*Answer D*).

Question 47

The correct answers are **A** and **B**. System-period temporal tables are created by executing the CREATE TABLE statement with the PERIOD SYSTEM_TIME clause specified. In addition, the table definition provided must include "system time begin" and "system time end" columns, which are used to track when a row is considered current, along with a "transaction start ID" column that DB2 can use to capture the start times of transactions that perform update or delete operations on a particular row. Once the resulting table is created, it cannot be populated until a corresponding history table is created and a link between the two tables is established—a history table can be created by executing a CREATE TABLE ... LIKE TABLE statement; a link between a system-period temporal table and a history table can be established by executing an ALTER TABLE statement with the ADD VERSIONING clause specified.

A primary key (*Answer C*) or unique index (*Answer D*) does not have to be included in the definition provided for a system-period temporal table. And while the definition provided must include "system time begin," "system time end," and "transaction start ID" columns, a "transaction end ID" column is not needed (nor recognized by DB2) (*Answer E*).

Question 48

The correct answer is **D**. A sequence is an object that is used to generate a sequence of numbers, in either ascending or descending order. Unlike identity columns, which produce data values for a specific column in a table, sequences are not tied to any specific column or to any specific table. Instead, sequences behave as unique counters that reside outside the database.

An alias (*Answer A*) is an alternate name for a table, view, or other alias; schemas (*Answer B*) are used to logically group objects in a database; and a package (*Answer C*) is an object that contains the control structures DB2 uses to execute SQL statements that have been coded in an application.

Question 49

The correct answer is **D**. The definition provided for a system-period temporal table does *not* have to include a "transaction end ID" column—such a column is not recognized by DB2.

However, the table definition for a system-period temporal table must include "system/row time begin" (*Answer A*) and "system/row time end" (*Answer B*) columns, which are used to track when a row is considered current, as well as a "transaction start ID" column (*Answer C*), which DB2 uses to capture the start times of transactions that perform update or delete operations on a particular row in the table. All three columns must be assigned a TIMESTAMP(12) data type, but they can be implicitly hidden.

Question 50

The correct answer is **A**. Views provide an alternative way of describing data stored in one or more tables; essentially, a view is a named specification of a result table that is populated each time the view is referenced in an SQL operation. Although views can be thought of as having columns and rows like base tables, they do not contain data. Instead, they obtain their data from the table(s) or view(s) they are based upon. Consequently, views *cannot* be enabled for compression.

With DB2 Version 10 (DB2 for z/OS) and Version 10.1 (DB2 for Linux, UNIX, and Windows), base tables (*Answer C*), temporary tables (*Answer D*), and indexes (*Answer B*) can be enabled for compression. (DBAs have control over which base tables and indexes get enabled for compression; DB2 has control over which temporary tables get enabled for compression.)

Question 51

The correct answer is **B**. Schemas provide a way to logically group objects in a database; they are used to organize data objects into sets.

An alias is an alternate name for a table, view, or other alias (*Answer A*); a sequence is an object that is used to generate a sequence of numbers, in either ascending or descending order (*Answer C*); and a view is an object that is used to provide an alternative way of describing data stored in one or more tables (*Answer D*).

Question 52

The correct answer is **D**. There is no such thing as a "write-only" view.

Views can be defined as being insertable (*Answer A*), updatable (*Answer B*), deletable, or read-only (*Answer C*).

Question 53

The correct answer is **B**. An application-period temporal table is a table that maintains "currently in effect" values of application data. Such tables let you manage time-sensitive data by defining the time periods in which specific data values are considered valid.

A system-period temporal table is a table that maintains historical versions of its rows (*Answer A*); insert time clustering (ITC) tables are used to cluster data according to the time in which rows are inserted (*Answer C*); and multidimensional clustering (MDC) tables are used to physically cluster data on more than one key or dimension, simultaneously (*Answer D*).

Question 54

The correct answer is **C**. Dirty pages that are written to storage are *not* automatically removed from the buffer pool they were stored in. Instead, they remain in memory in case they are needed again.

One buffer pool is created automatically as part of the database creation process (*Answer B*)—with DB2 for Linux, UNIX, and Windows, this buffer pool is named IBMDEFAULTBP; with DB2 for z/OS, it is named BP0. Each table space must be associated with a buffer pool (*Answer A*). And once a page has been copied to a buffer pool, it remains there until the space it occupies is needed or until the database is taken offline (*Answer D*).

Question 55

The correct answer is **D**. Procedures allow work that is done by one or more transactions to be encapsulated and stored in such a way that it can be executed directly at a server by any application or user who has been given the authority to do so. And views provide an alternative way of describing and presenting data stored in one or more tables. A procedure might reference a view; however, *a view cannot be derived from a procedure*.

Although views look similar to base tables, they do not contain data. Instead, they obtain their data from the tables (*Answer C*) or views (*Answer B*)—views can be derived from other views—they are based upon. Because an alias is an alternate name for a table or view, views can also be derived from an alias (*Answer A*).

Question 56

The correct answers are **A** and **D**. To facilitate the use of sequences in SQL operations, two expressions are available: PREVIOUS VALUE and NEXT VALUE. The PREVIOUS VALUE expression returns the most recently generated value for the sequence specified, while the NEXT VALUE expression returns the next value that a certain sequence will produce.

There is no PRIOR VALUE (*Answer B*), CURRENT VALUE (*Answer C*), or SUBSEQUENT VALUE (*Answer E*) expression.

Question 57

The correct answer is **A**. When table spaces, tables, indexes, *distinct data types*, functions, stored procedures, and triggers are created, they are automatically assigned to (or defined into) a schema, based upon the qualifier that was provided as part of the user-supplied name. If a schema name or qualifier is not provided as part of an object's name, the object is automatically assigned to a default schema, which typically has the name of the authorization ID of the individual who created the object.

Distinct data types *cannot* be defined into a package (*Answer B*), a database (*Answer C*), or a table space (*Answer D*).

Question 58

The correct answers are **A** and **C**. While packages can contain data access plans that were implicitly created, there is no way to explicitly create a data access plan. And because there is no such thing as a "scheme" object, scheme objects cannot be explicitly created.

Although servers, instances, and databases are the primary components that make up a DB2 database environment, many other different, but often related, objects exist. Typically, these objects are classified as being either data objects (sometimes referred to as database objects or data structures) or system objects. Some of the more common data objects available include schemas, tables, views, indexes, aliases, sequences (*Answer E*), triggers (*Answer B*), user-defined data types, user-defined functions (*Answer D*), stored procedures, and packages. Some of the system objects available include: buffer pools, table spaces, the system catalog, transaction log files, the DB2 directory, the bootstrap data set, the data definition control support (DDCS) database, resource limit facility tables, and the work file database.

Question 59

The correct answer is **D**. Applications that interact with DB2 databases have the option of using two types of connection semantics: Type 1 and Type 2. And each connection type supports a very different connection behavior. For instance, Type 1 connections allow a transaction to be connected to only one database at a time. Type 2 connections, however, allow a single transaction to connect to and work with multiple databases simultaneously. (*Answer C is incorrect because it states just the opposite*.)

With DB2 for Linux, UNIX, and Windows, when a database connection is established from the DB2 Command Line Processor (CLP), Type 1 connections—*not Type 2 connections* (*Answer B*)—are used, by default. With DB2 for z/OS, the opposite is true—Type 2 connections are used instead. Thus, Type 2 connections *can* be used with DB2 for z/OS (*Answer A*).

Question 60

The correct answers are **B** and **D**. A bitemporal table combines the historical tracking of a system-period temporal table with the time-specific data storage capabilities of an application-period temporal table. Consequently, when a bitemporal table is created, a corresponding history table must be created and a link between the bitemporal table and the history table must be established before the bitemporal table can be used. And whenever data in a bitemporal table is updated, a row is added to its associated history table.

If you want to query a bitemporal temporal table, you have the option of constructing a SELECT statement that:

- Does not contain any time-period specifications
- Contains a system time-period specification only
- Contains a business time-period specification only
- Contains both a system time-period specification and a business time-period specification

Bitemporal tables are user tables—*not system tables* (*Answer A*)—that are created by executing a CREATE TABLE statement with both the PERIOD SYSTEM_TIME *clause* (*Answer C*) and the PERIOD BUSINESS_TIME clause specified. And by including "system time begin," "system time end," "transaction start-ID," "business time begin," and "business time end" columns in the table's definition—*not "bitemporal-time-begin" and "bitemporal-time-end" columns* (*Answer E*).

Question 61

The correct answer is **C**. DB2 Connect provides a way for applications to establish connections to databases using a variety of standard interfaces for database access, such as JDBC, SQLJ, ODBC, OLE DB, ADO, ADO.NET, RDO, DB2 CLI, and Embedded SQL. The JDBC interface is widely used because it allows applications to run, unchanged, on most hardware platforms.

Because their use might require applications to be altered before they can be run on certain platforms, ODBC (*Answer A*), SQLJ (*Answer B*), and OLE DB (*Answer D*) are not as widely used as JDBC.

Question 62

The correct answers are **A** and **E**. An application-period temporal table is a table that maintains "currently in effect" values of application data. Such tables let you manage time-sensitive data by defining the time periods in which specific data values are considered valid. Because a bitemporal table combines the historical tracking of a system-period temporal table with the time-specific data storage capabilities of an application-period temporal table, it, too, can be used to manage time-sensitive data by defining the time periods in which specific data values are considered valid.

A system-period temporal table (*Answer C*) is a table that maintains historical versions of its rows. There is no such thing as a time-period temporal table (*Answer B*). And while application-period temporal tables are created by executing a CREATE TABLE statement with the PERIOD BUSINESS_TIME clause specified, *such tables are not called business-period temporal tables* (*Answer D*).

Question 63

The correct answer is **D**. Stored procedures allow work that is done by one or more transactions to be encapsulated and stored in such a way that it can be executed directly at a server by any application or user who has been given the authority to do so. Therefore, an application running on a remote client that needs to collect input values from a user, perform a calculation using the values provided, and store the input data, along with the calculation results, in a base table could use a stored procedure to perform all of the necessary processing *except* collecting input values from a user.

A trigger would be better suited for tracking every modification made to a table that contains sensitive data (*Answer A*). A user-defined function would be ideal for converting degrees Celsius to degrees Fahrenheit and vice versa (*Answer B*). And a sequence or identity column could be used to ensure that every new employee that joins the company is assigned a unique, sequential employee number (*Answer C*).

Question 64

The correct answers are **A** and **B**. An alias is an alternate name for a table, view, or other alias.

Aliases cannot be created for indexes (*Answer C*), sequences (*Answer D*), or procedures (*Answer E*).

Question 65

The correct answer is **A**. If a different data type is needed or desired for a particular sequence, that sequence must be dropped and recreated—the data type of an existing sequence *cannot* be changed with an ALTER SEQUENCE statement.

However, the ALTER SEQUENCE statement *can* be used to restart a sequence, change the way in which values are incremented, establish new minimum and maximum values (*Answer C*), increase or decrease the number of sequence numbers that are cached (*Answer D*), change whether a sequence cycles (*Answer B*), and alter whether sequence numbers are required to be generated in their original order.

Question 66

The correct answer is **B**. An index is an object that contains pointers to rows in a table that are logically ordered according to the values of one or more columns (known as key columns or keys). Therefore, before an index can be created, the table the index is to be created for must already exist.

Since indexes are not dependent on views (*Answer A*), schemas (*Answer C*), or sequences (*Answer D*), these objects do not have to exist before an index can be created. (If a schema name or qualifier is not provided as part of an index's name, the index is automatically assigned to a default schema, which typically has the name of the authorization ID of the individual who created the index. Therefore, a schema does not have to exist in order to create an index.)

Question 67

The correct answers are **A** and **C**. When the simplest form of the CREATE DATABASE command is executed, the characteristics of the database produced are defined according to a set of predefined default values. Specifically, the database will be an automatic storage database, it will have a page size of 4 KB, it will be created on the default database path that is specified in the *dftdbpath* database manager configuration parameter, and its default table spaces (SYSCATSPACE, TEMPSPACE1, and USERSPACE1) will be automatic storage table spaces. (Their containers will also be created on the default database path.)

The PAGESIZE 8192 option must be specified with the CREATE DATABASE statement used to create a database with a page size of 8 KB (*Answer B*). The AUTOMATIC STORAGE NO option must be provided with the CREATE DATABASE statement used to create a database that does not use automatic storage (*Answer D*). And the WITH "PAYROLL DATABASE" option must be specified with the CREATE DATABASE statement used to create a database that has the comment "PAYROLL DATABASE" associated with it (*Answer E*).

Working with DB2 Data Using SQL

Question 68

The correct answer is **D**. The ORDER BY clause is used to instruct DB2 on how to sort (order) the rows that are returned in a result data set. When specified, this clause is followed by the name (or position number) of one or more columns whose data values are to be sorted and a keyword that indicates whether the data is to be sorted in ascending (ASC) or descending (DESC) order. (If the keyword ASC or DESC is not provided, data is sorted in ascending order, by default.) The FETCH FIRST clause is used to limit the number of rows that are returned in a result data set. When used, the FETCH FIRST clause must be followed by a positive integer value, which in turn must be followed by the words ROWS ONLY.

Because only five rows of data were returned in the scenario presented, it can be assumed that the FETCH FIRST clause was used to limit the number of rows returned. However, this clause is coded incorrectly in two of the answers shown (*Answers A and C*). And it appears that the ORDER BY clause was used to instruct DB2 to sort the data for the AVG_INCOME column in descending—*not ascending*—order (*Answers A and B*).

Question 69

The correct answer is **A**. An inner join can be thought of as the cross product of two tables, in which every row in one table is paired with rows in another table that have matching values in one or more columns. Because only rows that have matching values in both tables are returned in the result data set produced, result data sets produced by inner join operations are typically smaller than those that are produced by outer join operations.

When a left outer join operation is performed, rows that an inner join operation would have returned, together with rows stored in the leftmost table of the join operation that the inner join operation would have eliminated, are returned in the result data set produced (*Answer B*). When a right outer join operation is performed, rows that an inner join operation would have returned, together with rows stored in the rightmost table of the join operation that the inner join operation would have eliminated, are returned in the result data set produced (*Answer C*). And when a full outer join operation is performed, rows that an inner join operation would have returned, together with rows stored in both tables of the join operation that the inner join operation would have eliminated, are returned in the result data set produced (*Answer D*). (Consequently, full outer join operations will normally produce larger result data sets than other join operations.)

Question 70

The correct answer is **C**. If a subquery is used with a DELETE statement and the result set produced is empty, <u>no</u> records will be deleted from the table specified and an error will be returned.

A subselect can be used with an INSERT statement (in place of a VALUES clause) to retrieve values from one base table or view and assign them to columns in a table (*Answer B*). And a subselect can be used with an UPDATE statement to supply values for one or more columns that are to be updated (*Answer A*). However, when used with an UPDATE statement, the subselect provided must not return more than one row! Otherwise, the update operation will fail and an error will be produced (*Answer D*).

Question 71

The correct answer is **C**. Although the TO SAVEPOINT clause can be used with the ROLLBACK statement to back out a subset of database changes that have been made by a single transaction (*Answer D*), the TO SAVEPOINT clause cannot be used with a COMMIT statement to apply a subset of database changes that have been made by a transaction to a database and make them permanent.

One or more savepoints can be used to break the work being done by a single large transaction into one or more smaller subsets (*Answer B*). And you can use as many savepoints as you desire within a single transaction, provided you do not nest them (*Answer A*).

Question 72

The correct answers are **B** and **E**. The UPDATE statement can be used to modify the values of specified columns in the rows of a table, view, or underlying table(s) of a specified fullselect. And update operations can be conducted in one of two ways: by performing what is known as a searched update or by performing what is known as a positioned update. Positioned update operations change data in a single row only, whereas searched update operations can modify several rows at a time—*not the other way around* (*Answer A*).

In addition to providing a way to change existing data values, the UPDATE statement can also be used to remove data stored in one or more columns—provided the columns <u>are</u> nullable (*Answer D*). (Such delete operations are performed by changing the existing data value to NULL.) And when the UPDATE statement is used to modify the values stored in parent key columns, the Update rule of the corresponding referential constraint is evaluated to determine whether the update is allowed—the values of corresponding foreign key columns are <u>not</u> altered (*Answer C*).

Question 73

The correct answer is **C**. The GROUP BY clause is used to instruct DB2 on how to organize rows of data that are returned in a result data set; the ORDER BY clause is used to instruct DB2 on how to sort (order) the rows that are returned in a result data set. Therefore, in the scenario presented, the "GROUP BY region_cd" clause will instruct DB2 to organize the data retrieved from the SALES table by region and the "ORDER BY COUNT(*)" clause will tell DB2 to order the data by the number of sales made (once it has been organized).

In the scenario presented, the "ORDER BY COUNT(*)" clause alone will not produce the desired results (*Answer A*)—instead, this clause will cause an error to be returned since DB2 expects the data to be grouped by COUNT(*). Neither will the "GROUP BY sales_amt" clause (*Answers B and D*); this clause will cause an error to be returned because the SALES_AMT column is either the wrong column to group by (*Answer B*) or it is not included in the select list provided (*Answer D*).

Question 74

The correct answer is **D**. The WHERE clause is used to tell DB2 how to select the rows that are to be returned in the result data set produced. When specified, this clause is followed by a search condition, which is a simple test that is applied to a row of data—if the test evaluates to TRUE, the row is returned in the result data set produced; if the test evaluates to FALSE or UNKNOWN, the row is ignored. By using parentheses and/or Boolean operators like AND and OR, it's possible to create a WHERE clause that is quite complex.

In the scenario presented, two different criteria are specified, but only one must be met. This implies that the WHERE clause used must contain a Boolean OR operator. And since the first criteria actually consists of two requirements, both of which must be met, the WHERE clause used must contain a Boolean AND operator as well. Because both requirements of the first criteria must be met, the AND operator—*not the OR operator* (*Answers A and B*)—must be used when examining the SALESDATE and AMT data values in a row. Therefore, the OR operator—*not the AND operator* (*Answer C*)— must be used to determine whether DEPARTMENT data values encountered meet the second criteria specified. Consequently, the only SQL statement shown that will meet the objective defined in the scenario presented is:

```
vSELECT * FROM sales
  WHERE (salesdate > '2012-06-01' AND amt > 40)
     OR (dept = 'Hardware')
```

Question 75

The correct answers are **B** and **C**. The number of values provided in the VALUES clause of an INSERT statement must equal the number of column names identified in the column name list. And the values provided are assigned to columns in the order in which they appear—in other words, the first value provided is assigned to the first column identified, the second value is assigned to the second column identified, and so on. In addition, each value supplied must be compatible with the data type of the column it is being assigned to, and each value must satisfy the conditions of any NOT NULL constraints, UNIQUE constraints, CHECK constraints, and referential integrity constraints that have been defined.

The INSERT statement can be used to insert rows into a table or updatable view, *but not a table function* (*Answer A*). When you want or are forced to insert partial records into a table or updatable view, you can construct and execute an INSERT statement in which only the columns you have data for are specified in the column names list provided. However, in order for such an INSERT statement to execute correctly, columns that do not appear in the column name list must either accept NULL values—i.e., have not been defined with a NOT NULL constraint (*Answer D*)—or have been defined with a default constraint (for example, NOT NULL WITH DEFAULT). And if the underlying table of a view that is referenced by an INSERT statement has one or more unique indexes, each row inserted into the view must conform to the constraints imposed by those indexes (*Answer E*).

Question 76

The correct answer is **B**. The GROUP BY clause is used to instruct DB2 on how to organize rows of data that are returned in a result data set; the ORDER BY clause is used to instruct DB2 on how to sort (order) the rows that are returned in a result data set. Therefore, in the scenario presented, the "GROUP BY month" clause will instruct DB2 to organize the data retrieved from the WEATHER table by month.

In the scenario presented, the GROUP BY clause—*not the* ORDER BY clause (*Answers A and D*)—is used to organize the data retrieved from the WEATHER table by month. The ORDER BY clause will merely cause an error to be returned since DB2 expects the data to be grouped by MONTH. A common mistake that is often made with the GROUP BY clause is the addition of non-aggregate columns to the list of columns that are supplied as the grouping expression. Because grouping is performed by combining all of the columns specified into a single concatenated key and breaking whenever that key value changes, extraneous columns can cause unexpected breaks to occur. (*Such is the case with Answers C and D*).

Question 77

The correct answers are **D** and **E**. The way in which a user-defined function (UDF) is invoked depends, in part, on what the UDF has been designed to do. Scalar UDFs are typically invoked as an expression in the select list of a query, whereas table functions are normally referenced in the FROM clause of a SELECT statement. In the scenario presented, the UDF named REGIONAL_SALES is a table function; therefore, it must be referenced in the FROM clause of a SELECT statement.

The keyword TABLE is needed to inform DB2 that the UDF being called returns a table; if that keyword is missing, the SELECT statement used will fail (*Answers A, B, and C*).

Question 78

The correct answer is **C**. The GROUP BY clause is used to instruct DB2 on how to organize rows of data that are returned in a result data set; the ORDER BY clause is used to instruct DB2 on how to sort (order) the rows that are returned. In the scenario presented, department number and average salary information will be retrieved from a table named EMPLOYEE (SELECT dept, AVG(salary) FROM employee). Then, the results will be organized by average departmental salary (GROUP BY dept) and arranged in ascending order (ORDER BY 2).

Because the EMPLOYEE table is being queried in the scenario presented (SELECT ... FROM employee), the average salary is being calculated using data stored in the EMPLOYEE table—*not in the DEPARTMENT table*, which is where two answers imply that salary information is to be retrieved from (*Answers B and D*). And since the DESC keyword was not provided with the ORDER BY clause used, the data returned is sorted in ascending order—*not descending order* (*Answer A*), by default.

Question 79

The correct answers are **A** and **D**. The WHERE clause is used to tell DB2 how to select the rows that are to be returned in the result data set produced. When specified, this clause is followed by a search condition, which is a simple test that is applied to a row of data—if the test evaluates to TRUE, the row is returned in the result data set produced; if the test evaluates to FALSE or UNKNOWN, the row is ignored. The BETWEEN predicate is used to define a comparison relationship in which the contents of a column or the results of some SQL expression are checked to determine whether they fall within a specified range of values.

Numeric values used in a search condition may contain a decimal point; however, they must not contain non-numeric characters such as those that are often used to separate each group of three digits—i.e., commas, periods, or spaces. (*Answers B, C and E are incorrect because the SELECT statements shown contain WHERE clauses with search conditions that have numeric values with commas in them.*)

Question 80

The correct answer is **C**. The way in which a user-defined function (UDF) is invoked depends, in part, on what the UDF has been designed to do. Scalar UDFs are typically invoked as an expression in the select list of a query, whereas table functions are normally referenced in the FROM clause of a SELECT statement. In the scenario presented, the UDF named MI_TO_KM is a scalar function; therefore, it must be referenced in the select list of a query.

The CALL statement is used to invoke a stored procedure—not a UDF (*Answers A and B*). And the specific name that is assigned to a UDF can be used to reference or delete (drop) the UDF, but not to invoke it (*Answer D*).

Question 81

The correct answers are **C** and **D**. A system-period temporal table is a table that maintains historical versions of its rows. SELECT statements that query system-period temporal tables can contain one of the following system time-period specifications:

- **FOR SYSTEM_TIME AS OF [*Timestamp*]**: Lets you query data as of a specific point in time

- **FOR SYSTEM_TIME FROM [*Timestamp*] TO [*Timestamp*]**: Lets you query data from one point in time to another

- **FOR SYSTEM_TIME BETWEEN [*Timestamp*] AND [*Timestamp*]**: Lets you query data between a start time and an end time

A system-period temporal table can also be queried without a time-period specification, in which case only current data will be returned.

System-period temporal tables *are not* used to store user-based period information (*Answer A*)— application-period temporal tables are used to store this type of information, instead. Consequently, application-period temporal tables are used to manage data based on time criteria specified by users or applications (*Answer E*). And unlike system-period temporal tables, application-period temporal tables do not require separate history tables (*Answer B*).

Question 82

The correct answer is **B**. The GROUP BY clause is used to instruct DB2 on how to organize rows of data that are returned in a result data set; the ORDER BY clause is used to instruct DB2 on how to sort (order) the rows that are returned. In the scenario presented, the GROUP BY name clause is needed to instruct DB2 to organize the data retrieved from the PARTS table, by employee.

In the scenario presented, if a GROUP BY clause is not provided with the SELECT statement used (*Answers A and C*), an error will be returned. The same is true if a GROUP BY clause is provided and the aggregate column used is COUNT(*) (or PARTS_MADE) and not NAME (*Answer D*).

Question 83

The correct answer is **D**. When a right outer join operation is performed, rows that an inner join operation would have returned, together with rows stored in the rightmost table of the join operation (that is, the table listed last in the OUTER JOIN clause) that the inner join operation would have eliminated, are returned in the result data set produced.

When an inner join operation (*Answers A and B*) is performed, every row in one table that has matching values in one or more columns found in a row in another table are returned in the result data set produced. (Non-matching rows found in either table are excluded from the result data set produced.) When a left outer join operation is performed (*Answer C*), rows that an inner join operation would have returned, together with rows stored in the leftmost table of the join operation (that is, the table listed first in the OUTER JOIN clause) that the inner join operation would have eliminated, are returned in the result data set produced.

Question 84

The correct answer is **B**. COMMIT and ROLLBACK statements are not allowed in the body of an SQL user-defined function (UDF).

CALL statements (*Answer A*) can be coded in the body of an SQL UDF to invoke one or more stored procedures; CASE statements (*Answer C*) can be used to control logic flow and/or what data values (if any) are returned; and SQL control statements (*Answer D*) can be used to define local variables, as well perform looping and branching operations.

Question 85

The correct answer is **C**. The FETCH FIRST ... ROWS ONLY clause is used to limit the number of rows that are returned in a result data set. The ORDER BY clause is used to instruct DB2 on how to sort (order) the rows that are returned in a result data set—when specified, this clause is followed by the name (or position number) of one or more columns whose data values are to be sorted and a keyword that indicates whether the data is to be sorted in ascending (ASC) or descending (DESC) order. And a subselect can be used with an UPDATE statement to supply values for one or more columns that are to be updated. Therefore, to achieve the desired objective, a subselect containing the FETCH FIRST ... ROWS ONLY clause and the ORDER BY clause must be used to retrieve the 10 rows with the lowest values in the COL1 column of the TABLE_A table. Then, an update operation must be performed on the rows that are returned by the subselect.

Since the FETCH FIRST ... ROWS ONLY clause *cannot* be used with the UPDATE statement (*Answers A and B*), it must be coded as part of the subselect or an error will occur. And since the objective of the subselect is to locate the 10 rows that have the lowest values in the COL1 column, the ORDER BY clause used must sort the data retrieved in ascending order—*not descending order* (*Answer D*). Consequently, the only UPDATE statement shown that will achieve the desired objective is:

```
UPDATE
   (SELECT * FROM table_a
      ORDER BY col1 ASC
      FETCH FIRST 10 ROWS ONLY) AS temp
      SET col2 = 99
```

Question 86

The correct answer is **D**. A transaction (also known as a unit of work) is a sequence of one or more SQL operations that are grouped as a single unit, usually within an application process. The initiation and termination of a single transaction defines points of consistency within a database—normally, a transaction is initiated the first time an SQL statement is executed after a connection to a database has been established, or when a new SQL statement is executed after a running transaction has ended. Once initiated, transactions can be implicitly terminated using a feature known as automatic commit or they can be explicitly terminated by executing either a COMMIT or a ROLLBACK statement.

A savepoint is a mechanism that allows applications and users to break the work being done by a single large transaction into one or more smaller subsets; *savepoints do not define points of consistency for a transaction* (*Answers A and C*). The system catalog is a set of special tables that contain information about everything that has been defined for a database system that is under DB2's control—*it has nothing to do with defining points of consistency for transactions* (*Answer B*).

Question 87

The correct answer is **B**. The FETCH FIRST ... ROWS ONLY clause is used to limit the number of rows that are returned in a result data set. The ORDER BY clause is used to instruct DB2 on how to sort (order) the rows that are returned in a result data set—when specified, this clause is followed by the name (or position number) of one or more columns whose data values are to be sorted and a keyword that indicates whether the data is to be sorted in ascending (ASC) or descending (DESC) order. And a subselect can be used with a DELETE statement in place of the name of a table or view. Therefore, to achieve the desired objective, a delete operation must be performed on a subselect that uses the FETCH FIRST ... ROWS ONLY clause and the ORDER BY clause to retrieve the last 10 rows in the TABLE_A table.

Since there is no FETCH LAST ... ROWS ONLY clause (*Answers C and D*), and because the ORDER BY clause used should instruct DB2 to sort the data for the TABLE_A table in descending—*not ascending* (*Answer A*)—order, the only UPDATE statement shown that will achieve the desired objective is:

```
DELETE FROM
    (SELECT * FROM table_a
        ORDER BY col1 DESC
        FETCH FIRST 10 ROWS ONLY) AS result
```

Question 88

The correct answer is **D**. The WHERE clause is used to tell DB2 how to select the rows that are to be returned in the result data set produced; when specified, this clause is followed by a search condition, which is a simple test that is applied to a row of data—if the test evaluates to TRUE, the row is returned in the result data set produced; if the test evaluates to FALSE or UNKNOWN, the row is ignored. By using parentheses and/or Boolean operators like AND and OR, it's possible to create a WHERE clause that is quite complex. In the scenario presented, two different types of criteria for row selection are provided (enroll date earlier than January 1, 2012 and GPA greater than 3.50), and both must be met (requiring a Boolean AND operator).

Because, in the scenario presented, two different criteria must be met, the AND Boolean operator—*not the OR Boolean operator* (*Answer C*)—must be specified with the WHERE clause used. And there is no `FOR` clause that can be used with a `SELECT` statement (*Answers A and B*). Therefore, the only clause shown that will meet the objective that was defined is:

```
WHERE enroll_date < '2012-01-01' AND gpa > 3.50
```

Question 89

The correct answer is **A**. An SQL (or Native SQL) stored procedure is a procedure whose body is written entirely in SQL or SQL Procedural Language (SQL PL).

An External stored procedure is a procedure that is written in a high-level programming language such as Assembler, C, C++, COBOL, Java, REXX, or PL/I that resides in an external library that is accessible to DB2 (*Answer B*). An External SQL stored procedure is a procedure whose body is written entirely in SQL, but that is implemented as an external program (*Answer C*).

With DB2, you cannot develop a stored procedure that accesses data using an Object Linking and Embedding, Database (OLE DB) provider (*Answer D*)—to access data in this manner, you must develop an OLE DB External Table function.

Question 90

The correct answer is **B**. The FLOWR XQuery expression is comparable to the `SELECT-FROM-WHERE` statement/clause combination available with SQL. The basic syntax for a FLOWR expression is:

```
XQUERY
    for $Variable1 IN Expression1
    let $Variable2 := Expression2
    where Expression3
    order by Expression4 [ASCENDING | DESCENDING]
    return Expression3
```

Consequently, the XQuery statement used in the scenario presented will return the expression "`<name>ACME Manufacturing</name>`". This expression is obtained by searching the XML data value stored in the `CUSTINFO` column of a table named `CUSTOMER` for the first opening tag found under the `customerinfo` root (outermost) element that is followed by a value.

Had the `text()` function been used with the XQuery statement, the opening and closing tags for the name would have been removed and the value "ACME Manufacturing" would have been returned (*Answer A*). And because the `customerinfo` element is the root element of the XML data value presented, it is typically referenced in the `for` expression of the XQuery statement and is not returned as part of the `return` expression (*Answers C and D*).

Question 91

The correct answers are **A** and **E**. When the `ROLLBACK` statement is used to terminate a transaction, all changes made to the database since the transaction began are backed out, the database is returned to the state it was in just before the transaction was started, and any locks that were acquired on behalf of the transaction are released. A savepoint is a mechanism that allows applications and users to break the work being done by a single large transaction into one or more smaller subsets; the TO SAVEPOINT clause can be used with the ROLLBACK statement to back out a subset of database changes that have been made by a single transaction. Once a savepoint is created, all subsequent SQL statements that are executed in a transaction are automatically associated with that savepoint until it is deleted—either explicitly by executing the RELEASE statement or implicitly by terminating the transaction the savepoint was created in. (When a ROLLBACK TO SAVEPOINT statement is executed, the savepoint specified is not automatically deleted as part of the rollback operation.)

Open cursors that were defined with the WITH HOLD option remain open and any locks that were acquired on their behalf are held when a COMMIT statement is used to terminate the transaction in which the cursors were opened. However, when a transaction is terminated with a ROLLBACK statement, any locks that were acquired on behalf of an open cursor are released—*not held* (*Answer C*)—and all open cursors are closed. When a ROLLBACK TO SAVEPOINT statement is executed, all locks acquired after the savepoint specified was created are released—*not the locks acquired after the most recent savepoint* (*Answer B*) *nor the locks acquired up to the most recent savepoint* (*Answer D*).

Question 92

The correct answer is **C**. Update operations can be conducted in one of two ways: by performing what is known as searched update or by performing what is known as a positioned update. To perform a positioned update operation, a cursor must be created, opened, and then positioned on the row that is to be updated. Then, to modify data stored in the row the cursor is currently positioned on, you must execute an UPDATE statement that contains a WHERE CURRENT OF [*CursorName*] clause. Therefore, the only UPDATE statement shown that will perform a positioned update operation is:

```
UPDATE sales SET amt = 102.45 WHERE CURRENT OF cursor1
```

If a WHERE clause is not provided with the UPDATE statement used (*Answer A*), the update operation specified will be performed on every row found in the table or view referenced. If a WHERE clause *is* provided (*Answers B and D*), a searched update operation will be performed on every row found in the table or view referenced that meets the WHERE condition supplied.

Question 93

The correct answers are **A** and **D**. An application-period temporal table is a table that maintains "currently in effect" values of application data. Such tables manage time-sensitive data by allowing users or applications to define time periods (using dates, times, or timestamps) in which specific data values are considered valid.

A system-period temporal table is a table that maintains historical versions of its rows. The definition for system-period temporal table must include "system time begin" and "system time end" columns, which are populated with database-manager maintained values and are used to track when a row is considered current (*Answer E*). A system-period temporal table's definition must also include a "transaction start ID" column that DB2 can use to capture the start times of transactions that perform update or delete operations on a particular row.

A bitemporal table combines the historical tracking of a system-period temporal table with the time-specific data storage capabilities of an application-period temporal table (*Answer C*). Consequently, bitemporal tables can be used to manage time-sensitive data by defining the time periods in which specific data values are considered valid; values for the time periods are explicitly supplied (*Answer B*).

Question 94

The correct answer is **A**. Although the DELETE statement can be used to empty a table, such operations can have unwanted side effects. For instance, every time a row is deleted from a table, a record about the deletion is written to a transaction log file. Thus, the removal of every row in a table can cause a large number of log records to be generated, particularly if the table being emptied contains hundreds of thousands of rows. Similarly, if any DELETE triggers have been defined on the table being emptied, those triggers can be fired multiple times. A better alternative is to use the TRUNCATE statement to empty a table of its contents. Truncate operations do not generate transaction log records, and they give you more control over any DELETE triggers that may have been defined.

A truncate operation will remove *all* rows from a table—*not just a few select rows* (*Answers B and D*). And if the IGNORE DELETE TRIGGERS clause is specified with the TRUNCATE statement used, DELETE triggers that have been defined on the table *will not be fired* as the data in the table is deleted (*Answers C and D*). (If the RESTRICT WHEN DELETE TRIGGERS clause is used instead, DB2 will examine the system catalog to determine whether DELETE triggers on the table exist; if one or more triggers are found, the truncate operation will fail and an error will be returned.)

Question 95

The correct answers are **A** and **E**. A transaction (also known as a unit of work) is a sequence of one or more SQL operations that are grouped as a single unit. Normally, a transaction is initiated the first time an SQL statement is executed after a connection to a database has been established, or when a new SQL statement is executed after a running transaction ends. Once initiated, transactions can be implicitly terminated using a feature known as automatic commit or they can be explicitly terminated by executing a COMMIT or a ROLLBACK statement.

While the CONNECT statement can be used to start a new transaction boundary, it cannot be used to terminate one (*Answer D*). The REFRESH command (*Answer B*) is a DB2 Query Management Facility command that has nothing to do with transaction boundaries. And although there is a RESTART

DATABASE command, which can be used to initiate a crash recovery operation on a DB2 for Linux, UNIX, and Windows database, there is no RESTART command (*Answer C*).

Question 96

The correct answer is **C**. The GROUP BY clause is used to instruct DB2 on how to organize rows of data that are returned in a result data set; the ORDER BY clause is used to instruct DB2 on how to sort (order) the rows that are returned in a result data set. Therefore, to meet the desired objective for the scenario presented, the "GROUP BY city" clause should be used to instruct DB2 to organize the data retrieved from the WEATHER table by city, and the "ORDER BY city" clause should be used to tell DB2 to order the data by city (once it has been organized).

In the scenario presented, the "ORDER BY city" clause alone (*Answer A*) will not produce the desired results—instead, this clause will cause an error to be returned. The "GROUP BY city" clause alone (*Answer B*) will not produce the desired results either—this clause will instruct DB2 to organize the data retrieved from the WEATHER table by city, but there is no guarantee that the data will be ordered by city. On the other hand, the "GROUP BY MIN(temp), MAX(temp)" clause (*Answer D*) contains non-aggregate columns in the grouping expression. Therefore, the only SELECT statement shown that will produce the desired results is:

```
SELECT city, MIN(temp), MAX(temp)
  FROM weather
  GROUP BY city
  ORDER BY city
```

Question 97

The correct answer is **B**. The XMLTABLE() function returns a result data set, in the form of a table, from an XQuery expression. The table returned can contain columns of any SQL data type, including XML (the actual structure of the table is defined by the COLUMNS clause of the XMLTABLE() function), and the data stored in the table can be used to populate other tables.

The XMLSERIALIZE() function converts a well-formed XML document into a character string or large object value (*Answer A*); the XMLPARSE() function parses a character string value and returns a well-formed XML document (*Answer C*); and there is no XML function that will produce a temporary table whose columns are based on the elements found in a well-formed XML document (*Answer D*). You would need to construct a query or XQuery expression to perform this type of operation.

Working with DB2 Tables, Views, and Indexes

Question 98

The correct answers are **B** and **C**. If you define a unique index for one or more columns in a table, and you later create a primary key for the same set of columns, the existing index will be converted to a unique, system-required index that is used to enforce the primary key constraint. When such an event takes place, a warning—*not an error* (*Answer A*)—that looks something like this will be generated:

```
SQL0598W  Existing index "nnn.nnn" is used as the index
for the primary key or a unique key. SQLSTATE=01550
```

The index conversion process is straightforward and relatively simple; consequently, the index is *not* marked invalid and rebuilt later (*Answer D*). Nor is it dropped so that another, similar index can be created (*Answer E*).

Question 99

The correct answer is **D**. A UNIQUE constraint is used to ensure that values assigned to one or more columns of a table are always unique. Once a UNIQUE constraint has been defined for one or more columns, any operation that attempts to place duplicate values in those columns will fail. If a UNIQUE constraint is created for column that accepts NULL values, that column will be allowed to have one, and only one, NULL value stored in it.

The NOT NULL constraint is used to ensure that a particular column in a table is never assigned a NULL value (*Answer A*); a CHECK constraint is used to control which values will be accepted for a column in a table (*Answer B*); and a default constraint is used to ensure that a column in a table will always be assigned some value (*Answer C*).

Question 100

The correct answers are **B** and **E**. A trigger is an object that is used to define a set of actions that are to be executed whenever a transaction performs an insert, update, or delete operation against a table or updatable view. Once a trigger is created, it cannot be altered. Therefore, if you create a trigger and later discover that you need to change its behavior, you must drop the existing trigger and then recreate it with the changes desired.

The triggered action of a trigger consists of an optional search condition and a set of SQL statements or SQL Procedural Language (SQL PL) statements that are executed when the trigger is fired. Therefore, a trigger *does* contain executable code (*Answer A*). Adding a trigger to a table that already has rows in it will *not* cause the trigger to be fired (*Answer C*). And the triggered action of a trigger can be executed just once (when the trigger event takes place) *or once for every row that the trigger event affects* (*Answer D*).

Question 101

The correct answer is **D**. A primary key is a special form of a UNIQUE constraint that uniquely defines the characteristics of each row in a table. When a UNIQUE constraint or primary key is defined, DB2 checks to see whether an index for the columns the UNIQUE constraint/primary key refers to already exists. If an appropriate index is found, that index is marked as being "unique and system-required"; if not, a new index is created and given similar characteristics (unique and system-required). In either case, the index is then used to enforce uniqueness in the columns the constraint/primary key was defined for.

While primary keys can be used to define a referential integrity constraint, every primary key that gets created *does not* have to have a corresponding foreign key (*Answer A*). Furthermore, a primary key can be created *at any time*—if a unique constraint already exists on the primary key's key columns, the existing index for those columns will be converted to a unique, system-required index that is used to enforce the primary key constraint (*Answer B*). And finally, a range partition *does not* have to be defined on the key columns found in a primary key (*Answer C*).

Question 102

The correct answer is **C**. Select properties of an existing table can be modified and columns and constraints can be added or removed by executing the ALTER TABLE statement. For example, to change the data of a particular column in a table, you would execute an ALTER TABLE statement that looks something like this:

```
ALTER TABLE [TableName]
    ALTER COLUMN [ColumnName]
    SET DATA TYPE [DataType]
```

where:

TableName   Identifies, by name, the table whose definition is to be altered

ColumnName   Identifies, by name, the column whose data type is to be changed

DataType   Identifies the new data type that is to be assigned to the column

The SET DATA TYPE clause—*not the ALTER DATA TYPE clause* (*Answer D*)—is used to change the data type (or the characteristics of the data type) that is assigned to a column in a table. There is no RESIZE COLUMN (*Answer A*) or ADJUST COLUMN (*Answer B*) clause for the ALTER TABLE statement.

Question 103

The correct answer is **C**. The NOT NULL constraint is used to ensure that a particular column in a table is never assigned a NULL value; after a NOT NULL constraint has been defined for a column, any operation that attempts to place a NULL value in that column will fail. In the scenario presented, both columns in the SALES table were defined with a NOT NULL constraint; therefore, three of the INSERT statements shown will execute successfully and one will fail. It is important to note that the fourth INSERT statement (INSERT INTO sales VALUES ('', 0.0);) is one of the INSERT statements that *will* execute successfully because an empty string ('') and the value 0.0 are treated as data values, not NULL values.

In the scenario presented, only one of the INSERT statements shown will fail—INSERT INTO sales VALUES (NULL, 224.37);. Therefore, the answers 1 (*Answer A*), 2 (*Answer B*), and 4 (*Answer D*) are incorrect.

Question 104

The correct answer is **D**. Informational constraints are used to tell DB2 which business rules data will conform to. However, unlike with other constraints, informational constraints not enforced. Instead, they are used to make DB2 aware of constraints that are being enforced at the application level—the DB2 Optimizer can use this information to choose an optimum access plan to use when retrieving data from the database. With DB2 for Linux, UNIX, and Windows, both CHECK and referential integrity constraints can be defined as informational constraints; with DB2 for z/OS, only referential integrity constraints can be informational constraints.

The NOT NULL constraint is used to ensure that a particular column in a table is never assigned a NULL value (*Answer A*); a CHECK constraint is used to control which values can be assigned to a column in a table (*Answer B*); and a referential integrity constraint is used to define a required relationship between select columns and tables (*Answer C*).

Question 105

The correct answers are **A** and **D**. Indexes are important because, among other things, they provide a fast, efficient method for locating specific rows of data in large tables (thereby allowing queries to run more efficiently), and they provide a logical ordering of the rows in a table.

Although a unique, system-required index is used to enforce a UNIQUE constraint, an index is *not* needed to enforce CHECK and NOT NULL constraints (*Answer B*). And while indexes provide a logical ordering of the rows in a table, *they do not order the columns* (*Answer C*). Indexes are typically used to improve query performance; therefore, tables in Online Transaction Processing (OLTP) environments or environments where data throughput is high should *use indexes sparingly or avoid them altogether* (*Answer E*).

Question 106

The correct answer is **D**. If the FOR BIT DATA option is used with a character string data type definition (i.e., fixed-length character string or varying-length character string), the contents of the column the data type is assigned to will be treated as binary data. This means that code page conversions are not performed if data in the column is exchanged between other systems, and that all comparisons are done in binary, regardless of the database collating sequence used.

The varying-length character string (VARCHAR) data type (*Answer B*) is used to store character string values; however, unless the FOR BIT DATA option is specified when a column is defined, the contents of a column with this data type will be treated as character data and code page conversions will be performed if data in the column is exchanged between other systems or if value comparisons are made.

The binary large object (BLOB) data type (*Answer A*) is used to store binary data values—*not character string data values*. And although the character large object (CLOB) data type (*Answer C*) *is* used to store single-byte or multibyte character set values, the FOR BIT DATA option *cannot* be used with the CLOB data type.

Question 107

The correct answers are **B** and **E**. A trigger is an object that is used to define a set of actions that are to be executed whenever a trigger event takes place; a trigger event can be an insert operation, an update operation, a delete operation, or a merge operation that inserts, updates, or deletes data.

The execution of an IMPORT command (*Answer A*), a TRUNCATE statement (*Answer C*), or a LOAD command with the REPLACE option specified (*Answer D*) will *not* cause a trigger to be fired.

Question 108

The correct answer is **C**. If the WITH <LOCAL> CHECK OPTION clause is specified with the CREATE VIEW statement used, all insert and update operations that are performed against the resulting view will be checked to ensure that the rows being added or modified conform to the view's definition. Essentially, the WITH <LOCAL> CHECK OPTION clause guarantees that an insert or update operation performed against a view will not create a record that the view will never see.

The RESTRICT clause (*Answer A*), CASCADE clause (*Answer B*), and WITH CONTROL OPTION clause (*Answer D*) are not valid clauses that can be used with the CREATE VIEW statement.

Question 109

The correct answer is **B**. Externally, timestamp values appear to be fixed-length character string values that are up to 32 characters in length. However, the internal representation of a timestamp value requires between 7 and 13 bytes of storage.

The timestamp (TIMESTAMP) data type is used to store six- or seven-part values (year, month, day, hours, minutes, seconds, and microseconds) that represent a specific calendar date and time (*Answer C*). The range for the year portion is 0001 to 9999; the month portion is 1 to 12; the day portion is 1 to 28, 29, 30, or 31, depending upon the month value specified and whether the year specified is a leap year; the hours portion is 0 to 24; the minutes portion is 0 to 59; the seconds portion is 0 to 59; and the microseconds portion is 0 to 999,999,999,999—the number of digits used in the fractional seconds portion can be anywhere from 0 to 12; however, the default is 6 (*Answer A*).

Because the representation of date and time values varies throughout the world, the actual string format used to present a date, time, or timestamp value is dependent upon the territory code that has been assigned to the database being used (*Answer D*).

Question 110

The correct answer is **D**. A distinct data type is a user-defined type (UDT) that shares a common representation with one of the built-in data types available with DB2. And the decimal (DECIMAL, DEC, NUMERIC, and NUM) data type is used to store numeric values that contain both whole and fractional parts separated by a decimal point. Both the *precision* and the *scale* of the value determine the exact location of the decimal point. (The precision is the actual number of digits needed to properly display the value; the scale is the number of digits used by the fractional part of the number).

The small integer (SMALLINT) data type (*Answer C*) is used to store numeric values that have a precision of five or fewer digits and no scale. The big integer (BIGINT) data type (*Answer A*) is used to store numeric values that have a precision of 19 digits and no scale. And the double-precision floating-point (DOUBLE) data type (*Answer B*) is used to store a 64-bit approximation of a real number. Consequently, none of these data types are ideal for storing data such as currency values, which usually have a scale of two digits.

Question 111

The correct answers are **A** and **C**. As the name implies, a BEFORE trigger is fired for every row in the set of affected rows *before* the trigger event takes place. Consequently, BEFORE triggers are often used to validate input data, to automatically generate values for newly inserted rows, and to prevent certain types of trigger events from being performed.

AFTER triggers—*not BEFORE triggers*—are often used to insert, update, or delete data in the same or in other tables (*Answer B*); to check data against other data values in the same or in other tables (*Answer D*); or to invoke UDFs that perform nondatabase operations. And INSTEAD OF triggers—*not BEFORE triggers*—are executed instead of the trigger event (*Answer E*).

Question 112

The correct answer is **C**. A primary key is a special form of a UNIQUE constraint that uniquely defines the characteristics of each row in a table (*Answer B*). Because UNIQUE constraints and primary keys are enforced by indexes, all the limitations that apply to indexes—such as no more than 16 columns with a combined length of 255 bytes are allowed, and none of the columns used can have a large object data type—apply. Thus, both UNIQUE constraints (along with their corresponding unique indexes) *and* primary keys can be defined over one or more columns.

The most significant difference between a primary key and a UNIQUE constraint is that only one primary key is allowed per table, whereas a single table can contain multiple UNIQUE constraints (and supporting unique indexes) (*Answer A*). And although a unique, system-required index is used to enforce a UNIQUE constraint, a distinction exists between defining a UNIQUE constraint and creating a unique index. While both enforce uniqueness, a unique index will accept one (and only one) NULL value. UNIQUE constraints and primary keys, however, will not accept any NULL values (*Answer D*).

Question 113

The correct answer is **A**. A CHECK constraint is used to ensure that a particular column in a table is never assigned an unacceptable value. Once a CHECK constraint has been defined for a particular column, any operation that attempts to place into that column a value that does not meet a specific set of criteria will fail. Consequently, a CHECK constraint can be used to ensure that a column's values fall within a specific range.

A UNIQUE constraint (*Answer B*) is used to ensure that values assigned to one or more columns of a table are always unique. A referential integrity constraint is used to define a required relationship between select columns and tables (*Answer C*). And an informational constraint (*Answer D*) is used to make DB2 aware of constraints that are being enforced at the application level so the DB2 Optimizer can use this information when choosing an optimum data access plan.

Question 114

The correct answer is **C**. Views can provide a different way of describing and looking at data stored in one or more base tables (*Answer D*). They *do not* enable a single SQL statement to work with a variety of tables.

Whenever a view is referenced in an SQL operation, a query is executed and the results are retrieved from one or more underlying tables (*Answer B*) and returned in a table-like format. Because of this, views are often used to restrict access to select data and rows in a table (*Answer A*). For instance, if a table containing employee information held sensitive information such as Social Security numbers and salaries, access to that data might be restricted by creating a view that contains only the columns that hold nonsensitive data. Then, only authorized users would be given access to the table, while everyone else would be required to work with the view.

Question 115

The correct answer is **A**. Schemas are objects that are used to logically classify and group other objects (such as tables, indexes, and views) in a database. When select data objects (that is, table spaces, tables, indexes, distinct data types, functions, stored procedures, and triggers) are created, they are automatically assigned to a schema, based upon the qualifier that was provided as part of their name. If a schema name or qualifier was not provided, the object is automatically assigned to a default schema, which is determined by examining the value found in a special register—with DB2 for Linux, UNIX, and Windows, this special register is the CURRENT SCHEMA (or CURRENT_SCHEMA) special register; with DB2 for z/OS, the CURRENT SQLID (or CURRENT_SQLID) special register is used instead. By default, the value assigned to these special registers is the authorization ID of the current session user; in the scenario presented, this would be "USER1".

With DB2 for Linux, UNIX, and Windows, objects cannot be created in the schemas that are automatically produced when a database is created—that is, in a schema whose name begins with the letters "SYS" (*Answers B, C, and D*). With DB2 for z/OS, objects cannot be created in a *system schema*, which is any set of schemas that are reserved for use by the DB2 subsystem.

Question 116

The correct answers are **C** and **D**. Referential integrity constraints are used to define required relationships between select columns and tables. Such relationships are established by comparing values that are to be added to one or more select columns (known as the foreign key) of a "child" table with values that currently exist for one or more columns (known as the parent key) of the "parent" table. (A table can serve as both the parent and the child in a referential constraint; such a table is called a self-referencing table, and the constraint is known as a self-referencing referential constraint.)

A foreign key can reference *only one* primary key (*Answer A*), a primary key can be referenced by *multiple* foreign keys (*Answer B*), and referential integrity constraints are enforced only during the execution of INSERT, UPDATE, DELETE statements. They are *not* enforced when SELECT statements are executed (*Answer E*).

Question 117

The correct answer is **A**. The columns used in a referential integrity constraint (also called a foreign key constraint) *do not have to be defined as being NOT NULL*. In fact, the ON DELETE SET NULL Delete Rule for referential integrity constraints ensures that whenever a row is deleted from the parent table of a referential integrity constraint, all records in the child table with matching foreign key values are altered such that the foreign key columns are set to NULL—provided the columns that make up the foreign key are nullable (that is, they do not have a NOT NULL constraint associated with them).

One or more columns that participate in one referential integrity constraint can be used in another referential integrity constraint (*Answer B*). The names of the columns used to create the foreign key of a referential constraint do not have to be the same as the names of the columns that were used to create the primary key; however, the data types of the columns that make up the primary and foreign keys must be identical, and the number of columns used in both keys must be the same (*Answer C*). And to define a referential integrity constraint, a primary key or unique key must already exist in the same or a different table (*Answer D*).

Question 118

The correct answers are **B** and **D**. If the INCLUDE clause is specified with the CREATE INDEX statement used, data from the columns specified with the clause will be appended to the index's key values. By storing this information in the index (along with key values), the performance of some queries can be improved—if all the data needed to resolve a particular query can be obtained by accessing the index only, data does not have to be retrieved from the associated base table. (If the data needed to resolve a particular query does not reside solely in an index, both the index and the associated table must be accessed.)

There is no clause that can be used with the CREATE INDEX statement to combine two or more indexes to form a single index (*Answer A*). The column names provided with the CREATE INDEX statement—*not the INCLUDE clause*—identify the primary columns that are to be part of the index's key (*Answer C*). And the PCTFREE clause—*not the INCLUDE clause*—is used with the CREATE INDEX statement to control the percentage of each index page that is to be left as free space for future insert and update operations that will cause the index to be populated (*Answer E*).

Question 119

The correct answer is **C**. The Extensible Markup Language Document (XML) data type is used to define columns in a table that can be used to store XML documents. By default, XML data that is inserted into columns that have been defined with the XML data type is stored in an XML storage object that is separate from the table's relational storage location.

The XML data type allows XML documents to be stored in their native, hierarchical format—*not as binary large objects or character large object strings* (*Answer A*). XML values are processed using an internal representation that is not comparable to any string value; therefore, the format used to present an XML value is *not* dependent upon the territory code that has been assigned to the database used (*Answer B*). And since no length specification has to be provided when the XML data type is assigned to a column, the amount of space set aside to store an XML value is *not* determined by the length specification provided when an XML column is defined (*Answer D*).

Question 120

The correct answer is **D**. INSTEAD OF triggers are fired only when specific trigger events (i.e., inserts, updates, and deletes) are performed against a subject view. Consequently, INSTEAD OF triggers are often used to force applications to use views as the only interface for performing insert, update, delete, and query operations.

BEFORE triggers (*Answer A*) and AFTER triggers (*Answer B*) are fired whenever a specific trigger event is performed against a subject table—*not a subject view*. And there is no such thing as a BETWEEN trigger (*Answer C*).

Question 121

The correct answers are **C** and **D**. A UNIQUE constraint is used to ensure that values assigned to one or more columns of a table are always unique. Informational constraints tell DB2 which business rules data conforms to; however, unlike other constraints, informational constraints are not enforced. Instead, they are used to make DB2 aware of constraints that are being enforced at the application level so the DB2 Optimizer can take this information into account when choosing the optimum access plan to use to retrieve data from the database.

Only *one* primary key is allowed per table (*Answer B*); however, a single table can contain *multiple* UNIQUE constraints (*Answer A*). Referential integrity constraints (also known as foreign key constraints) are enforced via a unique index on the *primary key* of the parent table and a foreign key on a child table that references the primary key (*Answer E*).

Question 122

The correct answer is **C**. BEFORE and AFTER triggers are only fired when a specific trigger event is performed against a *subject table*; INSTEAD OF triggers are only fired when specific trigger events are performed against a *subject view*.

BEFORE triggers are fired just before a trigger event (i.e., an insert, update, or delete operation) takes place (*Answer A*). Consequently, BEFORE triggers are often used to validate input data, to automatically generate values for newly inserted rows, and to perform tasks such as issuing alerts (*Answer D*). AFTER triggers, on the other hand, are fired after the trigger event has been successfully executed (*Answer B*). For this reason, AFTER triggers are often used to insert, update, or delete data in the same or in other tables; to check data against other data values in the same or in other tables; or to invoke user-defined functions (UDFs) that perform nondatabase operations (*Answer D*).

Question 123

The correct answers are **B** and **C**. Unlike base tables, which act as a long-term repository for data, temporary tables serve as temporary work areas. Consequently, temporary tables are often used for recording the results of data manipulation or for storing intermediate results of a subquery (when this information will not fit in the memory available). With DB2 10 and 10.1, two types of temporary tables are available: declared temporary tables and created temporary tables. Unlike base tables, whose definitions are stored in the system catalog of the database they belong to, declared temporary tables are not persistent and can only be used by the application that creates them—and only for the life of that application. When the application that creates a declared temporary table disconnects from the database (or is terminated, either on purpose or prematurely), the table's rows are deleted, and the table is implicitly dropped.

Insert time clustering (ITC) tables—*not temporary tables*—are used to cluster data according to the time in which rows are inserted (*Answer A*). There is no such thing as a declared local temporary table (*Answer D*). And when an application using a temporary table disconnects from the database unexpectedly, the temporary table is *not* converted to a base table (*Answer E*).

Question 124

The correct answer is **C**. A view is a named specification of a result table that gets populated whenever the view is referenced in an executable SQL statement.

Every time a view is referenced in an SQL statement—*not just the first time it is referenced* (*Answer D*)—the query that was used to define the view is executed and the results are retrieved from the underlying table and returned in a table-like format. A view is *not* populated when it is first created (*Answer A*), nor is it populated *only* when it is referenced by an INSERT statement (*Answer B*).

Question 125

The correct answer is **C**. The DECIMAL data type is used to store numeric values that contain both whole and fractional parts separated by a decimal point. For this reason, the DECIMAL data type is ideal for storing values that represent money.

The small integer (SMALLINT) data type should be used when you need to store numeric values that have a precision of five or fewer digits (*Answer D*). The big integer (BIGINT) data type should be used when you need to store numeric values that have a precision of 19 digits (*Answer B*). And the single-precision floating-point (FLOAT or REAL) data type should be used when you need to store a 32-bit approximation of a real number (*Answer A*).

Question 126

The correct answer is **A**. Select properties of an existing table can be modified and columns and constraints can be added or removed by executing the ALTER TABLE statement. For example, to add a new element such as a column to an existing table, you would execute an ALTER TABLE statement that looks something like this:

```
ALTER TABLE [TableName] ADD ([Element], ...)
```

where:

TableName	Identifies, by name, the table whose definition is to be altered
Element	Identifies one or more columns, UNIQUE constraints, CHECK constraints, referential constraints, and/or a primary key constraint that are to be added to the existing table's definition; the syntax used to define each of these elements varies according to the element specified

There is no INSERT COLUMN (*Answer B*), APPEND COLUMN (*Answer C*), or ATTACH COLUMN (*Answer D*) clause for the ALTER TABLE statement.

Question 127

The correct answer is **D**. When creating a clustering index, the PCTFREE clause of the CREATE INDEX statement can be used to control how much space is reserved for future insert and update operations. A higher PCTFREE value (the default is 10 percent) can reduce—*not increase*—the likelihood that index page splits will occur when records are added to an index.

If an index is created with INCLUDE columns (*Answer B*) or to support a UNIQUE constraint (*Answer A*), the UNIQUE clause must be specified with the CREATE INDEX statement used. And normally, a clustering index will improve query performance by decreasing the amount of I/O that is needed to access data (*Answer C*)—when a logical set of rows are physically stored close together, read operations typically require less I/O because adjacent rows are more likely to be found within the same extent instead of being widely distributed across multiple extents.

Question 128

The correct answers are **B** and **E**. The Delete Rule for referential constraints controls how delete operations performed against the parent table in a referential constraint are to be processed. Four different Delete Rule definitions are possible; the ON DELETE CASCADE Delete Rule ensures that whenever a row is deleted from the parent table of a referential constraint, all records in the child table with matching foreign key values are deleted as well. So, in the scenario presented, a primary key would need to be created on the DEPARTMENT table, and a foreign key would need to be created on the EMPLOYEE table that references the primary key of the DEPARTMENT table—the ON DELETE CASCADE Delete Rule would need to be specified as part of the foreign key's definition.

In the scenario presented, if a primary key is created on the EMPLOYEE table (*Answer A*) and a foreign key is created on the DEPARTMENT table, and that foreign key is defined with the ON DELETE CASCADE Delete Rule specified (*Answer C*), whenever a record is deleted from the EMPLOYEE table, any related records will be deleted from the DEPARTMENT table—the opposite of the desired behavior. And if a foreign is created on the EMPLOYEE table that references the primary key of the DEPARTMENT table and the ON DELETE RESTRICT Delete Rule is specified as part of the foreign key's definition (*Answer D*), any operation that attempts to delete a record from the DEPARTMENT table that has a corresponding record in the EMPLOYEE table will fail.

Question 129

The correct answer is **A**. A CHECK constraint is used to ensure that a particular column in a table is never assigned an unacceptable value; once a CHECK constraint has been defined for a particular column, any operation that attempts to place into that column a value that does not meet a specific set of criteria will fail. Consequently, in the scenario presented, a CHECK constraint can be used to ensure that the value of one column in a table is never less than the value of another column in the same table.

A UNIQUE constraint (*Answer B*) is used to ensure that values assigned to one or more columns of a table are always unique. An informational constraint (*Answer C*) is used to make DB2 aware of constraints that are being enforced at the application level so the DB2 Optimizer can use this information when choosing an optimum data access plan. And a referential integrity constraint (*Answer D*) is used to define a required relationship between select columns and tables.

Question 130

The correct answers are **A** and **C**. When features that provide Oracle compatibility are explicitly enabled, four additional Oracle-specific data types are made available for use. These data types are:

- DATE as TIMESTAMP(0)
- NUMBER
- VARCHAR2
- NVARCHAR2

Both the varying-length character string (VARCHAR or CHARACTER VARYING) data type (*Answers B and E*) and the national varying-length character string (NVARCHAR) data type (*Answer D*) are built-in data types that can be used with non-Oracle compatible DB2 databases.

Data Concurrency

Question 131

The correct answer is **A**. When a Share (S) lock is acquired, the lock owner can read, but not modify, all data (excluding uncommitted data) stored in the locked resource. Other transactions can read data stored in the locked resource (provided it has been committed); however, they cannot modify data stored in the resource.

When a Share With Intent Exclusive (SIX) lock is acquired, the lock owner can read and modify data stored in the locked resource—other transactions can read data stored in the locked resource but they cannot modify data stored in the resource (*Answer B*). When an Exclusive (X) lock is acquired, the lock owner can both read and modify data stored in the locked resource; however, other transactions can neither read nor modify data stored in the resource (*Answer C*). And when an Update (U) lock is acquired, the lock owner can modify all data (excluding uncommitted data) stored in the locked resource but they cannot read data stored in the resource—other transactions can read data stored in the locked resource; however, they cannot modify data stored in the resource (*Answer D*).

Question 132

The correct answer is **A**. If a transaction that is holding a lock on a resource needs to acquire a more restrictive lock on that resource, rather than releasing the old lock and acquiring a new one (*Answers C and D*), DB2 will attempt to change the state of the lock being held to the more restrictive state.

During lock escalation (*Answer B*), space in a database's lock list is freed by replacing several row-level locks with a single table-level lock. Usually, the table-level lock acquired is the same type of lock as the row-level locks that are released.

Question 133

The correct answer is **C**. A read-only transaction operating under Currently Committed semantics will not acquire a lock as long as DB2 can determine that the data needed has been committed. (Transactions performing read and write operations avoid lock waits on uncommitted inserts, and transactions performing read-only operations end up trading a lock wait for a log read when they encounter uncommitted updates/deletes from concurrent transactions.)

Only transactions running under the Uncommitted Read (UR) isolation level are allowed to see uncommitted data—transactions running under any other isolation level cannot see uncommitted data, and there is no mechanism that can be used to alter that behavior (*Answer A*). Likewise, there is no tool that can be used to force DB2 to write all data changes to the database as soon as the DB2 Database Manager can make a determination that those changes will eventually be committed (*Answer D*).

The use of Currently Committed semantics will result in an increase—*not a decrease*—in the amount of log space needed for update operations that are performed against tables that have been defined as DATA CAPTURE NONE (*Answer B*). This additional space is used to log the first update of a row by an active transaction; it is this data that is used to retrieve the currently committed image of the row.

Question 134

The correct answer is **C**. The Repeatable Read isolation level is the most restrictive isolation level available. It completely isolates the effects of one transaction from the effects of other concurrently running transactions; therefore, it offers the greatest protection of data but provides the least amount of concurrency.

When the Cursor Stability (CS) isolation level is used, lost updates and dirty reads cannot occur; however, nonrepeatable reads and phantoms can and may be seen (*Answer A*). When the Cursor Stability isolation level is used, if the same query is executed two or more times within the same transaction, the results produced can vary (*Answer D*). And because it provides the highest level of concurrency available (while preventing uncommitted reads), the Cursor Stability isolation level is the isolation level DB2 uses by default (*Answer B*).

Question 135

The correct answer is **D**. The LOCK TABLE statement allows a transaction to acquire a table-level lock on a particular table in one of two modes: SHARE and EXCLUSIVE. If a table is locked in SHARE mode, a table-level Share (S) lock is acquired on behalf of the requesting transaction, and other concurrent transactions can read, but not change, data stored in the locked table. In other words, concurrent transactions are *not* allowed to perform write operations against a table that has been locked in SHARE mode (*Answer C*).

If the ALTER TABLE ... LOCKSIZE TABLE statement is executed (*DB2 for Linux, UNIX, and Windows only*), DB2 will attempt to acquire table-level locks on behalf of any transaction that tries to interact with the table specified (*Answer A*); if the ALTER TABLE ... LOCKSIZE ROW statement is executed, DB2 will attempt to acquire row-level locks on behalf of transactions instead (*Answer B*).

Question 136

The correct answers are **C** and **D**. If a transaction that is holding a lock on a resource needs to acquire a more restrictive lock on that resource, DB2 will attempt to change the state of the lock being held to the more restrictive state. The action of changing the state of an existing lock is known as *lock conversion* (DB2 for Linux, UNIX, and Windows) or *lock promotion* (DB2 for z/OS).

Lock escalation (*Answer B*) is a process by which several row-level locks are replaced with a single table-level lock to free up space in a database's lock list. There is no *lock exchange* (*Answer A*) or *lock substitution* (*Answer E*) process with DB2.

Question 137

The correct answer is **C**. Intent Exclusive (IX) locks are typically acquired for transactions that convey the intent to modify (change) data; that is, transactions that contain SELECT FOR UPDATE, UPDATE WHERE, or INSERT statements.

Intent None (IN) locks (*Answer A*) are typically acquired for read-only transactions that have no intention of modifying data. Intent Share (IS) locks (*Answer B*) are typically acquired for transactions that do not convey the intent to modify data (i.e., transactions that do not contain SELECT FOR UPDATE, UPDATE WHERE, or INSERT statements). Share With Intent Exclusive (SIX) locks (*Answer D*) are typically acquired when a transaction holding a Share (S) lock on a resource attempts to acquire an Intent Exclusive (IX) lock on the same resource (or vice versa).

Question 138

The correct answers are **A** and **C**. The Repeatable Read isolation level is the most restrictive isolation level available; it offers the greatest protection of data, but provides the least amount of concurrency. With this isolation level, lost updates, dirty reads, nonrepeatable reads, and phantoms cannot occur.

When the Read Stability (RS) isolation level is used, lost updates, dirty reads, and nonrepeatable reads cannot occur, but phantoms can and might be seen (*Answer B*). The Uncommitted Read (UR) isolation level is the least restrictive of all the isolation levels available; therefore, it offers the lowest protection of data but provides the greatest amount of concurrency (*Answer D*).

The Repeatable Read isolation level <u>*completely isolates*</u> the effects of one transaction from the effects of other concurrently running transactions (*Answer E*).

Question 139

The correct answer is **B**. As the name implies, transactions running under the Uncommitted Read (UR) isolation level can see changes made to rows by other transactions before those changes are committed. Therefore, in the scenario presented, application APP_B will be able to retrieve all rows from table TAB1 without waiting for application APP_A to finish making updates.

Application APP_B will not have to wait for application APP_A to finish making updates (*Answer A*), it will not be limited to retrieving only the row currently being updated (*Answer C*), and it will not be prevented from retrieving the row currently being updated (*Answer D*).

Question 140

The correct answers are **B** and **D**. When a connection to a database is first established, a specific amount of memory is set aside to hold a structure that DB2 uses to manage locks (known as the lock list). Because a limited amount of memory is available and because every active transaction must share this memory, DB2 imposes a limit on the amount of space each transaction can consume in the lock list—to prevent a transaction from exceeding its lock list space limits, a process known as *lock escalation* is performed whenever too many locks have been acquired on behalf of a single transaction. During lock escalation, space in the lock list is freed by replacing several row-level locks with a single table-level lock. Consequently, the size of the lock list and the number of locks held are two factors that can influence lock escalation.

If a transaction that is holding a lock on a resource needs to acquire a more restrictive lock on that resource, DB2 will attempt to change the state of the lock being held to the more restrictive state— this is known as *lock conversion* (DB2 for Linux, UNIX, and Windows) or *lock promotion* (DB2 for z/OS). The lock mode needed (*Answer C*) and the lock mode currently held (*Answer E*) can influence lock conversion, but these two factors will have no effect on lock escalation. Lock size (*Answer A*) has no influence on lock escalation or lock conversion.

Question 141

The correct answer is **D**. When one transaction holds locks on a resources another transaction needs and the other transaction holds locks on resources the first transaction needs, a situation known as a *deadlock* (or *deadlock cycle*) will occur.

Only one transaction can hold an Exclusive (X) lock on a particular resource at any point in time (*Answer A*); any time a transaction holds a lock on a particular resource, other concurrently running transactions can be denied access to that resource until the transaction holding the lock is terminated or lock timeout detection causes a transaction waiting on a lock to be rolled back (*Answer B*); and if a transaction that is holding a lock on a resource needs to acquire a more restrictive lock on that resource, DB2 will attempt to change the state of the lock being held to the more restrictive state automatically—the more restrictive lock does not have to be "available" (*Answer C*) in order for this to happen.

Question 142

The correct answers are **C** and **E**. If a transaction that is holding a lock on a resource needs to acquire a more restrictive lock on that resource, DB2 will attempt to change the state of the lock being held to the more restrictive state. The action of changing the state of an existing lock is known as *lock conversion* (DB2 for Linux, UNIX, and Windows) or *lock promotion* (DB2 for z/OS). Consequently, the lock mode desired or needed and the lock mode currently held are two factors that can influence lock conversion.

When a connection to a database is first established, a specific amount of memory is set aside to hold a structure that DB2 uses to manage locks (known as the lock list). Because a limited amount of memory is available and because every active transaction must share this memory, DB2 imposes a limit on the amount of space each transaction can consume in the lock list—to prevent a transaction from exceeding its lock list space limits, a process known as *lock escalation* is performed whenever too many locks have been acquired on behalf of a single transaction. During lock escalation, space in the lock list is freed by replacing several row-level locks with a single table-level lock. Therefore, the size of the lock list (*Answer B*) and the number of locks held (*Answer D*) can influence *lock escalation*—not lock conversion. Lock size (*Answer A*) has no influence on lock escalation or lock conversion.

Question 143

The correct answer is **B**. *Intent None* (IN) locks are typically acquired for read-only transactions that have no intention of modifying data; that is, transactions that retrieve data with SELECT statements.

Intent Exclusive (IX) locks are normally acquired for transactions that convey the intent to modify data; that is, transactions that contain SELECT FOR UPDATE, UPDATE WHERE, or INSERT statements. Exclusive (X) locks are typically acquired for transactions that retrieve data with SELECT statements and then modify the data retrieved with INSERT, UPDATE (*Answer C*), or DELETE (*Answer D*) statements. And Super Exclusive (Z) locks are typically acquired on a table whenever the lock owner attempts to alter the table, drop the table (*Answer A*), create an index for the table, drop an index (*Answer A*) that has already been defined for the table, or reorganize the contents of the table by running the REORG utility.

Question 144

The correct answer is **B**. If a database's deadlock detector discovers a deadlock cycle, it randomly selects one of the transactions involved to roll back and terminate. The transaction chosen (known as the *"victim"*) is then sent an SQL error code and every lock the transaction had acquired is released. The remaining transactions can then proceed because the deadlock cycle has been broken—*they are not rolled back*.

Each database has its own deadlock detector, which is activated as part of the database initialization process (*Answer A*). When a deadlock cycle occurs, all transactions involved will wait indefinitely for a lock unless some outside agent steps in to break the cycle (*Answer D*). And if a database's deadlock detector discovers a deadlock cycle, it randomly selects one of the transactions involved to roll back and terminate (*Answer C*).

Question 145

The correct answer is **B**. When the Cursor Stability isolation level is used, only the row the isolating transaction is currently referencing is locked. (The moment a record is retrieved from a result data set, a pointer—known as a cursor—is positioned on the corresponding row in the underlying table, and that is the row that gets locked. This lock will remain in effect until the cursor is repositioned, usually by a FETCH operation, or until the owning transaction is terminated.)

In the scenario presented, if the Repeatable Read isolation level (*Answer C*) is used, other agents will be unable to assign seats as long as the transaction that generated the list remains active; therefore, the list will not change when it is refreshed. If the Read Stability isolation level (*Answer A*) is used, other agents will be able to unassign currently assigned seats (and these unassigned seats will show up when the list is refreshed), but they will not be able to assign any seat that appears in the list as long as the transaction that generated the list remains active. If the Uncommitted Read isolation level (*Answer D*) is used, other agents will be able to unassign currently assigned seats, as well as assign unassigned seats; however, uncommitted seat unassignments/assignments will show up when the list is refreshed, and the agent may make an inappropriate change based on this data. Therefore, the best isolation level to use for this particular application is the Cursor Stability isolation level.

Question 146

The correct answer is **C**. DB2 does not place locks on buffer pools.

DB2 can, however, place locks on table spaces (*Answer D*), blocks, tables (*Answer B*), rows (*Answer A*), and data partitions.

Question 147

The correct answer is **A**. When the Cursor Stability isolation level is used, only the row that the isolating transaction is currently referencing is locked. The moment a record is retrieved from a result data set, a pointer—known as a cursor—is positioned on the corresponding row in the underlying table, and that is the row that gets locked. This lock will remain in effect until the cursor is repositioned (i.e., moved to another row) or the owning transaction is terminated.

Updating or deleting the row the cursor is currently positioned on (*Answer B*) will not cause the lock that is currently held to be released; similarly, moving the cursor to a row that has been deleted by another application (*Answer C*) or moving the cursor to a row that is in the process of being updated by another application (*Answer D*) will not result in the release of a lock being held by an application running under the Cursor Stability isolation level—in all likelihood, such rows will have already been copied to the result data set that is currently being used by the application.

Question 148

The correct answer is **B**. Lock escalation is the term that is used to describe the act of releasing a large number of row-level locks a transaction (applications) holds to acquire a single table-level lock. (To prevent a transaction from exceeding lock list space limits, lock escalation is performed whenever too many locks have been acquired on behalf of a single transaction—during lock escalation, space in the lock list is freed by replacing several row-level locks with a single table-level lock.)

Lock conversion is the term that is used to describe the act of exchanging one lock an application holds on a resource for a more restrictive lock on the same resource (*Answer A*); lock timeout is the term that describes the process that is used to prevent one transaction from waiting indefinitely for another transaction to release a lock on a resource it needs (*Answer C*); and Currently Committed semantics is the term that is used to describe the process that allows scan operations to execute without locking rows when the data being accessed is known to have been committed (*Answer D*).

Question 149

The correct answer is **C**. The LOCK TABLE statement allows a transaction to acquire a table-level lock on a particular table in one of two modes: SHARE and EXCLUSIVE. If a table is locked in EXCLUSIVE mode, a table-level Exclusive (X) lock is acquired on behalf of the requesting transaction, and other concurrent transactions cannot perform any type of operation against the table while it is locked.

If a table is locked in SHARE mode, a table-level Share (S) lock is acquired on behalf of the requesting transaction and other concurrent transactions can read, but not change, data stored in the locked table (*Answer A*). The LOCK TABLE statement cannot be used to acquire an UPDATE table-level lock (*Answer B*) or a SUPEREXCLUSIVE (*Answer D*) table-level lock on behalf of a requesting transaction.

Question 150

The correct answer is **A**. Transactions running under the Uncommitted Read isolation level can see changes made to rows by other transactions *before* those changes are committed. Therefore, only applications running under the Uncommitted Read (UR) isolation level are allowed to retrieve rows that have been updated by a transaction that has not yet been committed.

Applications running under the Repeatable Read (RR) isolation level (*Answer B*), the Read Stability (RS) isolation level (*Answer C*), or the Cursor Stability (CS) isolation level (*Answer D*) are allowed to see changes made to records *only* after the changes have been committed.

Index